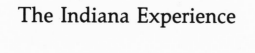

The Indiana Experience

The Indiana Experience

·❖·❖·❖·❖·❖·❖·❖·❖·❖·❖·❖·❖·❖·❖·❖·❖·❖·❖·

AN ANTHOLOGY

Compiled and edited
by A. L. Lazarus

INDIANA UNIVERSITY PRESS
Bloomington and London

Published in Canada by Fitzhenry & Whiteside Limited, Don Mills, Ontario
Manufactured in the United States of America

Library of Congress Cataloging in Publication Data
Main entry under title:
The Indiana experience.
Includes index.
1. American literature—Indiana.   I. Lazarus,
Arnold Leslie.
PS571.I6I56   1977   810.8'09772   76-50528
ISBN 0-253-32986-8 pa.
ISBN 0-243-14156-7 cl.   1 2 3 4 5 81 80 79 78 77

CONTENTS

Biographical and Autobiographical Sketches

Short Stories and Other Fiction

Plays

Folk Songs and Ballads of Indiana

Poems and Songs

ACKNOWLEDGMENTS

For the sabbatical leave that made this project possible I am indebted to Jacob Adler, Head of the Department of English; Robert Kane, Head of the Department of Education; and Robert Ringel, Dean of the School of Humanities, Purdue University. I should also like to thank William Whelan and Diane Dubiel of Purdue for their enthusiasm and dedication.

For screening candidate pieces, I acknowledge with thanks the help of the ICTE Editorial Board—especially Kenneth Nixon, Ball State University; Mescal Evler, former State Consultant in Language Arts; Edmund Sullivan, English Consultant, Evansville Schools; Lowell Coats, English Consultant, Fort Wayne Schools; Professors James Mullican and Charles Blaney, Indiana State University; and Edward Jenkinson, Director of the English Curriculum Study Center, Indiana University.

Several of the Purdue University Librarians had a hand in helping me locate selections—especially Anne Black, Jenny Knauth, Cheryl Knodle, Pamela McKay, Dennis Parks, Barbara Pinzelik, and Helen Schroyer; likewise, Lucille Washburn and Lois Andrew of the West Lafayette Public Library. A special thank-you is due Donald Thompson, Librarian of Wabash College, and R. E. Banta of Crawfordsville, compilers of *Indiana Authors and Their Books,* an indispensable biographical and bibliographical compendium. Other librarians and archivists to whom I am indebted include John Harris, Carol Waddell, and Paula Woods of the Tippecanoe Historical Society; and Gayle Thornbrough of the Indiana Historical Society.

For permission to reprint the following selections under copyright, grateful acknowledgment is made to the following publishers, authors, agents, and trustees of authors' estates:

Abbott Laboratories, Chicago, for Rex Stout's "Tough Cop's Gift" (also known as "Santa Claus Beat"), which first appeared in the magazine *What's New,* copyright 1953, by Abbott Laboratories.

Ball State University Press for A. L. Lazarus's "Boneless on the Monon" from Thomas Wetmore, ed., *Indiana Sesquicentennial Poets* (Muncie: 1967).

Beloit Poetry Journal and Donald Baker for "Twelve Hawks," which first appeared in *Beloit Poetry Journal,* Vol. X–4 (Summer, 1960), copyright 1960, by Beloit College, Beloit, Wisconsin.

Bobbs-Merrill Company, Indianapolis, and Richard Crowder for "Fame" [Comes to James Whitcomb Riley] from *Those Innocent Years,* copyright 1957, by the Bobbs-Merrill Company; and for "When the Frost Is on the

Harper & Row, Publishers, for Emily Kimbrough's "Our Waverly," *Innocents From Indiana*, copyright 1950, by Emily Kimbrough Wrench; also for George P. Elliott's "Miracle Play," *An Hour of Last Things*, copyright 1970, by George P. Elliott and his agent, Georges Borchardt; also for excerpts from William Gass's *In the Heart of the Heart of the Country*, copyright 1968— the excerpts exactly as printed here (*The Indiana Experience*) approved by special permission of William Gass; also for "The Studebaker Brothers of South Bend" from *More Than You Promise*, copyright 1949 and 1970, by Kathleen Anne Smallzried and Dorothy James Roberts.

Holiday Magazine for William E. Wilson's "Pioneers in Paradise," which first appeared in *Holiday*, XV (June, 1959) and is here reprinted by permission of Curtis Publishing Company and William E. Wilson.

Holt, Rinehart & Winston, Inc., for Will Cuppy's "George III" from *The Decline & Fall of Practically Everybody*, copyright 1950 by Fred Feldkamp and used with his permission; also for Brendan Gill's "Cole" from Robert Kimball, ed., *Cole*, copyright 1971. "Cole" first appeared as "Wouldn't It Be Fun?" in *The New Yorker*, September 18, 1971.

Houghton Mifflin Company for "Abe Lincoln's Indiana Boyhood and Youth" from Albert Beveridge's *Abraham Lincoln*, copyright 1928; also to the Beveridge estate.

Indiana Historical Society for permission to quote excerpts from *Indianapolis in the "Gay Nineties": High School Diaries of Claude G. Bowers* edited by Holman Hamilton and Gayle Thornbrough. Indianapolis: Indiana Historical Society, copyright 1964.

Indiana University Press for David Wagoner's "The Breathing Lesson" from *New and Selected Poems*, copyright 1969; also for John Woods' "The Deaths at Paragon" from *Turning to Look Back: Poems, 1955–1970*, copyright 1972, and for his poems "Guns" and "Striking the Earth," which, although first published elsewhere (as acknowledged below) were reprinted in *Striking the Earth*, copyright 1976; also for several folk ballads from Paul Brewster, ed., *Ballads and Songs of Indiana*, copyright 1940, by Indiana University.

Kansas Quarterly for Roger Pfingston's "Father & Gun," which first appeared as "The Gun" in the Summer, 1974, issue, Vol. VI–3.

Alfred Knopf/Random House and Mrs. George Jean Nathan for George Jean Nathan's "Attitudes Toward America" (Section 18, pages 109–115), Chapter VII, *Autobiography of an Attitude*, copyright 1925, by George Jean Nathan.

The Library of Congress for Elmer Davis's "Old Indiana and the New World," 1951.

The Little Magazine for permission to reprint Michael Allen's poem "Of Worms, the Earliest Harvest," which was first published in the Winter, 1975, issue, Vol. IX–1.

Eli Lilly for "A Trip to Wawasee in 1895" from *Early Wawasee Days* (Indianapolis: 1960).

Raintree Press for Richard Pflum's poem "Windfall," which first appeared in a longer version in *Moving Into Light,* copyright 1975, by Raintree Press. Mr. Pflum's shorter version is here *(The Indiana Experience)* printed for the first time.

Saturday Review for A. L. Lazarus's poem "An Indiana House Named Sylvia," which first appeared as "A House Named Sylvia" in the April 30, 1966, issue. Copyright 1966 by Saturday Review Associates and reprinted by permission.

Scripps-Howard Foundation and the Ernie Pyle Fund for Ernie Pyle's "Brown County" and "Ross, Ade, and Baker" from *Home Country,* copyright 1947, by Ernie Pyle and originally published by the William Sloane Associates.

Simon and Schuster, Inc., for excerpts from Chapters II and VIII of *Ross and Tom,* copyright 1974, by John Leggett—the exact excerpts approved by special permission of John Leggett; also for Wendell Willkie's "Our Reservoir of Good Will" from *One World,* copyright 1943, by Wendell Willkie, and renewed in 1971 by the late Philip Willkie; reprinted by special permission of Mrs. Philip Willkie.

Mary Ellen Solt for "Dogwood" from *Flowers in Concrete,* © 1966 by Mary Ellen Solt, published by the Fine Arts Department of Indiana University.

Southern Poetry Review and Philip Appleman for his poem "To the Garbage Collectors in Bloomington, Indiana, the First Pickup of the New Year," which first appeared in the Fall, 1967, issue, Vol. VIII–1, copyright 1967, by the Department of English, North Carolina State University. This poem was reprinted in Philip Appleman's *Summer Love & Surf,* copyright 1968, by Vanderbilt University Press and used by permission.

John Stover, Purdue University Department of History, for "Some Hoosier Railroad Memories," published here *(The Indiana Experience)* for the first time.

Felix Stefanile and Elizabeth Press for "How I Changed My Name Felice," "The Mourning Dove," and "Blizzard" from *A Fig Tree in America* (New Rochelle, N.Y.: 1970).

Swallow Press for John Matthias's poem "Swimming in the Quarry at Midnight," which first appeared as "Swimming at Midnight" in *Bucyrus,* copyright 1970, by John Matthias. This poem was originally published in a slightly different version from the one used here *(The Indiana Experience).* The changes (e.g., omitting "cops" from the watchers in lines 6 and 7) were made with the kind permission of Mr. Matthias.

Charles Toombs for "Master Timothy," © 1977 by Charles Toombs, which is published here for the first time.

Unified College Press and Dale Burgess for "Kokomo Helped Start the Whole Business," from *Us Hoosiers and How We Got That Way,* copyright 1966, by Dale E. Burgess.

University of California Press for the first ten pages of Chapter 1 of Irving McKee's *Ben Hur Wallace: The Life of General Lew Wallace,* copyright 1947 by the University of California Press and used by permission.

FOREWORD

Ask non-Hoosiers what comes to mind when they hear the word
Indiana, and they might mention the Indianapolis 500, the Fighting
Irish of Notre Dame, the Purdue Boilermakers, the Indiana Hurryin'
Hoosiers, or Hoosier hysteria. Chances are very good that non-Hoosiers are more likely to think about Indiana's contributions to sports
than to literature, the performing arts, education, medicine, engineering, space exploration, business, and industry. But the Hoosier
heritage is a vast, complex, and proud one that includes significant
contributions to every aspect of society and culture—not the least of
which is to literature.

Every well-read person knows the names of Lew Wallace, Theodore Dreiser, Booth Tarkington, George Ade, Lloyd C. Douglas,
Gene Stratton Porter, Ernie Pyle, Jessamyn West, Elmer Davis, Will
Cuppy, Emily Kimbrough, James Whitcomb Riley, Cole Porter, Joseph Hayes, and Kurt Vonnegut. And most of those writers are repre-
sented in this volume either by their own work or by writings about
them. But there is far more in this literary treasure chest which the
editor has divided into five compartments: essays, short stories, biographical and autobiographical sketches, poetry, and plays. Each
compartment contains its literary diamonds that demand close examination and that will reward you, the reader, for the time spent
looking beyond the sparkle to the hard core of brightness.

In the essay section, you will find the humor of Will Cuppy, Emily
Kimbrough, and Ruth McKenney. You will read the more serious
prose of Wendell Willkie, James Comer, George Jean Nathan, Eli
Lilly, Ernie Pyle, and Elmer Davis. And you will even be treated to
a sprightly essay on the origin of the word *Hoosier.*

The play section contains two surprises. George Barr McCutcheon's *The Double Doctor* has never been published until now. And
David Graham Phillips' *The Worth of a Woman* is a feminist play

that was produced in 1908—long before the public was ready to accept such thinking. In fact, Phillips was vilified by male chauvinists and assassinated by a fanatic who claimed that the playwright was smearing the ideal image of women.

In the section on biographical and autobiographical sketches, you will read about Abraham Lincoln's boyhood years in Indiana, about a high school commencement in 1898, about Cole Porter, and about Amelia Earhart at Purdue. And there are other jewels.

In fact, this anthology is filled with surprises. So I won't spoil them for you by indicating what you will find in the poetry and short story sections. Rather, I will simply wish you the happy and pleasant reading that you will enjoy because Arnold Lazarus, Professor of English at Purdue University, spent countless hours compiling this anthology for you. On behalf of the Indiana Council of Teachers of English, I wish to thank him for his hard work on, and dedication to, this excellent volume. I know that you, too, will be pleased with the treasure chest he has filled for you.

—Edward B. Jenkinson,
Director, English Curriculum Study
Center
Indiana University

President, Indiana Council of
Teachers of English—1974–76

The Indiana Experience

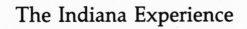

Essays

ELMER DAVIS

(b. Aurora, 1890–d. 1958) was educated in the Aurora schools, at
Franklin College, and at Oxford University, where he was a
Rhodes Scholar. After teaching at Franklin High School, he moved
to New York City, where he worked on the *New York Times.*
During World War II he was Director of the Office of War Information. Although his books include fiction, notably *Show Window,* he
is best remembered for his essays, especially *But We Were Born
Free* (1954) and *Not To Mention the War* (1940), containing his
celebrated essay on cats. The essay below was originally a speech
he delivered at the Library of Congress Exhibition Commemorat-
ing the Territory of Indiana, 30 November 1950, and later published by the Library of Congress, Washington, D.C., 1951.

Old Indiana
and the New World

I have no doubt that some of you felt that there was something a
little inappropriate in the selection of a speaker for this evening who
left Indiana 40 years ago, and has had only infrequent and casual
contacts with the State since then; and also one who did not come
from the region which has become generally known as the classical
and typical Indiana, the up-State flat lands. I came from the river
counties, which for many years past have been incorporated in the
life and culture of the State—thanks to the automobile; but which
had not been so incorporated in my day, when the automobile was
still a rich man's toy, and there were no roads for it to run on anyway.

In those days the river counties were something separate and
peculiar; they had little contact with the classic Hoosier culture up-
State, they belonged rather to the river culture, which from Pittsburgh and St. Paul down to New Orleans was pretty much all one
piece, a culture which even in the days of the railroad was long
dominated by the steamboat. The flavor of life in the river counties
in those days was much more the flavor of Kentucky than of Indiana;
and in my corner of the State we were still further denationalized;
we were part of the tri-State metropolitan complex of Cincinnati.

And in those days before the automobile there were also certain
other local cultures inside the State—cultures centering around, or

3

strung along, some of the railroads. The best known of them was the
Monon culture, thanks to the thousands of people from all over the
State who attended the four institutions of learning on the Monon;
but we had a local culture on the B. & O. too. I don't know whether
Senator Capehart is old enough to remember that far back, but if he
is I am sure he will bear me out. There were six principal towns on
the B. & O.—Lawrenceburg, Aurora, North Vernon, Seymour,
Washington, and Vincennes; and they all showed certain points of
resemblance—one of those points of resemblance being that each
one of the six would readily admit that the other five were the
hellholes of creation, and could bring up evidence to support it.

Yet when you survey the history of Indiana, as State and as Territory, for the past century and a half, it is clear that the river counties
were an essential and typical part of it, however they differed from
what later became the stereotype. We were after all the first of
Indiana, since the first settlers either came across the river from
Kentucky or down the river from Pennsylvania; we were building
stately homes and reading the classics when up-State Indiana still
consisted mostly of swamps, inhabited chiefly by water moccasins
and malarial mosquitos. That up-State life—at least as far up-State as
Decatur County—was later depicted by a river-county novelist, Edward Eggleston, in a book which was never popular among his fellow
citizens. And with some reason; for while *The Hoosier Schoolmaster*
was true as of the time he remembered, it was no longer true of the
time the book was published. By that time up-State had caught up
with the river counties; and was presently to go far beyond them, in
wealth, self-advertisement, and self-satisfaction.

Yet in those earliest days the river counties had established some
traditions to which the whole State has been loyal—in politics, for
instance. The Congressman from my district, in Andrew Jackson's
day, was Amos Lane—a violent anti-Jacksonian; and it has been reported by those who heard him that when he was denouncing his
enemies on the stump, the gritting and grinding of his teeth could
be heard 50 yards away. I defy any of our present congressional
delegation to improve on that. The river counties set the Hoosier
literary tradition; and it goes back beyond Edward Eggleston or even
Julia Dumont. My home town, Aurora, was founded by the first
Indiana novelist, Jesse Lynch Holman. It is true that his novel, *The
Errors of Education,* was not the first Indiana novel; he wrote it while
he was still living in Lexington or Frankfort, Kentucky, before he
came across the river. But Aurora, if it was not the place where *The
Errors of Education* was written, has a more melancholy distinction;

it was the place where the first Indiana novel was destroyed. In later life Judge Holman became convinced that his youthful work might have a deleterious effect on the morals of young people, so he tried to buy up the whole edition, and very nearly succeeded. (It was probably not too difficult a task, since the book, like the stock of certain family corporations, seems to have been closely held.) At any rate he seems to have got hold of all but two copies and according to tradition he burned them in the public square. The first and, so far, the only book-burning in Indiana.

Well—up-State eventually passed the river counties; yet we went on leading our own lives until the automobile finally reunited the State. What that life was like down on the river, 50 years ago, has lately been set down in a novel called *Ring In the New,* by Laura Buchanan Harris, who came from Rising Sun; it was riverbank stuff but a great deal of it is thoroughly recognizable as a picture of small-town life anywhere in Indiana, or indeed in the Middle West, at the turn of the century. It is incidentally about the best picture that has ever been done of life in the river counties; since our ablest novelist, David Graham Phillips, while he was an accurate and perspicacious reporter of Fifth Avenue and Wall Street, fell down badly in his one attempt to give a picture of life in Madison and at DePauw. So much for the river counties up till the time I left; but since then, with good roads and the cars that ride on them making the State all one piece, we have been incorporated into the general picture that Indiana presents to the world.

That is a remarkable picture—such a clear and familiar picture as perhaps no other State in the Union has ever presented. The picture written down in some of Tarkington's novels, some of Nicholson's essays, some of McCutcheon's cartoons, some of Ade's fables; and above all in practically all of Riley's poems—that is Indiana as it has presented itself to the world. It is an attractive picture; what is more, it is a coherent and credible picture. It was substantially true, for its time and place; but it dealt with only a part of Indiana—though the larger and wealthier part, the up-State flat lands; and for hardly more than a quarter of the commonwealth's existence as State and Territory—roughly, the 40 years following the Civil War. A picture of an essentially rural culture, though punctuated by and focussed on the county seats; a world of stovepipe hats and base-burner stoves, where people got around by horse and buggy and by spring wagon, unless they had to go so far that they took the accommodation train. A centripetal, introspective culture; pretty well satisfied with itself, but with better reason for self-satisfaction than most; a world with no aspiration to the loftier heights, but which also, in those days, managed to avoid the depths as well. . . .

But that was only a part of Indiana, in place and time; and the great merit of this exhibition which is opened here tonight is to remind us of the immense variety that has actually existed, over a century and a half, in a State whose stereotype is so familiar. You see here more of old Vincennes, and of the earlier French explorations, than Maurice Thompson ever told you. You see more of the early Utopian pioneers at New Harmony—men whom every Hoosier is taught to reverence but whom no present-day Hoosier would ever dream of imitating. Father Rapp's Utopia was celibate; and the taste for celibacy had disappeared from Indiana long before Dr. Kinsey's day. Robert Dale Owen is a hero because he has been dead a long time; if he lived in Indiana today he would probably be ridden out of town on a rail as a Communist agitator. Yet you see here records of those men and of many others, men of the river counties and of the lake counties as well as of the great interior; and you realize that in a State whose typical picture is so familiar, and so attractive, there were nevertheless at sundry times and in divers places many other things that were also Indiana.

That stereotyped picture drawn from Riley's poems and *The Gentleman from Indiana* and McCutcheon's Indian-summer cartoon— that picture was already beginning to be out of date in my day; and you can perhaps date its decline and fall by one of the best things George Ade ever wrote—*I Knew Him When*. . . .

Indiana was already changing. The brief age of the interurbans marked the beginning of the change; Indiana was ceasing to be rural, it was becoming industrialized. Not only Indianapolis but even the county seats, most of them, have become industrial towns with industrial problems, to which the old Hoosier credo offered no answer. I pass over the brief reign of the Klan, though I should like to believe that the spirit that made the Klan possible is as dead as the paraphernalia of hoods and sheets; but other problems came up with the new age and Indiana, like the rest of the country, is still trying to find the answer. . . .

Indeed there had been proof of that . . . in the spring of 1937, when the great wave of strikes—organizing strikes, steel strikes in particular—spread through the Middle West. There was bitterness and violence on both sides; plants were occupied by sit-down strikers; other strikers were shot down—retail shootings in Ohio and Michigan, wholesale shootings in Chicago. There were steel strikes in Indiana too; and Cliff Townsend, who was then Governor, settled them peaceably within 3 days—without violence, without bloodshed; and unfortunately without national publicity. The metropolitan newspapers in those days were not interested in the peaceful settlement of industrial disputes; all they cared about was brickbats and blood. But it was a demonstration that even in the new industrial age, the Hoosier temperament was disinclined to go to extremes.

Whether that temperament is a virtue or a fault has been much debated—the cult of the first-rate second-rate man, the avoidance of extremes, whether of virtue and of wisdom or of vice and folly. The argument has perhaps little point any more since it has come loose at one end; Indiana may still produce no saints and heroes, but . . . we did produce one man—the late Wendell Willkie—who was not afraid to go out on a limb for the things he believed in; who was not afraid even of that thing which Hoosiers of his generation and mine, and of the generation before us, were taught to fear above everything else; he was not afraid of being laughed at. He was a prophet not without honor, save in his own country; it is still to be seen whether he will have a successor. . . .

The old tight, introspective, self-satisfied Hoosier culture, which never aspired to the heights but never descended to the depths—which cultivated the doctrine of moderation in all things, of the golden mean—that is gone. . . .

For better or worse, the world had broken into Indiana; and Indiana had broken out into the world. An age in which I saw the Paris Opera House, which I had known well in other circumstances and in earlier years, filled with American soldiers, listening to other American soldiers performing the works of Hoagy Carmichael from Bloomington and Cole Porter from Peru.

The Indiana of tradition could handle the simpler problems of its day; but the problems of this new age take more thinking.

❖ ❖ ❖ ❖ ❖

MEREDITH NICHOLSON

(b. Crawfordsville, 1866–d. 1947) was educated in the Indianapolis schools. After working on Indianapolis newspapers, including *The Sentinel* and *The News*, he took to free-lance writing. Of his thirty publications two of the best known remain *The Hoosiers* (1900) from which this selection is taken, and *The House of a Thousand Candles* (1905).

The Rural Type
and the Dialect

The origin of the term "Hoosier" is not known with certainty. It has been applied to the inhabitants of Indiana for many years, and, after "Yankee," it is probably the sobriquet most famous as applied to the people of a particular division of the country. So early as 1830, "Hoosier" must have had an accepted meaning, within the State at least, for John Finley printed in that year, as a New Year's address for the Indianapolis *Journal,* a poem called "The Hoosier Nest," in which the word occurs several times. It is a fair assumption that its meaning was not obscure, or it would not have been used in a poem intended for popular reading. "Hoosier" seems to have found its first literary employment in Finley's poem. Sulgrove, who was an authority in matters of local history, was disposed to concede this point. The poem is interesting for its glimpse of Indiana rural life of the early period. Finley was a Virginian who removed to Indiana in 1823 and had been living in the State seven years when he published his poem. He was an accomplished and versatile gentleman, and his verses, as collected in 1866, show superior talents. One of his poems, "Bachelor's Hall," has often been attributed to Thomas Moore. The "Hoosier Nest" is the home of a settler, which a traveller hailed at nightfall. Receiving a summons to enter, the stranger walked in,—

> "Where half a dozen Hoosieroons
> With mush-and-milk, tin cups and spoons
> White heads, bare feet and dirty faces
> Seemed much inclined to keep their places."

The stranger was invited to a meal of venison, milk, and Johnny-cake, and as he sat at the humble board he made an inventory of the cabin's contents:—

> "One side was lined with divers garments,
> The other spread with skins of varmints;
> Dried pumpkins overhead were strung,
> Where venison hams in plenty hung;
> Two rifles placed above the door;
> Three dogs lay stretched upon the floor,—
> In short, the domicile was rife
> With specimens of Hoosier life."

"Hoosieroons" is never heard now, and was probably invented by Finley for the sake of the rhyme. Both Governor Wright and O. H. Smith were of the opinion that "Hoosier" was a corruption of "Who's here" (*yere* or *Hyer*); and Smith has sought to dramatize its history:
—

> "The night was dark, the rain falling in torrents, when the inmates of a small log cabin in the woods of early Indiana were aroused from their slumbers by a low knocking at the only door of the cabin. The man of the house, as he had been accustomed to do on like occasions, rose from his bed and hallooed. 'Who's here?' The outsiders answered, 'Friends, out bird-catching. Can we stay till morning?' The door was opened, and the strangers entered. A good log fire soon gave light and warmth to the room. Stranger to the host: 'What did you say when I knocked?' 'I said, Who's here?' 'I thought you said Hoosier.' The bird-catchers left after breakfast, but next night returned and hallooed at the door, 'Hoosier;' and from that time the Indianans have been called Hoosiers."

This is the explanation usually given to inquirers within the State. The objection has sometimes been raised to this story, that the natural reply to a salutation in the wilderness would be "Who's there?" out of which "Hoosier" could hardly be formed; but careful observers of Western and Southern dialects declare that "Who's hyer?" was, and in obscure localities remains, the common answer to a midnight hail. . . .

An Indiana visitor who had heard Lehmanowski lecture on "The Wars of Europe" and been captivated by the prowess of the Hussars, whipped one of the Kentuckians, and bending over him cried, "I'm a Hoosier," meaning, "I'm a Hussar." Mr. Woods adds that he was living in the State at the time and that this was the true origin of the term. This is, however, hardly conclusive. . . .

. . . Hoosier as a Christian name has been known in the Ohio Valley; it was borne by a member of the Indiana Methodist Conference in 1835. A Louisville baker named Hoosier made a variety of sweet bread which was so much affected by Indiana people that they were called "Hoosier's customers," "Hoosier's men," and so on; but no date can be found for this. The Rev. T. A. Goodwin, first heard the word at Cincinnati in 1830, where it described a species of gingerbread, but without reference to Indiana.

It is clear that the cultivated people of Indiana recognized the nickname in the early half of the century. Wright and Smith, as mentioned above, had sought to determine its genesis; and Tilghman

A. Howard, when a congressman from Indiana, writing home to a friend in 1840, spoke casually of the "Hoosier State." The word occurs familiarly in Hall's "New Purchase" (1855), and it is found also in Beste's rare volume, "The Wabash; or, Adventures of an English Gentleman's Family in the Interior of America," published at London in the same year, and in Mrs. Beecher's "From Dawn to Daylight" (1859). And when, in 1867, Sandford C. Cox published a book of verses containing the couplet,—

> "If Sam is right, I would suggest
> A native Hoosier as the best,"—

the word was widely known, and thereafter it frequently occurs in all printed records touching the State. It is reported from Tennessee, Virginia, and South Carolina by independent observers, who say that the idea of a rough countryman is always associated with it. In Missouri it is sometimes used thus abstractly, but a native Indianian is usually meant, without reference to his manners or literacy. . . .

The pioneers could not see then, as their children see now, that the wilderness was a factor in their destiny; that it drove them in upon themselves, strengthening their independence in material things by shutting them off from older communities, and that it even fastened upon their tongues the peculiarities of speech which they had brought with them into the wilderness. But their isolation compelled meditation, and when reading matter penetrated the woodlands it was usually worth the trouble of transportation in a day of few roads and little travel. The pioneers knew their Bibles and named their children for the Bible heroes, and most of their other books were religious. There have been worse places in which to form habits of thought, and to lay the foundation for a good manner of writing our language, than the Hoosier cabin. Lying before the fireplace in his father's humble Spencer County home during the fourteen years that the family spent in Indiana,—years that were of the utmost importance in his life,—Abraham Lincoln studied his few books and caught the elusive language-spirit that later on gave character and beauty to his utterances.

The social life of the first comers also drew its inspiration from their environment, and was expressed in log-rolling, house-raising, and other labors that could best be done by coöperation, and which they concluded usually, in a fashion quite characteristic, with a frolic. . . .

The Hoosier fiddle was a factor in all the festivities of the country folk. The fiddler was frequently an eccentric genius, ranking with the rural poet, who was often merely a maker of idle rhymes; however, the country fiddler in Indiana has held his own against latter-day criticism and the competition of the village brass band. Governor Whitcomb enjoyed local fame as a violinist, and Barry Sulgrove and General Lew Wallace, in their younger years, were skilful with the bow. Dr. H. W. Taylor, a conscientious student of early Hoosier customs, connects the Hoosier fiddler with the Scotch Highlanders, and has expressed his belief that the Highlander folk coming to the United States naturally sought the mountain country of Virginia, North Carolina, Tennessee, and Georgia, and that the Scotch fiddle and its traditions survive principally in these mountainous countries. We are told that the fiddle of the Hoosiers is an exotic and cannot long survive, though fifteen years after this prediction a contest of Hoosier fiddlers was held in the largest hall at Indianapolis, and many musicians of this old school appeared from the back districts to compete for the prizes. The great aim of the old time fiddlers was to make their instruments "talk." Their tunes enjoyed such euphonious names as "Old Dan Tucker," "Old Zip Coon," "Possum up a Gum Stump," "Irish Washerwoman," "Waggoner," "Ground Spy," and "Jay Bird."...

James Whitcomb Riley corroborates the impression of earlier writers in a characteristic poem, "My Fiddle":

> "My playin's only middlin'—tunes I picked up when a boy—
> The kind o'-sort o'fiddlin' that the folks calls 'cordaroy';
> 'The Old Fat Gal' and 'Rye-Straw,' and 'My Sailyor's on the
>   Sea,'
> Is the old cowtillions *I* 'saw' when the ch'ice is left to me;
>   And so I plunk and plonk and plink
>   And rosum-up my bow,
>   And play the tunes that make you think
>   The devil's in your toe!"

In several of the Southern Indiana counties the least admirable traits of the ancestors of the "poor whites" who came in from the South have been continued into a third and fourth generation; but these do not appear prominently in any fair or comprehensive examination of the people. Much has been written of the lawlessness of Indianians, and lynching and whitecapping have sporadically been reported from many of the southern counties. An attorney-general of the State who had brought all the machinery of the law to bear upon particular instances of lynching during his term of office, and who had given much study to the phenomena presented by these outbreaks, expressed his opinion that the right of way of the Baltimore and Southwestern Railway marked the "lynching belt" in Indiana. Statistics in confirmation are lacking, but it is safe to say that a large percentage of the lynchings reported in the State have occurred either in counties on the line of the road or in those immediately adjoining.... The milder form of outlawry, known as "whitecapping," has also been practised in Indiana occasionally, and sometimes with barbarous cruelty; but it, like lynching, is not peculiar to the State, and its extent has been greatly exaggerated by Eastern newspapers.

It has been insisted by loyal Indianians that the speech of the later generations of natives is almost normal English; that the rough vernacular of their ancestors has been ground down in the schools, and that the dictionaries are rapidly sanctioning new words, once without authority, that inevitably crept into common speech through the necessities of pioneer expression. It may fairly be questioned whether, properly speaking, there ever existed a Hoosier dialect. The really indigenous Indiana words and novel pronunciations are so few as to make but a poor showing when collected; and while the word "dialect" is employed as a term of convenience in this connection, it can only be applied to a careless manner of speaking, in which novel words are merely incidental. A book of colloquial terms, like Green's "Virginia Word Book," could hardly be compiled for Indiana without infringing upon the prior claims of other and older States to the greater part of it. The so-called Hoosier dialect, where it survives at all, is the speech of the first American settlers in Indiana, greatly modified by time and schooling, but retaining, both in the employment of colloquial terms and in pronunciation, the peculiarities that were carried westward from tide water early in the nineteenth century. The distinctive Indiana countryman, the real Hoosier, who has been little in contact with the people of cities, speaks a good deal as his Pennsylvania or North Carolina or Kentucky grandfather or great-grandfather did before him, and has created nothing new. His speech contains comparatively few words that are peculiar to the State or to communities within it; but in the main it shares such deviations from normal or literary English with the whole Southwest.

Lapses in pronunciation have never been punishable with death on the Wabash, as at the fords of the Jordan, where the shibboleth test of the Gileadites cost the Ephraimites forty and two thousand. The native Indianian is not sensitive about his speech and refuses to be humble before critics from the East who say "idea-r" and "Philadelphia-r." James Whitcomb Riley has made the interesting and just observation that the average countryman knows in reality a wider range of diction than he permits himself to use, and that his abridgments and variations are attributable to a fear lest he may offend his neighbors by using the best language at his command.... Sulgrove confirms Riley's impression:—

> Correct pronunciation was positively regarded by the Southern immigration as a mark of aristocracy or, as they called it, 'quality.' The 'ing' in 'evening,' or 'morning' or any other words, was softened into 'in,' the full sound being held finical and 'stuck up.' So it was no unusual thing to hear such a comical string of emasculated 'nasals' as the question of a prominent Indiana lawyer of the Kentucky persuasion, 'Where were you a-standin' at the time of your perceivin' of the hearin' of the firin' of the pistol?' ... To 'set' was the right way to sit; an Indian did not scalp, he 'skelped'; a child did not long for a thing, he 'honed' for it,—slang retains this Hoosier archaism; a woman was not dull, she was 'daunsy'; commonly a gun was 'shot' instead of fired in all moods and tenses.

While the French settlements in Indiana made no appreciable impression on the common speech, yet it has been assumed by some observers that the inclination at the South to throw the accent of words forward, as in gentle*men*, settle*ment*, was fairly attributable to the influence of the French.... However, Southern Indianians sometimes say *Tennes*-sy, accenting the first syllable and slurring the last, illustrating again the danger of accepting any theories or fixing any rules for general guidance in such matters. Dr. Eggleston remembers only one French word that survived from old French times in the Wabash country,—"cordelle, to tow a boat by a rope carried along the shore." The most striking influence in the Indiana dialect is that of the Scotch-Irish, who have left marked peculiarities of speech behind them wherever they have gone ... as, for example, the linguistic deficiency which makes *strenth* and *lenth* of *strength* and *length,* or *bunnle* of *bundle,* and the use of *nor* for *than,* after a comparative adjective. The use of *into* for *in* and *whenever* for *as soon as* are other Scotch-Irish peculiarities. These, however, are heard only in diminishing degree in Indiana, and many of the younger generations of Hoosiers have never known them....

The circulation of newly coined words has been so rapid in late years, owing to the increase of communication between different parts of the country, and to dissemination by the newspapers, that few useful words originating obscurely are likely to remain local. Lowell amused himself by tracing to unassailable English sources terms that were assumed to be essentially American; and if Chaucer and the Elizabethans may be invoked against our rural communities, the word-hunter's sport has grown much simpler when he may cite a usage in one State to disestablish the priority claimed for it in another. There is risk in all efforts to connect novel words with particular communities, no matter how carefully it may be done, and it is becoming more and more difficult to separate real dialect from slang. Lists of unusual words that have been reported to the American Dialect Society afford interesting instances of the danger of accepting terms as local which are really in general use. The word *rambunctious,* reported from New York State as expressing impudence and forwardness, cannot be peculiar to that region, for it is used in Indiana in identically the same sense. Other words, collected through the same agency and common in Indiana, are: *scads,* reported from Missouri, signifying a great quantity; and *sight,* meaning a large amount, noted in New England and New York. *Great hand for,* meaning a *penchant,* traced from Maine to Ohio, may be followed also into Indiana, but this, like *druthers,* for a preference or choice, belongs to the towns rather than to the country. *Go like,* in the sense of imitation, as *"go like* a rooster," is reported from both Maine and Indiana; and *foot-loose,* meaning free and untrammelled, observed in Georgia, is used in the towns, at least, of Indiana. The natural disposition of Americans to exaggerate led to the creation by the Southeastern element in Indiana population of *bodaciously,* a corruption of audaciously; and to the employment of *powerful,* indiscriminately with *big* or *little,* as a particularly emphatic superlative. Curiously enough *powerful,* which is usually identified with the earlier generations of the Southwest, is reported also from Eastern Massachusetts. *Sarcumstansis* for *circumstances, b'ar* for *bear,* and *thar* for *there* reached Indiana through Kentucky, and are now rarely heard. . . .

Mrs. Henry Ward Beecher, whose unamiable novel, "From Dawn to Daylight," is a dreary picture of Indiana life, gives a few interesting usages; as *a right smart chance of money, heap of plunder, sight stronger, proper hard,* showing that her acquaintance was principally with the Southern element, which she had known at Lawrenceburg and Indianapolis. *Plunder,* as a synonym for baggage, seems to be largely Southern and Western, and was probably derived from the Pennsylvania Germans. The insolent intrusiveness of dialect is illustrated by the appearance of the word in its colloquial sense in the first chapter of General Wallace's "Prince of India." Dr. Eggleston in "The Graysons" gives *weth* for *with, air* for *are, thes* for

just, sher'f for *sheriff,* and *yer's* for *here is.* Indianians usually pro-
nounce the name of their State correctly, though the final vowel
sometimes becomes *y.* Benjamin S. Parker remembers that in the
early days pioneers sometimes said *Injuns, Injiana,* and *immejut;*
but these usages are obsolete in the State . . . *Ornery,* a vulgar form
of ordinary, seems to be generally used, and has been observed in the
Middle States as well as in Indiana and Kentucky. The injunction
mind out, which is used in Kentucky in such admonitions as "*mind
out* what you are doing," becomes *watch out* in Indiana. *Wrench* for
rinse, used in the States contiguous to the Ohio, is *rense* in New
England. *Critter* for *horse* is still heard in parts of rural Indiana,
which derived population through Kentucky, where the same usage
is noted. *Fruit,* as applied to stewed apples (apple sauce) only, is a
curious limitation of the noun, heard among old-fashioned people of
Southern origin in Indiana. *Some place* for *somewhere* is not charge-
able to Indiana alone, but this and the phrases *want on* and *want off*
seem to be used chiefly in the West Central States, and they belong
to the borderland between slang and dialect. It would seem a far cry
from the Hoosier speech to the classic Greek, and yet Dr. H. W.
Taylor has pursued this line of philological inquiry with astonishing
results, tracing an analogy of sound and sense most ingeniously between Greek terms and words found in the American dialects.

In the speech of the illiterate, there is usually something of rhythm
and cadence. All slang shares a feeling for the balance and nice
adjustment of words, and slang phrases are rarely clumsy. The cry of
a boy calling his mate has its peculiar crescendo, and pedlers the
world over run the scale of human expression in pursuit of odd
effects. The drawl of the Southerner and Southwesterner is not un-
musical, though it may try the patience of the stranger. Even cultivated Indianians, particularly those of Southern antecedents, have
the habit of clinging to their words; they do not bite them off sharply.
G performs its office as final consonant in *ing* under many disadvantages; and it was long ignored, though the school teachers have struggled nobly to restore it. The blending of words, which begins with
childhood, is often carried into maturity by the Indianian; thus by a
lazy elision "did you ever" is combined in *jever,* and "where did you
get" becomes *wherjuget.*

It is unfortunate that there are so few trustworthy records of the
early Southwestern speech, and that first and last bad grammar,
reckless spelling, and the indiscriminate distribution of the printer's
apostrophe by writers who had no real knowledge to guide them,
have served to create an erroneous impression of the illiteracy of the

Indianians and their neighbors. It is likely that during the next quarter of a century the continued fusion of the various elements of Western population will create a dead level of speech, approximating accuracy, so that in a typical American State like Indiana local usages will disappear.

WILLIAM E. WILSON

(b. Evansville, 1906–) was educated at Central High School, where he was Editor of *The Centralian,* and at Harvard University. From 1950–1971 he taught at Indiana University. His twenty books include *The Wabash* (1940), *Abe Lincoln at Pigeon Creek* (1949), and *The Angel & the Serpent, the Story of New Harmony* (1964).

Pioneers in Paradise

Sometimes I think the trouble with the space age is that the traffic is all headed in the same direction. Perhaps what we need more than a rocket to the moon is an occasional angel plummeting from the sky to give us a piece of his mind. So far as I know, that hasn't happened in this country since Gabriel dropped in on New Harmony, Indiana, more than a hundred years ago.

Gabriel left his footprints in New Harmony as proof of his visit, and they are still there. There are also many other reminders of the two sets of Utopia seekers who settled that little town on the Wabash and dreamed of pie in the sky as well as heavenly messengers. There are ancient dormitories built of bricks made without straw, a towering thick-walled fort, a walled cemetery without headstones (the Harmonyites believed that anyone soaring into the hereafter would do better without ballast), a maze, an opera house, and a museum filled with the early inhabitants' belongings. And there is a spirit pervading the place that makes it different from any other Middle Western village I know.

When I was a boy, growing up in southern Indiana, I thought the best time for a visit to New Harmony was August. That is when the watermelons are ripe. There is nothing better than a red-ripe Posey County watermelon, but if I were going there as a sight-seer today, I would choose June or October. In June, the Trees of the Golden Rain are pouring their gold upon New Harmony's quiet walks and streets; and in October, the oak, the maple and the gum are aflame in the soft haze that rises like smoke from the river.

You can no longer reach the town by boat, like Father Rapp's pious German peasants or Robert Owen's starry-eyed cosmopolites when they came to experiment with Paradise in the wilderness. You couldn't go by boat in my boyhood either. I don't suppose there has been a passenger boat on the Wabash since Jenk Hugo ran the *Juno* aground at New Harmony in the 1860's and formed an island. When I was a boy, we went by train. Nowadays you can only drive.

The best approach is from Evansville by Indiana State Highway 66. That winding road takes you across the breadth of Posey, Indiana's southernmost and least accessible county, and lets you discover gradually that your journey is measured in years as well as miles. In New Harmony, it is not today, but yesterday. Drowsing in the sun, the village still dreams the dream of the men and women who lived there more than a century ago.

George Rapp dreamed the dream first. He was a German from Württemberg, the patriarch of a thriving colony of his countrymen in Pennsylvania, when he first saw the site of Harmony on the Wabash in 1814 and bought 30,000 acres of Government land. By the end of that year, Rapp and his followers had established the new community and were beginning to construct the buildings that still shelter many of New Harmony's 1360 inhabitants.

Rapp's Utopianism was a religious faith. Since God belonged to everyone, he argued, so should the world's goods. If men lived in a state of economic as well as spiritual equality, they would be better prepared for the millennium, which he believed was just around the corner.

But Rapp recognized that living on the brink of eternal peace was as difficult as living eternally on the brink of war. To keep men and women alert to the crisis, a master of brinkmanship was needed, and the master of George Rapp's choice was George Rapp. He told his followers that he was in direct communication with the Almighty— and they believed him. To keep his lines of communication clear, he said he needed a fine brick house where he could live apart from the communal hubbub of the dormitories—and his followers built it for him. They also dug a tunnel from his house to the communal fort, and after that the fort became the communal granary and warehouse.

Rapp had another theory about preparing for the millennium. He believed that Adam originally was both male and female and that Adam's "fall" was the loss of his female sex when Eve was created. To return to his original perfection, Rapp concluded, man must reunite the sexes within himself, and the way to accomplish that was to live a celibate life. Therefore, the patriarch put an embargo on marriage.

From across the Atlantic, no less a poet than Lord Byron raised a cynical eyebrow in the direction of the town on the Wabash. In *Don Juan,* Byron wrote:

> *Why called he 'Harmony' a state sans wedlock?*
> *Now there I've got the preacher at a deadlock.*
> *Because he either meant to sneer at harmony*
> *Or marriage, by divorcing them thus oddly.*
> *But whether Reverend Rapp learned this in Germany*
> *Or no, 'tis said his sect is rich and godly.*

Lord Byron's information was correct. With Father Rapp's adopted son, Frederick, as business manager, the sect became rich. And with Father Rapp himself as spiritual leader, it was godly. Those Germans in the Indiana wilderness made a religious ritual of everything they did. At sunrise, they marched to work singing hymns, and at sunset they marched back, still singing.

After that, to remove temptations, the men and women went off to their separate dormitories, and every hour of the night when the watchman made his rounds he reminded them of their purpose.

"Again a day is past," he chanted, "and a step made nearer to our end, our time runs away, and the joys of heaven are our reward."

But Communism—even religious Communism—apparently does not thrive on prosperity. At least, that is what Father Rapp concluded. He began to see signs of restlessness in his flock. It was not easy to continue living the life of austerity when their granary was bursting and their wine barrels were spilling over and strangers, coming from the towns and clearings roundabout, were buying up and enjoying the rich fruits of the community's labors. Father Rapp decided that the only thing to do was to sell out and start all over again, from scratch, somewhere else.

He feared, however, that his own opinion alone might not persuade his people to give up what they had earned. He needed divine confirmation. Luckily, about that time, the Angel Gabriel came down from heaven and agreed with him. What was more, Gabriel conveniently left a pair of giant-sized footprints on a limestone slab as proof that he had been there.

What George Rapp bought in 1814 for $61,050 he sold ten years later for about $150,000, and it must have been a fair price because the buyer was a businessman from Scotland, Robert Owen. Rapp then moved his colony to a site eighteen miles below Pittsburgh on the Ohio River, and there, in a town they named Economy, they prospered again. When Rapp died, in 1847, they were said to be worth several million dollars.

Owen, a textile manufacturer, had a dream of Utopia in his head too. But the millennium Owen dreamed of was social and intellectual, not theological. He staked his hopes on perfecting man's reason, not his soul. Most of the Owenites were distinguished men and women before they came to the Indiana wilderness. One of the keelboats that bore them down the Ohio and up the Wabash was so loaded with eggheads that it was called "The Boatload of Knowledge." Among its passengers was one of Owen's four sons, Robert Dale Owen. Another was the Dutch geologist Gerard Troost. Still another was a Philadelphian named Thomas Say, who later would be called "the father of American zoology."

It was Say who planted the first *Koelreuteria Paniculata* in the United States at New Harmony. The tree is more commonly known by its poetic Oriental name, The Tree of the Golden Rain, and, more commonly still, as the rain tree. In New Harmony, they call it the gate tree. Small and round-topped, it grows everywhere in the town, showering the streets and lawns with its golden blossoms in the spring and replacing them in autumn with clusters of yellow pods that are shaped like Japanese lanterns.

Besides the men on the Boatload of Knowledge, others of equal renown came to live or visit in the new Utopia. Among them were William Maclure, the geologist; Charles Alexandre LeSeur, a naturalist from the Jardin des Plantes of Paris; the teachers, Marie Fretageot and Joseph Neef, who set up an experimental school in the Rappite Community House No. 2, and the reformer, Frances Wright, who would establish her own community in Tennessee.

These Owenites gave lectures, wrote books, meditated, and danced and sang. Above all, they danced and sang. As one observer put it, "The dancing and the instrumental music engrossed more of energy than the more important considerations of community welfare."

Certainly the Owenites did not take kindly to manual labor. "The hogs have been our Lords and Masters this year in field and garden," one of the colonists complained. "We are without vegetables, except what we buy."

And not all of them found social equality congenial. The wife of one colonist wrote to a friend: "Oh, if you could see some of the rough uncouth creatures here, I think you would find it rather hard to look upon them exactly in the light of brothers and sisters."

Two years after he bought the town, Robert Owen had to admit that the experiment was a failure, and in May, 1827, he delivered a Farewell Address and went back to England, leaving his sons to manage his financial interests in the town. With Owen's departure, the communal effort fell apart in New Harmony, but the dream never entirely evaporated in Owen's head. He did not attempt to establish other communities, but he encouraged other dreamers to do so. The Yellow Springs Community in Ohio, for example, was an indirect result of his inspiration, and he gave comfort and counsel to the colonists of Brook Farm, at West Roxbury, Massachusetts. Owen died in 1858.

Today, when you visit the old town on the banks of the Wabash, most of what you *see* is the handwork of the Rappites—the substantial dormitories and the rooming houses, the fort, the cemetery, the maze, and, of course, Gabriel's footprints, which, skeptics have declared, were manufactured in St. Louis on George Rapp's order. But what you *feel*, if you linger a while in New Harmony and talk with its people, is the continuity of spirit that links it with its historic past. And this, of course, is the handwork of the Owenites.

After Owen's Utopia dissolved, many of his followers remained in the town, and they set a permanent mark upon its life. Robert Dale Owen was elected to Congress from New Harmony and was instrumental in founding the Smithsonian Institution; he labored in the cause of women's rights, and influenced Lincoln in the writing of the Emancipation Proclamation. His brother, David Dale Owen, set up a geological laboratory in New Harmony, and it is still there. For seventeen years, it was the headquarters of the U. S. Geological Survey.

Thomas Say stayed on and died in New Harmony in 1834. His tomb is in the yard of the old George Rapp homesite. In 1838, William Maclure founded the Library of the Workingmen's Institute, still one of the largest public libraries for a town of New Harmony's size. In 1859, Constance Fauntleroy, a granddaughter of Robert Owen, organized the first women's club in America, the Minerva Society. Her home, built in 1815 of hand-hewn oak, walnut and hickory, is on West Street and is open to the public.

As you drive into New Harmony from Evansville, the first of the Rappite buildings you see is the town's single bleak ruin. It is Rappite Community House No. 3 on Church Street. It was built in 1823 and converted into a hotel called The Tavern by the Owenites the next year. Robert Owen made his headquarters here and the place was operated continuously as a hotel for more than a hundred years. Seemingly beyond restoration, it probably will soon be torn down as a menace to safety.

The two-story brick house that Rapp's followers built for him was destroyed by fire in 1844; but on its site, at Church and Main Streets, you can see the home Alexander Maclure built immediately after the fire. It is one of the finest old houses in the Middle West. It is now private property, but it can be visited by special arrangement. In the yard is the huge slab of limestone—ten feet long, five feet wide and five inches thick—with the two enormous footprints that, Rapp said, had been made by the Angel Gabriel.

Catty-corner, as Hoosiers say, from the Maclure mansion is Community House No. 2, a three-story brick building and the most interesting survivor of the dormitories. When I was a boy, old No. 2 was a furniture store, owned by a descendant of the Owenites named Arthur Fretageot. In the spirit of his ancestors, Mr. Fretageot kept a large hall in the building open to the public. On Saturday nights we used to go there to sing and dance. The building is now being restored by the New Harmony Memorial Commission, and before long the old community house again will be open to the public.

The bricks with which old No. 2 was insulated were known locally as Dutch biscuits, slabs of wood wrapped with straw, cemented with clay. On the south wall of the dormitory hangs, or will hang when it is restored, a sundial that once ornamented Rapp's home. And under one of the stairways, there used to be an inscription written in German that read: "On the twenty-fourth of May, 1824, we have departed. Lord, with Thy great help and goodness, in body and soul protect us." I trust the timbers on which these words were scrawled have been preserved.

A little way down Church Street stands Community House No. 4, which was a dormitory for men in both Rappite and Owenite times. Later it was converted into a theater and it continued to present drama into the present century. Before the coming of movie palaces, it was the second largest theater in Indiana, in a town whose population never exceeded 1500. The building today serves as a garage, but the balcony of the Opera House is still intact and the outlines of the stage are still visible. Perhaps this old Opera House is the best testimonial to the culture that continued in New Harmony long after Owen's Utopia had failed.

There have been Fretageots among New Harmony's leading citizens ever since Madame Marie Fretageot came from France, by way of Philadelphia, to set up her experimental school, and members of the family still live in the old family home on Main Street. There are still Coxes and Fords and Sopers and Elliotts and Mumfords in the town, descendants of Owen's followers who bore those names. And there are still Owens. Recently, Kenneth Owen, a descendant of Robert Owen, returned to his birthplace, and he and his wife have bought and restored many of the old houses. All these people take a quiet pride in their ancestors and cherish the history of the old town on the Wabash.

Like the slab of limestone in George Rapp's yard, where Gabriel is said to have alighted, the New Harmony of today is a monument to the past, still bearing the impress of a spirit that moved men's minds a century and a half ago. It is well worth a visit before we all set off for the moon.

ELI LILLY

(b. Indianapolis, 1885–d. 1977), grandson of the founder of Lilly Pharmaceuticals, Inc., was educated in Indianapolis and at the Philadelphia College of Pharmacy. In 1937 he helped found the Lilly Endowment, a philanthropy that has supported several college libraries and the archeological projects at Angel Mound, Conner Prairie, and New Harmony. His publications include *Prehistoric Antiquities of Indiana* (1937), *The Conner Prairie Farm* (1941), *Early Wawasee Days* (1960), and *Schliemann in Indianapolis* (1961).

A Trip to Wawasee
in 1895

The young people of today have no idea of the complications involved in relatively short trips by rail before the turn of the century and the advent of the automobile. It may interest them to know that the logistics of a summer visit to Wawasee in the nineties were really complicated, to say the least! The filling of the back of the station wagon with a few suitcases and a two-and-one-half- or three-hour drive on cement roads, now so easily accomplished for a week-end visit, had not been dreamed of. Oh, no! The trip was such a Herculean task that only a long sojourn was adequate recompense.

Days before departure from Indianapolis, huge trunks had to be lugged from the attic, and the family were busily engaged in packing them. To take these to the Union Station, Frank Bird's Transfer Company's horse-drawn wagons were called. These were manned by stout, muscular mortals whose outstanding vocational attribute was a heady perfume, a mixture of sweat, fox nest, and livery stable. Whiffed once, it was never to be forgotten. Checking the trunks via the Michigan Division of the Big Four called for a trip to the railway station behind the slow "Clop! Clop! Clop!" of a horse or on the streetcar. A round-trip ticket to Wawasee cost $4.25.

Families would drive to the station in "the surrey with the fringe on top" or call Horace Wood's Livery Stable for a cab. That establishment was on the Circle. The youngsters always hoped that Jack would be the driver, for it was he who had the proud distinction of driving for the various presidents of the United States when they were visiting Indianapolis.

Each day, except Sunday, there were two local trains to the Lake, one leaving at about seven in the morning. After an interminable wait at Milford Junction and a transfer to the B. & O., the exhausted passengers would arrive at their destination about two in the afternoon (1:48, to be exact). Another possibility was to leave Indianapolis at eleven o'clock in the morning, reaching Wawasee about seven the same evening. The B. & O. train that completed this journey was called "The Milk Shake," because of the large quantities of this product that it collected at way stations. Later it was dubbed simply "The Shake." It well lived up to its name.

Day coaches were far from being as comfortable as those of today. Stiff, double, red plush seats whose backs were capable of being turned over enabled a family or a group of genial friends to ride facing one another if they boarded the train early enough to find two empty adjoining seats. Later, the Big Four added a chair car to the train, providing a more comfortable ride.

In the first decade of the century, Bob Johnson was a porter on the chair car. He was a popular, handsome, and accommodating Negro with the figure and grace of a bullfighter. Formerly a waiter at the Wawasee Inn, he usually won first prize at cakewalks held there, strutting and prancing to those rousing tunes "The Georgia Camp

Meeting" or "Alexander's Ragtime Band." At one time he had been stabbed in a fracas in the help's quarters.

"Accommodation" trains stopped at every town. There were twenty stops between Indianapolis and Milford Junction, a distance of about one hundred and twenty-five miles! There being no automobiles, all visiting between towns was done by rail. At each of the twenty stations, the conductor would call out its name in each coach, and groups of passengers, carrying babies, handbags, bandboxes, and bird cages, would file from the cars. They would be replaced by others, similarly burdened, going farther along the line.

One of the features of these trips was the tight-lipped contention between the fresh air enthusiasts who opened windows (there were no screens) and those who objected to the smoke and cinders pouring in from the coal-burning, steam locomotives. Cinders had an affinity for the human eye, and passengers frequently suffered from this cause.

There being no dining facilities on these trains, passengers had the choice of packing fried chicken, jelly sandwiches, fruit "in season," and other picnic fare into the proverbial shoe box, or dashing from the train at Anderson to snatch a sandwich or two from a small, stale-smelling restaurant next to the station. This restaurant was known to a small coterie as "The Tooth and Gorge" or "The Greasy Spoon." At Milford Junction, too, some time could be killed at a little eating establishment across the tracks, where the flies outnumbered the customers twenty to one. It was much more pleasant to resort to the shoe box in the shady little park back of the station, where the soft aeolian hum of the wind through the telegraph wires and the constant clicking of the instruments played an accompaniment to the usual cooling breeze.

A variation of this trip, avoiding the long wait at the Junction, could be made by wiring Miles Livery at Milford for a horse-drawn rig to drive the ten miles to the Lake—through frequent dust clouds and the ever-present perfume of the horses.

For the young fry, the journey from Indianapolis to the Junction was plain torture. The trip was delayed beyond reason by stops at Fortville, Ingalls, Pendleton, Anderson, Alexandria, Summitville, Fairmount, Jonesboro, Marion, La Fontaine, Treaty, Wabash, Urbana, Boliver, North Manchester (where many strangely garbed Mennonites invariably boarded the train), Silver Lake, Claypool, Warsaw, Leesburg, and, finally, Milford and the Junction.

Tension had mounted with each stop, relieved somewhat by fitful attempts at reading. After the lengthy wait at Milford Junction, at

long, long last came the boarding of the B. & O. for the remaining
ten miles to the Lake. Then, as the train slowed down, came the
ecstatic thrill for the youngsters—every bit as good as Christmas
morning—of catching from the car windows a blessed glimpse of the
back of the cottage, across the cornfields, almost hidden in its grove
of trees, with the glittering Lake beyond!

Then came the breathless haste for the jump down to the platform
of the old open-front shed station that stood by the road which still
crosses what is now the golf course. Trains were met by Mr. John
Riddle and his bus, which had seats along each side. A ride of half a
mile and then, glory of glories, the cottage and lakeside finally were
achieved.

DALE BURGESS

(b. Gaston, 1910–) was educated in Gaston and at Ball State University. He began his newspaper career on the *New Castle Times* and
worked up to the position of Indiana Editor of the Associated Press.

Kokomo Helped
Start the Whole Business

There are benighted areas in the world where Indiana is known
only as a place in North America where people race automobiles.
This linking of Indiana and autos is more sensible than many of the
images widely separated peoples have of one another.

The Hoosier state has manufactured 216 different autos. For one
reason or another, they lost out to the big Detroit automotive factories. The last Indiana-assembled car vanished Dec. 10, 1963, when
the venerable Studebaker firm of South Bend decided to limit its
auto manufacture to a Canadian branch.

Studebaker's luxury model, the Avanti, has been revived at South
Bend by new owners of the design and the expensive Duesenberg

is being assembled again at Indianapolis after a three-decade lapse. But these are tiny operations compared with Indiana's contributions to autos assembled in other states.

Indiana has 259 factories, scattered throughout the state, which make auto parts and equipment. In the manufacturing end of the transportation field, including 35 factories in aircraft and railroad equipment, Indiana produces more than $1 billion worth of products each year with about 90,000 workers who are paid over $600 million a year.

Much of the huge Indiana production of steel and other primary metals, worth almost $1.5 billion a year, goes into autos. This takes almost 100,000 workers making about $70 million a year. Add to that the workers with the state's 14 refineries, auto dealers and service stations and you will suspect that Hoosiers' involvement with autos goes considerably further than owning almost 2,000,000 of them.

The conspiracy to put the horse out to pasture probably started with a three-wheel steam vehicle made by Nicolas J. Cognot of Paris in 1769 and there were electric cars as early as 1887 in Brighton, England. The development of the internal combustion (gas) engine was spread over many years and hundreds of men contributed. One of the first practical was built by another Frenchman, Etienne Lenoir, in 1860.

The first true auto (not steam or electric) probably was the 1885 Benz in Germany. Almost every village blacksmith in the United States was inspired to create another. Among them was Charles H. Black of Indianapolis, whose 1894 Benz imitation is in the Children's Museum at the Hoosier capital.

The first Indiana auto to get into real production was designed by Elwood Haynes, built by Elmer and Edgar Apperson, and given its trial run July 4, 1894 on Pumpkinvine Pike southeast of Kokomo. Haynes, born in Portland and educated at Worcester Polytech of Massachusetts, had been working on his design since 1890, but J. Frank and Charles E. Duryea beat him into production with the first practical U. S. auto in 1891 at Chicopee Falls, Mass.

Haynes, pioneer in stainless steel, and the Appersons ran their first car 3 miles at 7 m.p.h. The vehicle weighed 820 pounds. The construction had been started at Greentown in 1890–91 but was moved to Kokomo in 1892. Haynes and the Appersons went separate ways in 1901 and the Apperson Jack Rabbit became a famous early speedster. Ed Apperson beat Barney Oldfield in the Pasadena Hill Climb in 1909.

Hundreds of auto makers appeared, mostly small scale operations, but their products had a general tendency to break down on the primitive roads. A group of Indianapolis auto makers headed by Carl G. Fisher built the Indianapolis Motor Speedway in 1909 as a place to separate the autos from the rattletraps.

The famous Memorial Day 500-mile race was started in 1911 on a new brick surface and was won by an Indianapolis Marmon driven by Ray Harroun. His speed was 74½ miles an hour. Jimmy Clark of Scotland won in 1965 in a Lotus-Ford at a bit over 150 m.p.h.

Famous Indiana auto racers have included Wilbur Shaw, Bob Sweikert, Rodger Ward, Harry Hartz and the old perennial breaker of transcontinental records, Cannon Ball Baker. The 500 field always has been led by a popular passenger car on the pace lap. The mortality rate among American auto builders is well illustrated by the list of pace cars for the first 20 races. Only four of them are still manufactured, counting Studebaker. The best list of Indiana car builders was compiled in 1961 by Wallace Spencer Huffman of Kokomo for the Indiana Historical Bureau.

Defunct cars, famous in their day, which Huffman listed included the Auburn of Auburn, 1900–1937; Bush, Elkhart, 1916–24; Cole, Indianapolis, 1909–25; Cord, Auburn-Connersville, 1929–37; Duesenberg, Indianapolis, 1920–37; Durant, Muncie, 1922–28; Elcar, Elkhart, 1909–32; Interstate, Muncie, 1908–18; Lambert, Anderson, 1905–17; Lexington, Connersville, 1910–27; Marmon, Indianapolis, 1905–33; Maxwell, New Castle, 1906–24; McFarlan, Connersville, 1910–28; Monroe, Indianapolis, 1914–24; Premier, Indianapolis, 1903–24; Richmond, Richmond, 1902–16; Stutz, Indianapolis, 1912–36.

The auto not only brought a new freedom and caused road builders to remould the landscape but also produced death and destruction far beyond Indiana's losses in all its wars. The State Board of Health began listing auto accidents as a cause of death in 1906 and recorded 3 fatalities that year. The annual total passed 100 in 1915 and passed 1,000 in 1928.

The board's figures vary a little from those the state police have been keeping in recent years. Before 1950, the board recorded all traffic deaths in the state, regardless of where the victim lived or whether the accident was inside the state lines. Since then, the board has listed all traffic accidents of Hoosiers, regardless of where they were hurt or died.

State police number traffic deaths inside the state lines, of both natives and visitors. The figures work out about the same and they are startling. Early in 1965, the board's list of Indiana traffic deaths passed 48,000. That's about the population of Kokomo, which helped start the whole business.

ERNIE PYLE

(b. Dana, 1900–d. 1945) was educated in the Dana public schools and at Indiana University. During World War II he accompanied our troops as a news correspondent and was idolized for his bravery, compassion, and candor. In 1945 he was killed by enemy fire in the South Pacific, having previously published several books, including *Brave Men* (1944). *Home Country* was published posthumously, in 1947.

Brown County

On the whole, I am ill at ease in the company of artists, for so much of the time I don't know what they are talking about. And yet I invariably like the places they have made into colonies. And so it was with Brown County, Indiana. I fell head over heels for the place, and the people, and the hills, and the whole general air of peacefulness. Good Lord, I even liked the artists there!

All northern and central Indiana is as flat as a board. Neat farms checker it, and the roads are straight as a ruler. Big barns and regular fences and waving fields of grain splash across the endless landscape. But some thirty miles south of Indianapolis the land begins to undulate, the hills are covered thick with forest, the roads wind, and the fields become patches on slopes. It is hill country because this is where the great glacier stopped and melted away and left its giant rubble piled.

Into this hill country of Indiana more than a hundred years ago came people from Virginia and Tennessee and Kentucky, pushing on into their new frontiers, though never out of the hills, for they were hill people. For a long time they lived their own lives in the woods and the tobacco patches and the little settlements, asking nothing of any man, and eventually they came to be known to the rest of Indiana as "quaint." That is what first attracted the artists to Brown County early in this century—the log cabins, the lounging squirrel hunters, the leaning sheds, the flowers and the autumn leaves and the brooks and hillsides. That, too, is what eventually attracted the sightseers. Brown County in the fall of 1940 was overrun with tourists and sightseers, and a few outsiders who genuinely appreciated not only the wildly colored hills of autumn but also the spirit of the people themselves.

Brown County was not the same as it was when the artists discovered it. The artists no longer considered it picturesque. They said it was "spoiled." They would have gone away, except that they said it was better than anywhere else. Fine roads and hotels had impinged upon the hills and villages. The patch farmer who lived up the holler was nearly pushed off the sidewalk by the gawkers from the city. There was little privacy left. And yet the deep fine attributes of the people endured. The native of Brown County was innately courteous. He would do anything for you, and not think of pay. His honesty was almost old-fashioned. Few people in Brown County locked their houses, and when they did they hung the key on a nail outside the door. They worked in a way that would paralyze an assembly line, yet their work got done, and friends told me there was something fundamental in the Brown County air that compelled an honest day's work for an honest day's pay. The typical Brown County man played a guitar, and sang in harmony, and loved to square-dance, and didn't get lost in the woods, and raised a little tobacco, and went to church, and drank whisky, and was a dead shot with a squirrel gun. Sometimes he was prosperous and sometimes he didn't amount to a damn —but it didn't matter whether he lived twenty miles up the crick in a clapboard cabin or worked in the garage downtown and wore a derby hat, still his code of gaiety and of honesty and his innate sense of dignity remained the same.

The log cabin is the mark of Brown County. I don't mean the log cabin of the western mountains, built of round logs with the bark still on. I mean the old-fashioned hewn log, roughly adzed into rectangular shape, and left unpainted and graying with age. The kind Abe Lincoln was born in. Such log cabins, modernized, have become a fad in Brown County. When people from the city build summer homes there, they are almost always log cabins. But don't let the term "cabin" fool you. I stayed in a little six-room-two-bath-and-basement log cabin, and there was a new one in Nashville that was said to have cost thirty-five thousand dollars. But it was still a cabin, and you'd better not call it a house.

A genuine cabin can't be built out of new logs. No, it must have antiquity. So you scout around the country and spot an old log house, or maybe a barn. This is called a "set of logs." Then you dicker with the owner, and buy it. You number the end of each log, take the whole place apart, haul it to wherever you want to build, and put it together again, with whatever improvements you want. Sets of logs are getting scarcer and scarcer. Walter Snodgrass said he had driven thousands of miles over the back hilly roads of southern Indiana, and even into Kentucky, looking for sets. He believed he knew every available log within two days' drive.

From the first, I knew I had no chance to become a great man, because I wasn't born in a log cabin. But I certainly know of nothing now to prevent me from dying in a log cabin—provided the people of Brown County would let such an ornery fellow die in their midst. So I guess I'll start looking around for a set of logs and a good undertaker.

Nashville, the county seat of Brown County, is only an hour from Indianapolis, and the road from the city is always heavily traveled. In the fall, when the leaves turn red and golden and yellow, Brown County seems to become a shrine for all the Midwest, and the local people have to stay home, for it is impossible for them to get anywhere. On autumn weekends, cars stand motionless in traffic jams for miles. On just one Sunday eighteen thousand people passed through the gates of Brown County State Park. But they were all gone by eight in the evening because they were afraid of the hills and of the darkness, and they wanted to flee before the night engulfed them. It made us old Brown Countyites snicker, but we were glad they'd gone, anyway.

Outsiders have never been too popular in Brown County. Too many of them stand on the street and laugh at the courthouse, which is certainly nothing to laugh at at all. They ask whether people can read and write. They are amazed to find there is a school in Nashville. They stand looking in a store window, and laugh and laugh, and the people inside don't like it. They make fun of the girls, and rudeness is on their tongues. The Nashville people tolerate a great deal in silence, but once in a while the younger ones break over into an old, old custom known as "egging"—which means just what you think it does. It doesn't happen often, and when it does it is more than deserved.

Nashville, the only settlement in the county that could properly be called a town, had a population of around four hundred in 1940. The only railroad in Brown County went through Helmsburg, eight miles away, but there were broad black roads out of Nashville in all directions. The town had no movie, but it had an old, old hotel that had been modernized, a tavern and a restaurant, an old log jail that was now a museum piece, a grocery and a hardware store and drugstore, shops for the craft buyers, and an art gallery. Nashville had no water system, and when a fire got started it was liable to be dangerous.

The courthouse lawn was always dotted with men sitting and talking, or lying in the grass asleep in the shade. Under one tree was a bench known as the Liar's Bench. Some years ago Frank Hohenberger, the photographer, took a picture from behind of six men sitting on this bench talking. The picture became famous, and was sold in every state in the Union. The bench I saw was not the same one, but people still sat on it all day long.

Nashville still abided by the old custom of taking up a public collection for people in distress. Flowers for the dead were the main reasons for collections, but if anybody burned out, or was caught by some calamity and needed help, the people helped him. It had gradually fallen to Mabel Calvin to be the town collector. She was in the hardware store with her father, and when somebody died the townspeople automatically started dropping in at the store next morning, leaving anything from a quarter on up. She estimated that in six years she had collected for a hundred funerals.

You didn't see artists trailing around Nashville in arty clothes. They didn't have a favorite bar where they congregated to discuss their genius in mystic tongues. They simply worked hard and lived like normal people, and hoped to Heaven somebody would buy their stuff. And practically all of them were self-supporting through their art—which speaks for itself. In many summers there were at least sixty artists painting in Brown County. They had rented a huge store building on Nashville's main street and remodeled it into an art gallery, which was open from late spring until early fall. The exhibitions were changed twice a year. In addition, each artist had a home studio, where visitors were welcome. Adolph R. Schulz became the dean of the Brown County art colony upon the death of the famous Theodore C. Steele. Schulz came from Wisconsin in 1907, and he left Wisconsin because, with the growth of dairying, the cows "ate up all the scenery." He was a tall man, slender, striking in appearance, youthful-looking despite his years, animated in his conversation and frank in his expression.

Close to Schulz in tenure was Will Vawter, of all the artists probably the most loved by the townspeople. He was a big man, heavy, with a large head made even larger by an immense thatch of white hair. He and Schulz both looked like artists, and yet Will Vawter also looked just like somebody's nice grandpa. Vawter illustrated one edition of Riley's poems. He had a nice sense of sarcastic humor about himself. Somehow we got to talking about smoking. He didn't smoke, but he chewed gum avidly and constantly, even when he was at a funeral looking at the corpse. He used to smoke cigars. He said he never could smoke halfway; he had to smoke perpetually or not at all, and it used to interfere with his art. He would load up his car of a morning with all of an artist's necessary junk, drive out in the country and find himself a likely spot to paint, then unload everything and set it up. "It was like setting up a circus," he said. "I'd get out my easel and fix it just right. And then the canvas. And then get my paints and brushes all out and ready. And then my stool. And finally set up a big umbrella over the whole thing, practically like a tent. Then I'd sit down to paint, and reach in my shirt pocket for a cigar. And of course I'd have left them at home. And do you know, I couldn't paint a stroke. So I'd jump in the car and rush back to town, taking corners too fast, killing chickens on the way, and being a general public menace. I'd lose an hour getting back to get those cigars so I could paint. So I just quit, and took up chewing gum."

Will Vawter talked about art the way I like to hear people talk. He said you go out and paint something the way you see it; somebody comes along to look at it, and if that scene happens to strike some memory, or cherished little scene, or a spot of appreciative beauty in whoever is looking at it, then he likes the picture, and if he's able he buys it. That's all there is to art. Nothing mysterious about it. When a man can talk like that, and still have no sense of time or direction whatever, and doesn't recognize his own house half the time when he sees it, then I say he has combined the functions of artistic detachment and common horse sense to a degree that nearly reaches perfection.

RUTH McKENNEY

(b. Mishawaka, 1911–) attended elementary school in Mishawaka but moved to Ohio before she reached high-school age. Aside from her humorous essays she wrote sociological treatises (perhaps the latter inspired the former), but she remains best known for the hilarious *My Sister Eileen* (1938).

No Tears, No Good

The nicely brought up child of today lives on a prissy milk-and-water movie diet of colored cartoons, costume pictures with noble endings, and banal dramas starring his favorite radio comic. The Mickey Mouse vogue among the juniors demonstrates what fearful changes Will Hays, the Legion of Decency and Aroused Parenthood have wrought in a mere twenty years or so.

My sister Eileen and I, movie fans when we were five and six, respectively, would have scorned Mickey Mouse in our youth; we preferred Theda Bara to Fatty Arbuckle, and that was the acid test.

We saw our first movie shortly after we saw our first airplane. The airplane was very nice, of course, and we had a school half-holiday to celebrate the glorious moment when an air machine first put landing gear on the dreary soil of Mishawaka, Indiana. That was the early spring of 1918, and airplanes were very patriotic and thrilling, but in spite of the glamorous fellow who ran the queer machine, we liked the movie better than the airplane. The movie lasted longer.

Our first film was Chapter 3 of a serial which had to do with bandits, high cliffs, and pistols. Eileen was so small she was able to sneak under the ticket-seller's high box and get in free. The serial was shown that spring daily, not weekly, in a made-over garage not far from our schoolhouse. Chapter 1 of the adventures of, say, Death-Defying Desmond started on Monday at four o'clock sharp and the last installment ended at the Friday-afternoon matinée, amid the hoarse cheers of the excited audience. Admission price was a nickel, but no self-respecting child in our fairly prosperous neighborhood would have thought of stumbling down the dark aisles and throwing himself into a creaking wooden seat unless he were equipped with a bag of peanuts, price also five cents.

The peanuts were not merely for the inner man; the shells were used by the large and energetic audience to enliven the dull stretches in the scenario. To us, even the liveliest Western had a good many sleepy sequences, and, indeed, the whole audience could be bored into mass fidgets at the mere sight of a long subtitle, for few, if any, of the paying customers at those four-o'clock matinées could read—not, at least, with any ease. Nobody in the theatre had the slightest idea of what the film was about, and nobody cared. We came to see the fights, and the horse races over the mountains, and the jumping across chasms. Our attention wandered as soon as the scene shifted indoors, and two subtitles in a row were enough to start a peanut fight.

Thus, when the heroine began to plead with the villain for the hero's life, Benny Burns, a big boy in the third grade, would rise and shoot a peanut shell at his old enemy, Freddie Meriman. Freddie would respond in kind, and soon the darkened theatre would be the scene of a fine free-for-all battle, with both sides eventually running out of peanut shells and resorting to books, hats, apples, and other deadly weapons. Piercing screams could sometimes be heard all the way out to the street, and the howls of the wounded would sooner or later seriously annoy the bored movie operator, upstairs in his booth. He and the ticket-seller were the only attendants, for in those days there were no laws about matrons, and for a nickel we did not have the dubious pleasure of hearing the regular pianist. In the midst of the joyous battle, then, the lights would suddenly go on, the heroine disappear from the screen, and the racket diminish slightly while the operator bawled, "Shut up, you brats, or I'll throw you all out."

"Ya-a-ah," we would all scream, Eileen's five-year-old shriek rising above the rest, "come on and do it!"

He never tried, though. He waited for comparative quiet, dimmed the lights, and put the heroine back on the screen, this time perhaps pleading, in one of those lightning developments, for her own life. The peanut battles were apparently more exciting than the serials. I remember little of that first spring movie season except a train wreck, but that train wreck will live in my memory as one of the most piquant experiences of my life.

In the film, a motorcar, a Model T Ford, was racing down a country road, pursued by something—I think it was a lot of bandits in another car. Just as the motorcar approached the crossing, a train appeared around a convenient bend. All this was old stuff; we were used to seeing motorcars and trains fight it out on the tracks.

But suddenly the camera switched from the general view of the automobile and the train, and on the screen appeared a huge pair of wheels—the train wheels. They grew larger and larger, revolving furiously. We were awed and horrified. The wheels were coming right for us; apparently, the motorcar was not to be run over, we were. Suddenly my sister Eileen screamed, and began trying to climb across the tense legs of the little boys in our row.

"Let me out, let me out!" she howled. "Ruth! Mamma! Help! It's coming!"

In the silence of the darkened movie house, Eileen's screams made a sensation. Other small girls burst into nervous sobs. Boys, even big boys in the third grade, began to whine dismally. On the screen the wheels were now rolling faster and faster, and the whole train loomed up, apparently about to descend upon us. In those days, when a cameraman had a good shot, he gave it plenty of footage, to let it sink in. Eileen's agonized howls and cries for help were now being drowned out by the panic-stricken roar of the whole audience. There was a tremendous din, and the scuffle of dozens of frightened children trying to stumble out into the aisles and run for home and mother. At this point the lights went on and the train, wheels and all, disappeared from the screen.

"For Christ's sake!" bawled the infuriated movie operator from his booth. The attention of the horrified audience was now shifted from the thought of escape, to horror at hearing a bad word, a swear word, shouted so baldly from above. This was a polite neighborhood.

"This ain't real," the movie operator continued in his stentorian tones. "Nobody's going to get hurt. It's just a movie."

You could hear the soft rustle of everybody saying "Oh" to his neighbor, the diminishing sniffles, the blowing of noses, the regaining of creaking wooden seats. But before the lights went down, the ticket-seller, a mean-looking lady of what we thought was vast age, with side puffs over her ears, walked down the aisle.

"Who started this?" she demanded sternly. A dozen fingers pointed to my fat, tear-stained sister. Eileen tried to hide under her seat, but in vain. She was ordered out to the aisle.

"How old are you?" the ticket-seller demanded, in front of everybody.

"Theven," Eileen lied, in her most unfortunate lisp. A dozen voices contradicted her. "She's only in kindergarten," various old pals shouted gleefully.

"Little girls in kindergarten aren't allowed to come to the movies," the ticket-seller said grimly, and grabbed Eileen's chubby arm. Weeping dismally, my poor sister was ignominiously led out, with me tagging sorrowfully along in back. Unfortunately, this event made such a scandal that our mother heard of it, via other little girls' mothers, and we were forbidden to attend movies until we were older.

Older was next year, after we had moved to Cleveland. There were three movie houses within walking distance of our new home, and we settled down to delightful years of Saturday and Sunday afternoon film orgies.

Nobody censored our movie fare except ourselves. Mother had no idea of what grim and gripping pictures we were seeing, for she

never went to the movies herself. She was something of an intellectual, and back in 1919 and 1920 people who had pretensions to
culture, at least in the Middle West, wouldn't have been caught dead
in a movie house. Mother thought the films were exclusively for
children and morons, like the comic strips in the newspapers. Cleveland had no Better Films for Children Committees in those days, and
Ohio preachers and newspaper editorial-writers did not thunder,
then, of the Movie Menace. Mother used to send us off to the neighborhood theatres with an innocent and loving heart.

"Don't sit through it more than twice!" she would shout from the
front porch as we skipped off, hand in hand, to the movies. We would
return, hours later, exhausted from the hard seats and emotional
duress.

We saw some bright and cheerful pictures, but I don't remember
many of them. There was Fatty Arbuckle, of course, and two wonderful children who threw dishes at each other—the Lee sisters. We
worshiped them. But most of the pictures we saw were, to us anyway,
grim and awful tragedies. If there were happy endings, we never
noticed them. Some of the pictures were so unbearably sad we could
hardly stay to see them twice. We did, though.

We wore large, round hats with ribbons for these excursions to the
movies. Once settled down in our seats, we held on anxiously to the
hats. At the least sign of trouble on the screen, we put the hats in
front of our eyes. Then we took turns peeking out to see if the film
had taken a turn for the better. It makes me blanch to consider what
we would have suffered if the films had been wired for sound when
we were children. As it was, we could generally tell when the trouble
was coming by the pianist, who used to begin thumping away at some
very dread music. Of course, since we saw every film twice, in spite
of our hat system of censorship we generally got the thread of the
plot on the second time around. If we still couldn't quite make out
what had happened, we stayed for the third show and were late for
dinner.

We had no favorite movie stars at first, for the truth was that we
hadn't really believed that movie operator. For a long time we
thought the movies were real, and that the tragedies we saw were
photographed, mysteriously, from real and horrible life. I gradually
came to understand that the suffering heroine was only an actress
and I used to reassure Eileen loudly as she wept. "Don't cry," I would
bawl through my own tears. "It's only a movie."

At last, though, we grew out of this primitive stage of movie response and developed into Wally Reid and Lon Chaney fans. Mr.

Chaney, of course, we admired in a rather backhanded way. Each Chaney film was, for us, a terrible ordeal, through which we suffered and bawled and wept. As we staggered out of the theatre, our pug noses swollen to red beets, we swore never to set eyes on the man again. But the next time we were back, groaning in our seats, fascinated and horrified. Finally "The Hunchback of Notre Dame" came along and very nearly finished me off. Even now, Eileen refuses to discuss that gruesome movie. Mr. Chaney was the hunchback, of course, and he suffered a peculiarly realistic and horrible beating in that old silent film. Eileen and I put our arms around each other, and howled steadily throughout the entire beating.

Mr. Reid, who came along a little earlier than the horror man, was a slightly more cheerful influence on our childhood, although his tragic death became, oddly enough, a family scandal. Our passion for Mr. Reid was shared by a young aunt of ours, who admired that jaunty actor with rather more enthusiasm than detachment. Now, my mother cared nothing for Mr. Reid but she was deeply attached to her only brother and she called him, as Mr. Reid's devoted fans called their idol, Wally.

Imagine her horror, then, one evening, when my young aunt called up and wept over the phone, in broken accents, "Maggie, Maggie, Wally's dead!"

"Dead?" shouted my mother, electrifying everybody at our dinner table. "No! No! It isn't true!"

My aunt said, amid her tears, that it was true, alas. My mother began, naturally enough, to cry. My father, white and shaken, rushed to the phone, tenderly pushed his wife aside while she sobbed, "Wally's dead," and picked up the receiver.

"How did it happen?" Father began, in that somber tone of voice you use for these trying occasions. Then we heard him roar, "What? You're crazy!" He hung up with a frightful bang and shouted, "It's Wally Reid, the film actor!"

Eileen and I began to howl at once. We didn't know our uncle very well, but we certainly knew Wally Reid, and felt perfectly terrible about his death. We simply couldn't understand Mother's calloused revival when she heard the good news that her brother still lived. That famous telephone conversation started a family feud that lasted for years. Mother never forgave her young sister, and my aunt stated freely and frankly that she thought Mother was a perfect idiot for not knowing that Wally Reid had been ill for days. People took their movies seriously those days, if they took them at all.

In spite of our devotion to Mr. Chaney and Mr. Reid, the film that made the deepest impression upon Eileen and myself when we were nine and ten or thereabouts starred neither of these gentlemen. The name of the film I never knew. We paid no attention to such trifles as titles, directors or the names of the cast. We saw it in a third-run house in the fall or late summer of 1921.

The movie opened with a charming domestic scene. The newly married wife was saving nickels for her Home. She had a special bank, made like a little house, for the purpose. But suddenly a handsome villain appeared on the scene, a business acquaintance of her husband. He invited the happy couple to a very swell party, and the little woman needed a new dress. So she pried open the quaint little bank (while Eileen squirmed and cried. "No, no!" in a perfect agony) and bought a wonderful dress for three hundred dollars. The couple trotted off to the party, the wife feeling pretty guilty of course, while the husband, the fool, bridled with pride. He told everyone who would listen to him that his wife's lovely gown was home-made by the clever little woman herself. How heartlessly Eileen and I laughed at that. We had no sympathy for the spineless husband; he was an oaf. Now the wife had planned to wear the gown but a single night and rush in back to the dress shop the next morning. Then she would put the money back in the cute little bank and her husband would never be the wiser. Eileen and I thought that was pretty risky. We always spilled things at parties, ourselves.

Sure enough, the party turned out to be a debauch. We weren't surprised. All grown-up parties were, in our opinion, debauches, and we were sure our parents, when they left the house in evening clothes, were bound for similar sinful sprees. This party, however, was a humdinger. It was climaxed by all the guests' tearing out of doors to go swimming in the ocean *with their clothes on.* We wouldn't have minded if they had gone in naked. We thought first and last of that three-hundred-dollar dress.

Eileen cried so at this point that the usher had to rebuke her; her sobs were distracting the pianist. We had our hats up, of course, but we were so stirred by the tragedy we couldn't help sneak looks at the screen. There she was, wading in; there she was, going in deeper. Then—oh, fearful tragedy!—a wave broke over her head and the dress was a goner. I forget how the movie ended. The husband found out and beat up his poor wife, I believe.

Rudolph Valentino came next in our movie career. We were having our teeth straightened when the Great Lover burst into our lives. We must have missed his early films or, worse, sat through them without a quiver, for we were twelve and thirteen before we began to take Mr. Valentino seriously, and then his career was very nearly over. But even so, I feel genuinely sorry for modern adolescents to think that their first sighs cannot be wasted on Rudolph Valentino. Alas, how much grosser is Clark Gable, how much milder is Robert Taylor! Ah, I can see, I can practically feel, Mr. Valentino's arms sliding and slithering around his prey; I can see his wonderful profile coming closer, bit by bit, his lips quivering, his eyes gleaming with that snake-eat-bird expression. Ah!

We saw Mr. Valentino's last film, "The Son of the Sheik," released in Cleveland after his death, six times all the way through and came back a seventh time just for the desert love scene. In those days no prudish censor cut the romantic footage, and we sighed gustily while the heroine struggled in the Great Lover's arms. We disliked that heroine, whoever she was, very much indeed. We thought it was both disloyal and stupid of her to put up a fight against Mr. Valentino. We would have given in at once.

When "The Big Parade" came to Cleveland, a year or so later, we were old enough to see the movies in the big downtown houses, providing, of course, that we had the cash. I remember we got the money to see "The Big Parade," in the best seats of the legitimate theatre showing the film, by coolly calling on the credit manager of a department store where our father had an account. With lowered eyes and swinging pigtails, we told him we were stranded; we had lost our purses. Would he please advance us four dollars for taxi fare home? He was stunned, apparently, by this novel approach, for he handed over the money and we rushed out, bought a two-pound box of the best chocolate-nut candy, and descended upon "The Big Parade."

Tragedies of a very real nature have overtaken us both since that spring day, but we have never cried so, either of us, again. We wept buckets. We wept through our own handkerchiefs, which for a change, we had remembered. We wept through the ruffles on our petticoats. When we started to sob on the back of our hands, a sympathetic gentleman sitting next to me gallantly offered his large handkerchief, and we wept together on that as the orchestra (this was a very special performance) played "My Buddy" and the guns thundered and the cast died, on the screen. Afterward we agreed it was the best movie we had ever seen, because we had cried the most. Our standard was simple but severe. No tears, no good.

"The Big Parade" was the last picture belonging to the idyllic, or honeymoon, stage of the movies for us. After that, our high-school beaux began to buy our movie tickets, and for many years, alas, the beaux took up more of our attention than the movies. By the time we had recovered from the shock of not paying our own way in, we were living in New York City and reading the *Times* moving-picture reviews. And somehow the movies have never been the same for us as they were in the days when we saw them in snatches from behind our big, round hats.

❖ ❖ ❖ ❖ ❖

GEORGE JEAN NATHAN

(b. Fort Wayne, 1882–d. 1958) was educated in the Fort Wayne schools and at Cornell University. He started his career on the *New York Herald* but is best remembered for his association with H. L. Mencken on *Smart Set* and *The American Mercury*. Nathan was one of the first critics to praise the work of Eugene O'Neill, F. Scott Fitzgerald, Willa Cather, and Theodore Dreiser. Nathan's thirty-three books include *The New American Credo* (1927), *Testament of a Critic* (1931), and *Entertainment of a Nation* (1942).

Attitudes toward America

Sings Ko-Ko in "The Mikado": " ... Then the idiot who praises, with enthusiastic tone, all centuries but this, and every country but his own."

I fear that I, for one, have in the past been not wholly free from the good Ko-Ko's disfavor, particularly as regards the second article of his animadversion. I have praised, with enthusiastic tone, English letters, French drama, German beer and music, Hungarian girls, Italian art, Turkish morals, Danish pastry, Swedish bathtowels, Greek sculpture, Spanish wines, Russian ballets, Swiss Alps and cheese, Dutch painting and Cuban cigars, as opposed to the like products of my own native land. I have praised, with not less enthusiastic tone, the British form of government as opposed to that of my own country, the free gayety of the French people as opposed to the blue and restricted gayety of my own people. . . . But, whether it be true that I am and have been an idiot or not, it seems to me to be time to shout "Whoa!" to the current sweeping disparagement, on the part of certain sepulchral and misguided citizens, of a Republic that, for all its obvious and transparent defects, has yet perhaps as many things to recommend it as any other country warmed by the sunshine of an all-wise and forgiving Siddhartha.

I resent the suppressed snickers of the butler that greet the United States whenever its name is mentioned at an alien dinner table. I resent the intimation of cultivated foreigners—and cultivated Americans no less—that the United States is a mere ethical and æsthetic outhouse for the obscene use of themselves and others like them. This is hardly the case. The United States may be run by rogues, but so is France, and so is Italy, and so is England. It may be a money-grubbing nation; so is France, and so is Italy, and so is England. It may be worked for all it is worth by profiteers; so is present-day Germany. And it may exalt the stockbroker above the artist and the automobile manufacturer above the conductor of a symphony orchestra; so, *as* a nation, does almost every other nation under the heavens. These are absurd charges. A nation, whatever its name, and whatever the color of its flag, is at bottom, and essentially, a mere mob. And a mob is always cheap, always shoddy, and infinitely ignorant. One thinks of a country, one's own or someone's else, not in terms of the millions of soup coloraturos who compose it, but in terms of its minority of educated and civilized men. My country has such men as other countries have them. It has them perhaps in not such great number, but it is getting more of them year by year. The old order changeth. The younger generation, so to speak, is . . . knocking at the back door. . . .

Let the band strike up with the existing facts. The United States is today, as it has been for the last fifteen years, the most thoroughly comfortable country to live in that one can find in the atlas. Its trains, taxicab service, bathrooms, ventilating systems, street buses, subways, elevated roads, hotels (in the aggregate), street-cleaning devices, the innumerable small things that contribute to make daily life easy and endurable—these are not matched by any other country. There is not a railroad in all of Europe one-fiftieth so well managed and so well run as the Pennsylvania. There isn't one that serves as respectable food in its dining-cars as the Baltimore and Ohio. There aren't in the world as satisfactory taxicabs as the original American "Yellows." Aside from the Ritz hotels, which are the same wherever one finds them, the United States can match every Adlon with a half dozen Plazas, every Bayerischer-Hof with a half dozen Statlers. The American bathroom—and here recall George Moore's celebrated philosophy—makes every other bathroom look like a country shanty amid the sunflowers. American heating apparatus, American barber-shops, American writing paper, American bootblacking entre-preneurs, American telephone service (in every large city save New York), American elevators, American drugstores, American coins and currency—these, too, lead the world in point of merit and effi-ciency. One need not emit a cackle at the crass materialness of such an argument. It is only the poseur who pretends that these are not, many of them, of a high importance in the scheme of life of mortal man and in his ever-present quest for tranquility of mind, peace of spirit, and bodily ease. Let the disbeliever try to find a decent pair of garters in Europe when he has broken the pair he brought over with him from America; let him go and have his hair cut; let him hurriedly try to buy a shirt that fits him; let him try his luck at having an aching tooth pulled or filled; let him try to find a comfortable pair of European shoes; let him try to get a satisfactory witch hazel to use after shaving; let him search for a strikable match in France, an ungreasy dish in Italy, a damp cigar in England, a dry bed sheet in Norway, a pen that he can write with in Greece, a mild cigarette in Russia, a hair brush in Spain, a dose of castor oil in Rumania, a decent cup of coffee in Portugal, or the most necessary if unmentionable article of human comfort in Denmark—let him essay this repertoire of likes and needs, or any part of it, and then ask him—if he is one part human—whether he cares to see New York harbor again, and how soon!

But have done with such base things, and to the higher reaches. The general literary taste of the United States at the present time—comparing the list of fiction and non-fiction best sellers with the same lists, where they are available, in Europe—is superior to that of En-gland, France, Germany or Italy. Save alone Berlin, the dramatic taste of New York is at the present time considerably higher than that of any European capital. It is five times superior to that of London, and three times superior to that of Paris. America provides a larger and more lucrative audience for opera, symphony concerts and the recitals of first-rate musicians than any other country. The level of intelligence and artistic perception is much lower in the higher stra-tum of the American people than in the same stratum of the Eu-ropean, but the mass of one country is not much different, as I have observed, from the mass of another. The American yokel and the German peasant, the American boob and the English boob, the

American hick and the French hick are brothers in ignorance under the cuticle. . . .

Our art is still in a crude state of development. Again true; but it is making progress. The American short story leads the world; the American etching is rapidly forging to the modern front rank; the American Victor Herbert, but recently laid to rest, is the superior of Lehar or Eysler or Kalmann or Fall; the American novel and drama gain stature and dignity steadily. Dreiser, Cabell, Lewis, Hergesheimer, Cather, O'Neill come on apace. And to return briefly to the shorter form of fiction, there is not a writer in Europe today doing finer work than the American Sherwood Anderson or Ruth Suckow. American criticism, on the higher levels, if inferior to the English and German, is miles ahead of the French and Spanish. American sculpture and painting and music are still either downright bad or in the process of finding themselves. These lie in the lap of time.

Character vs. Plot

That character is always more important than plot in literature and drama is proved by the fact that we usually remember character in proportion as we forget plot. One remembers Huckleberry Finn; but what was the plot of "Huckleberry Finn"? One remembers Uncle Tom; but what was the plot of "Uncle Tom's Cabin"? One remembers Ben Hur; but what was the plot of "Ben Hur"? And so, too, with Nicholas Nickleby, David Copperfield, Tess of the D'Urbervilles, King Lear, Tom Jones, Fanny Hill, Madame Bovary, Thérèse Raquin, Lord Jim, and a hundred others. The general trends of these one may recall, but the plots have vanished from memory. Only the characters remain.

How Many Workdays in a Year?

There are 365 days in the year. Of these, 52 are Sundays. That leaves 313 days. Of these, 52 are Saturdays or half-work days. Half of 52 is 26. That leaves 287 days. Of these, there are New Year's Day, Lincoln's Birthday, Washington's Birthday, Decoration Day, the Fourth of July, Labor Day, Columbus' Birthday, Thanksgiving Day and Christmas—all holidays, which leaves 278 days. In addition there are such State holidays as Arbor Day, such holidays as St. Patrick's Day and various religious holidays like Good Friday—an average of, let us say—to put it low—a half dozen. That leaves 272 days. The average human being, according to the best medical statistics available, is ill, taking one year with another, at least twelve days each year, and is then unfit for work. That leaves 260 days. The average working man's vacation period amounts to two weeks or, less the two Sundays and two half-Saturdays already counted, eleven days. That leaves 249 days. A day contains 24 hours, eight of which are the union limit of labor. Eight is one-third of 24, hence the working man works for one-third of 249 days. That is 83 days. On each of these 83 days he takes an hour off for lunch. Eighty-three hours amounts approximately to three and one-half days. That leaves 79½ days. Now, it is impossible for any human being to work continuously, without periodic rest, for seven hours. There must be time to stop for breath, to ease up the muscles, to take the crick out of one's back, to wait until one's helper is ready, to light one's pipe, to wipe the sweat from one's forehead—to do any number of such things. In a working period of seven hours, at least one hour is necessarily so wasted. That means, in 79½ days, 79½ hours—or approximately three and one-third days. That leaves approximately 76⅙ days. The average [person] thus actually works just 76⅙ days out of the 365.

The Eve before New Year's Eve

Of all the days in the year, there is at least one regarding which the moralists need have no concern. That day is the thirtieth of December. A study of statistics for the last twenty-two years shows that on this particular day the morals of the community are higher than on any other day of the calendar: there are fewer crimes, fewer arrests, fewer wife-beatings, fewer bawdy divertissements, and fewer cases of alcoholism. It is on this day that the Americano takes a rest from sin in preparation for the grand and glorious New Year's Eve debauch due the following night.

How Not to Begin a Story

I have, in my editorial capacity, been reading fiction manuscripts now for exactly eleven years and four months. In that period, I have read perhaps 30,000. Meditating these 30,000, I am brought to the conclusion that I have never yet found a good one that began in any one of the following ways: 1. "It was in the year so-and-so"; 2. "Now, dear reader"; 3. "Long ago, before this story begins"; 4. "This is the true story of"; 5. "Out beyond the line where the sea touched the sky"; 6. with the description of gathering clouds; 7. with a quotation from Horace; or 8. with the word "imagine."

Ministry of Fine Arts

The Americano has at least one reason for getting down on his knees every night and offering up a prayer of thanks to the Almighty, and that is the absence at Washington of a Ministry of Fine Arts such as that maintained by the French government. Imagine a department of this kind as it would be filled and operated in these grand and glorious States! A gala annual banquet would be held [at which the members of the] National Institute of Arts and Letters would march *en masse* to the ceremonies in cap and gown, and would be headed by Isham Jones' jazz band playing George Gershwin's latest masterpiece. Harry Hansen would get salubriously stewed and bite off William Lyon Phelps' ear, and Phelps, in turn, would spill his *consommé Créole* on the heiress to Amy Lowell's cigar. A toast would be offered to the memory of those two great *litterateurs,* the MM. Woodrow Wilson and Theodore Roosevelt, and Dreiser, Cabell, Red Lewis and the rest of such dismal failures [would] be left out in the cold. . . .

❖ ❖ ❖ ❖ ❖

EMILY KIMBROUGH

(b. Muncie, 1899–) was educated in the Muncie schools and at Bryn Mawr College. From 1922–1929 she was an editor of *The Ladies Home Journal.* Her works, besides cinema and TV scripts, include *Innocents from Indiana* (1950), and (with Cornelia Skinner) *Our Hearts Were Young and Gay* (1954).

Our Waverly

A year after we had moved to Blackstone Avenue, my father bought an electric for Mother. It was a Waverly like the one Grandmother Kimbrough had in Muncie, Indiana. Grandmother didn't drive her Waverly, but Grandfather did, and said that he found it more satisfactory in many ways than his Pierce Arrow, which Hubert drove. Grandfather had sold the horses, Maude and Prince, when he bought the Pierce Arrow, and promoted the hired man, Hubert, from driving them to driving the Pierce Arrow.

Grandmother felt that Hubert's promotion took place too rapidly. It made her uneasy, she told Grandfather, to see Hubert rise and pull far back whenever he put on the brake. Other people she saw driving automobiles didn't do that. Grandfather considered this an unfair criticism. He said it was just a reflex action due to the facts that Prince had had a hard mouth and Maude had been congenitally indifferent. In Grandmother's voluble opinion, it made her nervous, whatever it was.

The Waverly, however, suited them both to a T, particularly when touring, because Grandfather had the front seat removed. Since the Waverly was operated from the back seat, and entirely by hand, he could stretch his legs at full length while he drove. Grandmother's legs did not reach so far as his, so he put their two suitcases in front of her when they motored over to Wilmington, Ohio, to see his brother, Jervis, and Jervis's wife, my great aunt, Wilmina.

The distance to Wilmington from Muncie is about one hundred and twenty miles, and the Waverly would get them, on one charge, to Dayton, eighty-two miles. This was as far as Grandmother and Grandfather cared to go in one day. They would spend a comfortable night in the hotel there, have the electric recharged, and arrive in Wilmington by the following afternoon.

The maximum speed of the Waverly was thirty-two miles an hour; as fast, Grandfather said, as anyone who was not a fool cared to travel. He reserved twenty-five for emergency spurts, and held generally to a cruising speed of eighteen to twenty.

They rolled along at that pace over the flat, dusty roads of Indiana and the gentle hills of Ohio. Grandmother crocheted, and sometimes read aloud to him, though when she read he had to slow down to twelve. Going faster than twelve made her sick at her stomach if she read, she said, but it was all right for crocheting. Grandfather, leaning back, his legs stretched out, or crossed in front of him, smoked a cigar.

The Waverly was the only place, he declared, where he could sit and smoke in peace, and that further endeared the machine to him. When he smoked at home, Grandmother always came in with a folded newspaper which she waved around the room and around him, blowing gustily at the same time, and making such a strong draft at the back of his neck he had to tuck a large silk handkerchief around his collar when he took out a cigar. She did this even in his own den, an invasion that never failed to rouse him to incredulous and angry surprise. A den was a place to which a man retreated in order to smoke, wasn't it? Grandmother's answer never changed. The smoke settled in the curtains unless you drove it out—no matter *what* the room was for. But in the Waverly she let him smoke peacefully, so long as he kept the window beside him open a little—not too much on account of her neuralgia and his own tendency to a stiff neck.

When farmers hailed them along the road, Grandfather usually stopped the electric for conversation. He was grateful to them for this evidence of friendliness. It distressed him to have them throw stones at the Pierce Arrow and distressed Grandmother to the point of refusing to ride into the country in it. The farmers were doing their best to get gasoline automobiles off the road because they caused so much damage by frightening the horses into runaways.

An electric in the country was a rarity, but the farmers approved of it—thought it a fine way to travel, they told Grandfather, without tormenting horses or folks. Grandfather used this testimony in the letters he wrote us advocating the machine. "The farmer can teach us many things," he said.

In spite of his recommendation, however, my parents did not settle on a Waverly until we had looked over other makes.

The first one we tried was a Detroit. One Monday afternoon a man brought this machine for a demonstration. He went first to my father's office and drove him out. He said the electric took very little more time than the train—they just came spinning along very smoothly.

The demonstrator was pleased. He took us all for a ride in different combinations. Five could ride at one time, but it was crowded. When I rode with Mother he showed her how it was driven.

There were two parallel metal bars, one shorter than the other. They stood upright at the left of the driver and out of his way when he got in and out of the machine. The driver's place was on the left side of the back seat. The demonstrator showed Mother how the rods came down, as simply as closing the lid of a box, because they were each on a hinge. Brought down by a touch, they extended across in front of the driver, one above the other. The longer one was for steering, the shorter for speed control. If you wished to turn left, you pushed the long bar away, or pulled it toward you to turn right. Pushing the shorter bar away would send the machine from first, through the notches of higher speeds, to fifth. Before it would start, however, you had to insert a thick, flat key in a slot. This would turn on the current.

While the demonstrator explained all this, I could see Mother growing restless. Finally, he asked if she would like to try just sitting in the driving seat, and manipulating the speed and steering bars; he would get out, come round to the other side and sit beside her. He opened the door as he was speaking. Mother was in the driver's seat before he had uttered the last syllable.

I sat diagonally across from her on the front seat that ran the full width of the machine. I knew she was not going to let the man get in on the other side; she had had enough of him, and I had a feeling she was going to do more than manipulate the bars. She did—so fast that I hadn't time to brace myself, and was knocked to the floor instantly by the abruptness of our departure. I wasn't hurt, but I stayed where I was until we stopped. We didn't go very far, but we went fast. When I raised up, I saw that we had come out the driveway, across the street, over the curb and the sidewalk between two trees, and were in front of the iron gate to the Stephens' house. Mrs. Stephens, and her son, Jack, were on their front porch trying to open the screen door and get into the house. Mother called through the car window to them, "I've found the brake."

When Father arrived, with the demonstrator and Brother just behind him, Mother explained how it had been her intention to turn left at the foot of the driveway, but instead of the steering, she had pushed the speed bar away from her. She told the demonstrator that perhaps he hadn't sufficiently emphasized the difference between the two bars. He was walking around the electric while she said this, looking, I think, for signs of damage. He seemed to be surprised at the way we had come between the trees without hitting either of them, or scratching the paint on the electric. He only said if Mother would turn the electric over to him, he would try to back it into the street. She and I returned on foot with Father and Brother.

When we reached the curb in front of our building, Father sat down on it. He felt weak, he said. Mother patted his shoulder, but she was preoccupied, and presently she walked away. Brother and I sat down beside Father.

It took the demonstrator a considerable time to retrace the distance Mother had driven in almost nothing, and he scraped a fender against one of the trees that she had cleared nicely. When he did draw up in our driveway again, Mother rejoined us. She had been thinking about the machine, she said, and had decided it was badly designed. She urged the demonstrator to have the company produce a model with a wheel for steering. A wheel was the normal appurtenance; the very sight of it indicated its purpose. The demonstrator told her few, if any, electrics were made with a real steering wheel, because a wheel took up too much room.

Mother described for him Mrs. Frank Ball's electric in Muncie, made to order for her and the five Ball children. There were three rows of seats in it and the steering apparatus was a wheel, only set flat, like a motorman's. The car was open, too, like a summer trolley. It had proved most satisfactory.

Father suggested from the curb that before she had a special electric built, we investigate other makes, and the demonstrator took his Detroit back downtown.

The next make we tried was an Ohio. Another demonstrator brought one around the next day. It also had a steering bar, but the speed control was a round knob the size of a door knob. It was above and to the left of the steering bar and you revolved it in your left hand to move from one speed notch to the next. Mother was glad to try the machine. She said it was like being thrown from a horse; you had to ride again immediately or you never would; and she insisted that I go too, for the same reason. But she was not relaxed, which was perhaps the reason she tried to revolve the steering bar with her right hand while she was making the rotating motion with her left hand to advance the speed. She was cautious, too. She advanced only to first, then retreated to neutral, then came up to first again. We alternately jerked forward, coasted, jerked forward, coasted, while Mother echoed on the steering bar each rotation of the speed knob. When we had lurched to the corner of the next cross street, Mother stopped the machine and got out. She made me get out, too.

She talked from the curb to the demonstrator, describing the steering wheel on Mrs. Frank Ball's electric, and recommending its adoption by the manufacturers of the Ohio. The demonstrator said he would tell them, but he urged her to try once more the mechanism already on the machine. Once she got used to it, he promised, she would never be bothered again. Mother told him that after practice one could also become skilled in patting the head and rubbing the stomach, but she felt there were other activities more rewarding of that concentration. This disposed of the Ohio.

One afternoon a few days later a demonstrator brought a Waverly for a demonstration. She liked it the minute she saw it. She had never driven Grandmother's, but she said she was sure anyone could drive a Waverly without previous experience, and without confusion because the speed control was an upright, short lever at the left hand side of the driver, and low down, at about the level of the seat itself. There was nothing else in that same zone, Mother pointed out to the demonstrator, except a small lever into which the key fitted, and which, after unlocking, you set into backward or forward gear as needed. It suggested she said, the throttle on a locomotive. The steering rod broke at a hinge, like the two rods on the Detroit, to lie across the front of the driver, somewhat like the safety strap in a baby coach. You pushed it away to turn left, pulled it toward you to turn right. There was a foot brake, and you could also brake by pulling back on the speed lever, the demonstrator said. Neither brake should be operated when you were in gear or you would burn out the motor.

Father was at his office when the Waverly arrived. After the man had driven Mother and Brother and me around the neighborhood and given Mother a turn at the controls, he suggested that he drive Mother in town, pick up Father, and bring them both back. Mother was exhilarated by her success with this machine and the demonstrator's insistence that she was the quickest to catch on of all the women he had ever taught. She said she thought she could handle a Waverly without any further help—except perhaps in the downtown traffic—but she made my brother and me get out.

We waved good-by from the sidewalk, but Mother didn't take her hand off the bar to wave back. She nodded several times instead, looking straight ahead of her.

When Mother and Father returned home Brother and I were at the living-room windows watching for them. We had been there such a long time that it was dark. Our parents seemed to be all right when they got out in the driveway, and the Waverly, as well as we could see from the street light, seemed all right, too. The demonstrator drove away in it.

Brother and I opened the front door and waited for them. As soon as Mother saw us she called out, "Children, the Kimbroughs own a Waverly."

Brother and I went immediately to the kitchen to tell Hilda the news, and we didn't hear any further details until we were having dinner. Mother explained then, that the Waverly had her confidence not only because of the intelligent arrangement of its steering and speed controls but also because going down Michigan Avenue on the way uptown, the demonstrator, who had by then taken over the driving—another time it would not be necessary—had blinked the lights on and off as they passed the Waverly salesroom. It was just dusk.

"He told me that everyone who owns a Waverly always does that," Mother said. "I knew then that Waverly owners and Waverly makers are good friends. That signal was like a fraternity handclasp, so the machine must be dependable."

Our Waverly was delivered the next day, and all that month we went for a ride every pleasant evening. Mother had dinner moved up to six o'clock so that we could catch the sunset afterglow on the lake and over the lagoon in Jackson Park. We would rush through the meal. Brother was inclined ordinarily to dawdle over his food, but one warning from Mother that he would be left behind would set him briskly on the march again. Hilda told Brother and me she distrusted anything that came of hurrying. She said she would not care to ride in the electric until we all got more settled down. But she approved of early dinner.

Brother and I would race down the stairs ahead of Mother and Father and wait for Mother to get the Waverly out of the barn, now called the garage, insisting to her that the sun had practically set. Father waited on the sidewalk at the end of the driveway to make sure, he said, that the street was clear. I think he couldn't let go of the memory of our first sortie from the driveway to the Stephens' front gate, and wanted to be certain that Mother had an unob-structed getaway, in case she should confuse her motions again.

She never did. She drove with a firm hand and a firm foot. Her footwork was of a special sort. It served as a kind of extra brake for Brother and me. He and I always sat at either end of the front seat, which was narrow and extended the width of the machine. The conventional way to use this seat was to face the driver, with both feet on the floor and one's back against the front window. But Brother and I sat facing each other, our backs against the side door windows, to allow Mother full view ahead. In this position we could not put our feet on the floor, we had to stretch them in front of us along the seat, my feet against Brother's thigh, and vice versa. In this position we had nothing to hold on to, so whenever Mother stopped suddenly, or swooped around a corner, as she liked to do, she simulta-neously put her foot up hard against our legs to keep us from falling off sideways to the floor. The action became so involuntary with her that once rounding a corner fast, when she was taking for a drive old Mrs. Dyer, a neighbor, and two other ladies, she put her foot up into Mrs. Dyer's lap and pushed hard against her stomach. Mrs. Dyer was sitting on the front seat in the conventional position, her back to the window, her feet well braced on the floor.

Mother told me later what she'd done, adding that it had made Mrs. Dyer nervous, and that when I learned to drive, I must remem-ber not to put my foot up.

After the first two weeks, the novelty of riding in the Waverly wore off for Brother and me, but it was supplanted by an exciting by-product: visits to a motion picture theater. We never knew when these might take place, because they happened only when the power in the electric ran down. We charged the machine ourselves by means of an apparatus that Father had had installed in the garage.

This apparatus gave off a crackling sound and a blue light which disturbed the neighbors at night. One evening we even had a visit from the police who had a report that our garage was haunted. After that Mother, out of consideration and over Father's protest, would run the charger only in the daytime and in short spurts. That was why the electric frequently ran down on an evening's drive. But Mother found that if you let the electric rest for an hour or two, it would in some mysterious way generate enough power all by itself to get us home. So we would abandon the dead car and march off to the nearest motion picture. This was Father's idea; Mother didn't approve of motion pictures, but she agreed to the arrangement because she felt that to wait in any other place for two hours, or more, would make us conspicuous. Brother and I got to see three installments of *The Adventures of Kathleen* by turning off the switch of the charging machine on days we knew the serial was playing.

In April that year I went to Muncie, as usual, to spend my spring vacation with my grandparents. While I was there, Grandfather taught me to drive Grandmother's Waverly. His method was simple, and hair-raising. He drove me up Main Street, that had a streetcar track down the middle of it, and explained, as he drove, every detail of the machine. I had heard it all from the demonstrators, and their language was easier to understand, because Grandfather was an orator. I had also been watching Mother drive, which I told Grandfather. He was aware of that, he said, and had therefore given only a recapitulating summary. He then stopped the electric and got out.

"Take the machine, Emily," he said to me through a window. "I have clarified your own observations on how to conduct it. Your grandmother is waiting at the house. I think she wishes to be taken to market. You can give her a surprise by driving her yourself." He looked up the street and added, "I perceive the trolley coming, but it must be at least two blocks away. You had better turn around and clear the tracks before it reaches you. Good-by. I have an errand here."

I did not drive Grandmother to market. By the time I reached the house I was bawling, though I had been helped and encouraged by the motorman, the conductor, and most of the passengers on the trolley. Perhaps Grandfather didn't see the performance. At any rate, he didn't come back to help me, and when that evening Grandmother rounded on him, for putting me through such an ordeal he looked amazed and wounded.

"Why, Margaret," he told her, "Emily said she wanted to learn to drive."

When I returned to Chicago at the end of vacation, I was lofty about my driving, and told Brother it was a pity he was too young to learn. Father said he considered my age equally inappropriate, but Mother told him she had worked out a plan for me that was perfectly safe, because it was only three blocks, and she had never heard of anyone's having an accident on a drive of only three blocks. I was to drive myself to and from Miss Faulkner's School, at Forty-eighth Street and Dorchester Avenue, on the two days when we had afternoon sessions. One was for basketball, the other for dancing class. Walking home alone in the late afternoon *was* dangerous, she thought. It was, however, on the three-block trip in the Waverly, that I came to grief.

I was driving home from dancing class, when, on the turn from Dorchester Avenue to Fiftieth Street, the speed lever stuck between third and fourth speeds. I jiggled it, I tried to push it ahead, to pull it back. I couldn't budge it. It was frozen, and I was rounding the corner at a clip of about twenty miles an hour, or better. I couldn't stop because I had been severely warned that in an electric, if you put on the brake while the current was on, you burned out the motor after first setting it on fire, and the motor was immediately under the driver's seat. You could tap the brake lightly for a very slight pause, but for a genuine slowing down, you had to pull the speed lever back to neutral, and then apply the brake. After that you started all over again, neutral to first, et cetera.

I only remembered about tapping the brake after I had got round the corner and settled on to four wheels again. I tapped my way around the corner at Fiftieth and Blackstone. Simultaneously, I began to ring the bell, which was a button at the end of the steering rod. I had only half a block to go before reaching our apartment. I knew I couldn't stop there, but I thought I might attract someone's attention.

The first time past brought no results, so I went on around the block, brake-tapping at the corners, though the seat beneath me was beginning to feel hot. I had also gathered speed, so I approached the apartment on the second try at a mileage per hour that I had experienced before only on a Flexible Flyer. But I was ready with my message in flight, in case there was anyone to receive it. At the corner I stopped ringing the bell, braced my knee against the steering rod to hold a steady course, leaned out the window, my hands cupped around my mouth, and roared over and over, "Mother, come help! Mother, help! *Mother!*"

I was afraid that people in the apartments would be the only ones to hear me and have to relay the news to Mother, but miraculously it was Hilda who heard and recognized my voice and the bell of our electric. I saw her come out on the porch my next time round the block. But she shook her finger crossly as I flashed by, and yelled after me, "Shame on you."

Part way around the block I was confused by this; then I guessed she had thought I was showing off how I could drive no-handed, and wouldn't on any account let Mother see. But the next time past, I saw Mother beside Hilda on the porch. "Come in this minute," she called down very loud and she repeated it. This prevented her from hearing what I was saying. Going around the corner, I burst into tears. I had been sure that once I got Mother's attention, she would know what was wrong and what to do.

That lap was the most dangerous of all the trips around the block. The noise of my bell made several people who were crossing the street jump into the air and then scurry to the sidewalk. They were angry, too, because an electric didn't make any noise, so the first warning they had was the bell. Motorcars and horse-drawn delivery wagons should have impeded me, but I zigzagged around all of them. When I rounded on to Blackstone Avenue again, Mother had guessed that I couldn't stop. She was standing in the middle of the street. A number of people from our building were on their porches, watching. She pantomimed by bending her knees and swinging her arms that she was going to jump onto my runningboard. As I reached her, I tapped the brake so hard that the motor sizzled under me. She made it, swinging on to the runningboard on the side opposite me, and held on by thrusting her arm through the window, which fortunately was open. She crouched to talk to me through the window. "You're doing nicely," she said "What's the matter? Stop crying."

"The speed lever's stuck." I jiggled it to show her, and I stopped crying. When she had satisfied herself that the lever *was* stuck, she straightened up, looked over the top, and shouted, first to people in our way, then equally loud but sticking her face suddenly through the window, to me.

"Out of our way, little boy. . . . We could keep on driving 'til the power dies. . . . Look out, *please*, we're out of control. . . . Not around and around like this, Emily, we'll be dizzy. . . . Keep *back*, please. . . . But in a straight line we might be in Gary before we stop. Ring the bell louder. . . . Don't be a fool (this to a man on the curb who called something to us), we're not doing this on pur. . . ." We had shot past him by this time and were in our own street again, which was quieter. It gave Mother time to think. She leaned reflectively over the window ledge.

"I *will* not pass all those people again," she said. "They don't seem to understand what we're doing. They make me feel like a fool."

"Where do you want me to go?" I asked her. She had an inspiration. "Go across Fifty-first Street," she directed, "and up Lake Park. There's a nice garage somewhere along that block. Mrs. Dyer told me. Very courteous, she said. We can ask which it is."

We crossed Fifty-first Street, turned left, and right on Lake Park Avenue. There seemed to be several garages on each side of the street.

"Ring the bell again," Mother told me, "but stop when someone comes out so I can talk to him."

I rang steadily, but no one came. So I drove once around *that* block. At the second round, Mother changed the plan of approach. "Don't ring," she ordered, "shout 'ahoy' with me. That's more unusual. It may bring someone."

It did. It brought two or three men out of almost every garage on the run.

Mother said, "Quiet, Emily," and straightened to her full height. "Are you Mrs. Dyer's garage," she called as we whirled by. No one answered.

"I surprised them, I think," Mother said as we went around the block again. "You have to present ideas slowly to people like that. They work with their hands. It makes them deliberate. And yet surgeons, they tell me, respond quickly to a crisis. Broader preliminary education probably."

We turned into Lake Park for the third time. Some of the men who had come out at our shouts were still in front of the garages. Mother addressed them, leaning out from the running board, her one arm upraised.

"My daughter," she said rapidly but clear and loud, "my daughter has had an accident. Not really an accident. She only drives three blocks. To Miss Faulkner's School . . . for basketball. I am Mrs. H. C. Kimbrough, 5019 Blackstone Avenue." We passed the last garage . . . "and dancing, on Wednesdays," she called back.

We had reached the corner. Mother didn't talk as we made the next circuit, but at Fifty-first and Lake Park she got ready again. This time I saw only one man in the whole block. He was young and thin and dirty. He slouched over to the curb as we rushed toward him and dropped into the gutter a cigarette he'd been smoking. He was on my side of the machine. I don't think Mother even saw him. She called down to me, "Ring again, Emily, and shout. We'll have to start all over again."

I was watching the young man. He stepped into the street and put up his hand, palm toward me, like a traffic policeman. I tapped the brake as hard as I dared. He stepped with no particular effort on the running board next me. I stopped tapping and the Waverly shot forward again. He held the sill of my window in one hand, leaned inside, reached down beside me and pulled out the key that connected the current. The machine slowed down. I put on the brake hard, and we stopped.

Mother apparently didn't realize at once that we had stopped. Her face appeared in the window, and she seemed about to speak to me when she saw the face of the man in the opposite window. She spoke to him instead.

"Oh," she said, "I'm glad to see you. Are you Mrs. Dyer's garage?"

"No, ma'am," he said finally, "I don't think so." He looked at me, and pointed to the speed lever. "That happens every once in a while," he said. "All you got to do is disconnect the current. People never seem to think of it. They don't think quick, I guess."

❖ ❖ ❖ ❖ ❖

JOHN STOVER

(b. 1912–), a native of Kansas, has taught at Purdue since 1947. A specialist in the history of transportation, his books include *A History of American Railroads* (1967), *Turnpikes, Canals, & Steamboats* (1969), and *The Life & Decline of the American Railroad* (1970).

Some Hoosier Railroad Memories

In an earlier age hundreds of railroad depots served Indiana. Most middle-aged Hoosiers remember the small well-painted—boxcar red or brown or green, according to company policy—station down at the end of Main Street. Such depots provided much of the warp and woof of the society in the innocent generation before World War I. With its telegraph office, its mail and express service, its less-than-carload-lot-freight, and its complement of passenger and freight trains, the station was the major focal point of communication with the outside world.

Most intercity passengers in the early decades of this century rode the green plush or yellow straw seats in the day-coaches and smoking-cars of the frequent and nameless local trains. Drummers and traveling salesmen, families moving to new homes, students going off to college, and children on their way to visit grandparents or a favorite aunt, all went down to the depot to board the cars. Even as America became a nation dedicated to the automobile, the timetables of most railroads were crowded with the schedules of local, fast-mail, and express trains. Probably no single community facility in Indiana, or any other state, today provides the variety of important services associated with the railroad depot of yesterday.

But it is different in our town today. The Monon depot of a generation ago became a used-furniture auction house when a smaller station was located away from the center of town. This smaller building in turn was relegated to being a feed store with the loss of the last Monon passenger train. The Big Four-New York Central station, down near the river bank, has suffered the same decline in traffic that the river steamboats were facing a long century ago when the first steam locomotives appeared. The local passenger business became so poor that when the Big Four railroad restaurant suffered a serious fire the picturesque building was not repaired or rebuilt. The Wabash depot was also in decline, and soon there was more action in a nearby tavern called the "Depot" than could be found at the railway station.

Railroads came to our town back in the 1850s, and quickly rail passenger service became common. By the end of the Civil War more than a dozen trains served the city, and at the turn of the century a total of nearly thirty daily trains were stopping at the three depots. Even in the early years after World War II over a dozen trains gave us daily service to such rail centers as Chicago, Indianapolis, Cincinnati, Detroit, St. Louis, and Louisville.

Much of this passenger service was quite good. On the Monon, often called the Hoosier Line, three trains provided daily service to a quartet of Indiana colleges: DePauw, Indiana, Purdue, and Wabash. Some older and more affluent alumni might even take a Monon Pullman down to the private car siding at the French Lick Hotel in southern Indiana.

Several Wabash trains furnished service between Detroit and St.

Louis, but the best known was the *Wabash Cannon Ball*. This train's route in fact bore little relationship to the geography found in the words of the popular song: "Atlantic to the wild Pacific . . . California to ice-bound Labrador." On its route through Indiana the *Cannon Ball* followed the Wabash River much of the way. The track also often paralleled the faint depression in nearby fields which marked the old Wabash and Erie Canal, an early waterway which had had only a decade or so of good traffic before succumbing to the iron horse.

Perhaps the best known Big Four passenger train in our state was the streamliner named for the folksy Indiana poet, the *James Whitcomb Riley*. The *Riley* was fast enough to be included in the annual speed surveys in *Trains* magazine, and had a schedule which permitted many Hoosiers a daylight run to and from Chicago plus a brief afternoon shopping tour in the Windy City. Travelers going in the other direction had adequate rail connections in Cincinnati for eastern points.

Soon so many Hoosiers, and Americans generally, had been lured away from the downtown depot by the speed of the jetliner and the convenience of the automobile that railroads were losing money on nearly every passenger train. Train after train was discontinued, and finally we were left with only an aging *James Whitcomb Riley*, now operated by Amtrak. Inadequacies of track maintenance plus a deteriorating road bed resulted in so many "slow orders" that finally the *Riley* was transferred to an alternate line. The Big Four depot, now Penn Central, still sells Amtrak tickets, but one must go out of town in order to board any train. The conductor's "all aboard," that had for so many years echoed along the platforms of three small Hoosier depots, was no more.

❖ ❖ ❖ ❖ ❖

WILL CUPPY

(b. Auburn, 1884–d. 1949) was a descendant of the French Huguenots who settled Whitley County. He spent his boyhood in South Whitley, where his mother, transplanted from the Pennsylvania Dutch, was the teacher. Will pumped the organ in the Presbyterian Church and attended Auburn High School. He also spent twelve years as a student at the University of Chicago. When he turned to free-lance writing, his pieces appeared in the *New York*

Herald Tribune and *The New Yorker*. His books of irreverent essays include *How to Tell Your Friends from the Apes* (1931) and
The Decline and Fall of Practically Everybody (1950).

George III

George III was King of England during the American Revolution.
Naturally, our side won. The English had plenty of ammunition and
were very good at fighting. They just picked on the wrong people,
that's all.[1]

As his name implies, George III was the third of the Georges, of
whom there were four from 1714 to 1830, or an average of one every
twenty-nine years. Nobody seems to have realized that this was an
awful lot of Georges.

The trouble with having so many Georges all at once is that they
tend to become blurred and to be known vaguely as the four
Georges, or any old man in a wig. How to tell the Georges apart is
something of a problem.[2]

Anyway, George I was the one who couldn't speak English and
didn't try. He was Elector of Hanover, a place in Germany, but was
regarded as heir to the throne because he was a descendant of Mary
Queen of Scots. He was brought over by the commercial interests
and reigned until 1727 without the least notion of what anybody was
talking about.

During this time there was no Queen of England. George I kept
his wife in prison because he believed that she was no better than he
was.[3]

Although George I was extremely dull, his subjects were very
sporting about it. They felt that, after all, the Georges were just
getting started and the next few might be different.

George II, however, was practically the same thing, except that he
was smaller and noisier and redder in the face. When agitated or
angry he would throw his wig across the room and kick his toes
against the wall.[4]

1. *On July 9, 1776, the statue of George III in Bowling Green, New York,
was torn down. To compound the insult, the lead of which it was made was
cast into bullets to shoot at King George's soldiers.*
2. *At the time it may have been easy enough, but today it is almost a lost
art.*
3. *He was wrong there.*
4. *After a while his feet began to hurt. He thought it was because his shoes
were too tight.*

He was a brave man, too. He was not a bit afraid of Bonnie Prince Charlie or any of the seven gentlemen he had brought with him to raise the North and win back his rightful throne. When the Young Pretender was at Derby in '45 and the courtiers turned pale with alarm, George II simply exclaimed, "Pooh! Don't talk to me dat stuff!" and ate a hearty supper of *Schweinskopf* and *Specksuppe*.

Personally, I am for Bonnie Prince Charlie and I don't care who knows it. Only he *would* drink and he had a disconcerting way of powdering his wig during the most inauspicious moments of a battle. Gentlemen, the King over the water! And another for Flora Macdonald!

George II also got his country into several wars, including the War of Jenkins' Ear, caused by the rumor that a Spaniard named Fandino had cut off the ear of Captain Jenkins.[5] There was some question afterwards whether Captain Jenkins hadn't lost his ear in the pillory, but meantime the English captured a Spanish galleon worth ten million smackers, so it all turned out happily.

Caroline of Anspach was a model wife to George II. Though tormented by gout, she would plunge her feet into cold water, force herself to smile, and go out walking with him. She loved him.[6]

George III was the grandson of George II. He began his reign in 1760 and the next year married Princess Charlotte of Mecklenburg-Strelitz, concerning whom a charming tale is told. "Who will take such a poor little princess as me?" she murmured one day, and at that very instant the postman appeared with a proposal from George, who wouldn't take no for an answer.

So the poor little princess jumped for joy and got some lovely new dresses and sailed for England in the royal yacht and married the King and spent the next sixty years thinking it over. George is said to have winced when he saw his bride.[7]

They had fifteen children, who were bathed, according to Queen Charlotte's strict orders, on alternate Mondays. Historians have quarreled bitterly over the wisdom and unwisdom of this domestic scheme. Would it not have been better, some ask, to bathe one child a day for fourteen consecutive days and the odd child every other Saturday night? Or in groups of five on Monday, Friday, and the following Thursday? Such questions are rather futile. The main object was achieved, wasn't it?[8]

5. *Fandino threatened to do the same to King George.*
6. *She must have.*
7. *And he didn't wince easily, either.*
8. *Or was it?*

George III was very fond of children, especially other people's children, as is prettily shown by the episode of the beefeater's little boy, upon meeting whom one day the King inquired with a kindly pat on the head, "Whose little boy are you?" "Please, sir," replied the urchin, "I am the King's beefeater's little boy." "Then kneel down and kiss the Queen's hand," said the King, to which the beefeater's offspring retorted, "No, I won't for if I do I shall spoil my new breeches."

George III's coronation, at Westminster Hall, was most unusual. The Queen had a toothache and neuralgia, and was feeling out of sorts to begin with. Then things were late getting started. The chairs of State for the King and Queen were forgotten, and so was the sword of State.

When the King complained, Lord Effingham, the deputy Earl Marshal, said it was true there had been great neglect, but that he had now taken such care of registering directions that the next coronation would be conducted in the greatest order imaginable.

The King was so flattered by this diverting speech that he asked the earl to repeat it several times.[9]

Lord Talbot, the steward, had trained his horse to walk backwards, so that he would be able to withdraw correctly from the royal presence. But when the animal entered the hall, it remembered its lesson, turned about, and backed the whole distance to the table, where the King was.[10]

Things were all fouled up in general.

George was not one for traveling. But in 1789 he went to Weymouth, a seaside resort. There an old man, overwhelmed by the King's presence, kissed the royal back as the King left the water and was informed by the royal attendants that he had committed an act of high treason.

Another time he went to Portsmouth, to inspect a battleship. He said it was all right and returned home.

For part of his reign, George III had as his Prime Minister William Pitt the Younger.[11] Lady Hester Stanhope, who vouched for Pitt's love of ladies, was an earnest transvestite. She was adopted by Pitt, her uncle, and presided at his table "with brilliance." She and Pitt had a habit of nearly getting married. She once lost all her clothes in a shipwreck and put on a male Turkish costume, which she liked so well that she made it part of her wardrobe. "Though there seems

9. *He forgot that he wouldn't be around at the next coronation to appreciate the earl's efforts.*
10. *This is what comes of teaching animals tricks.*
11. *Son of William Pitt the Elder.*

no reason to suppose that she was sexually inverted," she sometimes dressed as an Albanian chief, a Syrian soldier, a Bedouin, or a Pasha's son. *Very* interesting.[12]

The reign of George III was the beginning of the machine age. Stephenson invented the locomotive, Watt the steam engine, and Hargreaves produced his spinning jenny. Dr. Johnson was going strong, and Adam Smith was spouting off about *laissez faire.*[13] And the Whigs and the Tories were at it hot and heavy.[14]

George once said wars were useless. The news from America didn't seem to upset him greatly. When he heard of the surrender of Cornwallis at Yorktown, George said: "It's nothing." But Lord North, his Prime Minister at the time, resigned.[15]

George sometimes forgot what the fuss had been all about. The colonists, it seems, had to "pay taxes to which their consent had never been asked."[16]

George III acted pretty strangely at times, but so did the other Georges. Perhaps the most nerve-racking thing about George III was his habit of sputtering "What-what-what" every so often, apropos of nothing in particular, so far as anybody could see. He would use this "What-what-what" alone, or in a combination with the matter in hand, as "So it's five o'clock, what-what-what," or possibly "What-what-what, so it's five o'clock."

He was often heard to mutter "What-what-what" while he was wondering how the apple got into the dumpling. In his later years he wondered this once too often.[17]

For pure, all-around meanness, George IV is your man. His wife, Queen Caroline of Brunswick, was insulted at every turn and finally tried on a charge of committing adultery, on some very flimsy grounds.

12. *After Pitt's death, she nearly married Sir John Moore.*
13. *Adam Smith once remarked: "What an extraordinary man Pitt is! He makes me understand my own ideas better than before." That indicates which way the wind blew.*
14. *Don't feel badly if you can't tell the Whigs from the Tories. The Duke of York, brother of George IV, "could never distinguish clearly in his mind the difference between a Whig and a Tory, and as a consequence always argued both ways at the same time." Whigs are more tolerant towards people in trade. Tories drink a great deal of port. After they'd had a few, they cried, "Sack the lot," doubtless referring to their opponents.*
15. *Van Loon tells us that Lord Frederick North belonged to a family that gave England a large number of distinguished politicians and Epsom Salts.*
16. *Today we pay taxes but our consent has been asked, and we have told the government to go ahead and tax us all they want to. We like it.*
17. *It's best not to go into those things.*

It's a long story, but after the coronation, George IV rode to West-minster Abbey in his carriage, and the Queen followed in another, with the blinds drawn. The King left his carriage finally and strode into the Abbey. The Queen left *her* carriage and walked towards the gate. But the iron bars were slammed shut in her face. She died three weeks later, uncrowned.[18]

❖ ❖ ❖ ❖ ❖

WENDELL WILLKIE

(b. Elwood, 1892–d. 1944) was educated at Culver Academy and at Indiana University. Both his parents were lawyers, his mother the first woman attorney in Indiana. In 1940 he was the Republican nominee for President of the United States but lost the election to Franklin Roosevelt. Willkie's books include *Free Enterprise* (1940) and *One World* (1941).

Our Reservoir of Good Will

We left Chengtu on October 9, traveled almost a thousand miles in China, crossed the vast expanse of the Gobi and the Mongolian Republic, crossed thousands of miles of Siberia, crossed the Bering Sea, the full length of Alaska and the full width of Canada, and arrived in the United States on October 13. We had gained a day by crossing the international date line.

When you fly around the world in forty-nine days, you learn that the world has become small not only on the map, but also in the minds of men. All around the world, there are some ideas which millions and millions of men hold in common, almost as much as if they lived in the same town. One of these ideas, and one which I can report without hesitation, has tremendous significance for us in America; it is the mixture of respect and hope with which the world looks to this country.

Whether I was talking to a resident of Belém or Natal in Brazil, or one toting his burden on his head in Nigeria, or a prime minister or

18. *The English paid very little attention to George IV. By that time they were numb.*

a king in Egypt, or a veiled woman in ancient Bagdad, or a shah or a weaver of carpets in legendary Persia, now known as Iran, or a follower of Ataturk in those streets of Ankara which look so like the streets of our Middle Western cities, or to a strong-limbed, resolute factory worker in Russia, or to Stalin himself, or the enchanting wife of the great Generalissimo of China, or a Chinese soldier at the front, or a fur-capped hunter on the edge of the trackless forests of Siberia —whether I was talking to any of these people, or to any others, I found that they all have one common bond, and that is their deep friendship for the United States.

They, each and every one, turn to the United States with a friendliness that is often akin to genuine affection. I came home certain of one clear and significant fact: that there exists in the world today a gigantic reservoir of good will toward us, the American people.

Many things have created this enormous reservoir. At the top of the list go the hospitals, schools, and colleges which Americans— missionaries, teachers, and doctors—have founded in the far corners of the world. Many of the new leaders of old countries—men who are today running Iraq or Turkey or China—have studied under American teachers whose only interest has been to spread knowledge. Now, in our time of crisis, we owe a great debt to these men and women who have made friends for us.

Good will has also been stored up for us, like credit in a bank account, by those Americans who have pioneered in the opening of new roads, new airways, new shipping lines. Because of them, the peoples of the world think of us as a people who move goods, and ideas, and move them fast. They like us for this, and they respect us.

Our motion pictures have played an important role in building up this reservoir of friendliness. They are shown all over the world. People of every country can see with their own eyes what we look like, can hear our voices. From Natal to Chungking I was plied with questions about American motion-picture stars—questions asked eagerly by shop-girls and those who served me coffee, and just as eagerly by the wives of prime ministers and kings.

There are still other reasons for our reserve of good will abroad. The people of every land, whether industrialized or not, admire the aspirations and accomplishments of American labor, which they have heard about, and which they long to emulate. Also they are impressed by American methods of agriculture, business, and industry. In nearly every country I went to, there is some great dam or irrigation project, some harbor or factory, which has been built by Americans. People like our works, I found, not only because they help to make life easier and richer, but also because we have shown that American business enterprise does not necessarily lead to attempts at political control.

I found this dread of foreign control everywhere. The fact that we are not associated with it in men's minds has caused people to go much farther in their approval of us than I had dared to imagine. I was amazed to discover how keenly the world is aware of the fact that we do not seek—anywhere, in any region—to impose our rule upon others or to exact special privileges.

All the people of the earth know that we have no sinister designs upon them, that even when we have in the past withdrawn from international affairs into a false self-sufficiency, it was without sinister purpose. And they know that, now we are in this war, we are not fighting for profit, or loot, or territory, or mandatory power over the lives or the governments of other people. That, I think, is the single most important reason for the existence of our reservoir of good will around the world.

Everywhere I went around the world, and I mean literally everywhere, I found officers and men of the United States Army. Sometimes they were in very small units; in other places they filled enormous army camps which covered acres of some foreign country. In every situation in which I found them, they were adding to the good will foreign peoples hold toward America.

A striking example of this was the crew of our C-87 army plane. None of its officers or enlisted men had ever been abroad before except on a fighting assignment. They were not trained diplomats. Most of them spoke no foreign language. But everywhere we landed, they made friends for America. I shall remember for a long time the sight of the Shah of Iran, just after we had given him the first airplane ride of his life, shaking hands with Major Richard Kight, our pilot, and looking at him with what I can only describe as a mixture of admiration and envy.

I was proud of American soldiers everywhere I saw them. I felt a confidence that our citizens' army, uninterested in entrenching themselves as professional army men, would automatically help to preserve the reservoir of good will which our generation inherits, and would at the same time find out, through firsthand experience, why this is America's war.

For, as I see it, the existence of this reservoir is the biggest political fact of our time. No other Western nation has such a reservoir. Ours must be used to unify the peoples of the earth in the human quest for freedom and justice. It must be maintained so that, with confidence, they may fight and work with us against the gigantic evil forces that are seeking to destroy all that we stand for, all that they hope for. The preservation of this reservoir of good will is a sacred responsibility, not alone toward the aspiring peoples of the earth, but toward our own sons who are fighting this battle on every continent. For the water in this reservoir is the clean, invigorating water of freedom.

Neither Hitler nor Mussolini nor Hirohito, with their propaganda or by their arms, can take from us the unifying force of this good will —and there is no other such unifying force in the world—or divide us among ourselves or from our allies, as long as we do not make a mockery of our protestations of the ideals for which we have proclaimed we fight. A policy of expediency will prove inexpedient. For it will lose us the invaluable spiritual and practical assets that come from the faith of the people of the world in both our ideals and our methods.

If we permit ourselves to become involved in the machinations of Old World intrigue and religious, nationalistic and racial blocs, we will find ourselves amateurs indeed. If we stand true to our basic principles, then we shall find ourselves professionals of the kind of world toward which men in every part of it are aspiring.

J. C. FURNAS

(b. Indianapolis, 1905–) was educated in the Indianapolis schools and at Harvard. His works include *So You're Going to Stop Smoking* (1939), *Voyage to Windward: Life of RLS* (1951), and *Life & Times of the Great Demon Rum* (1955).

The Franklin Wonder Five

. . . Basketball was invented in Springfield, Massachusetts (under the auspices of the same Gulick who founded the Camp Fire Girls), by a YMCA physical director, James Naismith, to give the boys in the gym something more competitive than Indian clubs. Since it used a smaller playing area and was independent of weather, this bouncy, swirling, upward-seeking blend of soccer and hockey made a better spectator sport than either.

The YMCA's took it all over the country. A version for girls with an extra player and special rules developed. Professional teams began to exploit it. The AEF took it to Europe, where it struck roots as baseball did not. By then college athletic directors, particularly in the Midwest, were booming intercollegiate basketball. Student admissions to knockdown bleachers in the gym more than paid for the coach and the simple equipment. Much of that was infection upward from the high schools, among which the game was feverishly organized before most colleges were strongly affected. Here was something really worth doing in that shiny-floored gymnasium intended to foster physical fitness for all pupils in Decaturville's new high school. Many country high schools lacked enough pupil population to field football elevens. But once standard rules fixed the basketball team at five, an enrollment of say eight or nine senior and a dozen or so junior boys often supplied enough athletic potential. And the nippier or huskier among them were likely to be good basketball timber because on the gable end of every barn for miles around protruded a hoop at which Junior was looping a basketball whenever he was not eating, doing chores or in class.

Teams from small high schools often held their own or better with those from large city schools with hundreds of boys to choose from. In 1920 a Midwestern high school basketball tournament at the University of Chicago, including also teams from the Deep South, was won by Wingate, Indiana, a very small school indeed, defeating Crawfordsville, Indiana, a county seat with a very brisk small sectarian college; a few weeks earlier, Crawfordsville had won a Tri-State championship at Cincinnati with Wingate as runner-up; the two towns were only 12 miles apart. Simultaneously the high school of Franklin, Indiana, another county seat with a small sectarian college, was developing a "Wonder Five" who may well have been the best nonprofessional basketball team that ever trotted out on a court.

The five boys making the nucleus of this demonstration that, for some inscrutable reason, Indiana was then basketball incarnate had all been in the same Sunday school class taught by the high school basketball coach. As high school sophomores they not only won the state title but went into its finals with a win/lose record of 29/1. They won it again in 1921 and 1922; 89/8 was their three-season record against the sharpest opponents in the nation. Moving on into Franklin College, coach and all, as freshmen they went undefeated against a tough schedule of Indiana college teams. As their renown grew, they occasionally scheduled one or another big Midwestern university—by then basketball was important in the Big Ten—and in the next three seasons knocked off, once or several times, Wisconsin, Notre Dame, Purdue, Michigan State; no team from outside Indiana ever beat them. They had become a ten-legged, ten-armed, five-headed but single-minded organism never in a hurry, passing the ball without looking to see if the other fellow was there—he'd be there because he always was. You don't need to look at your left foot to know it's there. They specialized in the Garrison finish, eliciting from a sportswriter on the Indianapolis *News:*

> You can beat them in the first half,
> You can always have the ball;
> But when the game is over
> They ain't been beat at all.

Theirs was not the high-scoring game by beanpole freaks familiar today. The Wonder Five were average-sized or not much larger, and their average scores per season ran between 33 and 39 points. But otherwise the word "average" is shudderingly inappropriate for the virtuosity of their passing game and the uncanniness of their eye for the basket. In my memory they were more impressive than Notre Dame's Four Horsemen football team of a few years later. That, as those familiar with the 1920's will recognize, is the optimum compliment. . . . .

JAMES COMER

(b. East Chicago, 1934–), Associate Dean of the Yale University School of Medicine, was educated in the East Chicago public schools and at Indiana, Howard, and Michigan Universities. He interned at St. Catherine's Hospital, East Chicago, and devotes much of his time to children's mental health projects. He has published several articles on adolescence, and two of his recent books are *Beyond Black and White* (1972) and *Black Child Care* (1975; co-edited with Elvin F. Puissaint).

The Functions of the
Urban Black Church

The church played a big role in the development of the black man's self-respect and dignity. Because of the church's dominant role, Sunday was always a big day at our house. We awoke to the smell of bacon and the sound of gospel music. Every house down the street seemed to be tuned in to the same station. Our favorite vocal group was the "Wings over Jordan." My father was a deacon, a position of great importance in the black church, and a deeply religious man. He said a very long grace and we often got a little restless around the table. Sometimes my two brothers and I would make faces and I could hardly keep from laughing—my younger sister would get mad at us and we would look up and find our mother giving us a withering glance. All eyes closed and there was silence again. She would not tolerate any disrespect for our father. The black woman often zealously protected the dignity of the black man, because his dignity was under such constant assault outside the home.

The major roots of our family were in the church; ours was the Zion Baptist. Some of the ministers could touch the congregation deeply. One approach always caused people to shout and cry: these were the sermons that were full of assurances that conditions would be better in the hereafter. They were also designed to help a rejected and abused people feel good about themselves and enjoy a sense of purpose and worth.

During such sermons, the minister would gradually build to a high emotional pitch and then in a repetitive fashion cry out, "He's a Rock in a weary land! He's a Shelter in a mighty storm! He rescued Daniel from the lion's den! He's a Father to the fatherless! He's a Light in the darkness! He's Eyes to the blind and a Cane to the cripple! He brought the children of Israel out of bondage and He'll take care of you!" With each assertion, the "Amens," "Yes, Reverends," and "Yes, Lords" would become more frequent and the excitement would grow. When he reached "He'll take care of you," the shouting and crying would start.

Some of the women would lurch back in the pews, as if having a fit, their arms flailing back and forth. I often thought the force against the pews would pull them from their moorings. Two or three ushers would rush up to control them. One man in our church shouted and others would occasionally weep quietly with one hand over their eyes. I often wondered why grown men would cry. As a child, I never did quite understand the shouting and crying and the explanations I received always left me more curious: 'Well, Negroes have had it hard"; "Some people have to let it all out." Later, when I met many of these people in the steel mills and in the world beyond the church, I began to understand what the shouting and weeping were all about. While an element of African and even Southern black and white religious culture was involved, the intensity of the response reflected the sense of frustration and helplessness the people felt. The church was the place to discharge frustration and hostility so that one could face injustice and hardship the rest of the week.

The black church had another important function: it was a place for participation and belonging. The deacons, trustees and ushers were ten feet tall on Sunday. This was not Inland Steel, Miss Ann's Kitchen nor the bank. This—the church—was theirs. In retrospect, the trustees were like the city board of finance and the deacons were like the city council. There was a little bit of respect for everybody.

One Sunday I visited a storefront church with a friend of mine. Several of the choir members and ushers were people I knew from school. It seemed to me odd that some of these people were quite withdrawn in school and were hardly known to the teachers and staff, but in their church they were lively, active participants. At the storefront church that day, I found at least part of the answer. The choir gave a rousing rendition of a spiritual. The soloist responded to the audience's enthusiasm with these words, "One thing I like about this church is that if you have a speck of talent you can use it, and the people will love you and respect you for it." I had noticed this in my own church as well. In the Baptist Young People's Training Union Bible Drill, girls who barely participated in school could quickly find the chapter and verse. Many black children were not respected in school even when they attempted to use their talent. I still observe that many black children who are turned off in school and considered dull are turned on in church and in other less alien places.

The biblical and hereafter sermons bothered my mother. "What's he talking about David, John, Moses and Paul and all those people for? ... Why does he talk about golden streets and rewards in Heaven? ... I'm worried about these cement sidewalks I have to walk down every day. He ought to be teaching our people about saving their money and buying homes and taking care of their families."

Occasionally a minister would come to town who could preach two sermons—one spiritual and one intellectual. Then many of the educated people, old and young, who had abandoned church would come back. But it would never last. Soon the people who wanted to hear the spiritual sermon would complain that he "wasn't preaching." These people were the backbone of the church: the church was their major investment and they were the major contributors. They did not want the church branching out and getting into areas like business, education, or even recreation. I recall that one of the major debates in my church was over a plan to have a youth night. The officers would not have any dancing in our church! Some members argued that it would be better to have the youth dancing in the church than in some "smoke-filled den of iniquity." Others countered that if young people are going to sin, they should not sin in the House of the Lord. The church was for listening to the Word of God!

Divisions of this sort were usually between the group who turned toward the values and interests of the total society and those who remained primarily tied to the substitute culture—the black church. Education and opportunities in the "outside world" enabled some to keep their feet in two cultures—the church and the total society. Others, for various reasons, remained enmeshed in the culture of the church alone.

One Sunday, a sixteen-year-old girl brought her born-out-of-wedlock baby to church and created quite a stir. A few women fussed over the baby. The minister talked about forgiveness and understanding. Most of the women did not see it that way—they grumbled about "people carrying on over the baby like it had a daddy." Some of the women who complained were of the "black puritan" background. This "better class of Negroes," as some have referred to themselves, attempted to "out-middle-class" or "out-decent" the white middle and upper classes in vain efforts to win respectability. Because of the stereotype of the immoral Negro, sexual morality was an issue of special concern. In the academy my father had attended as a youngster, girls were always accompanied by a matron in the front of the line and at the rear. Until very recently, supervision of female students was much stricter at black colleges than at white.

Because the minister and the church could gratify so many social and psychological needs, he and the institution were very powerful.

My parents occasionally disagreed about the church. I sometimes thought my mother was less religious than my father. I asked her about it once. She replied that it was not that she was less religious, just that she did not trust all the people who claimed they were called to spread the gospel. Gradually I came to understand what she meant. One Sunday the minister was preaching a "race sermon." This is a sermon in which the minister "gives white folks the business." The congregation responds with loud and enthusiastic "Amens," as the sins and wrongs of white America are spelled out. Just as the minister was warming up to the subject, the head usher rushed down the aisle and onto the pulpit and whispered something in the minister's ear. This was highly unusual; nobody ever disturbed the minister after he started his sermon. The usher returned to the vestibule and brought two white visitors to the rostrum. They were given the honored seats of the assistant pastors and the minister continued his sermon. But there was an abrupt change in his tone. He began to preach about love and brotherhood and how white folks and colored folks could get along together.

The visitors were from the Inland Steel Company. As I recall, Inland Steel gave a large check to the church every Christmas. (Some say it was as much as $1,000.)

My mother's distrust of certain ministers was again vindicated when I was in the seventh grade. The older black students asked me to talk with a minister I knew to get his support for our side in a disagreement in our school. There was a black Paul Robeson Glee Club and a white glee club. The black students did not think we needed both. When I explained the argument to the minister, he paused thoughtfully and said, "Well you see there's a difference in our voices. We have richer, stronger voices and that's the reason for separate glee clubs." Although I had been taught to respect my elders, particularly ministers, I argued that if our voices were stronger and richer it would appear that the white glee club could use our help. He did not appreciate my point of view and told me that some day I would understand. I understood at the end of the year when I saw him on the school stage giving the benediction at the high-school graduation. He was the only Negro on the stage; in fact, I am told it was a black first for East Chicago. He had had to "go along with 'the Man's' program" to appear on the program—to take one step forward.

In the recent flurry of major studies of the black experience, only E. Franklin Frazier and Carter Woodson, both blacks, have given more than a passing glance at the role of the black church. The director of a black-studies program told me that he could not find collections of church sermons in the libraries of major universities. Some young students would like to ignore it all together. But how can we? The root, heart and soul of black culture in America are in the black church—whether we blacks like it or not.

Biographical and
Autobiographical Sketches

❖❖❖❖❖❖❖❖❖❖❖❖❖❖❖❖❖❖❖❖❖❖❖

ALBERT BEVERIDGE

(b. 1862–d. 1927), a graduate of Asbury College (now De Pauw University), Greencastle, in 1885, began practicing law in Indianapolis in 1887. In 1899 he was elected to the U. S. Senate. His biographies of Chief Justice Marshall, Frances Willard, and Abraham Lincoln have won wide acclaim for their scholarly research and their painstaking rendering of detail.

Abe Lincoln's
Indiana Boyhood and Youth

Not earlier, then, than the approach of December, 1816, the Lincoln family started for the Indiana solitudes. Two horses bore husband, wife, and children as well as household belongings. Upon one horse rode the father, his little son mounted behind him; on the other horse was Nancy Lincoln, with their nine-year old daughter. How they carried through Kentucky on two horses thus laden articles needful in journey and forest abode, does not appear; but it was managed in some fashion.

Thus Thomas Lincoln 'packed through,' as such methods of travel and conveyance were then called, to the Kentucky shore of the Ohio. Their route lay through Elizabethtown where, however, it seems they did not tarry. In two days, the ferry was reached, where, leaving the horses, the Lincoln family was taken across the river to Posey's farm on the Indiana side.

There, it is said, Thomas Lincoln borrowed a wagon to take wife, children, and household articles to Pigeon Creek. If he went in a wagon, it is well-nigh certain that it was wholly of wood, with solid wheels made from sections of great logs, since few if any other kind of vehicles were used in the backwoods at that time; and it is probable that this clumsy contraption was drawn by oxen. But it is more likely that he used the common conveyance of those days, a stout heavy sled, which generally was employed for rough going, even in summer time.

Footnotes that appeared in the original publication of this selection have been omitted in this edition. A.L.

Two days, at the very least, it must have taken to reach the knoll which the father had selected several weeks earlier; no road whatever existed, and only a trail, 'Blazed out part of the way By a Man By the [name] of Jesse Hoskins,' served to guide them. 'The Ballance of the way ... Lincoln had to Cut his way,' writes Dennis Hanks. So Thomas felled trees, cut underbrush and vines and made openings through which the oxen could drag the sled or wagon forward. Over stumps and rocks, across gullies, bogs, mounds, and soggy ground, they crept onward and, finally, reached the spot 'Rite in the Brush,' where Abraham Lincoln was to spend the next fourteen years.

Winter was at hand—it may be that the thin snow even then was beginning to fly. Thomas hastily built a shelter for his family. It was a 'half-faced camp,' such as hunters were wont to throw up as a protection against the weather, not unlike that sometimes found in sugar-camps at a later day. . . .

Within and about this camp of poles and brush existed Abraham Lincoln, then in his eighth year, together with his sister and parents throughout the winter of 1816–17. Hanks relates that the second day after the family arrived, the boy killed a turkey 'with his farthers Riffle,' more by accident than skill, since 'Turkies two Numer[ous] to Mention.' No other food but game brought in by Thomas Lincoln was possible at first; and water was to be had only by melting the snow, or by carrying in a kettle from the distant spring. Luckily Thomas Lincoln did not have far to go to get sustenance for his family, game filling the thickets that surrounded the small hill on which the half-faced camp was built. 'We did not have to go more than 4 or 5 hundred Yards to Kill deer, turkeys and other wild game,' Dennis Hanks relates of the following year.

At last came the spring of 1817. Wild rose, swamp lily, wild honeysuckle, blue flag and yellow flag, Sweet William bloomed; crab apple, wild plum, haw trees blossomed; grape clusters began to form; abundant dogwood made spots of white among the brush and trees. The waters of Pigeon Creek rose in their banks and, warmed by the season, invited those begrimed by winter's unwashed months. . . .

In the autumn of 1817, Nancy Lincoln's heart was gladdened by the arrival of her aunt and uncle, Betsy and Thomas Sparrow, who with Dennis Hanks, now eighteen years of age, had come to live permanently with the Lincolns. 'Lincoln had Bilt another Cabin By this time,' says Hanks, 'and got in it a Bout 40 Rods apart' from the half-faced camp. This cabin was of the usual type, round logs with the bark on and roof of poles and slabs. It was larger than any the Lincoln family had lived in, being eighteen feet wide and twenty feet long;

and it was high enough for a loft beneath the roof, reached by pegs driven in the log walls.

But no floor was laid, no door contrived, no window; even the roof was not finished when cold weather came. Nor did the approach of another winter quicken the domestic enterprise of Thomas Lincoln; and Hanks chronicles of this and later years, that 'we all hunted pretty much all the time, Especially So when we got tired of work —which was very often I will assure you.'

In the uncompleted cabin Thomas, Nancy and their children spent the fall of 1817 and the following winter; Thomas and Betsy Sparrow with Dennis Hanks, occupying 'that Darne Little half face camp,' as Dennis called it, near by. No dogs or cats cheered the Lincoln hut; no chickens, hogs or cows were about. The only light was from hog fat. For most of the day the two men roved with their rifles, they, Nancy, and the children, living well-nigh exclusively on wild animals and birds—'ate them as meat, water and bread,' as Hanks told Herndon. Sometimes Lincoln and Hanks varied their hunting by search for wild honey and 'found bee trees all over the forest.' In the autumn nuts and wild fruit added variety to their fare. Hanks records that 'the country was full of chesnuts, Paw paus, . . . wild-turkey peas'; and hickory-nuts, walnuts, hazel-nuts were plentiful.

Now and then, when not hunting, the men cleared a patch of about six acres; and a little corn and other vegetables were raised. If any corn ripened, the kernels were broken by pounding with a stone or axe-head in a mortar made by hollowing a place on top of a hardwood stump, as was done by most people of the backwoods. No mill was nearer than seventeen miles on the banks of the Ohio 'close to Posey's'; and when we got there, laments Dennis Hanks, 'the mill was a poor concern . . . a little bit of a tread horse mill the ground meal of which a hound could Eat as fast as it was ground.'

It was more than a year after he had squatted on the land, that Thomas Lincoln bethought him of the necessity of entering it legally. So he made his way through the forests ninety miles to Vincennes where the land office then was, and, on October 15, 1817, entered the Southwest quarter of Section 32, Township 4 South, Range 5 West, paying the preliminary instalment of sixteen dollars, for which a receipt was given him. This tract of one hundred and sixty acres, for half of which, as will appear, Thomas Lincoln finally succeeded in getting a patent, was at that time in Hurricane Township, Warrick County, which within a year became Carter Township, Spencer County. But four other entries of land had then been made in the whole township, each for an entire section or more.

Thus dragged along the slow dull weeks. Another winter went by, another spring and summer. Then in the autumn of 1818 a disease, mysterious as forest shadows, came suddenly upon Pigeon Creek. 'The milk sick' the settlers called it, because it attacked cattle and particularly milch cows as virulently as men and women. No cure was known and those seized generally died, and died quickly. The nearest doctor lived thirty-five miles from Pigeon Creek, and, if accessible, could have done no good, since medical treatment proved wholly inadequate then, or for many years afterward.

Betsy and Thomas Sparrow, who were known in the settlement as 'Mrs. Lincoln's father and mother,' were stricken in the half-faced camp and there on skins and leaves covering the ground they died, about eighteen months after their coming. A tree was felled, a log of right length cut and whip-sawed into rough, uneven boards. These Thomas Lincoln fashioned into rude boxes, fastening them together with wooden pegs driven into holes made by a small auger, for no nails were at hand. Into these boxes the bodies were placed, and, upon a wooded hill some quarter mile distant, were buried.

To the sick old man and woman Nancy Lincoln had given all the help she could; she had visited, in her last illness, the wife of Peter Brooner, a hunter chiefly, whose cabin was only half a mile away. Mrs. Brooner died, too; and, at the same time, Nancy Lincoln fell sick. Neighbors attended her and one of them, William Wood, recalls that he 'sat up with her all one night.' Thus 'she struggled on' for a week; and at the last, calling Sarah and Abraham to her side, told them to be good to their father, to each other, and to reverence God. She died in October, 1818, on the seventh day of her illness.

Thomas Lincoln made a coffin for his wife as he had for the others; and on a sled, as the first pioneer woman in that region had been taken to her grave, the body of Nancy Lincoln was hauled to the knoll and buried by the side of her foster parents. No stone or board was placed to mark where she lay, nor during the life-time of her husband or son was a monument of any kind erected over that neglected grave.

Abraham was now nine years old, and there is no evidence that his emotions were unlike those of other children of similar age and in the same situation. Back to their doorless, windowless, floorless cabin, went Thomas Lincoln and his children; and there, with Dennis Hanks, they lived through the remainder of the winter, through the spring, the summer and the autumn of 1819. Sarah, now in her thirteenth year, did the cooking.

The father and Dennis Hanks kept on hunting, between infrequent intervals of work in the clearing and when Thomas was not
doing some small job of carpentering for other settlers. 'We always
hunted,' Dennis reiterates, 'it made no difference what came for we
more or less depended on it for a living—nay for life.' Abraham
brought water from the spring and creek, or from holes dug to catch
the seepage from rains; but this device was a 'tempo[ra]ry
affair.' . . .

Other settlers were taking up claims in the region, cabins of un-
barked logs were rising here and there, children multiplying, society
forming. In common with most people of the Western country, those
on and about Pigeon Creek were very ignorant, rough mannered,
vividly superstitious. The waxing and waning of the moon marked for
them, the times to plant and sow. The howling of a dog meant the
certain coming of death among them; and if a shovel or edged tool
was brought into a cabin there could be no doubt that a coffin would
be taken out. Nothing must be begun on Friday; a bird alighting at
the window or flying into the house meant coming sorrow. Ghosts
visited earthly scenes and haunted the unworthy. Witches, too, were
real beings of evil; dreams were forecasts of events to come. Faith
doctors and charms were 'implicitly believed in.' . . .

Cabins usually were packed, husband and wife, children, guests,
relatives, and hired men living in a single small room—cooking,
eating, and sleeping there, a loft sometimes relieving the congestion.
The sense of modesty was embryonic, and men took off their clothes
before women without a thought by either of any impropriety. Men
and boys wore deerskin trousers and coats and coonskin caps; the
clothing of women and girls was of linsey-woolsey, home-made from
wool and flax. Usually everybody went barefoot during spring and
summer; and when they did not, wore moccasins made of hide, until
shoes appeared.

Incredible quantities of whisky were consumed, everybody,
women and preachers included, drinking the fiery liquid. A bottle
was in every cabin—to offer it was the first gesture of welcome, to
refuse unpardonable incivility. All used tobacco, chewing, smoking,
snuffing; and corn-cob pipes in the mouths of women were a not
uncommon sight. Men were quick to fight and combats were brutal.
Profanity was general and emphatic.

Yet an innate love of justice, truthfulness, and fair dealing perme-
ated every community, and generous and ready hospitality was the
highest ordinance. The desire that their children should get 'learning' was well-nigh a passion, second only, indeed, to their respect for

law and insistence upon that regular procedure afforded by courts. The upright judge, was, by them, the most respected of men; the capable lawyer, the most admired. Religion, too, was a vital part of their lives; and churches were organized as soon as there were settlers enough to form small congregations. Preaching was crude, direct, vociferous; but it was an effective force for good.

Schools were started almost as soon as churches—in fact church and school were companion influences for decency, knowledge, and morality in pioneer life. And grave was the need of them. . . .

A peculiar and distinctive dialect resulted from the untaught and unrestrained speech; and this dialect became common to the vast majority of people who had crossed the mountains to occupy the forests and prairies of the Western Country. If a man was feeble he was 'powerful weak,' and when he grew better he was 'fitter.' The word 'sot' meant sit, set, or sat. Nobody fought, they 'fit.' You did not stay awhile, but 'a spell.' How do you do, was expressed by the exclamation 'howdey.' You came 'outen,' not out of, the house, or field; and when there was much or many of anything there was a 'heap.' Wages were 'yearned,' not earned, and children always were called 'young uns.' When a person was persuaded or induced, he was 'hornswoggled.' Where was 'whar'; came 'kum'; heard 'hearn'; took 'tuck'; care 'keer'; than 'nor'; because, 'kase.' Distance and direction were expressed by 'way back' or 'over yander.' When addressing the chairman of a public meeting the speaker said 'Misteer Cheermun.' Many of these idioms and pronunciations Lincoln retained throughout life—he began his famous Cooper Union speech by saying, 'Mr. Cheerman.' In addition to this dialect, plain, short words were used which now are avoided. In short, says Esarey, the language of the pioneers was that of the peasantry of the eighteenth century.

The amusements of the people were so contrived as to get needed work done; but they were boisterous with rampant jollity. The felling of the splendid forests to make clearings left great quantities of logs that could not be used for cabins or stables; and these logs were burned. So at 'log rollings' everybody helped mightily, ate heavily, and drank much whisky; and robust was the play and rough the jests at meal-time or when the logs were gathered and set on fire. Much the same happened when neighbors came to help put up the frames of houses or build cabins, 'raisings,' as these events were called.

'Corn shuckings' were the scenes of greatest enjoyment. Men and boys were chosen by two captains and thus divided into equal groups, each strove to husk the most corn. Songs were sung, stories told, jokes cracked; 'and pass the bottle around' was the order of the hour.

Sugar-boilings, wool-shearings, and hog-killings were scenes of similar festivities.

'Quilting bees,' where women met to make coverings for beds, were times of scarcely less cheer. . . .

Such were the surroundings and the society in which Abraham Lincoln's formative years were to be spent; and we shall now witness his development under these conditions, from his tenth to his twenty-first year.

When there were enough children in the settlement to justify the starting of a school, Andrew Crawford opened one in a cabin of unhewn logs, two or three miles from the hut of Thomas Lincoln. Like all others of the time it was a subscription school, the teacher taking his pay in skins or farm produce, far more valuable than the 'wild-cat' paper, which then was the only form of money. Indeed Dennis Hanks testifies that throughout their sojourn in Indiana deerskins, 'Hogs and Venison hams was a Legal tender and Coon Skins all So.'

The Lincoln children went to Andrew Crawford's school for a while during the winter of 1818–19. The school was held in 'a rude pole cabin with huge fire-place, rude floor of puncheons and seats of same, and a window made by leaving out a log on the side to admit the light, often covered with greased paper to keep out the wind.' Spelling, reading, writing, and 'ciphering to single rule of 3 no further' were taught in the haphazard manner of the period and region. It was a 'blab' or 'loud school,' the children studying vocally. Punishment was administered by whipping or making the child wear the 'dunce cap.' 'When we went to Crawford he tried to learn us manners,' relates Nathaniel Grigsby, showing the pupils how to enter a room, the formalities of introduction and the like.

But the teacher gave up after one season, it appears, as frontier school promoters sometimes did. Thereafter Andrew Crawford disappears from the chronicles of Pigeon Creek pedagogy. Lincoln was then in his tenth year and he did not again go to school until 'he was about 14 or 15.' What he learned from Crawford we do not know; a little simple reading, perhaps, and how to form words with a quill pen—certainly not much more, since he could not write well until four or five years later.

Back and forth during the winter months of 1818–19, went the Lincoln children from the log schoolhouse in the woods to the unfinished cabin on the knoll. Thomas Lincoln and Dennis Hanks were the providers, protectors, mentors. Hanks complains that they had 'to work Very hard Clair ground for to Keep Sole and Body to

Geather and Every Spare time that We had we picked up our Rifle and feched in a fine Deer or turkey and in the winter time we went a Coon Hunting;' but Dennis seems to have included in this description of their toil all the years spent in Indiana. . . .

A time came when even Thomas Lincoln could stand it no longer. So back to Kentucky he journeyed for another wife. He knew where to go, it appears, for he went directly to Elizabethtown where the woman he had first courted, Sarah Bush, still lived. She was now a widow, her first husband, Daniel Johnston, having died of the 'cold plague' in 1814, leaving three children for Sarah to care for, John D., Sarah [Elizabeth], and Matilda. Immediately on coming to Hardin County, Lincoln must have seen Sarah's brother, Isaac Bush, and collected from him at least part of the money which he had paid Isaac for the Sinking Spring farm eleven years before. If so, it is but natural that the two men should have talked of the plight of widow and widower and the good sense of their marriage.

Certainly Lincoln made quick work of the business when he saw Sarah in Elizabethtown, and as certainly he was in funds. As related by Samuel Haycraft, then deputy clerk of Hardin County Court, Thomas Lincoln, on December 1, 1819, went to the house of Sarah Johnston in Elizabethtown, reminded her of their mutual bereavement and proposed that they get married 'right off.' The widow said she could not 'right off as she owed some little debts which she wanted to pay first.' Lincoln asked for a list of the debts, 'got the list paid them off that evening. Next Morning I issued the license and they were marr[i]ed . . . right off.'

Without delay Thomas and Sarah, with her three children, started for Indiana. They took with them the household goods and furniture which had been gathered by the thrifty Sarah during the lifetime of her first husband. In comparison with the store taken by Thomas and Nancy Lincoln in the winter of 1816, Sarah Lincoln's domestic effects must have been opulent; for it took a wagon and team of four horses, borrowed from Ralph Crume, a brother-in-law of Lincoln, to haul the load to the Ohio. Pots, pans, skillets, blankets, covers, a feather bed, a bureau which 'cost 45 dollars in K[entuck]y,' were among the things piled in the wagon.

So, in mid-winter 1819–20, came Thomas and Sarah Lincoln to the dirty, unkempt cabin near Pigeon Creek, where his neglected children and the vagrant Dennis Hanks were maintaining a bare existence. So, too, began a new and distinct period in the life of Abraham Lincoln. Sarah Lincoln was blessed with energy and sense, was a good housekeeper, prudent, systematic, and with a passion for cleanliness. She was, says her grand-daughter, 'a very tall Woman, Straight as an Indian, fair Complection and was when I first remember her, very handsome, Sprightly talkative and proud, Wore her Hair curled till Gray, Is Kind hearted and very Charitable and also very industrious.'

No more hunting for Thomas Lincoln and Dennis Hanks until they had split and smoothed puncheons and made a floor, finished the roof, put in a door, cut a place for greased paper to let in the light. The children were washed, combed and 'dressed . . . up' so as to look 'more human'; the cabin cleansed, decent bedding put on the 'bedsteads made . . . of poles and clapboards.' The fire-place was overhauled, ample cooking utensils installed; and Thomas was stirred into making a proper table, better stools and, perchance, a hickory chair or two. The change was so pronounced that, nearly thirty-five years afterward, Lincoln remembered and described it.

Eight persons, three adults and five children, now inhabited the Lincoln cabin. Three or four years later, in 1823, John Hanks, the half-brother of Dennis Hanks, joined the Lincoln family and lived with them for four years, thus making nine who dwelt within those crowded walls. But, under Sarah Lincoln's guidance, there were comparative order and harmony. The increased size of the family required more food and clothing of course, but this was easily managed by the efficient housewife. The burden of supplying provisions was chiefly upon Thomas Lincoln and Dennis Hanks; this did not trouble them greatly.

But often the family larder was allowed to run very low, it seems. Once all they had to eat was potatoes, which led Abraham to remark, when his father asked 'the blessing,' that they were 'very poor blessings.' Food little concerned the boy, however, for 'Abe was a moderate eater,' his stepmother assures us. 'He ate what was set before him, making no complaint; he seemed careless about this. I cooked his meals for nearly 15 years.' And Mrs. Lincoln adds that 'he always had good health.' . . .

When Abraham was old enough, he was sent to the mill with a bag of corn, and these journeys left upon his mind the most pleasing recollections of his boyhood. Thomas Lincoln had acquired a horse or two, and trips to the mill were made bareback with the sack of grain or meal carried in front of the rider. After young Lincoln had learned to read he poured into the ears of companions on these mill rides everything he had read.

A year or two after the coming of Sarah Lincoln, another school, about four miles away, was started by one Azel W. Dorsey. It was exactly like that of Andrew Crawford except that Dorsey did not try to 'learn manners' to the children. Abraham went to this school for a short time. A schoolmate tells us that he was 'long and tall . . . wore low shoes, short socks and his britches made of buckskin were so short that they left bare and naked 6 or more inches of Abe Lincoln's shin bone.' The school books from which the teacher gave out his lessons were the Bible, Webster's or Dilworth's *Spelling Book,* Pike's *Arithmetic* and a song book.

It was at Dorsey's school that he perfected that clear, distinct chirography, so like that of Washington and Jefferson; and here too he learned to spell with that accuracy which was to become a tradition in the neighborhood. He did all the writing for the family and indeed for everybody in the settlement. Even more important to his avid mind was the fact that he learned to read with ease and fluency.

So ended the education of Abraham Lincoln in schools, except for a short and broken attendance in 1826 at a similar school taught by William Sweeney. Including the two schools in Kentucky the boy went to school for less than a year. 'His father has often told me,' relates John Hanks, that Abraham 'had not gone to School one year in all his life'; and Lincoln himself, long afterward said the same thing. Nathaniel Grigsby thinks that Lincoln went to the Indiana schools for not less than eighteen months, altogether; but Dennis Hanks insists that 'he got about Six Months Schooling while he lived in Indiana,' and this estimate is probably the more accurate.

There was, indeed, no reason for him to go longer to these backwoods teachers—they 'could do him no further good; he went to school no more.'

In the Indiana schools he excelled, it appears, particularly in spelling and could 'spell down' the whole class when, at the close of the school every Friday, the older children were placed in line against the log wall for a contest in spelling. He was unselfish with his proficiency. One day he showed a girl schoolmate, Anna C. Roby, the proper letter in the word 'defied,' by covertly placing a finger on his eye.

He was notably studious in everything—'head and Shoulders above us all,' confesses Dennis Hanks. He would help the other pupils, 'would learn us get our cip[h]ers.' His stepmother tells us that, when at home, Abraham 'cyphered on boards when he had no paper or no slate and when the board would get too black he would Shave it off with a drawing Knife and go on again: When he had paper he put his sums down on it.' He made a copy-book by sewing together blank sheets which Dennis Hanks gave him: 'I bought the paper

[and] gave it to Abe.' In this he did his work in arithmetic, scribbling at three places this legend:

> 'Abraham Lincoln, his hand and pen
> he will be good but God knows when.'

He early showed that kindness of heart which distinguished him throughout life. At Crawford's school the boy reproved other children for cruelty to animals, particularly the placing of glowing coals on backs of turtles; and, even then, wrote 'short sentences' against it. While at Dorsey's school he wrote poetry. 'Abe took it up of his own accord,' relates Grigsby. He kept this up at Sweeney's too, and at both schools also wrote 'compositions against Cruelty to animals,' which barbarity seems to have been a favorite practice of his schoolmates, and young Lincoln's particular aversion. Indeed, revulsion at brutality, sympathy for the suffering, animals as well as humans, constituted the dominant note of his character, even in boyhood. He always came to school good humored and laughing and 'he scarcely ever quarreled.'

He continued to write poetry as well as prose compositions long after his school days were over, it appears, and took his pieces 'straight' to the interested neighbor, William Wood, for comment and criticism. Even thirty-seven or thirty-eight years afterward, Wood could remember that one of Abraham's compositions was 'a poem' entitled 'The Neighborhood broil.' The copy-book in which his school figuring was done, contains these lines in his youthful hand:

> 'Time what an empty vapor tis
> And days, how swift they are
> Swift as an Indian arrow
> Fly on like a shooting star
> The present moment just, is here
> Then slides away in haste
> That we can never say they're ours
> But only say they're past.'

The ability to read meant more to him, however, at this period of his development than did all else acquired at school. It opened to him the world of books—a world hitherto closed to him, well-nigh unknown, indeed. From this time forward, reading was the passion of the youth and, as will be seen, continued for more than twenty years to be the passion of the man.

About the time he learned to read, the boy was big enough to do work upon the ungracious farm, and to labor for others, his earnings going to the father, a legal right which Thomas Lincoln exacted rigidly until Abraham reached the full age of twenty-one. He worked for several of the small farmers of the settlement, for Romine, for Wood, for Taylor, for Crawford, for Turnham, ploughing, making rails, 'daubing' with mud the chinks between the logs of the cabins. . . .

Between Thomas Lincoln and his son, so different in intellect, character and appearance, there was little sympathy or understanding; and for some reason the father treated Abraham roughly. Sometimes a blow from the old man's fist would hurl the boy 'a rod.' 'I have Seen his father Nock him Down of the fence when a Stranger would call for Information to NeighBour house,' testifies Dennis Hanks, who adds that 'the Old Man Loved his Childern.' Thomas Lincoln also thrashed the lad, who took his punishment in silence, tears the only outward sign of what he felt and thought. . . .

The father's ill-treatment of the son seems the more extraordinary in view of Abraham's remarkably good nature; for he was conspicuously obliging, eager to please everybody, his parents most of all. 'Abe was a good boy . . . the best boy I ever saw,' declares his stepmother. 'I can say,' she continues, 'what scarcely one woman, a mother can say in a thousand . . . Abe never gave me a cross word or look and never refused . . . to do anything I requested [of] him. I never gave him a cross word in all my life. . . . His mind and mine, what little I had, seemed to run together—move in the same channel.' Abraham's devotion to Sarah Lincoln, whom he always called 'mama,' is striking. Many years later he told Chapman of 'the encouragement he always had received from his Step Mother' and declared that 'she had been his best Friend in this world and that no Son could love a Mother more than he loved her. . . .'

Even the alertly partial Dennis Hanks admits that Abraham 'was lazy—a very lazy man. He was always reading, Scribbling, writing, ciphering, writing Poetry,' etc. This too is the testimony of his stepsister: 'Abe was not energetic except in one thing—he was active and persistent in learning—read everything he could—ciphered on boards, on the walls.' The son-in-law of Dennis Hanks declares that 'Lincoln was not industrious as a worker on the farm or at any kind of manual labor' and that 'he only showed industry in the attainment of knowledge.'. . .

The distasteful toil in field and wood was lightened by Abraham's fun and wit; and, although he had no voice for singing, he would join the other hands in shouting the songs of the time and place—in the language of Dennis Hanks, 'Hail Collumbia Hap[py] Land if you aint Broke I will be Damned,' or 'the turbentuck [turbaned Turk] that Scorns the world and Struts aBout with his whiskers curld for No other Man But himSelf to see and all Such as this.' Other and rougher songs there were. Nathaniel Grigsby tells us that: 'we sung what is called carnel Songs and love songs. i cannot repeat any of them at this time we sung a song called Barbra allen also we sung the Silk Merchant daughter and others.'...

So the tall, bony youth, with a coonskin cap on his head and clad in deerskin shirt and homemade trousers which were still always far too short, exposing many inches of 'sharp, blue and narrow' shins, went about the countryside doing, in languid fashion, the jobs he was hired to do, or working reluctantly on his father's stumpy farm; but always cracking jokes, telling stories, joining, though poorly, in the songs of the other workers; and, whenever his father or employer was not about, making speeches to his fellows. Strangely enough Abraham did not care for fishing or hunting, rarely joining the pursuit of even coon and turkey, although, boasts Dennis Hanks, 'we sure were excellent bow shots—a squirrel couldn't escape.'

Reading, however, was the outstanding phase of Lincoln's life at this time. Much as he loved pranks with other youths, he would forego their jollity and lose himself in some new volume....

Thus he consumed the scanty store of books brought to the Lincoln cabin by his stepmother, when she came to Pigeon Creek near Christmas time, 1819, wrought in cabin and surroundings the miracle we have witnessed, and rescued the children from the dirt accumulated since their mother died a year before. There had been a few books in her Kentucky household and, although Sarah Lincoln could not read, she knew the value of them, it seems, and brought them with her. There were but four or five volumes—*Robinson Crusoe, Pilgrim's Progress, Sinbad the Sailor, Æsop's Fables*. It appears that this was the first time a Bible found a place in the cabin, for Hanks records that 'Thomas Lincoln brought the Bible in 1818 or 19.'...

In 1823, seven years after Thomas Lincoln came to Indiana and four years after his marriage to Sarah Johnston, he joined, by letter, the Pigeon Creek Baptist Church....

To this church, after 1823, the family went when a preacher of that sect came to Pigeon Creek. When Abraham was in his fifteenth year, he would repeat to his companions and others, almost verbatim, the sermons he heard, imitating the delivery of the preacher, for he was an excellent mimic. His stepmother declares that 'he would hear sermons preached, come home, take the children out, get on a stump or log and almost repeat it word for word.'

Although others of the family became members of the Pigeon Creek congregation, Abraham did not then or afterwards 'join church.' His stepmother explains that 'Abe had no particular religion —didn't think of that question at that time, if he ever did. He never talked about it.' 'i cannot tel you what his notions of the bible were,' wrote Nathaniel Grigsby to Herndon; 'he talked about religion as other persons did but i do not now his view on religion he never made any profession while in Ind[iana] that i now of.'...

The books at home exhausted, he ranged the countryside in search of more, an intellectual prowler for the sustenance of the printed page. His step-mother asserts that 'Abe read all the books he could lay his hands on.' In 1823 when Abraham was fourteen years of age, Levi Hall who had married Nancy Hanks, aunt of Nancy Lincoln and mother without marriage of Dennis Hanks, came with his family to the Pigeon Creek settlement. They brought the copy of Bailey's *Etymological Dictionary*, which Mordecai Lincoln had bought in 1793. The fact that this dictionary was at his hand must be borne in mind while considering the books read by Lincoln during the years that he remained in Indiana....

From some source and in some way he got hold of a copy of Grimshaw's *History of the United States*. Of all the American histories in one volume published at that time none had such peculiar qualities as that by William Grimshaw. The first chapter explains the advances made in astronomy, geography, and navigation; and, thus, the reader has before him at the start the existing condition of the world. Then follows the account of the discovery of America and the development of the colonies.

Quickly the author reaches the subject of slavery, bitterly condemning it. 'What a climax of human cupidity and turpitude!... The colonists ... place the last rivet to the chains!' Throughout the little volume the student is not permitted to lose sight of the shackle and the lash. The early New England persecutions are set forth in wrathful terms and an earnest plea made against intolerance. The causes of the Revolution are stated clearly, the patriot writings named, the War for Independence and later events described. The book ends with the cession of Florida to the United States; and, as a climax, the progress of literature, science and art is described....

Abraham had worked for David Turnham, who lived near Grandview on the Ohio. Turnham, six years older than Lincoln, was a prosperous farmer, a Justice of the Peace and a man of uncommon ability. As will presently appear, he had much influence on Lincoln's life. He owned the *Revised Laws of Indiana;* and sometime before he left the State, Lincoln borrowed this formidable volume of nearly five hundred long pages and read it repeatedly and with care. This was the first law book he ever read. It contains the Declaration, the Constitution, the first twelve Amendments, the Virginia Act of cession of the Northwest Territory, the Ordinance of 1787, the Act admitting Indiana, and the first State Constitution. Then follow about four hundred pages of laws on every subject which then required legislation—rights and remedies, crimes and punishments, courts and procedure, offices and fees, and all the machinery of civil government. Through this volume Lincoln acquired a fair understanding of the elements of law and government.

During this period, too, he read another book which had more and greater qualities making for general culture than any one volume he is positively known to have read. This volume was popularly called 'Scott's Lessons.' Its formal title was *Lessons in Elocution, or Selections of Pieces in Prose and Verse for the Improvement of Youth in Reading and Speaking,* by William Scott, of Edinburgh. The book opens with short essays upon public speaking, the object of which should be to convey a 'precise idea.' Scott urges simplicity and intelligence of gesture, distinctness of enunciation, right placing of emphasis, pausing at the end of one sentence before beginning the next, and other items of the technique of delivery.

Then come what the compiler calls 'Lessons in Reading,' beginning with five pages of maxims. Brief selections from the classics follow, mostly fables and parables, but including essays on points of character and conduct, with sketches of Alfred, Catiline, Cæsar, Elizabeth, and other historic characters. Excerpts from many poems are next; and then a good selection of pieces for recitation, including parts of speeches by the Earl of Chatham, Lord Mansfield, Cicero, and Demosthenes, as well as the imaginary addresses of Hannibal and other commanders to their armies. Hamlet's advice to the players is printed as prose, as is the appeal of Brutus after Cæsar's death, Hotspur's soliloquy, and Falstaff's praise of sack. Antony's Oration, Hamlet's analysis of death, and the exhortations of Henry V before Harfleur and Agincourt, are given. Short and pointed quotations are made illustrative of various forms of speech—antithesis, climax, enunciation, query, and the like. . . .

The other two books worthy of note, which are known to have been read by Lincoln while in Indiana, are Weems's *Life of Washington* and the same writer's *Life of Franklin.* It has not been discovered where he got the *Life of Franklin,* but he borrowed Weems's *Washington* from Josiah Crawford, a young farmer of the neighborhood, who had brought the book with him from Kentucky. Abraham worked for Crawford, at times, having 'daubed' his fifteen feet square log cabin when the Crawfords arrived in 1824. It seems that the youth left the book where rain injured it, a calamity of which he promptly told Crawford, who gave him the volume and he 'pulled fodder a day or two for it.'. . .

Such were the volumes, each of which it should be remembered Lincoln read so thoroughly that he could repeat, word for word, parts that best pleased him. 'When he came across a passage that struck him he would write it down on boards if he had no paper and keep it there till he did get paper, then he would rewrite it, look at it, repeat it. He had a copy-book, a kind of scrap-book in which he put down all things and thus preserved them.'. . .

At Rockport, where Abraham often went, he made the acquaintance of John Pitcher, the first resident attorney of Rockport, who afterwards became prosecuting attorney for Spencer County. Pitcher had a good library which, as he declared sixty years later, included the 'standard works of that day,' as well as law books; and the use of this library was given to young Lincoln. The youth also went to Boonville, some twelve or fourteen miles distant from the Lincoln cabin, and there saw the prosecuting attorney for Warrick County, John A. Brackenridge, who is said to have had an immense library for the time and place, consisting of at least four hundred and fifty-seven volumes. Inference has been made that Lincoln borrowed many of these volumes and frequently visited the house of Brackenridge to read his books and take counsel of him. . . .

Along with the pleasing fiction of midnight study by the log fire, we must dismiss the unhappy legend that Thomas Lincoln interfered with Abraham's incessant reading. The father yielded to the influence of Sarah Lincoln, it appears, and did not disturb his son's devotion to books. 'As a usual thing,' says his wife, 'Mr. Lincoln never made Abe quit reading to do anything if he could avoid it. He would do it himself first . . . he himself felt the uses and necessities of education [and wanted] his boy Abraham to learn and he encouraged him to do it in all ways he could.'. . .

Young Lincoln liked to tell what he knew—insisted on telling it. In fact, self-expression was indispensable to the youth, and he became a very geyser of loquacity, talking incessantly to all who would listen—and most were eager to hear him. For he never bored anybody. His talk was informing, to be sure; but it was witty too and full of humor. Nobody could resist his funny stories, and he was as fond of jokes as he was of reading. Yet Mrs. Lincoln relates that when neighbors came to visit her: 'Abe ... was a silent and attentive observer, never speaking or asking questions till they were gone and then he must understand everything—even to the smallest thing, minutely and exactly.' ...

Still he went to all the social gatherings—'always attended house raisings, log rolling corn shucking and workings of all kinds.' There was a small prairie on the South Fork of Pigeon Creek and there members of the local militia gathered for muster. Lincoln was always on hand at these jolly assemblages. And no other person in the now comparatively well populated settlement was so welcome everywhere, for he always was cheerful and tried to make others happy too. No situation was too gloomy for his fun-making, no man so sour that Lincoln could not make him laugh. . . .

Then, too, he 'naturally assumed the leadership of the boys.' But he was never dogmatic, it appears, never aggressive in his views, never turbulent or offensive in stating them, never insistent that others should think as he thought. 'He wounded no man's feelings' and even his jokes 'were at no man's expense.' ...

But 'Abe did not go much with the girls ... didn't like girls much, too frivolous' says Mrs. Allen Gentry, then Anna C. Roby, who saw as much of Lincoln at that time as any girl in the settlement except, of course, his sister and step-sisters. His step-mother confirms Mrs. Gentry's opinion, saying: 'He was not very fond of girls.' Joseph C. Richardson also relates that Abraham 'never seemed to care for the girls'; and David Turnham bears witness that 'he did not seem to seek the company of the girls and when with them was rather backward.' The girls liked him, however, because he was 'friendly, somewhat sociable, not so much so as we wanted him.' Certainly there was nothing attractive in Abraham's appearance, for he was 'a long, thin, leggy, gawky boy dried up and shriveled.' Even by his sixteenth year he was '6 feet high' and 'bony and raw, dark skinned.'

Lincoln began to make speeches as early as his fifteenth year. He would mount a tree stump, or stand upon a fence and talk to his fellow workers, who would leave their jobs in fields or woods to listen. 'His father would come and make him quit, send him to work,' says his step-sister who saw and heard these incidents. Her mother tells us the same thing. 'His father had to make him quit sometimes, as he would quit his own work to speak and made the other children as well as the men quit their work."

Of greater moment, however, than the fact that he made them at all, was the arrangement of his speeches and the style of his delivery. Considering the examples of exclamatory and emotional oratory furnished by preachers, lawyers, and candidates to whom he listened, the most reasonable explanation of young Lincoln's method and manner of speaking, is that he had taken Scott's *Lessons* seriously and that the advice of the Scotch schoolmaster was in harmony with his own thoughts on the subject. For all who heard him make these backwoods speeches, lay emphasis on the logical clearness of them and Lincoln's composure in delivery.

The clearness and simplicity of these youthful speeches, so striking that all made note of and remembered those qualities, were partly the result of his writing and rewriting what he read and thought. Sometimes he wrote essays on weighty subjects. William Wood, then about forty-five years of age, relates that one such paper, written in 1827 or 1828, was on 'national politics,' saying that 'the American government was the best form of Government in the world for an intelligent people, that it ought to be kept sacred and preserved forever; that general education should [be] fostered and carried all over the country; that the constitution should be [held] sacred, the union perpetuated, and the laws revered, respected and enforced.'

Wood was so impressed by the essay that he gave it to the leading lawyer of Spencer County. 'I showed it to John Pitcher who was travelling over the circuit on law business and stopped at my house one night: he read it carefully and asked me where I got it. I told him that one of my neighbor boys wrote it: he couldn't believe it until I told him that Abe did write it. . . . Pitcher said to me "the world cant beat it." He begged for it—gave it to him and it was published.'

Wood was a member of the United Brethren Church and a foe of hard drinking. He was a subscriber for a temperance paper published in Ohio; and 'Abe used to borrow it, take it home and read it and talk it over with me. . . . One day Abe wrote a piece on Temperance and brought it to my house. I read it carefully over and over and the piece excelled for sound sense anything that my paper contained. I gave the article to one Aaron Farmer, a Baptist Preacher: He read it, it struck him: he said he wanted it to send to a Temperance paper in Ohio for publication: it was sent and published. I saw the printed piece, read it . . . over and over again.'

One outstanding fact of Lincoln's life at this time is that, although his associates, and indeed everybody, drank a great deal of whisky, Abraham seldom touched liquor. To be sure he 'did drink his dram as well as all others did, preachers and Christians included,' testifies Grigsby; and his devoted friend and mentor, William Wood, reluctantly admits that 'Abe once drank as all people did here at that time.' But this slight and casual drinking seems to have been entirely for the sake of comradeship and Lincoln's strong dislike of offending anybody. Equally striking is the fact that, although profanity was general and intense, Lincoln never fell into that habit. 'I never knew him to swear,' testifies Wood; 'he would say to . . . other boys, leave off your boyish ways and be more like men.' Wood explains this attitude by concluding that 'Abe was always a man though a boy.'

Yet, as we have seen, he was no prig; instead he was inordinately sociable, even familiar, and had faults extremely human, such as his love of a certain type of anecdote—a taste which he never overcame and the expression of which, as will appear, was so marked a feature of his manhood and so shocking to the eminent men among whom he did his historic work.

In his seventeenth year his sister Sarah, then aged nineteen, married Aaron Grigsby, son of a farmer and one of the important men in the settlement. Even then social distinctions were sharply drawn and upon the lines of property; and the Grigsbys were of aristocracy of the backwoods. Abraham composed some doggerel in verse, which, it is said, was sung at the wedding by 'the Lincoln family.' . . .

But in the meantime he adventured far, though briefly, into the world beyond the fifty-mile circuit of the Pigeon Creek settlement. He had seen something of river life, having been hired in 1825 by one James Taylor to help run a ferry boat across the Ohio from near the mouth of Anderson Creek. . . .

Lincoln also built for himself a scow in which he would take travellers to passing steamers hailed in midstream. Another ferryman, John T. Dill, a Kentuckian, angered by this competition, haled Lincoln before a Kentucky Justice of the Peace, Samuel Pate, for running a ferry without a license. Lincoln said that he did not know that it was against the law to take passengers to steamboats in midstream, especially when the ferryboat was on the other side and the steamers would not land or wait. The plaintiff pointed out, however, that the jurisdiction of Kentucky ran to low water mark on the Indiana shore. But 'Squire' Pate decided that taking persons to passenger craft in midstream, was not 'setting them over' the river and, therefore, that Lincoln had not violated the statute. Abraham was deeply impressed and, thereafter, went to this rural court when cases were heard and decided. In such fashion began Lincoln's interest in the study and practice of the law.

But running a ferryboat now and then, across the Ohio, taking an infrequent traveller to a steamer, ploughing, splitting rails and killing hogs for Taylor and others, gave Lincoln little more experience of human activities than Pigeon Creek had afforded.

In his nineteenth year, however, the chance was offered to make a far journey; and the opportunity came as the result of Lincoln's good fellowship and integrity, and the friendship and confidence inspired by these qualities. The richest man in Carter Township was James Gentry, a native of North Carolina who in April, 1818, had come from Kentucky with his young wife to the Pigeon Creek settlement. He entered a thousand acres of land and afterward bought several hundred acres more. He had a large family, two of whom married into the family of another wealthy man, Gideon W. Romine. Gentry soon began to keep a small stock of goods for sale at his farm house; thus began the town of Gentryville. Soon William David, a blacksmith, came and in time a few cabins were built near by. Gentryville became the social as well as the trading centre of the countryside.

Gentryville was less than a mile and a half from the Lincoln cabin; and to the backwoods hamlet young Lincoln would speed like a homing pigeon when work was done for the day. For there gathered other youth and men who craved companionship and the story-telling, talk, and discussion which took place in country stores. About this time, one, William Jones, came from Vincennes and opened a little store. Soon he and Lincoln became fast friends and Jones hired the boy to help him. But it was the village blacksmith who was 'Abes pertickler friend.' Gentry and Jones formed a partnership, with Abraham sometimes assisting as man of all work.

As long as Gentry or Jones would keep the candles lighted and the log fire burning, Abraham would remain, talking, forever talking, relating his jokes, telling his rude and often unsavory tales; flashing his kindly repartee, propounding his theories about everything. 'He was so odd, original and humorous and witty that all the People in town would gather around him,' Dennis Hanks told Herndon. 'He would Keep them there till midnight or longer telling Stories [and] cracking jokes. . . . I would get tired, want to go home, cuss Abe most heartily.' And 'Sumtimes we Spent a Little time at grog piching waits,' says Dennis. . . .

Lincoln had great physical strength, so great that tales of his performances are well-nigh unbelievable. Long afterward one elderly person recalled that the young Hercules of Pigeon Creek bore away easily heavy posts which 'some of the men' were preparing to carry by means of bars. 'Abe could sink an axe deeper in wood . . . He could strike with a mall a heavier blow than any man I ever saw,' testifies William Wood. Stature, physical power, good humor, intellect, integrity, are the outstanding features of the picture of Abraham Lincoln during these years.

In April, 1828, James Gentry hired this strong, capable, and trustworthy youth to go with his son, Allen, on a flatboat loaded with produce to New Orleans, then the best market for such things as the upper Mississippi country had to sell. The boat started from Gentry's landing on the Ohio, about three quarters of a mile from Rockport. Lincoln acted as a bow hand, 'working the foremost oar and was paid eight dollars per month from the time of starting to his returning home.' It was no ignorant lout but a fairly well-informed young person of grasping and absorbing mind, who, with quip and quiddity, droll story and quaint common sense, enlivened the hours, as Gentry's flatboat floated down the Ohio and Mississippi to the great Southern mart. . . .

So came Abraham Lincoln to New Orleans, the first city and the first place bigger than the Boonville or Rockport, Indiana, of 1828, he had ever seen. . . .

At the market, the common place of meeting, could be found nuts and fruits of the tropics; fish from lake and gulf; sugar, grain, and meats. Lincoln saw and heard the bustle and heaving labor on the river front, sea-going vessels made ready, crews of strange speech. He could note the medley of people and dress—French, Spanish, Mexicans, Creoles, even Indians, and slaves, from the full negro through many degrees of mixed blood. It all gave a new experience to the two youths from the backwoods of Indiana, but there is no evidence of the impression made upon Lincoln by this, his second contact with slavery.

The cargo sold, the young men returned to their Indiana homes in June, making the journey up stream on one of the big and sumptuous steamboats of the time, the elder Gentry paying the fare. On Pigeon Creek Lincoln took up again the old routine, unchanged in speech or manner by his trip to the metropolis of the South. He was still the avid reader of books, the incessant talker, the bubbling fountain of good cheer.

But Gentryville no longer satisfied him; he had caught a glimpse of the world beyond Pigeon Creek, beyond Rockport and Boonville. The spell of the river had stolen over him; he wanted to be 'a steamboat man' on a big river craft like the one on which he had returned from New Orleans. In 1829, relates William Wood, 'Abe came to my house one day, and stood round about timid and shy. I knew he wanted something. I said to him, "Abe what is your care?" Abe replied, "Uncle, I want you to go to the River (the Ohio) and give me some recommendation to some boat." I remarked, "Abe, your age is against you. You are not 21 yet." "I know that, but I want a start," said Abe. I concluded not to go for the boy's good.'

So he stayed on at the Pigeon Creek cabin, doing the familiar work of the backwoods farm, felling trees, splitting rails, ploughing fields, helping Thomas Lincoln now and then in his casual carpentering. But he read and wrote more than ever, and lost no opportunity to hear speeches, especially legal arguments. When court was held in Rockport on the Ohio or at Boonville, county seats of Spencer and Warrick counties respectively, Lincoln would go, making careful notes of all that was said and done. . . .

Thus by reading, listening, absorbing, Abraham's knowledge grew. 'How did Lincoln and yourself learn so much in Indiana under such disadvantages?' Herndon diplomatically asked Dennis Hanks. The answer is the best explanation yet given. 'We learned by sight, scent and hearing. We heard all that was said and talked over and over the questions heard, wore them slick, greasy and threadbare.' . . .

❖ ❖ ❖ ❖ ❖

LEW WALLACE

(b. Brookville, 1827–d. 1905), Crawfordsville's ornament, is best known as an author. His novel *Ben Hur* (1880), for example, sold in the millions. But he also played the roles of soldier ("Zouave"), lawyer, violinist, and painter. (See, further, "A Hoosier Schoolboy," p. 99.) Wallace's biography *Benjamin Harrison* (1888) reconstructs the early law career, in Indianapolis, of the man who was to become twenty-third President of the United States. This man was a grandson of William Henry ("Tippecanoe") Harrison (1772–1841), our ninth President, and a great-grandson of the Benjamin Harrison (1726–1791) who signed the Declaration of Independence.

The Lawyer
[Young Benjamin Harrison]

The Indianapolis bar at the time young Harrison sought admission to it was composed of gentlemen of unusual ability and reputation. . . . In that day speaking-ability was especially required; the tyro who was without it was thought to be a hopeless case in advance. The mere office lawyer was a subject of pity, if not contempt. If in the family there was a boy who had what was called the "gift of gab," his parents and friends foreordained him to the law. Opinion in that respect has undergone a somewhat radical change; but without dwelling upon it every one familiar with the gentlemen named would see at a glance the difficulties before young Harrison. He would have to prove not merely his knowledge generally but his ability to cope before a jury with any one or all of the formidable array given. Amongst others, Jonathan W. Gordon, in the fall of 1854, was regarded with great popular favor. Of unquestioned ability, an enthusiast but eccentric, he was serving the people as prosecuting attorney; and, having made the acquaintance of Harrison, he formed a high opinion of him and led him to his first appearance.

There was on the docket an indictment against an individual for burglary. The case came up for hearing in the afternoon, and by chance Horace Mann was announced for a lecture in the evening. Major Gordon was anxious to hear that distinguished person; and, fearful that the trial would be continued into the night, to accommodate himself he requested his new friend to assist him. The invitation was accepted. Judge Majors was presiding. The defence was conducted by Governor Wallace and Sims Colley. As anticipated the evidence was heard, and Major Gordon for the State and Mr. Colley for the defendant finished their speeches in the afternoon; whereupon an adjournment was had.

The interior of the old court-house was dingy, gloomy and forbidding in the daytime; at night it was funereal. When young Harrison came in to make the concluding argument he found a large assemblage waiting to hear the débût. On the fixed desk before the judge there were two tallow candles lighted. The clerk in his place below the judge protected by a stout railing sat with his book opened, in a light similarly derived. On the pillars in the centre of the room, and here and there upon the walls, were old-fashioned tin sconces, casting a glow red and murky with smoke, partly of cigars, partly from a leaking stove. At the judge's left sat the sheriff, and at his left again the panel. At the feet of each juror was the inevitable spittoon, and in pauses the plug of tobacco was passed from man to man. In crises of the evidence and the speeches the expectoration was incessant; sometimes the amber fluid missed the targets at which it was projected. Altogether the scene was not such as to impart inspiration to the debutant upon his entry. On the other hand, the wonder grew when he rose to begin, so boyish-looking was he.

He had taken full notes of the evidence, and, like all beginners, fearful of mistakes in statement, was resolved to read from them copiously. A table had been drawn between him and the jury, and when he began, to his consternation, he discovered the light was wholly insufficient. The sheriff had provided but one candle! What should he do?

There was dead silence throughout the dusky room. His voice, sharp, clear, penetrating, was being heard to the farthest corner. The audience was already in sympathy with him. The situation was embarrassing. He referred to his notes. He wished to be absolutely correct. He shifted the candle. He turned the paper to every angle. It would not do. The pencilling refused to come out. Then, in desperation, he flung the notes away. To his own amazement he found his memory perfect. Best of all he found he could think and speak upon his feet flash-like and coherently. There were not only words at command, but the right words, enabling him to express himself exactly. He found too the pleasure there always is in the faculty of speech with freedom superadded. Confidence came with the discoveries. From that day to this, whether addressing himself to court or jury, or the vaster audiences who furnish the delight of oratory on the platform or stump, he has been an impromptu speaker.

At the conclusion of this maiden effort he was congratulated by everybody.

Under the code of that day the defence had the closing speech, and as the duty devolved upon Gov. Wallace, he was profuse in complimentary references, and dwelt with feeling upon the kindness of the young man's grandfather to him when he was a lad.

The audience dispersed to exploit "that little fellow, Harrison." "What a swinge-cat he is! Who would have thought it? He is only a boy yet!" they said to each other.

The jury, after retirement sufficient to take the usual votes, returned a verdict of guilty—and Harrison's first trial was a triumph and more.

IRVING McKEE

(b. 1909–), a native of California, taught at Culver Academy, Indiana, from 1937 to 1953. Besides writing his award-winning biography *Ben Hur Wallace*, he has served as an editor for the Indiana

Historical Society. Many readers have read, or seen a film version of, *Ben Hur*—one of the three most popular novels of all times (along with *Uncle Tom's Cabin* and *In His Steps*). But few readers, aside from those of Crawfordsville, know very much about *Ben Hur*'s author, General Lew Wallace—soldier, diplomat, romanticist. Death overtook Wallace before he finished his autobiography, but Irving McKee gained access to previously unexplored Wallaciana and persuaded the University of California Press to bring out the biography, from which comes the following excerpt, "A Hoosier Schoolboy." That title brings to mind the titles of two celebrated novels—*The Hoosier Schoolboy* (1883) and *The Hoosier Schoolmaster* (1871) by Edward Eggleston, a native of Vevay.

A Hoosier Schoolboy

Brookville, all of twenty years old in 1827, was the first big town in Indiana, and Indiana in turn was the shining goal of farm-hungry settlers by thousands. A land office had followed the retreating Indians to Brookville and now offered plow-resistant acres at a dollar and a quarter. In response, as soon as the Ohio River became navigable and the road passable in the spring, came the immigrants, poling flatboats up into the Whitewater or prodding teams across the state line.

For a time the tavern at Brookville was conducted by Andrew Wallace, a third-generation Scotch-Irishman whose experience, at forty-nine, made him a capable host: he had kept a store at Carlisle, Pennsylvania, completed the first land survey at Troy, Ohio, published books and a newspaper (the *Liberty Hall Gazette*) at Cincinnati, and fathered seven sons and a daughter. He had rubbed elbows with William Henry Harrison, farmer and Indian-fighter; since then, of course, Harrison had routed the red-skinned Prophet at Tippecanoe, Indiana, and had been elected Senator. As evidence of his connection Andrew cited the success of his eldest son, "Colonel" David Wallace, whose brick house stood not far from the tavern; brick was a sign of substance in this world of logs. Harrison had placed at the disposal of his Cincinnati neighbor, Andrew, an appointment to West Point originally earmarked for one of Harrison's own sons. After graduation David taught mathematics at the Academy for two years and then, no war being in sight, resigned from the army to go to Brookville with the title of colonel. A year's study at the office of Judge Miles C. Eggleston—whose first cousin, once removed, was to write *The Hoosier Schoolmaster*—won him admission to the bar. A year later he had enough laid by to justify marriage with Esther French Test of Brookville, brown-eyed and seventeen, daughter of a judge and sister of a judge-to-be. Dark-haired, clean-shaven, sternly self-contained, David at twenty-eight was "a man of noble presence in the slender elegance of youth," wrote David's son.

This last, Lewis Wallace, was born on April 10, 1827, and named after Major Samuel Lewis, U.S.A., an uncle by marriage. Other uncles, blood kin, were to attain distinction: Benjamin Franklin Wallace in the Iowa legislature, John Thomson Wallace in the Adjutant General's Office at the national capital, and William Henson Wallace, Governor of Washington, Governor of Idaho, and delegate to Congress from both Territories in turn; but their fame lay in the future. So none of the colonel's four sons—William, born in 1825; Lewis, 1827; John Test, 1829, nor Edward Test, 1831—was named after one of his three successful brothers.

Months of each year David saw little of his family. At first he accompanied the Third Judicial Court, astride "Ball," a horse valued at as much as forty dollars. Then, elected on the Whig ticket, he attended three consecutive sessions of the Assembly at Indianapolis; the pay was two dollars a day. Meanwhile the land office, like the "pillar of a cloud" in Exodus, had moved westward to the state capital. The colonel, now Lieutenant Governor (also at two dollars a day), read the signs; joining his brother Benjamin in "merchandising," he moved his family by horse and wagon across Indiana to Covington on the Wabash in the spring of 1832. On the way, two of his sons contracted scarlet fever; John died at Indianapolis, but Lewis, dosed with scalding saffron tea, recovered—and remembered his mother's eyes brimming with tears.

Covington was in an uproar, like Cincinnati twenty years before. (So the frontier went.) In May a large body of hostile Sauks under Black Hawk swooped out of the West to within thirty miles and killed two settlers; another attack was expected every day. No sooner had the Wallaces settled down in their one-story frame house than the colonel was raising and drilling a company of militia (like gawky Abraham Lincoln at New Salem, Illinois). The "milish" never marched to war, for Black Hawk was soon laid by the heels, but the incident left a deep impression with five-year-old Lewis. He saw that military prowess as well as civil enterprise was building America, that soldiers were carvers of destiny. None of his father's after-honors excited him as much as the cadet's gray uniform with the bullet buttons. And both of the son's names were those of soldiers! Henceforth he yearned with facile imagination to wear a hero's sword.

In school at Covington he was awed by the first stove he had ever seen. But he soon embarked upon an education in the best American —especially Indianian—tradition: daydreams punctuated by flog-gings, truancies evoking maternal tears and the paternal rod. His parents were realistic in a time when only one Hoosier child in six could expect to be enrolled in a school. The maternal tears were soon only a memory, for in 1834 Esther Wallace died of "galloping" con-sumption. Her friends remembered her as a devout and charitable Methodist, but withal so irrepressible in social enjoyment that she could dance from Sunday to Sunday. Her son Lewis, at seventy, paid tribute to "her eyes, large, sparkling, and deeply brown—they follow me yet."

Schooling continued sporadically at Crawfordsville, thirty miles east, where the three Wallace boys were boarded out while their father earned a solid reputation as president of the Indiana Senate. The preparatory department of Wabash, Crawfordsville's new Pres-byterian college, as well as the county seminary there, was unconge-nial to the towheaded Lewis (whose hair was soon to darken); in each the inevitable bullying master ruled, and, fleeing each, the truant learned more of woods and fields than of grammar, arithmetic, and Latin. "I ran wild in the great woods of my native State," he recalled in 1887. "I hunted, fished, went alone, slept with my dog, was happy, and came out with a constitution." And the hunting was done in a day when woods were meat market.

At the end of three years the lieutenant governor returned to Crawfordsville with his party's nomination for the governorship and with a new wife, the former Zerelda Gray Sanders, nineteen and handsome, daughter of a well-to-do Indianapolis physician.* David Wallace had been one of the foremost proponents of Indiana's gran-diose Internal Improvement Act of 1836, fuse of an ultimately disas-trous speculative boom; but he won handily in the gubernatorial election of 1837. With his wife and four children (the new union quickly bore fruit) he moved back to Indianapolis. In spite of a cur-

---

*Sister-in-law of Dr. Richard J. Gatling, inventor of the "Gat," she became the first president of the W.C.T.U. and, according to one historian, was "recognized everywhere as the foremost woman speaker of the State."

rent bank panic, the new governor, whose salary was $1,200 a year, assured everybody that the outlook was glorious.

The Hoosier capital had been laid out hopefully, sixteen years before, on a plan similar to Washington's; it shouted its newness and lived in the future. Stumps were common in its vacant lots, there was no railroad, and it was a ten days' haul to the Ohio River, main line of extrastate commerce. Nevertheless, immigrants were swelling the population beyond the four thousand mark, digging canals, laying track. Imminent wealth dominated the dusty odors of construction. Nothing in Covington or Crawsfordsville compared with the State House, gala in its fresh stucco; in his flat-topped oilcloth cap, visored before and behind, Lewis Wallace was overawed by this sixty-thousand-dollar edifice. He would have been the last to concur in the historian's judgment that it was "spoiled by a contemptible little dome, about as suitable as an army cap on the Apollo Belvedere."

New diversions, however, served merely as new motives for truancy, and the local seminary compared favorably in brutality with those left behind. Watching Jacob Cox, pioneer Indiana artist, execute a portrait of the governor apparelled in his best broadcloth dignity, the boy discovered an affinity for brush and pigment; it was temporarily stifled by his realistic father, but burst out often in later life. In the State House library he made the acquaintance of Irving and Cooper, whose vistas succeeded those of Olney's *Geography* and *The Life of Daniel Boone*. "My name was Idleness," he testified fifty years later, "except that I read—every moment that I was still I was reading." The book that stayed with him longest was Plutarch's *Lives;* here were military heroes far enough removed from the turgid Hoosier scene, but he had the magic ability to see them and hear them and forget that he was turning pages.

But he was not a recluse. He took part in one of the Indianapolis Thespian Corps' performances of *Pocahontas,* a vigorous blank-verse play by Robert Dale Owen; William Wallace was the heroine, and Lewis, her sister "Numony." Here was first manifested a lifelong sympathy with the theater. Henceforth Wallace often thought and acted dramatically, even melodramatically.

He proved that he could compete in more ordinary extracurricular pursuits as a member of "The Red Eye and Hay Press Club," with quarters accessible only by trapdoor (long before *Penrod*); he engaged in garden raids, feasts, bell pullings, and athletic contests in the woods. And of course he was a truant when, late in May, 1840, Indianapolis was the rallying point for a Harrison-for-President celebration which was to be held at Tippecanoe battleground. Whig delegates and delegations, twenty thousand strong—in carriages, in carts, on horseback, on foot,—formed a column twenty-five miles in length up the four-day route to the battleground. His father away, Lewis Wallace joined the parade and for twelve days lived thrillingly under the "Log Cabin and Hard Cider" banner. Harrison was the hero of that far-reaching victory of 1811 which had flung open the Northwest; grateful Indiana had named counties after Harrison and his fellow officers (in fact, the counties commemorated all the celebrated military heroes of America). Harrison had befriended young Wallace's father, and in return Governor Wallace had worked ceaselessly for Harrison. So Lewis took the '40 campaign, the most enthusiastic in Indiana's history of enthusiastic campaigns, as a family triumph, and was finally and irrevocably confirmed at the age of thirteen in his decision to become a soldier.

The governor rejoiced for Harrison even as his own downfall came. His fortunes had risen with the Internal Improvement Act, and they rapidly declined with it. At the close of 1838 he dolefully addressed the Assembly concerning the State's balance sheet, riddled with bad planning, incompetent administration, and outright embezzlement. His proclamation of November 28, 1839, as the first Thanksgiving Day in Indiana was bitter irony in view of the fifty years' debt and humiliation which the State faced. He was personally upright, able, and eloquent, and had carried on for Harrison by helping Federal agents to drive the last troublesome Indians beyond the State's borders, but he had bet on a wrong horse. Inevitably his own party convention of 1840 repudiated him. The former governor moved his household to a one-story, weather-boarded log building on Massachusetts Avenue, with a farm attached, and turned to consider the refractory Lewis again. In four years the boy had failed in as many schools; people were branding him, still only thirteen, as wicked and destined for hanging.

As president of a much-needed educational convention held at Indianapolis in 1839, David Wallace had heard a good speech by one Samuel K. Hoshour; to Professor Hoshour at Centerville, a settlement seventy miles east, went Lewis. He and his older brother William, the model student whom errant boys always have in the family to be compared with, were boarded with Aunt Rebecca Test of Centerville. The expedient turned out surprisingly well. Hoshour was the first sympathetic teacher Lewis had met, or recognized; it did not seem to matter that the Professor had yellow wattles. On occasion, the boy still got a flogging, but the pain was ameliorated by discrimination and sound justice. Moreover, Hoshour revealed the attractions of John Quincy Adams' *Lectures on Rhetoric and Oratory*, *The Spectator*, *The Vicar of Wakefield*, and the verses in the Gospel of Matthew telling of the Wise Men (later on, the genesis of *Ben-Hur*).

Back at Indianapolis' seminary after a year, Lewis suddenly found he could more than hold his own there. On Friday evenings the classroom was the scene of the Union Literary Society's meetings, throbbing with debates, recitations, readings, and parliamentary exercises. The chairman meted out assignments and levied uncollectible fines; strangely enough, the Society lived for eighteen years. With various young ladies for inspiration, lyrics flowed freely from Wallace's pen and were not only read to the members but, occasionally and anonymously, were published in an indulgent newspaper.

Still stimulated by *Pocahontas*, he wrote, in the style of "Marmion" and "The Lay of the Last Minstrel," a long historical poem with John Smith for its hero. The several hundred lines concluded, to the author's entire satisfaction, with the rescue of Pocahontas. He followed this effort with a sort of epic called "The Travels of a Bed-bug," in which the chief character emerged from the quarters of a local lawyer, and passed from office to office and from hotel to hotel until, like Alexander, it succumbed to too much drink. Here a poetic career also expired, for no sooner was the epic in circulation than the poet was sought out by several gentlemen with canes in their hands.

With more profit the apprentice, now sixteen, turned to the novel. "Even then," he recalled a half century later, "the importance to a writer of first discerning a body of readers possible of capture and then addressing himself to their tastes was a matter of instinct with me." At the moment, the Literary Society's tastes ran to (among others) G. P. R. James, who had reiterated *Richelieu* (1829) with six other weighty tales of knighthood. James was easier to imitate than Scott, James's model, as Thackeray's *Burlesques* had demonstrated.

> Oft in the sunrise somewhere, he would build
> Tall castle piles, and wall and moat them round.

The boy who was doing this became in fifty years the man who wrote the lines, in "The Wooing of Malkatoon"; castles in Spain and elsewhere filled the interval.

His *The Man-at-Arms: A Tale of the Tenth Century* owed much of its romanticized history and extravagant sentiment to James. For battle scenes the young Hoosier acknowledged a debt to Macpherson's 'Ossian'; the passion for chivalry, military feats, and an audience was peculiarly his own. In the course of two hundred and fifty closely written sheets of foolscap, Pedro, a valiant page, ran the gamut from agony to bliss in his devotion to Inez, the Rose of Guadalajara (mean-ingfully aged sixteen). Clandestine meetings led to Pedro's banish-ment, à la *Romeo and Juliet,* but a nurse and a hermit, also faintly Shakespearean, conspired to effect a secret marriage. Betrayed, Inez was incarcerated by wrathful parents and her marriage fraudulently annulled. She escaped a threatened match with an eligible prince by feigning madness. A helmet hiding his identity, Pedro became a hero of the First Crusade, and in time Inez' father was so overtaken with remorse that he too, with his family, embarked on a pilgrimage to Jerusalem. There, with Pedro apparently (but only apparently) dy-ing, Inez' sanity returned and the two were reunited.

The foolscap disappeared, happily, in the Mexican War years. But at the time it absorbed ink in David Wallace's law office, above a shoeshop, and was read to an attentive Society, it served a significant purpose. It left with the tyro the lifelong conviction that the senti-mental historical novel was not only a popular medium, but one which his hand could easily manage.

The impulse of truancy, though more often dormant, still re-mained. It broke out one day when Lewis and Aquilla Cook, two years older and "bright,"* had been reading accounts of the fall of the Alamo a few years before, and of the giants who there met their death. Perhaps a vague desire to avenge that barbaric massacre—or maybe the threat of a new Mexican attack—impelled the two to leave home and school to reinforce Commodore Edwin W. Moore of the Texan navy. In any event, after a vain attempt at recruiting, the boys embarked on a skiff down the White River, intent upon overtak-ing a flatboat bound for New Orleans. Unfortunately for their hopes they were pursued and caught by Lewis' grandfather Sanders and a constable.

For David Wallace there was nothing picturesque about the Alamo incident; it was the last straw. The former governor had served a term in Congress (at eight dollars a day), had been defeated for reëlection mainly because he had championed fantastic Professor Samuel F. B. Morse's side of the "electro-magnetic telegraph" issue, and was now reëstablishing a legal practice. He felt it his duty to speak realistically and decisively to the tall, thin, and olive-hued but withal robust youth who suddenly seemed a stranger. He did it with his accustomed good address and unexceptionable manners:

"Were I to die tonight, your portion of my estate would not keep

*Son of the State House librarian, he subsequently married a dancer in Cincinnati, killed a man on her complaint that she had been insulted, and was never heard of afterward, except in a letter to a Cincinnati paper boast-ing how he had fooled the police and escaped arrest.

you a month. I have struggled to give you and your brothers what, in my opinion, is better than money—education. Since your sixth year I have paid school bills for you; but—one day you will regret the opportunities you have thrown away. I am sorry, disappointed, mortified; so, without shutting the door upon you, I am resolved that from today you must go out and earn your own livelihood. I shall watch your course hopefully."

The two parted with mutual politeness, father inscrutable, son dazzled by the vast prospect of life unshadowed by home or school. Not that he gazed without regret, at least in later recollection. David Wallace assumed an awesome stature as his son recalled his love of literature, especially of Macaulay and the English quarterlies, and his fireside readings, with voice and expression of remarkable sensitivity, from the fiction of Lamb, Shakespeare, Milton, Scott, and Byron; from the sermons of Chalmers, Hall, Bossuet, and Bourdaloue, and from the chronicles of Thucydides and Geo. Bancroft. The elder Wallace had assigned declamations to his sons and appraised the performance, with special attention to enunciation. Material included Campbell's "Hohenlinden," Halleck's "Marco Bozzaris," extracts from Webster, Emmet's "Vindication," Phillips' "Washington," Collins' "Ode to the Passions," Byron's "Corsair," and Scott's "Marmion" and "Battle of Beal' an Duine."

"My education, such as it is," Wallace declared in 1887, with little exaggeration, "is due to my father's library." Without his father, he would not have received a judicious schooling at home, or outside, where it was difficult to find in early Indiana. More particularly, his father's example developed in Wallace a deep-grained habit of courtesy which never left him.

He now turned to the office of County Clerk Robert B. Duncan, who was courting Aunt Mary Sanders (whom Lewis considered a friend) and coaching brother William in law. Duncan gave the younger Wallace boy records to copy—captions, pleadings, orders, judgments, dates of filing—at ten cents a hundred words. Soon he was earning eighteen dollars a week, living in a boardinghouse, attending sociables, and practicing the quadrille in a class conducted by a bandy-legged little Frenchman dubbed "Do-ci-do."* When this

---

*About this time, young Wallace presented to Miss Elizabeth Bedsall, aged sixteen, a treatise on the language of the flowers, tenderly inscribed on the flyleaf: "To Elizabeth, from Lew Wallace." At the bottom of the page, in another hand (probably Miss Bedsall's), appeared the notation: "See page 16." Page 16 expounded the symbolism of the marigold; it was supposed to convey the taunt, "You think you're bold, but you're not." Apparently this was the young lady's teasing riposte to a presuming swain.

respectable routine failed to quench the thirst of the spirit, he found time in the hush of the courthouse vault to apply himself to Lindley Murray's *English Grammar,* and Professor Hoshour's ghost looked approvingly over his shoulder. Then, late that year (1843), he took down from David Wallace's shelves, still accessible, a new three-volume work by the great Prescott: the *History of the Conquest of Mexico.* In this the apprentice hewer of tales saw his block of marble: "As a history, how delightful it was!" he rhapsodized in 1896, "as a tale, how rich in attractive elements!—adventure, exploration, combat, heroisms, oppositions of fate and fortune, characters for sympathy, characters for detestation, civilization and religion in mortal issue." And, not having heard of two forgotten novels by Robert Montgomery Bird, he believed that the field was "absolutely untouched" in fiction.

He recommenced weaving the plot and establishing the background of *The Fair God,* which was to be his first published novel, springing Phœnix-like from *The Man-at-Arms.* He loaded Prescott with marginal notes, and then, after learning Spanish, Bernal Diaz' *Historia verdadera de la conquista de la Nueva España.* Later, as on occasion he visited Washington, were to come annotations from other sources—Hervara, Sahagún, Torquemada—as he familiarized himself with the cloud-capp'd towers, gorgeous palaces, and solemn temples of old Mexico. The manuscript was begun in a blankbook one winter's night with no thought of publication, according to the author. For no fewer than thirty years thereafter, with some long interruptions, it served as a pastime, something to pick up—by memory if, as often happened, the blankbook had been left behind—when business slackened, a train ride grew dull, or a wait extended itself. Then, indeed, "Shining Popocatepetl the dusty streets did rule."

KATHLEEN SMALLZRIED

(b. Wabash, 1909–) is a graduate of Wabash High School. She started her writing career by engaging in local journalism projects but got her first major assignments in reporting for the *South Bend News-Times,* where she worked from 1929 to 1936. From 1942 to 1946 she was an editor for the U.S. Committee for Economic Development, and from 1948 to 1951 she served as the Director of Information for the U.S. Council, International Chamber of Commerce.

The Studebaker Brothers
of South Bend

. . . Henry shook his head. He was not well. Work in the forge had not agreed with him, and he wanted to get out of town, onto a farm. It was a good idea, but not for him.

So John, with $3,000 of his savings, bought his older brother's share of the business and became full partner with Clem. A day after he came home he was at work, hammering out ideas bigger than the job on his anvil. Clem, fired by John's ambition, slaved with him, shoulder to shoulder. In that same year of 1858, the company, still known as H. and C. Studebaker, ran its first advertisement in the local paper.

Encourage Home Industry
Northern Indiana
Carriage and Wagon Factory.
H. &. C. Studebaker
Would call attention of the public to their large and splendid assortment of Carriages, Buggies, Wagons and Sleigh-cutters. They can now assure the public that the work in their establishment cannot be excelled in Northern Indiana for durability or fineness of finish. None but the best workmen are employed in the Factory, consequently it is the only establishment in this part of Indiana that will warrant their work. Blacksmithing, painting, trimming, custom work, and repair done on short notice in the best style. The new brick factory is on Michigan Street south of the American Hotel.

* * *

Peter began to brag to his brothers that they were the best retailers in the country. The carload lots dealers of Kansas, Missouri, Nebraska, the Oklahoma Territory and the Indian Territory, and Arkansas he christened the Jayhawks, in honor of the Kansas guerrilla fighters of the Civil War, and around them he centered his selling campaigns.

Iron had fallen so much in price that the cost of standard models could be dropped. With the farm wagon and the Izzer buggy the Jayhawks went to work to counteract the depression in more expensive lines. Peter gave them all the help he could, sending out literature and advertising matter from the home office, making collections, and doing general trouble shooting. The kind of connection he established with his dealers is taken for granted today, but it was a new thing then. He was among the first American businessmen to realize that the force in the field was the most vital part of the central organization.

Somewhere on his staff Peter harbored an anonymous poet who wrote advertising copy for the Jayhawks. Sound in rhyme and meter, his productions circulated largely on the prairies. "Farmer Jones's Wedding Day" was a composition designed to appeal to the feminine pride of ownership.

As Farmer Jones and his worthy wife one night by the fire
    were sitting,
She suddenly said with a quiet smile, as she raised her eyes
    from her knitting,
"Joe! Tomorrow's our wedding day, my dear, and I should like
    to know
What you are going to buy for me when into town you go."

"Yes, love," quoth he, "we've wedded been these ten long
    happy years,
And I am proud and glad to say there's been more smiles than
    tears.
So I intend to mark the day by buying something neat
That all may see we do agree as we drive down the street.

"I'm told the Izzer buggy, of Studebaker fame,
Outclasses all the other rigs of every style and name.
Old Banker Smith has got one, and Mayor Tompkins, too,
And if they suit such swells as they, well, why not me and you!"

Said Mrs. Jones to Farmer Joe, "Oh, Joe! You are too kind!
For that same Izzer buggy was running in my mind.
Old Mrs. Smith turns up her nose at our poor two-wheeled cart,
And Mrs. Tompkins stares so hard it well nigh breaks my
    heart."

So Farmer Jones in town next day an Izzer buggy bought.
He found the Studebaker rigs the public fancy caught.
And Mrs. Jones was happy made upon her wedding day,
And proves to all who choose to call that Izzers lead the way.

Not only to women did the bard of South Bend address his lines. He composed other verses to persuade male customers that Studebakers were reliable, inexpensive to operate, and long lasting, as well as socially desirable.

> The rain and shine and dew came down.
> The farmers' crops would fill the town.
> But worn out wagons spoil it all.
> When prices suit, he cannot haul.

Chorus:

> Oh, farmers all! Poor farmers all!
> To save your cash on you I call.
> For Studebaker offers you
> The very best that he can do.
> Then to it quick your horses hitch.
> 'Twill last until you all get rich.

> The Studebaker won't wear out
> No matter how you drive about.
> Pile on your rocks, this is no joke,
> This wagon is as stout as oak.

> Road cars and buggies, best you've seen
> In finest style fit for a queen,
> For Studebaker made them so.
> They can't be beat where'er you go.

> The dollars in your pocket laugh
> A Studebaker costs but half
> You pay whenever others break
> That Studebaker didn't make.

> Eureka Springs, sir, is the place.
> George Martin with a smiling face
> Will loads of wagons show to you
> And prove that what we tell is true.

Largely through the energetic selling of the Jayhawks, business at the wagon works spurted ahead in the closing months of 1895. In the rest of the country recovery was not in sight, failures and bankruptcies still overtaking commercial houses everywhere. Peter was so sure his western dealers had performed wonders that he began to revolve in his mind some sort of recognition the brothers could make them, a magnificent token which would bind them and the company together with even stronger ties.

"Why couldn't we bring the whole lot of them here to South Bend for a party?" he asked J.M.

The two sat down together and figured the expense. If they chartered a train, if they reserved floors in the hotel, if they planned food and entertainment, say, for three days, the cost would not be prohibitive.

"It's a crazy idea," J.M. told him, "but we'll do it. All the same, I think we'd better wait for a year or two to see whether business is really going to pick up."

Peter agreed. But before the Jayhawks came to South Bend he fell ill. And before he had time to realize his malady was to be fatal, he was dead.

His death was such an unbelievable thing to his brothers that they hardly knew how to adjust themselves to it. So the Jayhawk party was forgotten until 1898. In that year the company's annual sales had touched three million dollars for the first time, and J.M. and Clem decided the moment had come to give Peter's party to the dealers who had been so largely responsible for the figures on the annual balance sheets. Accordingly they planned the celebration for the next year and in 1899 the western sales force came to South Bend.

A special train picked them up at Kansas City. Its sides were hung with huge banners: "Excursion of Car Load Buyers to the Largest Vehicle Factory in the World. ANNUAL CAPACITY, 75,000 VEHICLES."

The party began with a reception in the president's office at which Clem shook hands all around and told his guests something of the company's history. Then they were shown through the factories and yards on a car of the private railroad which the brothers maintained to connect their forty-eight departments spread over more than a hundred acres. Ten miles of tracks were laid within the plant limits. The Jayhawks stared in appreciation at the 50 million feet of lumber in the yards, the 300 tons of steel in 125 different patterns, the 12,000 wagons stored in the shipping department, at the electric elevators and the dynamos and generators in the power plant, at the plating room in which tinning, plating in nickel and even silver and gold for fancy harness was being done, at all the great separate divisions which were turning out thousands of skeins, wheels, axles, hubs and boxes for assembly by crews working together.

CLAUDE BOWERS

(b. Westfield, 1878–d. 1958) was brought up in Hamilton County and was a graduate of Indianapolis High School. From 1901 to 1933 he worked on such newspapers as *The Indianapolis Sentinel, The Terre Haute Star, The Fort Wayne Gazette,* and *The New York World.* He later served as U.S. Ambassador to Spain (1933–1939). His best known books include *Spanish Adventures of Washington Irving* (1940), *The Young Jefferson* (1945), and—perhaps his masterpiece—*The Tragic Era* (1929). While in high school he kept a journal from which came the following excerpts, complete with misspellings.

High School Commencement, 1898

Jan 23 This evening Spencer came over. I am very glad to find him pretty blue. He is begi[nni]ng to realize that fame and greatness are not born but made after heroic struggle. He feels the inadequacy of his literary power, the lack of historical knowledge and the immaturity of his mind, and then too he realizes that this Law School shoves out superficial lawyers with a limited knowledge of the Ind. statutes and with no knowledge what-ever of the general principles upon which the law is grounded. He regrets that he has not five years of preparitory study before him, and has determined to study literature, history and sociology for the next two years in connection with his legal studies.

Jan 24 Harold Jones is the most melancholy fellow I have ever known. He is subject to fits of blues and they come frequently and linger long. Fatherless, motherless . . . and living from hand to mouth he has every reason for discontent. Today he is particularly blue because his books for the next term amount to about $3.00 and he has not a cent with which to purchase. His pantiloons are ruffled at the bottom, buttons are off his coat, and he has sworn to stay out of school this week, go to Lebanon and try to scare up some funds. I can always break his blue spells however and have him laughing that peculiar ha! ha!

High School Exit

Jan 29 Last night was the limit of my high school experience. My class is one of the very finest that ever graduated. The boys are big-souled fellows, and the girls are accomplished and above all, spirited.

Class Day

On last Saturday we held our Class Day Exercises in the High School Hall. It was a very gloomy, rainy day but that did not interfere with the crowd that gathered to hear our farewell words. The boys glee club which has been practicing for some time made the welkin ring with melody—striking hard at members of the faculty and prominent members of other classes. I had to read the class will—a mere device for hiting any person. Sara Messing read the class prophecy which had me elected to the U.S. Senate in a short time. It also made an embarassing mention of a cellar window exit which I once made to escape a certain friendly young lady. The boys had a spirited yell which they gave with terrific force—

> "Ali vevo, ali vivo
> Ali vevo, vivo, vum,
> Go get a rat trap bigger than a cat trap,
> Go get a cat trap bigger than a rat trap,
> Canibal, canibal, Sis boom, bah,
> January '98—Rah! Rah! Rah!"

The girls, more harmonious, more spirited, and enthusiastic than any class of girls before had a yell of their own, which under the leadership of Edna Kuhn, and Florence Dunning they gave with a vim, which all the boys in the High School could not drown.

> "Onery Twoery, eckery, ery
> Always, happy, jolly, and merry
> Always early, never late
> Girls of January '98"

After the program had been exhausted, we drew ourselves up on the platform and faced the boys of the June class, far out-numbering us, and Ott. Kettenbach stepped forward and challenged the June boys to put us off the platform if they could. The June boys did not stir. We were much surprised, and so to give them some encouragement we sang a derisive song—"Oh I don't know—your not so hot." They still retained their seats. Then we assumed a look of superiority and disgust and, drawling out "Well,—Well—Well"—retired from the platform without the sheding of blood.

Commencement Day

Last night graduating exercises were held in Plymouth church before a large audience. Everything was beautifully, and tastefully decorated with palms and trailing vines. Music was furnished by the brilliant blind musician—Prof. Hanson who rendered parts of "Trovatore"—the wierd "Miserere" and dashing "Anvil Chorus." I sat on the front row with Sara Messing.

Lilyan Habich spoke first on the "Ideal of Service." Daisy Hale followed with an impressive imaginary sketch to the home of Chas. Dickens. She did all right, but imagining herself an elocutionist, she delivered it in a manner somewhat affected. Next came Jesse D. Wall whose oration on Puritanism was very dry. His delivery was very poor, and he forgot once or twice. Andrea Furgerson who came next looked almost angelic in her white robes as she stood before her audience and talked of the relations of God to Nature.

Abraham Cronbach had a deep, philosophical, and deeply religious oration, couched in the many-syllabled words of which he is so fond, and delivered very well, considering his thin voice, and his inability to speak in but one tone. Ada Braddocks sketch of a new England village was very dull.

Sara Messing did far better than any of the girls. She spoke naturally forcibly, clearly. Once when speaking of the Cuban's fight for independence, she was interrupted by applause. I came next, and was given an enthusiastic reception and hearing. I was interrupted by vigerous applause three times. Martha Allerdice was tame. All concede mine to have been the best, and all place Sara next. The boys carried me on their sholdiers after the exercises. Prof. Doty said I had a fine speech, tho he acknowledged that he listened to none other. Langsdale said I was "a diamond set in a brass band." Cronbach's father came to me and said I did better than Abie. Prof. Hufford said it did better than many a college oration. I was completely lionized for the evening. Before leaving the stage the boys yell rang out, followed at once by that of the girls.

Mother gave me a magnificant book case, a young lady presented me with a splendid copy of the drama—"Richeleau," Davis gave me a fancy paper cuter, and Doll Bowers sent me a silver handled hat brush with my initials.

The Class

Martha S. Allerdice the first honor student, is very short and somewhat chubby. She has a sweet fat face, which is quite attra[c]tive when she smiles. She is very quite and modest.

Grace D. Berry is tall and slender, with light hair and blue eyes. She is so very good and proper that no one pays much attention to her.

Ada Braddock is low, and slender—with no form at all to speak of. Her forehead is low, her complexion very fine. She is quite a talented drawer—and but for her awkardness inexperience and over modesty, she might be better known than she is.

Juliet R. Brown is the daughter of Judge Edgar A. Brown. She is tall and well built. She has a pretty face—large blue eyes, and light hair. She has considerable executive ability, and is a beautiful yet sensible girl.

Abraham Cronbach—see a very small awkard, emaciated figure— black hair, none too well kept, small eyes, black, dreamy and sunken, cheeks colorless and caved in,—cloath him in a dirty shirt, shoes unblacked—give him a big vocabulary of long words—have him talk philosophy and religion—and give him a thin voice—an extremely clear articulation—and you have Abie Cronbach the so-called genius of our class. He is extremely poor and his father has a stand on Market. His mother was born in Poland and is very ignorant disliking books. Abie is destined for the holy Profession and will one day probably be a Rabbi.

Florence Lilian Dunning the charming daughter of Dr. Dunning is small but with the perfect form and features of a fairy. Her hair is light, her eyes are blue—her lips are red and inviting. We boys used to admire her shapely legs when she wore short dresses. She has more spirit than a hundred war horses. She is energetic, enthusiastic, and has the elements of a leader. She is a talented musician. She was voted the most popular girl in the school.

Andrea Furgerson is our poetess. She is tall, and slender—has black hair and brown eyes. She has a pretty, healthy, glow upon her cheeks. But she shines best when silent. She is not a brilliant conversationalist. She can write very pretty poems. She was born in Cork, Ireland.

Lorin Green is a fine brown-haired, ugly faced, healthy hearted Irishman—just up from Georgia.

Victor Keene is a pretty boy—with all the shallowness requisite for social success. His father was a prominent politician. Vic. is quite a ladies man—has a dress suit—wears his black hair—don't care a damn. Thats all.

Edna M. Kuhn is tall and stately. She is a well rounded form that is the admiration of every boy. She has a pretty face—some what too independant. There was a time when she was very spoony, but she is now settled down—at least she is not now so loud. Still she has many admirers who stream to her home to enjoy her entertaining manners. She too has the elements of a leader. She is the one who originated the girls yell and she leads it. Her father is the wealthy merchant.

Geo. Langsdale needs no notice. I shan't forget him.

Margaret McCullough daughter of the great preacher Oscar McCullough is a great beauty of the aristocratic order. Her facial features are perfect. Her eyes, dark, and dreamy. She has a form that rivals Edna Kuhns.

Sara Messing, daughter of the Jewish Rabbi, is not pretty, but she is attractive. She is brilliant in some respects—can write brilliant verses at least. She is a natural politician.

Feb 1 This morning I heard the brilliant young musical genius Oliver Willard Pierce lecture on Wagners "Flying Dutchman." He is short, symetrical. His face is peculiarly beautiful and animated. His eyes are very brilliant. While he talks a smile lingers about his lips. He is not a lecturer or master of Rhetoric—and he made frequent gramatical and Rhetorical mistakes. Some-times he could not think of a word and would let it go.

Ever now and then he would rush to the piano and with intense feeling and rare skill play snatches from the Opera.

Tonight I went to the Law School Deb Club to listen to a debate upon the money question between M. L. Daggy and John Morrison, on the silver side and two insignificant others on the other.

John Morrison who is President of his class and was first President of the Debating Club. He graduated from Butler College several years ago and has since been in business in Frankfort. He is a big, fat fellow and though smooth-faced, he looks to be at least 30 years old —his age. He has been on the stump, and last year during his visit to Frankfort, Bryan was introduced by him. He made a very good speech which consisted mostly in unqualified denunciation of the bond-holders and John Sherman. There was neither originality or argument or arrangement and the denunciation was rather crude. . . .

ERNIE PYLE

(b. Dana, 1900–d. 1945). For biographical notes see "Brown County," above, page 28.

David Ross, George Ade,
and Cannon Ball Baker

David Ross, who had been referred to as "Indiana's No. 1 Citizen," was sixty-nine, and had never married. He was an inventor, an engineer, a chemist, a manufacturer, a farmer, an educator, and president of the board of trustees of Purdue University. He was all wool, without embroidery. He had Jack Garner eyebrows, except that they were steely instead of white. He pursed his lips, folded his hands across his stomach, and paused long and frequently in the middle of a sentence, and you wondered if he'd forgotten what he was saying. But he hadn't.

Ross graduated from Purdue in 1893, and he had been paying back his alma mater ever since. He had an almost religious sense of obligation to the world for what it had done for him. He had given the university a lot of his time, and more than a million dollars. Among his gifts to Purdue were its airport and, with George Ade, the Ross-Ade Stadium. Purdue was his life—the only family he had, and Purdue students made him a father confessor.

When he went to Purdue it was for an engineering course, but shortly after graduation he almost died of typhoid, and the doctors told him he'd have to stay in the open. So he went back to the farm, and never left it for thirteen years. Out there on the farm, he thought up his first invention, a steering gear for autos. When he was thirty-five, he ventured into the industrial world. He built his first factory in 1906, and now in 1940 it was still going. Many of our 1940 passenger cars were steered with Ross gears and more than half the trucks on America's highways.

Later he built another gear factory, and one for making a processed shale composition that looks like stone. He had scores of patents. But once he had invented and perfected a thing, he was through with it—never wanted to monkey with it again. He had retired from his factories long ago, and stepped back in only when they needed pulling out of a hole. He had never worked for anybody a day in his life. Always his own boss. And he had never kept on doing a job himself a minute after he had trained someone else to do it. He said he had never had any desire for money, and yet almost everything he touched made money.

He owned about a thousand acres of farm land, and had three families running it. He didn't call them tenants, but partners. Two of them had been with him nearly thirty years. Ross himself was living on one of his farms, eleven miles out of Lafayette. It had been farmed continuously by the Ross family since 1820, and he said it was in better shape now than the day it produced its first crop.

Ross drove to his office in Lafayette every morning, carried on the business of Purdue University, received callers and students, made decisions about his factories. At noon he drove back to the farm and stayed there. If you visited him in the afternoon you'd find him wearing only "three pieces of clothing," as he put it—two shoes and a pair of shorts. He liked to get his hoe and monkey around out in the sun.

One day in 1933 Ross's tenant farmers, Ona Myers and Harry Bartlett, said to him, "Our bins are all full. Our haymows are stacked to the roof. Our outside cribs won't hold another bushel of anything. What shall we do?"

Ross looked at them a long time, from under his bushy eyebrows, and then in his short, bluff sentences he said, "Indiana has one of the best state park systems in the country. There's a World's Fair in Chicago. You've got relatives in Dakota. You've got enough money. Take a year off. Quit farming for a year. Put everything down to clover, and then go see this country."

The farmers were aghast. "What will the neighbors say?" they asked.

"I don't give a damn what the neighbors say," said Ross.

And so the two farmers packed up their families and went away to see America. Next spring they were back. The granaries were still full. "You've still got money, haven't you?" said Ross. Yes, they had. "Take another year off, then." So they did. That year came the western drought. Hay was at a premium. They sold every ounce of all three cuttings at twenty-five dollars a ton, and made more money than they ever had before.

One day they came into the office and said, "Things are bad out in the Dust Bowl. Cattle poor and dying. Feed scarce out there. We've got plenty of feed. We could pick up some of these weak cattle pretty cheap in Nebraska."

"What the hell you stoppin' here for?" said Ross. "Get on your way."

So they went to Nebraska, brought back the cheap and half-starved cattle, fed them out, and sold them. Made more money than ever—made enough in those two "vacation" years to buy a farm apiece. So Ross started looking around for new "partners." The two farmers heard about it and came storming into his office. "Well, you've bought farms of your own, haven't you?" said Ross. "I'll have to have new tenants, won't I?" No, he wouldn't. "Those farms are for us to retire to in our old age," they said. "Until then, we're staying with you." And they were still with him in 1940, prosperous and happy.

George Ade was a wonderful man. He was one of that famous quartet that made Indiana great in letters. The others were James Whitcomb Riley, Booth Tarkington, and Meredith Nicholson. Riley died before I got around his way. Once I drove for half an hour around Tarkington's home at Kennebunkport, Maine, and never got up nerve enough to go in. I spent an evening with Meredith Nicholson in the American legation in Nicaragua, when he was United States minister. And now I wanted to meet George Ade.

Ade was seventy-four, and he had not been well for several years. I didn't know whether he would see anybody or not. So a friend at Purdue called his farm near Brook, fifty miles away, and left a message. In a little while Ade called back. Sure he would see me, and I'd have to stay for lunch.

I found him sitting on a long couch in the cool living room of the comfortable home he had built thirty-five years before. He had on gray trousers and shirt, summer shoes, neat tie, no coat; he was spick and span as a bandbox, tall and slender and graceful as a youth. It took a minute for him to place me, and then he realized it was my columns he read every day in the Miami *Herald* in the wintertime. I was tremendously flattered. He called them my "letters."

"And so you're from Indiana?" he said. "From down around Dana? Yes, I know Dana. You find Hoosiers no matter where you go, don't you?"

He liked to revert to the old days and tell stories of Riley and Tarkington. He was full of yarns about Riley, and as he told them he would laugh and laugh. He said Riley was without question the most amazing and interesting personality he ever knew. He had framed letters from him in his study, and the drawers were full of them.

Ade's kind are the salt of the earth—sharp, witty, gently caustic, quick on the understanding, and blessed with an ordinariness that helps to make them great men. Ade had a humility that I loved. Not a studied humility, but just a plain Hoosier appraisal of himself. It showed when he was telling how Indiana University gave him an honorary Doctor of Laws degree in 1926. "They gave them to Tarkington and Nicholson and me," he said, "and that was pretty fast company for me to be moving in!" And he meant it. He beamed over that degree like a little boy.

He had received three degrees—his original one from Purdue, from which he graduated in 1887; a Doctor of Humane Letters from Purdue; and his I.U. doctorate. He had all three diplomas on his study wall. "But I can tell you one degree that will never come my way," he said, "and that's the Doctor of Divinity. No, sir, I'll never get that." Then he told about the cyclone of the year before. He had missed it by going over to Rensselaer to a movie that afternoon, but it swung across his farms, touching nothing on either side, and smashed down four different sets of his buildings and most of his beautiful shade trees. "People around here said it was a visitation of divine wrath for the way I've always lived," he said, and he laughed. "That's all right as far as I'm concerned, but why did it pick on those tenants of mine? They live all right." And he went on: "That divine-wrath business was blown up, you know, when the San Francisco fire left a block-square warehouse full of whisky standing right in the middle of a whole section of the city that was absolutely burned down." Ade told things like that with chuckles and a born storyteller's zest. And if divine wrath were really holding sway, I doubt that it would pick on George Ade at all. He had done too much for his fellow man.

He had always been generous, and in his younger days had been famed in Indiana as a host. He had an unusual capacity for enjoyment, and he could make other people enjoy themselves. Nearly thirty years earlier he had started a golf course on his farm. He gradually enlarged it, and finally gave it to the community. It was called the Hazelden Country Club. Ade himself hadn't played golf for several years, although he was once of championship caliber. He seldom walked out of the house nowadays, though indoors he seemed agile and not at all in poor health. He spent nearly all his time reading and playing solitaire. He had occasional callers, though not too many, and he still loved picnics—had a picnic ground and swimming pool and dance hall right on his lawn.

Ade had contributed to Purdue nearly all his life, probably close to a hundred thousand dollars, Purdue officials told me. He had helped build the Sigma Chi fraternity house, and, of course the Ross-Ade Stadium. He and Dave Ross were old and fast friends. The stadium was Ross's idea, and he badgered Ade into coming in with him on it. Then it came time for a name. "Purdue Bowl wouldn't do," Ade said, "because it wasn't a bowl. So I thought why not get my name on it? Hell, I wanted my name on it. I was shameless about it.

Why, a hundred years from now nobody will remember me for any books or plays or fables I wrote, but they're gonna remember me for that stadium. Yessir, I wanted my name on there." He didn't seem to realize how much he had contributed to the gaiety of the world with his pencil. (Yes, pencil, for he never learned to use the typewriter.)

Ade was born at Kentland, a few miles from Brook. After leaving school he worked on newspapers in Lafayette, and then for two years with a patent medicine company. "We guaranteed absolute cure of the tobacco habit," Ade said, "provided the patient faithfully followed the directions on the bottle. The very first direction was, 'Give up the use of all forms of tobacco immediately'!"

It was from newspaperwork in Chicago that he sprang into the literary limelight around 1900. He said he never did have much ambition, that somebody else pushed him into every good thing that ever happened to him. By 1905 he was rich. He bought the farm at Brook and built his house that year. He had lived there in the summers ever since. He spent his winters in a rented house at Miami Beach.

He always used to go to Florida by auto, but the trip now exhausted him so that he went by train. "The trouble is I want to see very damn thing," he said, "and I sit there for four days jerking my head from one side of the road to the other like somebody watching a tennis game, and when I get there I'm dizzy." He had his first auto back in the days when they guided the things with a handle bar instead of a steering wheel. But he hadn't driven a car himself since 1910.

He never married. His household consisted of Katie Krue, who was combination housekeeper and nurse, and a cook, a gardener, and a chauffeur. The house, which was large and rambling, looked like a gabled country clubhouse of a generation ago. In a corner of the first floor was his study, where thirty years ago he had written some of America's most popular books and plays. There he wrote *The College Widow* in three weeks. The study was lined with old photographs, medals, and letters from people like Riley. On one side was a large safe which contained most of his manuscripts. The house was full of little statues and images and trinkets that he had brought back from his travels. He had been around the world two or three times.

He had achieved real fame and fortune, yet at the height of his career he had come back there a few miles from his birthplace, and built a home to spend the rest of his life in. He was the compleat Hoosier. . . .

Cannon Ball Baker was an Indianapolis institution. In that automotive city he had been making a living for thirty-five years by setting
automotive records, and at fifty he was still doing it. He held more
auto records than any five other men combined. The Baker home
was full of silver cups and medals and testimonials. He had driven
forty thousand miles on the Indianapolis Speedway in test work,
though he drove in the big race only twice. He had driven five
thousand miles just up and down Pikes Peak. He had crossed the
continent a hundred eighteen times, and had driven hundreds of
miles in the western sandy deserts on railroad tracks, before there
were any roads. He had ridden across the Isthmus of Panama before
the Canal was finished, following railroad tracks and foot trails. He
had ridden a motorcycle the entire length of Cuba, around the island
of Oahu, all over Australia, and across Tasmania.

There was a time when speed records were being set right and left,
but like the hoop skirt and the hair on my head, those things were
gone for ever now. Autos had become so perfect that all of them
could go too fast. So Cannon Ball Baker's records nowadays were of
a different stripe. They were records of mileage per gallon. He had
proof that he had motored at the rate of 55.8 miles to the gallon of
gasoline—that was with the wind. But when he drove right back
again against the wind and averaged up the two, he came up with
39.2 miles to the gallon. He did it with a manifold-and-carburetor
development of his own. He'd been working on it for years. He said
it was perfect now, and he expected it to make him a million dollars.
He had it installed in his own Graham sedan, and he said that car
would go farther and faster on one gallon of gas than any other car
in the world.

And he had another thing, a perfection of the old rotary-valve
engine, which he had worked out in a one-cylinder motorcyle. With
that motorcycle he had got 154 miles on a gallon of gas. Furthermore,
the thing was so smooth that he could ride uphill and down at five
miles an hour without a buck or a tremble. This thing would make
him another million. That makes two.

Cannon Ball Baker was a hearty fellow. He had a big hooked nose,
and loved to talk and laugh and show you around. I went out to his
house to see him (used a pint and five-eighths of gas getting there)
and spent the afternoon with him and Mrs. Baker. His real name was
Erwin George Baker. He started motorcycle racing in 1906, then
began setting transcontinental records on his motorcycle. As his
records grew, he acquired such names as Demon, Warhorse, Dare-
devil, and The Fox. But it was when he rode into New York in 1914,

at the end of a new transcontinental, that he got the name Cannon Ball; a reporter on the *Tribune,* George Sherman, gave it to him. He was in the Indianapolis phone book as Cannon Ball Baker, but Mrs. Baker called him Erwin, and friends called him Bake.

As late as 1934, he was racing across the continent on the public highways at speeds as high as a hundred miles an hour. But not any more. His top limit now was the same as mine—fifty miles an hour. He liked to set records at that speed. Once he shook hands with the engineer of the *Lark* just as it was leaving Los Angeles, and then beat the train into San Francisco by forty minutes, though he never drove over fifty miles an hour. He said it wasn't so much the speed as the gawking around that got you into trouble. You had to sit there one-minded and staring, as though you were shooting a gun—which you really are, only you're riding on the bullet. He said one of the first requisites of safe driving was to get your stomach right up against the wheel, so you'd have a good purchase on it, and then keep your eyes peeled. . . .

RICHARD CROWDER

(b. Remington, 1909–), a graduate of De Pauw University, has taught American literature at Purdue since 1937. He has written biographies of Carl Sandburg, Edwin Arlington Robinson, and Michael Wigglesworth, but is perhaps best known for *These Innocent Years* (1957), a biography of James Whitcomb Riley (1849–1916).

Fame
[Comes to James Whitcomb Riley]

When Professor William Lyon Phelps came out from Yale to lecture, he and Riley struck up a warm friendship. Phelps took particular pleasure in hearing the Hoosier swear—never vulgarly, never vehemently, often in laughter. He would swear when his own name was misspelled; he would swear when Edgar Allan Poe's middle name was misspelled (even though he had no affinity for Poe's verse).

He would swear at the very thought of Walt Whitman. He would swear at disappointments, at delights. But always gently, always with imagination.

[Riley's] reputation was now solid enough that Phelps felt justified in requiring his Yale undergraduates to write papers on *Poems Here at Home* and *Neghborly Poems*. Another Yale professor, Henry A. Beers, had devoted three pages to Riley in his *Studies in American Letters* in 1895. The Hoosier Poet was conquering a very discriminating clan, the college teachers of literature.

Riley had sent *Scribner's Magazine* a poem "On a Youthful Portrait of Stevenson," which was to appear with a picture of the subject. When in September he received payment, he returned the check, requesting instead a complete set of Stevenson's works. To his great pleasure the books arrived on October 7, his forty-eighth birthday (though hardly anyone knew it).

His relationship with Scribner's was indeed cordial, but he was having untold difficulty meeting one requirement: for publicity Arthur Scribner wanted him to compose a paragraph in *prose!* He worried, he fumed, he finally got some words together. But, when he sent it off, he gave Scribner a free hand. Prose was simply out of his line; any change for the better would be welcome.

Scribner's were preparing the first two volumes of the Homestead Edition, *Neghborly Poems* and *Sketches in Prose.* They were both to be published this fall. There was some question about the spelling of *Neghborly,* but the poet won out. The pronunciation would not have been different with the correct spelling. Riley's insistence on omitting the letter *i* was an effort at keeping the "country" flavor even in the title. He had a precedent in Huck Finn's "sivilization."

The question occurs whether this careful misspelling was snobbish or not, since it did not alter the pronunciation. Riley invariably enjoyed himself among his unsophisticated friends—a Hancock farmer, an Indianapolis storekeeper. Was he unconsciously betraying the simple people by this calculated gaucherie?

There is the further question of Riley's accuracy in his transcript of Hoosier speech, for it is a manner of expression not now current. If, as some say, Riley's children and farmers speak an invented language, then the spelling, the elisions and the contractions are of little permanent importance. On the other hand, if Riley's verse is the lone depository of an authentic dialect now disappeared—and there are stout defenders of this view—then language historians should vindicate the poet's almost frenetic concern with jots and tittles.

In November—publishing business out of the way for a while—Riley took a reading tour across the Mississippi: Topeka, Kansas City, Omaha, Lincoln, Des Moines. He spent Thanksgiving quietly in Omaha. He had been invited to church at All Saints' and to the rectory for dinner afterward, but was happy to be able to refuse because he had not brought along a Prince Albert coat proper for the occasion. He wrote letters and read those he had received. And he yearned for Lockerbie Street. But he was in good health now, and after all he was back home in a week.

The Rubaiyat of Doc Sifers, dedicated to Dr. Hays, was offered for sale on December 4. A few days later the Century Company made a hundred autographed copies in red silk binding available to collectors and Christmas shoppers.

Riley was feeling expansive. He read far into several nights in a row, enjoying Twain's *Following the Equator.* He sent a check for a hundred dollars to the fund for a library in Greenfield. In mid-month he set out for New York, partly on business, partly for pleasure.

Three days before Christmas he was the guest of the New England Society of New York, the only man present who was not a New Englander by birth or residence. After his assigned toast, "Hoosierdom and Yankeedom," he delighted his hearers with "The Old Man and Jim," which always brought tears, and with "The Old Soldier's Story," which never failed to produce laughter.

Next day he went out to Bronxville to spend Christmas with Stedman. After the hubbub of the metropolis he was happy for the Lockerbie-like quiet of this pleasant suburb. He could never acclimatize himself to the noise and rush of any city.

He came back to New York late on Christmas Day and spent the following week among his friends and publishers there. On New Year's Eve he could at last attend a function of the Authors' Club, of which he had been a member for some time. At the Watch-Night party he fell into conversation with a friend of Bliss Carman's. As they talked, the man revealed that Carman had taken great pleasure in Riley's poetry and was, as a matter of fact, preparing an article of considerable extent praising the Hoosier's work. He was under contract to publish it in the *Atlantic Monthly.* The *Atlantic!* Riley had for years been struggling to conquer that bastion. He still had not been published in it, but he was to be the subject of an essay. Was that not a foot in the door? . . .

Meanwhile Marcus Dickey had been arranging for some programs out of town. In this month Riley was in St. Louis and Kansas City. Then he returned home. The Indianapolis streets had been renumbered recently, so 26 was now 528 Lockerbie Street; but it was still the same wonderful refuge. Riley was always glad to get back.

He had been preparing his books for the Homestead Edition. They were coming out at the rate of about one a month. To all these volumes he added material; they were not just reprints of the earlier editions. He had really been hard at work.

Indianapolis was never loath to show its appreciation of what Riley —and other writers in the state, too—had accomplished. On the day after Riley's program in Kansas City, the Indianapolis *Sentinel* had published an anniversary edition. One section is devoted to "What Indiana Has Done for Literature in Ten Years." Riley had returned to find an article on his contribution as well as short pieces on the work of his colleagues, Wallace, Thompson and the rest. It was good to be recognized at home, the place he loved above all else.

Riley spent almost the entire month of April in the South. He stayed in Nashville over the Easter week end. Rain came down on Saturday, but he went sightseeing anyhow—to Murfreesboro and to the site of the Battle of Stone River. In the afternoon he was taken to the home of Mary Noailles Murfree ("Charles Egbert Craddock"). He found a quiet, well-ordered little family of three. Mrs. Murfree, the mother, aged eighty, was still following her life-long custom of an hour's daily piano practice. Miss Fanny busied herself with the details of housekeeping, but found time to write—had in fact published a novel in the *Atlantic* eight years before. (Ah, the *Atlantic!*) Miss Mary had from childhood suffered lameness which made her dependent on her sister for support. But *she* had had *two* novels in the *Atlantic.*

The next day was Easter. Nashville citizens turned out in beautiful new clothes, to eye and be eyed, to go to church respectably. Riley, not to be outdone—Riley, the glass of fashion—donned his own new suit and joined the parade.

The following ten days brought him to Memphis, to Chattanooga, to Lookout Mountain for a brief look, to Birmingham, to Atlanta (where he saw Joel Chandler Harris at the *Constitution* office), to Macon, back northward to Knoxville on his way home. En route Dickey arranged a date at Asheville. So Riley's homecoming and further work on the Homestead Edition was delayed. He visited the grave of Nye at Asheville and paid a call on his widow. Always he was confident that Nye was right beside him.

May was a busy month. Scribner's wanted to finish the Homestead Edition as soon as possible; so Riley began work at once on *Green Fields and Running Brooks.* He had been invited to submit a poem for the September issue of the *Atlantic* (at last!) And he was on the annual banquet program of the Indianapolis Literary Club. He read the first version of "The Name of Old Glory," but was not satisfied. He had been trying for a long time to clear it of any hint of Hoosier farm speech and idiom. He saw that he had a long way yet to go. Many people of critical taste read or heard it read that summer. Riley tried his best to profit by their comments. He was trying it out on as many audiences as he could in his effort to polish it and make it acceptable to the Eastern magazines.

He attended the Western Association's convention in spite of a general debility. He was on the program, in reporting which the minute book overflowed with love:

> Mr. Riley was suffering a great weakness from a recent illness and was exceedingly pale—but as he mounted the platform steps, cheer upon cheer rallied him to the emergency, and for almost an half hour he held his audience either in tears,—awe-stricken,—or side-splitting laughter—as best pleased his fancy. I wish every Indianian could have heard him! God bless and keep our Hoosier Poet! There are no words with which we can describe anything Riley does when he contributes to entertainment.

When in June Riley had learned that his long-time correspondent Benjamin Parker of New Castle would not be able to afford the week at Eagle Lake with the Western Association, he instructed George Cottman to invite him as a guest of the Association. Riley himself would foot the bill on condition that Parker not be told. Parker was properly mystified and did not find out who his benefactor was until long afterward. In his present good fortune Riley was not forgetting his old friends who were in need. When he heard that one of them was in trouble, he would pay the necessary hospital bill or send the necessary clothing, asking nothing in return except the continued sincerity of friendship that he now valued above all else.

The *Bookman* for September carried several announcements concerning Riley. The current *Atlantic*, said the *Bookman*, was publishing "The Sermon of the Rose" by Riley and an appreciation of him by Bliss Carman. The tenth and last volume of Scribner's Homestead Edition would come out this month. Riley was at work on a volume of child verse, collected from his earlier poems. *The Golden Year*, a year book based on Riley verses and compiled by Clara E. Laughlin, would be in the stores before Christmas. Furthermore, there was nothing to the rumor that Paul Laurence Dunbar and Riley were collaborating on a comic opera. This was a great deal of news even for a man of Riley's reputation.

Riley was grateful to Carman for the article, for he thought of the *Atlantic* as the world's top-ranking periodical. Carman had certainly not been stingy with his praise. He had said that "Riley is about the only man in America who is writing any poetry." What he did not realize, apparently, was that most of the poems in Riley's books had been written five, ten, even twenty years earlier. In a way he was agreeing with Edwin Arlington Robinson in decrying the paucity of poetic depth in these decades of trifling sonneteers, in these innocent years.

Late in September Riley did some last-minute work on "The Name of Old Glory," then sent it off to the *Atlantic*. One success deserved another. Two poems in the *Atlantic* in one year would be success indeed.

In mid-October he began a month's tour of the Great Lakes cities and New England, beginning in Cincinnati, where the afternoon of October 17 was wet and cold. The weather discouraged a number of people who had bought tickets from attending Riley's reading in the Music Hall that evening, but a good-sized crowd was there, nonetheless.

There was some dissatisfaction with the performance. In the first place, the hall was so large that the reader's voice could not be heard with comfort beyond the first twelve rows. In the second place, the great orchestra pit gaped between the stage and the audience. An intimate art like Riley's demanded closer physical contact with the audience than such an arrangement permitted. "The Object Lesson," though still funny, was beginning to seem a trifle long to those who had heard it many times before. The audience enjoyed "The Old Soldier's Story," but its gory detail was just beginning to pall.

At the close Riley was given a silver loving cup engraved with the names of twenty-four of his Cincinnati friends. He looked at the cup and at the cluster of roses that had been laid at his feet and was completely overcome. He was able to recover himself, however, so that he could close his program with some child rhymes and stories. The old readings might be getting a little dull, but his charm, the rapport between readers and hearers, was as binding as ever.

Detroit, Ann Arbor, Cleveland, Buffalo, Rochester, and on to Boston, where he was introduced by Julia Ward Howe, who leaned on his arm as they came to the platform. While Mrs. Howe was speaking, Riley turned pale; but, as he gradually overcame his nervousness, he regained his color, delicate though it had always been. That same night Hall Caine, the British novelist, was lecturing in another audi-torium in Boston. So great was Riley's drawing power that Caine's audience numbered fewer than twenty people.

By November 22 he was back home, where the Century Club honored him at a banquet in the Denison. The after-dinner program was long. Everyone wanted to pay tribute to Riley, who at last rose and made a little speech: he had always regarded himself as an amateur, he said, for he felt that was the only way to maintain the childlike quality of wonder and primal pleasure with which he tried to saturate his poetry. His modesty and candor drew long applause. Before the evening was over, Riley—inevitably—read some of his poems.

That fall Clara Laughlin's collection of Riley verse was published in London. Bowen-Merrill had agreed to handle its sales in America. Reviews on both sides of the Atlantic were favorable. The *Academy* of London expressed the opinion that it was too bad that Riley was known to so few Englishmen, but then even English dialect writers were neglected. If British readers would bring themselves to exam-ine this book they would find that

> There is no humaner poet now writing, and no tenderer and gen-tler; and no one loves children with a sweeter love than he. This little book provides a very comprehensive introduction to his work, and will, we hope, send readers to it.

In America reviewers were commenting on the Homestead Edi-tion. Maurice Thompson in the *Critic* saw Riley's work at its best as related to Riley on the platform:

> ... the secret of his success is in a certain slender but pure vein of dramatic power.... Mere caricature does not fill a large space in Riley's poems; pure drollery does; and this fits them to the elocu-tionary mood and to the needs of the facial contortionist.... In the open field of genuine literature Mr. Riley's success has been nota-ble but limited.... The poet seems not quite at home....

Riley's "notable but limited" achievement ... The public might still acclaim him with uncritical fervor, but men of literature were begin-ning to commit themselves to the opinion that he was not a poet of great stature.

On the other hand, he was attaining a victory he had dreamed of all his life. The December *Atlantic* published "The Name of Old Glory." Two poems in three months! Was his early "Leonainie" theory working out? Was the *Atlantic* accepting him just because he was Riley? Probably not. The editor had made him work at this new poem until it had met his standards.

Except for the patriotism of "Old Glory" the Spanish-American War had scarcely touched Riley. One morning in January 1899, however, the state of Indiana accepted a gun captured from the Spanish and the battle flag from the man-of-war *Indiana*. Into the first-floor corridor and rotunda of the State House were crowded Assemblymen and many other important citizens to witness the ceremonies. The theme of the program was, of course, patriotism. At its climax Admiral George Brown presented Riley to the gathering. The customary storm of applause roared through the halls. Riley announced his "homely poem to the dear flag, a homely tribute by a voice from the crowd." Then he began to recite "Old Glory." They had all read it, if not in the *Atlantic*, at any rate in the *News*. Many of them had heard him recite it in one of its early versions. But this was the finished product delivered by its writer in a context already full of patriotic emotion. As he read the lines with all the fervor at his command, he lifted his head to gaze at the flag waving above him. The throng before him was totally silent.

> By the driven snow-white and the living blood-red
> Of my bars, and their heaven of stars overhead—
> By the symbol conjoined of them all, skyward cast,
> As I float from the steeple, or flap at the mast,
> Or droop o'er the sod where the long grasses nod,—
> My name is as old as the glory of God.
>   ... So I came by the name of Old Glory.

As his clear, nasal, beloved Hoosier voice ceased, there was a clapping of hands which increased in intensity until, when the impact of what had taken place struck, the entire General Assembly jumped to their feet and shouted and waved their arms so enthusiastically that Riley had to bow over and over again. Then he came forward and announced quietly: "I have nothing else I can offer you. I thank you again and again." He had not needed dialect to appeal to his audience. He had scored another triumph. . . .

Bliss Carman was an admirer of Riley, but he had never been privileged to meet him until one day in front of Willard's Hotel in Washington he and his partner, Richard Hovey, ran into the Hoosier, who had read their *Songs from Vagabondia* with pleasure. After Hovey introduced the other two, Riley shifted his chew of tobacco, looked Carman up and down, and commented on his extraordinary

height. Carman recorded the event in a dialect poem, "How I Met
Jim Riley." Riley, he reported, had said,

> "Guess your parents used a trellis
> Fer training you. . . ."

Carman was speechless, but he was

> " . . . proud
> O' meetin' Jim Riley. . . ."

This spring the New York *Times* paid him tribute. His long poems
and his prose, said this paper, were flat and unsatisfying. On the other
hand, he excelled all other American poets in the short dialect piece.
His farmers were "intelligent, keen-eyed, purposeful." His children
were real. These short poems had "taken sanctuary from the critics
in the hearts of little children and of 'the common people' who 'hear
him gladly'."

Riley devoted the latter half of May to a tour of Indiana cities. He
opened at Earlham College, Richmond. The exuberant and sympathetic audience encouraged him to a superior performance, but toward the end of the announced program his voice gave way
considerably, and he was forced to decline any encores.

The next night he read at the Princess Rink in Fort Wayne before
the largest crowd that city had seen since Thomas B. Reed had
campaigned for the Presidency. Advance ticket sales had reached
nearly two thousand. Before their arrival in the city Dickey had
received a telegram: "Please have Mr. Riley rehearse his 'turn' suspended from the ceiling. There will be no room for him in the
auditorium. Seat sale largest but one in the history of the city." That
one had been for a performance of Edwin Booth.

In Lafayette, Riley was assisted by a local quartet of ladies who sang
"There, Little Girl, Don't Cry" with such fine effect that Riley said
he would not soon forget it. The next day was rest day. Riley would
have preferred to stay in his room at the Lahr House in Lafayette.
But Dickey, an insatiable tourist, insisted on their going out to view
the Tippecanoe Battle Ground. In company with two Purdue professors they combed very thoroughly the sixteen-acre park, site of the
battle. At the conclusion of the inspection one of the academic guides
asked Riley whether he had any questions. In his slow, nasal
drawl, he asked, "How in the devil did the Indians get over that iron
fence?"

He had recited, this time by request, "The Name of Old Glory." The crowd had been enthralled. Next morning's *Journal* described his delivery:

> His gestures in reciting this heroic poem are a marvel of grace. Two simple movements of his arms illustrate the waving of a flag from the halyards in a remarkably impressionistic manner, and another as equally simple movement limns the outlines of the flag as it droops.... There is a peculiar quality to his voice ... that really thrills, a quality that actually inspires patriotism.

Twice in a week Riley had cleared for his sponsors over a thousand dollars. In spite of this evidence of his popularity Riley decided that he ought not to read again in Indianapolis for a long time.

He was not feeling well. He passed a quiet summer working on another book. In early September he went up to northern Michigan with the Hays family. He determined, however, not to undertake a tour during the next season. The decision was a wise one, for he was an invalid most of the winter.

At a reception he did meet Robert Louis Stevenson's widow, who had been born Fanny Vandergrift in Indianapolis. But two weeks later he was not able to go to Hauté Tarkington Jameson's dinner for William Dean Howells. On the day after, though, Howells came to Lockerbie Street. He stayed an hour, talking with "the poet of our common life."

Riley Love Lyrics, the poet's book for Christmas shoppers that year, contained forty-five poems, only one of which had not been in a previous book—"The Sermon of the Rose," his first *Atlantic* poem. Not only was he composing no new pieces nowadays, but he was also principally reissuing verses his worshipers had read in previous volumes. A new Riley book did not have to have new lines: a new title was enough to make it sell.

EDGAR LEE MASTERS

(b. 1868–d. 1950), although a native of Kansas, took Indiana and Illinois personages as subjects of his prose and his verse biographies. One of the characters in *Spoon River Anthology* (1915) was inspired by Dreiser.

Theodore the Poet

As a boy, Theodore, you sat for long hours
On the shore of the turbid Spoon
With deep-set eye staring at the door of the crawfish's burrow,
Waiting for him to appear, pushing ahead,
First his waving antennae, like straw of hay,
And soon his body, colored like soap-stone,
Gemmed with eyes of jet.
And you wondered in a trance of thought
What he knew, what he desired, and why he lived at all.
But later your vision watched for men and women
Hiding in burrows of fate amid great cities,
Looking for the souls of them to come out,
So that you could see
How they lived, and for what,
And why they kept crawling so busily
Along the sandy way where water fails
As the summer wanes.

THEODORE DREISER

(b. Terre Haute, 1871–d. 1945). For biographical notes see "The
Lost Phoebe," page 209.

My Brother Paul [Dresser]
and the Birth of
"On the Banks of the Wabash"

It was the same with "On the Banks of the Wabash," possibly an
even greater success, for it came eventually to be adopted by his
native State as its State song, and in that region streets and a town
were named after him. In an almost unintentional and unthinking
way I had a hand in that, and it has always cheered me to think that

I had, although I have never had the least talent for musical composition or song versification. It was one of those delightful summer Sunday mornings (1896, I believe), when I was still connected with his firm as editor of the little monthly they were issuing, and he and myself, living with my sister E—— that we had gone over to this office to do a little work. I had a number of current magazines I wished to examine; he was always wishing to compose something, to express that ebullient and emotional soul of his in some way.

"What do you suppose would make a good song these days?" he asked in an idle, meditative mood, sitting at the piano and thrumming while I at a nearby table was looking over my papers. "Why don't you give me an idea for one once in a while, sport? You ought to be able to suggest something."

"Me?" I queried, almost contemptuously, I suppose. I could be very lofty at times in regard to his work, much as I admired him—vain and yet more or less dependent snip that I was. "I can't write those things. Why don't you write something about a State or a river? Look at 'My Old Kentucky Home,' 'Dixie,' 'Old Black Joe'—why don't you do something like that, something that suggests a part of America? People like that. Take Indiana—what's the matter with it —the Wabash River? It's as good as any other river, and you were 'raised' beside it."

I have to smile even now as I recall the apparent zest or feeling with which all at once he seized on this. It seemed to appeal to him immensely. "That's not a bad idea," he agreed, "but how would you go about it? Why don't you write the words and let me put the music to them? We'll do it together!"

"But I can't," I replied. "I don't know how to do those things. You write it, I'll help—maybe."

After a little urging—I think the fineness of the morning had as much to do with it as anything—I took a piece of paper and after meditating a while scribbled in the most tentative manner imaginable the first verse and chorus of that song almost as it was published. I think one or two lines were too long or didn't rhyme, but eventually either he or I hammered them into shape, but before that I rather shame-facedly turned them over to him, for somehow I was convinced that this work was not for me and that I was rather loftily and cynically attempting what my good brother would do in all faith and feeling.

He read it, insisted that it was fine and that I should do a second verse, something with a story in it, a girl perhaps—a task which I solemnly rejected.

"No, you put it in. It's yours, I'm through."

Some time later, disagreeing with the firm as to the conduct of the magazine, I left—really was forced out—which raised a little feeling on my part; not on his, I am sure, for I was very difficult to deal with.

Time passed and I heard nothing. I had been able to succeed in a somewhat different realm, that of the magazine contributor, and although I thought a great deal of my brother I paid very little attention to him or his affairs, being much more concerned with my own. One spring night, however, the following year, as I was lying in my bed trying to sleep, I heard a quartette of boys in the distance approaching along the street in which I had my room. I could not make out the words at first but the melody at once attracted my attention. It was plaintive and compelling. I listened, attracted, satisfied that it was some new popular success that had "caught on." As they drew near my window I heard the words "On the Banks of the Wabash" most mellifluously harmonized.

I jumped up. They were my words! It was Paul's song! He had another "hit" then—"On the Banks of the Wabash," and they were singing it in the streets already! I leaned out of the window and listened as they approached and passed on, their arms about each other's shoulders, the whole song being sung in the still street, as it were, for my benefit. The night was so warm, delicious. A full moon was overhead. I was young, lonely, wistful. It brought back so much of my already spent youth that I was ready to cry—for joy principally. In three more months it was everywhere, in the papers, on the stage, on the street-organs, played by orchestras, bands, whistled and sung in the streets. . . .

BRENDAN GILL

(b. 1914–) is a Contributing Editor to *The New Yorker*.

COLE PORTER

(b. Peru, 1893–d. 1964), scion of a wealthy family, was given piano and violin lessons at the age of five. He attended Worcester (Mass.) Academy, Yale College (where he was a member of the Eliza-

bethan Club), and Harvard Law School. He later devoted himself
more seriously, however, to music. In Paris at the Schola Cantorum
he studied under the classicist composer D'Indy and also learned
much about jazz from Black musicians. Porter had joined the
French Foreign Legion but during World War I transferred to the
French Army. Back in the United States he began to earn recognition, in the 1920s, for his lyrics in such Broadway musical comedies
as *Greenwich Follies* and *Fifty Million Frenchmen;* and, in the
1930s, for *Anything Goes* and *Du Barry Was a Lady.* Despite the
horseback-riding accident in 1937 which crippled him for life, he
continued to win successes with such musicals as *Something for the
Boys* (1943) and *Kiss Me, Kate* (1948); and with his lyrics for such
films as the autobiographical *Night and Day* (1945) and *High Society* (1956). For these and other stage and screen musicals he composed such memorable lyrics as "Begin the Beguine," "True
Love," "C'est Magnifique," and the urbane, often witty, verses
which appear on page 392.

Cole

Begin with the face, familiar from so many photographs. It was
small, round, smooth-skinned, delicately modeled, invincibly boyish.
Even in age, after decades of suffering, it held hints of the implike,
lovable child that we see pictured in a starched blouse and broad-
brimmed straw hat at four, already eager to seek out and embrace
the world. It was a world that would become his oyster, his cham-
pagne, his caviar, and in the small city of Peru, Indiana, in the
flagrantly misnamed gay nineties, it must have been plain to the
ambitious mother of the child if not to the child himself that the
sooner one held out both arms to such a world the better.

People who hug life to them, though they grow older, never grow
old: Cole carried with him to the grave not the ravaged face of an
old man but the ravaged face of a young one. The family knack for
longevity—his grumpy millionaire grandfather J. O. Cole lived to be
ninety-five, his mother to ninety—proved a curse to him; he was
ready for death, indeed he pleaded for it, but the stout heart inside
his mutilated body indignantly refused to consent. Cole had not
marched with conventional inattentive acquiescence into his late sad
years; he had been battered into them by an intemperate and
preposterous fate, and when he died, in 1964, at the age of seventy-
three, he had endured no telling how many centuries of continuous

physical pain. In the light of this dreadful fact, it is curious to observe in the last photographs, along with the looked-for signs of anguish, signs of an undiminished trustingness, as if the promises of a long life, however little they had happened to be fulfilled for him, remained, all touchingly and beautifully, promises for others.

We are haunted by the face in part because it is so unchanging— because, in a sense, it haunts itself, being its own at first jaunty and playful ghost and then its pitiful one. In any casual snapshot of an outing held who knows when in Paris, Cairo, Venice, or Hollywood, it is Cole that one instantly singles out and gives a name to. The face of the little boy on ponyback in the apple country and the face of the elderly, crippled recluse dividing his time between an apartment high in the Waldorf Towers and a cottage in Williamstown is the face of the debonair undergraduate at Yale, already an accomplished charmer, who by an adroit manipulation of exceptional talents and an exceptional intelligence is offered whatever he covets and avoids whatever he dislikes. What a spoiled young man he must be! But then what excellent value he gives! All his life he will be accused of being a snob and all his life he will deny the charge, but his snobbery, real or imaginary, is beside the point, which is that at every turn, unfailingly, he furnished the world with far more joy than he got back. In the unspoken bargain struck between genius and the rest of us, it is the rest of us who come home with full hands and, in this instance, dancing feet.

There are several classbook photographs of Cole, posing with this or that distinguished undergraduate group before a length of nineteenth-century wooden fence from the Old Campus at Yale. (The official college photographers kept this sacred remnant of fence, no more likely to be genuine than slivers of the True Cross, in their Chapel Street studio for football captains and other heroes to be propped against. Behind the fence was a backdrop of tastefully painted Old Campus elms, looking not unlike a rain forest in Brazil.) Cole is well-dressed, not to say dudeish, in these official photographs, and the face, under dark hair parted in the middle, is always in dead earnest. It is obvious that he is proud to be who he is and where he is, and why not? By a number of years, he has anticipated the ordeal and triumph of a favorite protagonist of Scott Fitzgerald's daydreams and fictions: a rich young nobody from the uncharted here-be-dragons hinterland West of the Alleghenies makes his way East and succeeds in taking the gilded citadel by storm. In Cole's case, the East consisted of New Haven and New York, but how much more mere territory was it necessary to capture in order to count as somebody?

As for the gold, to a newcomer from Pee-ru, to say nothing of St. Paul, it looked like the real thing. Both Cole and Scott would assert with Henry James "I can stand a good deal of gold."

That short, trim, rather bookish-looking boy, with his crisp tenor voice and his dislike of contact sports and indeed of any exercise except riding and swimming—surely it was odd in the Yale of that day, shortly before the First World War, that such a figure could have been a big man on campus. Yet Cole was. Dink Stover and Frank Merriwell were long past, but their descendants have a way of incarnating themselves continuously out of the damp night air of all those narrow one-syllable eighteenth-century New Haven streets—Elm and York and Grove and High and Wall—and one cannot help wondering what the handsome, burly athletes of the Porter era, with their suspicion of cleverness, their pursuit of the manly, their strenuous Christianity, thought of the exquisite pagan hedonist in their midst. Well, it appears that they liked him very much. He made Deke (thanks, it is true, to the influence of an upperclassman and fellow hedonist named Gerald Murphy), and he made Keys, and he was the Leader of the Glee Club and a member of the Whiffenpoofs, and he was also, in his nearest approach to the sweat and towel snapping of the locker room, a cheerleader. His best friends were Monty Woolley and Len Hanna, notable specimens of what were thought of euphemistically in those days as perennial bachelors. The Woolley-Hanna set was inclined to spoof the pieties of Mother Yale and their favored habitat was New York, to which Cole often accompanied them; nevertheless, he was friendly enough with the Stovers to win their admiration with a couple of football songs—*Bingo Eli Yale* and *Bull Dog*—that to this day remain the best-loved musical furniture in the minds of many Old Blues.

We glimpse the bright, mascotlike face smiling above elegant white tie and tails when at Christmas the Glee Club would travel its thousands of miles by rail around the country and Cole at the piano would bring down the house with a series of encores consisting of his own perky (and shrewdly self-censored) ditties. We glimpse the face again when Cole, back in New Haven, attends a meeting of an arcane and prankish group known as the Pundits. Having spoken of ghosts, one is tempted to linger a moment over that quizzical Pundit face of his and to impose on its unmarked freshness all that we know will someday befall it. Among the courses that Cole took at Yale, and neglected less than he did others, was William Lyon Phelps's celebrated "T & B," the then universally recognized abbreviation of "Tennyson and Browning." Billy Phelps was a bravura performer, who manifested a shameless, endearing pleasure in his platform skills; his students never forgot that they had taken a course with him, though what he had taught them might soon slip from memory. Phelps had founded the Pundits, limiting the club to ten undergraduates, and he considered Cole an ideal member. The motto of the Pundits pretended to conceal itself from the barbarian world by being reduced to initials: "T.B.I.Y.T.B." These initials stood for "The best is yet to be" and came from Browning's famous and once frequently quoted exhortation from "Rabbi Ben Ezra": "Grow old along with me!/The best is yet to be,/ The last of life, for which the first was made."

Browning, incomparably skilled at rhyme and a master of syncope and of what Hopkins called sprung rhythm, made a profound impression on Cole. Long before he went off to New Haven, his father read Browning to him and urged Browning upon him. (Samuel Fenwick Porter, whom everyone in the family, including Cole, appears to have either pitied or disliked, was a remarkable man. He began life as a good-looking, penniless druggist and his marriage to the heiress Kate Cole ought to have proved a stroke of good fortune. He had a strong literary bent and a passion for agricultural experiments, which he was able to indulge with the help of his wife's wealth. He seems to have been slowly crushed to death between the fiercely go-getting Kate and his powerful, contemptuous father-in-law, neither of whom made any bones about preferring the cheerful son to the sorry father.) Browning's unquestionable influence upon Cole can be found in many of the more acrobatic of Cole's lyrics; indeed, the chances are that he learned at least as much from Browning as he did from another and more obvious source, W. S. Gilbert, and from his younger contemporary, Ogden Nash. By an agreeable coincidence, Cole was to spend several summers at the Palazzo Rezzonico, where Browning died. It is hard to resist speculating on what Cole made of Browning's incorrigible optimism when his dark days came. With what a wry mockery he must have repeated to himself in his last years the Pundit motto, "The best is yet to be." In spite of Browning and Billy Phelps and Mother Yale, life had not turned out that way.

Ten or twelve years pass, and the face is still uncannily that of a stripling. The smooth skin is tanned now, for the season in the photographs is nearly always summer and the place nearly always somewhere in France or Italy, as like as not the Lido. Cole is said to have considered himself unprepossessing; a man's opinion of his looks, especially if it is unfavorable, is not to be trusted over his photographs, and in his Venetian period Cole is downright handsome. His eyes are his best feature—large and dark brown and slightly popped, with heavy lids and something lemur-like in their playful, darting alertness. Also rather simian, and appealingly so, is the big mouth open in laughter, with its formidable array of square white teeth. In these carefully preserved snapshots, Cole is a healthy, happy animal, his bare body, slender and nut-brown, shining with the oil that protects it from the Mediterranean sun; he stands or sits or lies on the endless blazing Lido beach, mugging into the camera, while behind him we make out serried rows of bathing cabanas, with perhaps a jacketed servant emerging from between the rows with drinks on a tray and, in the middle distance, Monty and Noël making silly faces.

If Cole has a reputation in the nineteen twenties, it is not that of a composer who happens to be having an awfully good time on the side but that of an international playboy who writes an occasional witty song to be played and sung by him in the corner of one or another of the innumerable fashionable parties he gives or goes to; subsequently, the song may be allowed to drift out and down into the ordinary workaday world and gain a certain vogue there among a deliberately limited cult. (Of all the songs that Porter wrote up to, say, 1925, only one became what is known in music-publishing circles as a standard, a tinkly little tune called *Old-Fashioned Garden,* which was a hit in the Raymond Hitchcock revue, "Hitchy-Koo of 1919.") Cole's reputation at that time could be summed up in the facile accusation that he was being "social" instead of "serious"; like most reputations, this contains a truth and deforms the truth, for Cole was, in fact, being both at once. Social in his tastes but Middle-Western-Protestant-Puritan in the seriousness of his aspirations, he was every bit as eager to make good as his mother and grandfather had been before him. Although he took care to uphold the tiresome undergraduate tradition that to be seen to be working hard is bad form, in truth he worked very hard indeed. In Paris, he studied composition under the austere classicist Vincent d'Indy and familiarized himself with the entire range of nineteenth-century "art" songs, particularly the *lieder* of Schubert and Schumann. At the same time, he was making friends with a number of black musicians and performers in Paris. Well ahead of most of his white contemporaries, he began to experiment with jazz rhythms, and his clever pastiche, *The Blue Boy Blues*—a song inspired by the sale of Gainsborough's painting, "The Blue Boy," to an American millionaire—was, for a while, highly popular in England. In 1923, Porter composed the score of a ballet for the Swedish Ballet company; the book was by his old Deke sponsor Gerald Murphy, who also designed the sets and costumes. The ballet, a triumph in Paris, was regarded with almost equal admiration in America, where it was given over sixty times in the course of a two-month tour. It was Cole's first and last public appearance as a "serious" composer. The ballet, entitled "Within the Quota," anticipated certain musical ideas that were to cause a stir when, several months later, they found expression in *Rhapsody in Blue*, by Cole's friend George Gershwin. Cole undertook to write a second ballet, for which Bakst was to provide the costumes. Bakst died, and Cole abandoned work on the ballet. The score of "Within the Quota," which Cole himself believed had been lost forever with the dissolution of the Swedish Ballet, was brought to light in 1970 and the ballet given a revival in New York. Many musicologists find the score of interest, and not alone because of its historic significance.

To remain a sort of gentleman-composer, moving at a measured height above the squalid scramble of the market place, was important to Cole as a young man and proved a considerable stumbling block to his career. Irving Berlin warned him that if he wanted to get work from theatrical producers he had better acquaint himself with the corner of Broadway and 42nd Street, where, if his name was recognized at all in the twenties, he was written off as an expatriate highbrow. Seeking to avoid Broadway and yet hoping to be pursued by it, Cole would go so far as to rent a large and costly apartment on Fifth Avenue and invite theatrical people to parties there; but it appears not to have occurred to him that, except geographically, Fifth Avenue was even farther from Broadway than Paris and the Lido were. The desire to seem a charming amateur who just happened to enjoy all the perquisites of a hardened professional was based less on a sense of caste and class than on a deep-seated and, as it proved, ineradicable lack of confidence in himself. This was an emotion that, if it was unknown to Cole's mother and grandfather, must have been familiar enough to the father he despised. It directly contradicts the principle enunciated by Freud to the effect that no man who has been his mother's favorite knows what it is to fear failure. (The teasing of one's dead betters is often an irresistible temptation; let it be noted that Freud himself was his mother's favorite. In his seventies, white-bearded and world-famous, he was *"mein goldener Sigi"* to Frau Freud, who contrived to live even longer than Kate Porter did and to keep her beloved closer to her apron strings. Not all mama's boys have been great men, but a remarkable number of great men have been mama's boys.)

Cole wished ardently to succeed; still more ardently, he wished not to be known to have failed. Hints of this double goal are to be found scattered everywhere throughout his life. He was to give ample proof of his courage, but his refusal to defend his own work in the rough-and-tumble of preparing a show led more than one Broadway director to describe him flatly as a coward. At the peak of his popularity, if someone connected with a Porter show in rehearsal expressed skepticism about a song, Cole always preferred discarding it to re-writing it; a fresh start struck him as the safest way to avoid the odious close give-and-take of criticism. The discarded song might turn up years later, slightly altered, in a new show or movie; meanwhile, the moment of dangerous self-doubt had been got past. Cole's passion for travel may have been a covert method of problem-solving for him. Who can tell what the tireless sightseer has left unexamined at home? Cole was never to be offered as much work as he wanted, or claimed to want, but he rejected many of the projects that agents and producers brought to him because he doubted that he would be able to bring them off. Not that he would give this as a reason; it was an aspect of the discipline he practiced in respect to fear that it seemed to the casual observer an emotion totally alien to him. Gentlemen had no nerves, and on the opening night of a Porter show he made a point of sitting well down front with a party of friends, laughing and applauding the show as if he hadn't the slightest doubt of its success. His behavior was gallant, and it was also protective: by wearing a mask of unshatterable aplomb, he was putting himself beyond reach of critics and envious rivals, to say nothing of a public always eager to observe who in the pecking order is the latest to be made to bleed. The finest of the musicals he was to write—"Kiss Me, Kate"—was the one he hesitated longest over committing himself to; he pretended that the reasons for his hesitation were that the project was too intellectual, that revivals of Shakespeare never did well at the box office, and that he didn't understand the book that Bella and Samuel Spewack had prepared. The truth was that Cole had had a couple of failures and was aware that people were saying he was through; he was simply afraid that "Kiss Me, Kate" would prove to be beyond his powers.

Playboy. Expatriate. Highbrow. Snob. The names flung at him in his youth he slowly, manfully outgrew by the exercise of an extraordinary musical talent working in the closest possible union with high intelligence. (The Porter lyrics, composed at the same time as his music and indissolubly wedded to it bar by bar, syllable by syllable, were a product of intense intellectual concentration; the seemingly

effortless rhymes came not from heaven but from a rhyming dictionary.) Cole literally sweated to make good, though it was part of what
was later to become known as a "life style" for him never to be
observed to be sweating at all: a mild Mediterranean glow was the
permissible limit. In Venice, back of the drawn blinds of the Palazzo
Rezzonico while the rest of the household napped, or in Paris, in the
chaste, art-deco elegance of the silvery house at Number 13, Rue
Monsieur, or in New York, on the forty-first floor of the Waldorf
Towers, he gave himself to his difficult craft. It was donkey work, but
he did it, and as far as one can tell at this distance in time the person
who, after unfalteringly loyal "Ma" in far-off Peru, gave him the
courage to persist in his years of largely unrecognized and unre-
warded labor was Linda, his wife.

For Cole, astonishingly, had married. Unlike most of his close companions and without, it appears, disturbing his relations with these
companions, he had fallen in love with and courted and won an
American divorcée named Linda Lee Thomas. She was a good many
years older than Cole and, perhaps because of her uncertain health,
looked older than she really was; she was also far richer than he, for
his millions were to sift down to him only after the deaths of his
grandfather and mother. (Cole always doted on the rich, and, everything else being equal, he preferred what he called the "rich-rich"
to the single, unhyphenated, and, in effect, poverty-stricken rich, like
himself.) At one time, Linda had been described as the most beautiful
woman in the world; when Cole met her, in 1918, the superlative,
though reduced in scale, was still impressive: she was spoken of as the
most beautiful woman in Europe. A compendium of the qualities
that Cole then admired most in people, she was well-born, intelligent, and what was then known as sophisticated; she could manage
a large household with her left hand; she gave amusing parties; and
she gossiped amusingly about other people's parties. She was said to
have perfect taste and perfect manners and, knowing everyone that
mattered, she passed her days in the company not only of decorative
idlers but of such ideal companions as Berenson, Lord Carnavon,
Bakst, Churchill, and Shaw. Does all that sound, to our ears, sufficiently impressive? To young Cole, it must have seemed everything.

As an eighteen-year-old belle from Louisville, Kentucky, Linda
had married a "fast" young Yale man of proper lineage named Edward Russell Thomas, destined to enter history as the first husband
of Cole Porter's wife and, still more unluckily, as the first person in
the United States known to have killed somebody with an automobile. Thomas soon proved an indefatigable philanderer; according to

rumor, he was also something of a sadist in the discharge of his conjugal obligations, and it is possible that by the time Linda won a divorce from him, in 1912, she had had enough of the sexual side of marriage. Be that as it may, having accepted a handsome settlement from Thomas, she moved to Paris and became a leader of what, even during the years of the First World War, was a lively international social set. It was in Paris that Cole met her and in 1919, to the surprise of many friends on both sides, they were married. The marriage lasted for thirty-five years, until Linda's death from emphysema, in 1954. She had wished to be buried in Williamstown, where, in a house called Buxton Hill, they had passed happy summer days. Cole chose, instead, to bury her in the family plot in Peru, arranging matters so he could lie in death between Kate and Linda. He was always compulsively neat.

The marriage was not without intermittent warfare and cobbled-up truces. A recurring crisis concerned Hollywood, which Linda (perfect manners . . . perfect taste) disliked and which Cole adored, in part because of its climate and in part because he was genuinely interested in the sharklike ignoramuses and ex-fur salesmen who had swarmed up out of the gutter to assume control of the movie industry. Like any Keys man, he had a certain curiosity about the gutter. When a song he wrote for the movie "Rosalie"—*In the Still of the Night*—made Louis B. Mayer weep, Cole was beside himself with pleasure; he had a high opinion of Mayer's aggressive animality, and to see such a bully in tears! Linda was not impressed by bullies. It was one thing for her to play den mother to Cole's entourage in Venice or Paris or Williamstown or New York, but it was another to play that not always pleasant role in Hollywood. She was a model of the accommodating aristocrat, yet there were limits. An awareness of limits, she might have said, is precisely what distinguishes aristocrats from the lower orders, and it was a bad mark against Cole for him not to have kept this necessary social truth in mind. No doubt Cole had merry days beside the sun-struck swimming pool in Brentwood, but over him and his young friends fell, for her, the shadow of innumerable Mayers and Warners and Harry Cohns. To Linda, they and their imitative myrmidons were so many foul-mouthed, cigar-chomping Genghis Khans, and if it had not been for Cole's accident, in the autumn of 1937, she would almost certainly have left him.

Cole's accident. It is the central episode of his life—not the most important one but the one that everything else stands in relation to. We ask of a Porter song or movie or party or broken friendship or newly decorated apartment whether it was before or after the dreadful October morning at the Piping Rock Club, in Locust Valley (the setting met the usual Porter requirements in respect to social cachet). Cole's old friend, the Duke di Verdura, designer of the celebrated bejeweled cigarette cases that Linda gave Cole to mark the openings of new Porter shows, was a member of the houseparty that had gathered at the Countess di Zoppola's that weekend on Long Island, and he recalls that Cole, with a characteristic impetuous need to *do* something, had worked absurdly hard at organizing a group to go horseback riding. "He hadn't been riding in a long time," the Duke has said. "It was a sudden caprice, but Cole's caprices seemed sometimes to be made of steel." Against the advice of a groom at the stable at Piping Rock, Cole chose for his mount a mettlesome, nervy horse. A few minutes out along the bridle path, the horse shied at some bushes, reared, and fell back upon Cole, who, being out of practice, found himself unable to disengage his feet from the stirrups. As the horse struggled to get up, it fell back upon Cole and crushed one of his legs. Again, the horse sought to rise and again it fell back, this time rolling over and crushing Cole's other leg.

The accident took but a few seconds, and Cole maintained afterwards that he scarcely realized that he had been hurt. A member of the riding party, Benjamin Moore, was the first to reach Cole. Although Cole made light of the accident, Moore saw at once that he was terribly injured, and he galloped off to get help. As Cole later told the story—and he liked a good story—lying there, he took out a pencil and notebook and set to work on the lyrics of a song that became *At Long Last Love*.

In the ambulance that Moore summoned and that carried Cole to a nearby hospital, he went into shock and remained unconscious for two days. The attending doctors were convinced that both legs would have to be amputated. Linda was in Paris (by an ironic chance, she and Cole were not speaking to each other at this desperate moment in their lives) and on being notified of the accident and of the threat of amputation, Linda insisted that no decision be reached until she arrived in New York. She consulted with Kate Porter in Indiana by long-distance telephone and between them they decided that, no matter what the doctors said, Cole's legs must not be amputated. (By a further ironic chance, Linda had been living apart from her first husband when he, too, suffered a grievous accident and was threatened with the loss of a leg. Linda returned to Thomas, forbade the doctors to cut off his leg, and nursed him back to health before leaving him for good, several years later. She must have thought she could do as much for Cole.) In respect to the recommended amputations, Linda and Kate reasoned that Cole would die of despair if with his pride in his body he were to be so conspicuously maimed and humiliated, and perhaps they were right. In any event, they had no way of knowing then that Cole's legs were never to mend; that after some thirty-five operations on both legs, one of them would have to be amputated at last; and that in the twenty-seven years left to Cole from the time of his accident until his death, there would scarcely be a day that he was free of pain.

Cole was forty-six when the accident happened. Given his preternaturally youthful appearance, he seemed a man who was only just beginning to approach his prime. It amounts to a miracle that even following the accident the boyish face did not vanish altogether; there comes to mind a photograph of him being carried into a theater in white tie and tails a couple of years after Piping Rock—a rueful, dapper banty of a man, held high by chauffeur and valet, one foot heavily bandaged, the other in a brace—and to this day there are people who speak with awe of seeing him hobble, with the help of two canes, into a Hollywood nightclub on Sunset strip, his eyes black and enormous with suffering and his mouth grinning with glee—with glee!—in anticipation of an evening's pleasure. He was brave, oh, he was very brave, but as Kate's son and Linda's husband he had little choice: to those unbending nineteenth-century aristocrats, courage was an assumed commonplace. Moreover, they were sure that the important thing was for Cole to go on working hard and playing hard, and he did. By no telling what power of concentration of mind and dismissal of body, he provided the scores for more Broadway musicals and Hollywood movies after the accident than he had done before it; among the musicals were such substantial hits as "Leave It to Me," "Panama Hattie," "Kiss Me, Kate," "Can-Can," and "Silk Stockings." The number of Porter songs to achieve the status of standard continued to mount. Berlin, Rodgers, and he were said to be the three most popular composers in America. Cole's earnings from ASCAP threatened to move him out of the familiar category of rich into what he considered the much more appealing category of rich-rich. In his late years, Cole learned with delight that, according to an ASCAP survey, five of his songs had made a list of the thirty most popular songs of all time. He shook his head over that: not bad for a highbrow.

Which was Cole's way of saying that of course he never *had* been a highbrow. Applied to him, the tag was as unjust as the tag of lowbrow applied to those of Cole's contemporaries who lacking his musical scholarship, seemed to stumble upon their beguiling tunes by serendipity. Cole was delighted to be popular and he was all the more delighted because his popularity was so unexpected: who would have guessed that the style he had spent so long forging and refining—a style idiosyncratic, making no concessions to the then common taste, and often difficult to play and sing correctly—would become, along with Gershwin's, the most readily recognizable voice of the American musical theater in the thirties? Of all decades, the thirties, with its sour aftertaste of the extravagant twenties and its gritty grayness of prolonged, unliftable depression, would seem the least apt to choose the wealthy, playful, and totally apolitical Cole for a spokesman, but so it happened. Porter musical comedies encompass the period with a Porter neatness. Cole wrote the score for the last Broadway musical of the twenties, "Wake Up and Dream," which opened on December 30, 1929, and boasted the hit song, *What Is This Thing Called Love?* He also wrote the score for the last Broadway musical of the thirties, "Du Barry Was a Lady," which opened on December 6, 1939, and offered, among its twenty-odd songs, *Well, Did You Evah!, Friendship, But in the Morning, No,* and *Do I Love You?*

Between those pleasing parentheses, in the sullen year 1932, there arrived "Gay Divorce," with Fred Astaire singing *Night and Day,* and two years later was born the quintessential Porter musical, "Anything Goes"—to the extent that such things can be defined, the quintessential American musical of the period. In the cast were Ethel Merman, William Gaxton, and Victor Moore, and among its hit songs were *I Get a Kick Out of You, All Through the Night, You're the Top,* and *Anything Goes.* A year later came "Jubilee," with *Begin the Beguine, Why Shouldn't I?* and *Just One of Those Things,* and in 1936 there was "Red, Hot and Blue" with *Ours, Down in the Depths (on the Ninetieth Floor),* and *It's De-Lovely.* The list of hits is so long that it threatens to become simply a list and therefore to strike us as less fantastic than it really is. There were to be plenty of other hits in the forties and a few in the fifties as well, but Cole had changed and the country had changed, and with age and sickness it was harder and harder for him to take in what was happening beyond his high fortress at the Waldorf and the little fortress in Williamstown. For the movie, "High Society," besides the title song, he wrote *I Love You, Samantha, You're Sensational, True Love,* and *Who Wants to Be a Millionaire.* Under the circumstances, it was a remarkable score. Because Louis Armstrong was in the cast Cole wrote a song for him called *Now You Has Jazz.* He worked on it like a schoolboy on a term paper, diligently but without confidence; he was no longer sure what such a song should be, and, as always, he dreaded being seen to have failed. The year was 1956, but to Cole it felt like the year 2000.

True, Cole had stayed younger longer than most, but now he was growing older earlier than most. He was often petulant and forgetful and lonesome, and there were times when he was irrational, as when he claimed in unbecoming panic to be going broke. Nevertheless, there were good days, or, rather, good hours, or hours that managed to be simultaneously good and bad. An old Yale classmate, the historian Arnold Whitridge, would come to dinner at the Waldorf with his wife Janetta (it was Cole who had introduced the Whitridges to each other in those long-past Paris days), and in an attempt to cheer Cole up Whitridge would sing from memory, stanza after stanza, some Porter song from an undergraduate smoker of forty-odd years before. And Cole would smile and say, in the saddest voice, "Did I write that? Is that really mine?"

End with the last song Cole ever wrote. It was for a television musical entitled "Aladdin," broadcast in 1958 and roundly deplored by the critics. The song was supposed to be sung by the Emperor of China, and Cole called it *Wouldn't It Be Fun!* It is an amusing song to us, as it must have been to Cole, because it stands everything he believed in right on its head. Never can Cole have uttered so succinctly and merrily a credo the direct opposite of his own. The song outrageously asks

> Wouldn't it be fun not to be famous
> Wouldn't it be fun not to be rich!
> Wouldn't it be pleasant
> To be a simple peasant
> And spend a happy day digging a ditch!
> Wouldn't it be fun not to be known as an important VIP,
> Wouldn't it be fun to be nearly anyone
> Except me, mighty me!

The song is like a casual, mocking wave of the hand, where a proper farewell would have proved unbearable, both to him and to us. "Mighty me!" The voice is that of the elfin boy in the straw hat and starched blouse, Kate's son, Linda's husband, lover and friend of many; the face and the voice and the songs are one and they will never grow old, never die.

❖ ❖ ❖ ❖ ❖

GEORGE PALMER PUTNAM

(b. 1887–d. 1950) was a New York publisher and the husband of

AMELIA EARHART

(b. 1898–d. 1937), the first woman to fly across the Atlantic, across
the Pacific, and across most of the world. Earhart was also the first
woman to teach aeronautics, thanks to an invitation from President Elliott of Purdue. In the following biographical sketch Amelia
Earhart is referred to affectionately as "AE."

Amelia Earhart at Purdue

Although AE could never become quite reconciled to her high-
sounding title—Counselor in Careers for Women—I think that even
in the fortuitously shortened period in it, she found her job at Purdue
University one of the most satisfying adventures of her life. It came
about as so many things—apparently quite by chance; yet somehow
it seemed almost foreordained, so surely did it fit into the pattern of
her unfolding interests.

In 1934 she was a speaker at the annual "Women and the Changing World" Conference of the New York *Herald Tribune*. She felt
that in itself the Conference was one of the ablest of the many
brilliant contributions to their times of Mrs. Ogden Reid and Mrs.
William Brown Meloney, and she was particularly happy to be invited as a speaker.

"I present to you evidence against a 'lost generation,' " Mrs. Meloney said, introducing her, "for I remind you that no generation
which could produce Amelia Earhart can be called a lost generation.
She has set a pace for those of her age and her time. She has never
been content to rest on her laurels. She has worked, and is working,
and will continue to work hard to further the science to which she
has dedicated her life."

And AE began by saying that, although she had been instructed to
address her brief talk to youth, it was with trepidation that she did
so, because it occurred to her that "the ancients, such as I am, should
be listening to young ideas rather than pointing up opportunities in
a world which has the elders decidedly on the run!"

I wonder if that was not the point at which Dr. Edward C. Elliott, President of Purdue University, who was in the audience, got the idea which crystallized not long after into AE's association with his institution.

At any rate, Dr. Elliott later dined with us at the Coffee House Club in New York. He is a lean, powerful man who combines the brisk attributes of a dynamo with the important qualities of scholarship and human vision. He has a habit of referring to himself, with humorous deprecation, as just a Hoosier schoolmaster, but no gentleman from Indiana ever knew his way about more competently than he.

That evening we three had to ourselves what I imagine is the most civilized and homely clubroom in America. We sat at a little table in that second floor front room with its books and paintings, the grand piano and diminutive stage where some of the most lively didos of theatrical tomfoolery in our time have been presented—the Fish drawings, the cartoons and photographs of Frank Crowninshield, Bob Bridges, Charlie Towne, George Chappell, and the others, the Benda masks, and all the rest of it. With the ubiquitous Williams, steward extraordinary, in attendance, the setting was superlatively pleasant for the launching of any project.

After dinner we sat on the couch beneath the Maxfield Parrish bulletin board, AE with her feet tucked up under her like a little girl. Elliott, from a chair facing us, came to the point.

"We want you at Purdue," he said, smiling wisely at AE.

If she was surprised, she didn't show it. "I'd like that," she said as simply and as directly, "if it can be arranged. What would you think I should do?"

He told her about Purdue's enrollment of some six thousand students. "About eight hundred of them are girls. And we've a feeling the girls aren't keeping abreast of the inspirational opportunities of the day nearly as well as might be."

AE's eyes shone, as they always did at the suggestion of a challenge. Not in the excited way of an anticipation that burns itself out of its own fire before it can produce anything lasting, but with a certain steady glow.

"I think you could supply some spark which would help to take up the lag between the swift eddying of the world around modern women and the tardier echoes of the schoolroom."

For two hours we turned the whole idea over between us. And when Elliott set off at his characteristic pace to get a midnight train from Grand Central, headed for a morning conference in some distant state, the plan, as it later went into effect, was pretty well jelled. AE was to put in at Purdue as much time as she could—it would be in the neighborhood of a month out of the college year. She would have pretty much of a free hand in "ventilating" her philosophy of things as they are to the girls, for Elliott said he had come to have a great trust in her ways of thinking. And she would also be Adviser in Aeronautics, for the University was then the only one in the United States with its own fully equipped airport providing for day and night flying.

On June 2, 1935, President Elliott announced the appointment, saying, "Miss Earhart represents better than any other young woman of this generation the spirit and the courageous skill of what may be called the new pioneering. At no point in our educational system is there greater need for pioneering and constructive planning than in education for women. The University believes Amelia Earhart will help us to see and to attack successfully many unsolved problems."

And so, in November, AE became a visiting faculty member at Purdue. I find a little word-picture of the new "professor" as others saw her, apparently by a student, one Miriam Beck. "Tall, skinny, handsome, tousle-headed, smiling; the students were transported with delight, and even the most skeptical of older residents charmed."

It was about a year and a half later that she purchased the "flying laboratory," the ten-passenger Lockheed Electra transport, out of the resources of the Amelia Earhart Fund for Aeronautical Research. This fund was set up by the Purdue Research Foundation for the purchase, outfitting and maintenance of the ship as a laboratory in which she was to have a free hand working out continuous problems arising from her own experience in aviation.

She went to Purdue armed with the conviction that educators often should shift over to more practical points of view in their instruction. "Too much emphasis, it seems to me, has been placed on learning a skill without finding out whether the student has a natural bent or talent for that particular work, or whether the working world needs that person when he or she is trained.

"We have watched the colleges produce countless graduates who could only demand jobs for which, notwithstanding the adequacy of their formal education, they might be totally unprepared or unfitted, and in which they were often even just plain not interested. It's a fundamental problem, and I can imagine that reform may involve the entire reconstruction of our educational system. Because Johnnie liked to play with tin soldiers, his mother has jumped to the conclusion, since the Year One, that he wanted to be a soldier! So she packed him off to military school—which he hated—though maybe she never found it out—all because what really interested him about tin soldiers was that they were made of lead, and lead is metal, and you heat metal and melt it and make it into lots of things—steel for skyscrapers, decorative ironwork, leading for stained glass windows. . . .

"Anyhow, the reason I've come to Purdue, at Dr. Elliott's most satisfying suggestion, is because Purdue seems to me to be headed so much in the right direction. If I must relate it to my own personal interests, the mere fact of the University's own airport, with equipment not to be found even at many well-appointed commercial airports, would be all I needed to know as an index of the Purdue vision about education. . . ."

Glad as AE was to be at the University—"it is my kind of school, a technical school where all instruction has practicality, and where a progressive program for women is being started too—" she shrank from being thought a vocational guide, because in the six or seven weeks of the academic year she could be there, she couldn't possibly do a well-rounded job of vocational guidance. "I just have a philosophic interest in the various aspects of careers."

Of course I suppose it was natural that the largest part of her delight was in the University airport. She felt the University had so wisely chosen a middle course between forbidding and ignoring student interest in and aspiration to flying by setting up a comprehensive machinery of supervised flying "where students who want to learn how to fly can do so at reasonable rates." The whole matter of flying-lesson expense worried her. Whereas most girls were not able to earn as much money as boys—no one wanted feminine grease monkeys around hangars to do the odd jobs which often pay a good part of a young man's rudimentary training—they had to pay the same price as the boys for their lessons.

Then, of course, she found it exciting that laboratory tests made in the aeronautics department could be immediately put into practice at the field which, by the way, is also an emergency landing field, maintained by the government. "You see my interest in aviation goes into every part of the industry. It isn't flying alone. To be interested exclusively in pilots would be like being interested solely in the engineer in the railroad industry. It takes from forty to a hundred men on the ground to keep one plane in the air. That is from forty to a hundred jobs per plane—and I don't think all those jobs need forever be held by men!"

"I feel that education has been failing to discover individual aptitude soon enough," she explained in talks with faculty members. "I hope the time will come soon when psychologists and psychology will be able to determine a child's bent at preschool age. Then the child won't waste so much time studying and working in the wrong direction.

"I don't mean that people should study only the subjects related to their future business interests—even if those interests could be accurately determined far in advance. Such a procedure would be hopelessly narrowing. Besides, very often the individual's cultural development makes him content and successful in a field he stumbles on largely by accident.

"But the waste effort when a student just muddles along in college 'learning to be a lawyer'—when that student has, really, an engineering mind! If he keeps up his grades no one bothers about his fitness —and I believe many a student has kept up such grades as a matter of personal pride even knowing that the field of concentration, per se, was the last thing he was really vitally interested in! Or maybe it was parental preference that kept the student in line. 'My father always wanted me to be a doctor—so—I'm going to be a doctor.' I think that is educational tragedy!"

From the questionnaires, she found that 92 percent of the women students who answered wanted to go into gainful occupations. . . .

Possessing the capacity to have a terribly good time, turned loose among elements she liked, she had a good time in her office, of course, keeping her appointments with girls who wanted to talk about work they could get zest out of doing. But I think sometimes she had even more fun at meals, with a different group of girls sitting at her table each time. She had a room in one of the dorms too, and was right among girls "where they lived," in more senses than one.

I have heard it said that no one could quite make out how she was able to fit so well into the mysteriously rigid life of a dormitory, but she seemed to enjoy every minute. Sometimes she absent-mindedly broke the rules. She came to dinner once in her flying clothes, and the freshmen waited ecstatically to see if she wouldn't be sent back to get properly dressed for dinner. Very early in the proceedings she asked if she could have buttermilk—whereupon calls from the student body for buttermilk increased forty-fold overnight.

Conceiving her job as being an exploration of vocational needs, the discovery of new fields which girls could go into and help develop, she couldn't, as has been said, set herself up as a vocational guide. She couldn't even consult individually with all of the eight hundred girl students, and she didn't try. She met various student groups and spoke to the senior, junior, and sophomore women on vocational opportunities, besides addressing the University convocation and various other campus gatherings.

She sent out a questionnaire to students to explore their after-college plans because she thought finding out about this would help the college authorities to reconstruct courses so they would be more useful. She thought too that such exploration might help the students themselves to clarify their own thinking, to agree with themselves on a general objective, perhaps even a specific one.

... I have no doubt that the idea of a Purdue "flying laboratory" for AE if, as, and when, took rough shape in Dr. Elliott's mind as he listened to what she said about youth and aviation at the Tribune Conference—though I doubt he was aware of it at the time.

"It is true," she said, "that there are no more geographical frontiers to push back—no new lands flowing with milk and honey this side of the moon to promise surcease from man-made ills. But there are economic, political, scientific and artistic frontiers of the most exciting sort awaiting faith and the spirit of adventure to discover them.

"Probably no field presents greater lure for young people—explorers—than aviation. It has the color and movement of flying to kindle the imagination, and its growing importance as an industry is tempting to those who plan serious careers in transportation, for aviation is simply the newest form of transportation—the climax of the pageant of human progress from oxcart to airplane."

Then launching into an analysis of what aviation offers youth, and of its quirks she cautioned:

"Though I list a few of the transportation problems to be solved, I cannot promise that ability, the desire to work, or experience, or any other attribute will guarantee the privilege of solving them and earning a living thereby. The economic structure we have built up is all too often a barrier between the world's work and the workers. If the younger generation finds the hurdle too absurdly high, I hope it will not hesitate to tear it down and substitute a social order in which the desire to work and earn carries with it the opportunity to do so."

Although when she took off on the Round-the-World flight it was too early to judge the results of her work, I cherish some of the student reactions to her, for they seem to me to indicate a certain measure of the effectiveness she hoped she would have on the campus.

There was Marguerite Coll, enrolled in electrical engineering. She and two girls taking chemical engineering talked to AE.

"She explained to us very clearly," Miss Coll said, "what some of the obstacles are in the way of women who want to go into what's always been known as a man's field. She was encouraging though. She didn't see why, if a woman had special talents along that line, she couldn't go out and show 'em! She realized that there was radio work, for instance, that didn't require hard, manual labor and that a girl could do quite as well as a man. And she told us a lot about opportunities in television and in radio operation."

It was Marian Frazier who drew a picture of AE as I like to think of her in her university tour of duty.

"One night I was sitting in my room studying, and Miss Earhart stuck her head in the door and asked if she could borrow my pen," Miss Frazier said. "She said, 'I'll bring it back in just a sec',' just like any girl would do. I guess I couldn't keep it to myself because, when she did bring it back, there was a bunch of girls in my room—just to get another look at her. But really, you know, I don't think she gets enough sleep. She's terribly busy. I often hear her typewriter clear up to midnight."

When it came to AE's own academic explorations with the Lockheed Electra which the Research Foundation made possible for her but insisted should stand in her name, she summed it all up as "Finding out the effects of flying on people."

She thought that in aviation's rapid advance too much attention had been concentrated on mechanical matters and too little paid to the human elements of flying. She was tremendously interested in technical progress, but she was even more interested in determining the effects of speed, altitude, air pressure, fatigue, and diet on human beings who flew. She was anxious too to conduct some experiments in the relation of alcohol to the demands made on a pilot.

Contrary to a blast directed at her by one writer for setting herself up as an explorer into medical and psychological facts of the human element in flying, she had had some medical training, much more than he knew, because she absorbed knowledge quickly. Having been interested almost since childhood in chemistry and physics, she was no stranger in the realms in which she wanted to experiment.

Her abilities so impressed those who helped set up the machinery for her to use that they concluded, "We who have observed the effects of Miss Earhart's words and work realize what she is accomplishing for the fundamental promotion of sound aeronautics. Even aside from her pioneering feats, which seem to us to be the most potent single influence today in encouraging American air travel, certainly she is pre-eminent in breaking down sales resistance to aviation. It can't be broken down just by words. The words have got to be backed by knowledge which people are convinced has been secured in a trustworthy way. Our opportunity to co-operate with her is a happy one for us."

There seems to have been a single dissenting voice in all this. I did hear of one professor—a Donald Meek-ish kind of man, I imagine— who found himself disturbed by AE's activities.

"I'm afraid," he said plaintively, "that if she keeps on, the coeds won't be willing to get married and lead the quiet life for which Nature intended them."

I wonder.

❖ ❖ ❖ ❖ ❖

EDWIN WAY TEALE

(b. 1899–), although a native of Illinois, was descended from a long line of Indiana farmers. He spent his boyhood summers on his grandfather's farm in northern Indiana near Lake Michigan, and learned to love its sandy shores along with their flora and fauna. A dedicated naturalist, he worked during the 1930s as the naturalist editor for *Popular Science* before turning to free-lance writing and teaching. His best known books include *Dune Boy: Early Years of a Naturalist* (1943), *The Wilderness World of John Muir* (1954), and *Journey Into Summer* (1960).

The Far Dunes

Across the soot-stained and mossy roof of a low farmhouse, a narrow streak angled upward like the thin trail of a garden slug. It started at the lower edge of the kitchen roof, where a melon-crate leaned against the side of the house, and extended to the ridgepole of the dwelling. The trail was the product of innumerable scuffings and clingings. At its far upper end, a small boy, bareheaded and clad in blue overalls, hugged the peak of the farmhouse and gazed into the north.

The sun pressed its heat on his back; poured its heat on the ancient shingles around him. The smell of a pitchy hemlock tree was strong in the air. Mud-dauber wasps droned past on blurring wings, going and coming in their labors beneath the eaves. The countryside lay still in the heat of the midsummer morning.

A mile and a half away, across woods and swamps, the boy could see hills of gold shining in the sun. They were the crests of the great Indiana dunes which lifted their mountains of wind-blown sand above the level of the Lake Michigan shore. High above him, sliding along the blue of the sky, a bald eagle soared in their direction. The boy, squinting upward, followed its flight. Lower down, and passing directly over the white-and-green farmhouse, a gray sandhill crane flapped by, riding on six-foot wings and trailing its awkward legs, rudder-like, behind it.

The boy lay still in the sunshine. With his head on his hands, he watched the two great birds shrink in size. In his mind, he began to picture how the farm and the marsh and the distant dunes must appear to the eagle and the crane. His eyes again sought the far dunes. They rose like a shining, mysterious land of gold beyond the tree-tops. Hardly more than fifty miles from America's second-largest city, that stretch of lonely sandhills was a fragment of untamed wilderness. The boy had heard that wolves still howled among the snow-clad dunes on winter nights.

It was only in later years that he learned the history of this world beyond the treetops: how in a distant past bluffs had eroded into the waves on the western shore of Lake Michigan; how currents set up by the prevailing winds had carried the quartz grains to the southeastern tip of the lake where wind and wave and ice had forced them out onto the shore to create the almost fluid hills of the dune country. There, they formed a strange, tormented battleground where the wind and the root were ever at war—the wind striving to move the sand along, the vegetation seeking to anchor it down. Sometimes the wind won and, year after year, a sand-mountain moved ponderously forward, engulfing, like a glacier of quartz, the plants, the bushes, and even the trees which lay in the path of its advance. Again, this tug-o'-war ended in triumph for the root and a wandering dune became stationary, carpeted with green.

If the boy had viewed these sandhills from the altitude of the eagle, they would have had the appearance of a curving chain of green and golden beads. If he had seen them from the winding sand-road which skirted the bordering swamp, instead of from his more distant roof-top, the great hills would have resembled stooping giants, facing toward the east. Shaped by the prevailing wind from the northwest, their longer slopes were toward the west, their more abrupt descents toward the east. The dunes themselves, as well as the great blowouts and the small ribbed patterns on the beach sand, were autographs of the wind. But, to the boy, clinging to the rooftop in the hot sunshine, it was not the history of these sandhills which attracted him. It was the mystery of the far-away and the wildness of the dunes which stirred his imagination.

It was thus, as the boy in the blue overalls, that I spent many hours during the long summer days of my earliest boyhood.

Always, just west of my rooftop perch, I could see the bulk of an immense white oak. It towered a hundred feet into the air. Standing by itself, it gave my grandfather's farm its name: Lone Oak. I used to look up and up along the sheer rise of its great bole. The oak seemed propped against the sky. On days when the upper branches stood out against a background of drifting clouds, the old tree sometimes appeared to be moving, swinging in an arc toward me. I remember that once the impression became so overpowering that I scrambled away in a panic down the roof-slope.

The old farmhouse at Lone Oak stood at almost the exact physical center of the ninety-odd acres of marsh and woods and sandy soil which comprised my grandfather's farm. From my lookout I could see this farm spread out around me: the apple orchards; the rye fields; the asparagus patch; the red barn and the granary and the outbuildings; the straggling sand-road which appeared over a hill to the west, ran past the front gate of Lone Oak, and disappeared amid woods to the east; the swampy south pasture with its crisscrossing trails and its small elevated tract we called the Island; and, below the Island, the tracks of the Père Marquette Railroad, running east and west and forming the southern boundary of the farm. Beyond, away to the south—across a wide valley of low-lying farms and marshland—the blue hills of the Valparaiso moraine rose against the lighter blue of the summer sky.

Inch by inch, I knew our farm. I knew its chip-laden woodyard where I collected kindling and gathered stove-wood for the kitchen range. I knew its vast mow where I jumped from beams into the hay, sending up multitudes of glinting motes of dust. I knew its ditches, their sides filled with the massed green of juicy spearmint. I knew its spring where horses drank from a mossy trough formed of a hollowed-out poplar log. I knew its north woods, a mysterious realm of little trails and piles of yellow sand dug from burrows, and its even more mysterious marshlands, with their stagnant waters, their tangled vegetation, and their strange inhabitants.

Compared with the black loam of the riverbottom or the productive acres of the prairie, Lone Oak Farm probably was an unpromising tract. But to a boy, alive to the natural harvest of birds and animals and insects, it offered boundless returns.

Life, during these early years, was divided into a kind of mental Arctic night and day. During winter months, I lived in a city, went to school, moved in a crepuscular and foreign realm. Summers, and at Christmas, Thanksgiving and Easter vacations, I covered the seventy miles which separated Joliet, Illinois, from this dune-country farm of my grandparents.

That seventy miles seemed to carry me to the other side of the world.

At Lone Oak there was room to explore and time for adventure. A new world opened up around me. During my formative years, from earliest childhood to the age of fifteen, I spent my most memorable months here, on the borderland of the dunes.

ROSS LOCKRIDGE

(b. Bloomington, 1914 – d. Bloomington, 1948) took his own life at the age of 34 in the same year that his enormously successful novel, *Raintree County*, was published.

JOHN LEGGETT

(b. 1917–), a former editor at Houghton Mifflin Company, publishers of *Raintree County*, is author of *Ross and Tom* (1974), which explores the reasons for the tragedy.

Ross

. . . I brought this melancholy curiosity about Ross Lockridge back to my office one afternoon and fetched his publicity folder out of my file. On top, an editorial from the *Washington Post* puzzled over the irony of Lockridge's suicide, noting that although *Raintree County* had set off a moral controversy and some critics had scored its length and diffuseness, critics had been almost unanimous in their praise of the book's passionate, lyric vision of America. It was as important a debut as any in recent years and it had made Lockridge rich and famous. What more could he ask?

The *Post*'s editorial pointed out that a major theme of the book was its repudiation of materialism and affirmation of faith in the American dream and destiny. How, the *Post*'s editorialist asked, had Lockridge himself lost that hope and optimism?

I unfolded the *Raintree County* reviews. They were of a prominence and profusion that is no longer seen. Although it was a first novel by an unknown author the critical community had joined to celebrate the book's publication. With the *Life* excerpts, the huge MGM prize and the Book-of-the-Month selection it had become an institution even before publication day, shimmering on high ground beyond the reach of detractors.

James Hilton had opened his review on the cover of the *New York Herald Tribune* book section by suggesting that *Raintree County's* impact on America would be similar to that of Sinclair Lewis's *Main Street*, since both books had appeared at the close of a great war to offer America a self-portrait, towering in victory and prosperity over a shattered world.

The Sunday *New York Times* added its laurel wreath, describing *Raintree County* as a work of art, enormously complex and with a cosmic, brooding purpose. Even the skeptical critics agreed that Lockridge had fashioned a triumphant hero: John Wesley Shawnessy was outsize, yet touchingly human.

I could recall that in 1948, the year *Raintree County* was published, I had carried it along on my honeymoon, and that Shawnessy had won me very early in the book with his feelings toward women. He was desirous, yet sensibly shy of the creatures. He carried such a burden of conscience about them that his reason was sometimes impaired. He could not believe so attactive a girl as Nell Gaither loved him.

The character Shawnessy is a dreamer rather than a doer. He leaves the making of fortunes and careers to others and yet he is driven by ambition. As teacher and poet he must influence everybody, and this scorning of the game and still wanting to prevail was, I found, just as sympathetic a conflict as his sexual one.

Shawnessy's wish and rationale about fame are openly borrowed from Hawthorne's tale *The Great Stone Face*, which tells of a small boy named Ernest who lives in a valley dominated by a cliff shaped like a human face. The legend is that a child from this valley will become the greatest and noblest person of his time, and in manhood his face will resemble that of the Great Stone Face.

Throughout Ernest's lifetime, men leave the valley to become successful and return, hoping to find they have fulfilled the prophecy. The rich merchant, the illustrious commander, the eminent statesman are all disappointed—and so is Ernest, until a poet, seeing the sunset shining on his face, cries, "Behold! Behold! Ernest is himself the likeness of The Great Stone Face!"

The boyish Johnny Shawnessy calls it the most wonderful story ever told and only the modesty of the maturing one keeps him from announcing his candidacy for the Ernest role.

So far Shawnessy is an exceptional fellow, but flesh. However, there is more. His young manhood unfolds to reveal parallels with the young nation as it plunges toward Civil War, is shattered by it and survives in a new, more cynical consciousness. Clearly Shawnessy has become the Republic itself in eruption and change.

Nor is that all of him. In his mystical, philosophical quest for life's meaning, continually seeking his lost Eden and in the end finding it, he is apparently Mankind.

As if this were not enough grand design, Lockridge tells Shawnessy's story by a clock similar to the one Joyce used for *Ulysses.* It starts at dawn on July 4, 1892, when Shawnessy is fifty-three, and moves through the hours and celebrations of that Independence Day, then spins back erratically into Shawnessy's past, assembling it like a vast jigsaw puzzle, the climactic pieces withheld until last.

In reading the book I had been wholly caught up in the story of Shawnessy the exuberant boy, recognizing the honesty of the portrait and the skill with which Lockridge had built his Raintree County, a patch of Indiana so vivid it had to be authentic and yet so bustling with sharp-eyed, sharp-tongued boys and provocative girls it was far more desirable than any Eden I had imagined.

But then I lost Shawnessy in transition, in those toils of conscience which deliver him from Nell Gaither, his river nymph and true love, into that sinister marriage with Susanna Drake and the South. It is the moment when Shawnessy becomes more man than boy, and more symbol than individual.

His New Orleans honeymoon, his loss of wife and child, his campaigning with the Union Army—Chickamauga, Chattanooga, the capture of Atlanta and the March to the Sea—his postwar wanderings and his baffling relationship with the actress Laura Golden made a vast, impressive structure into which the real Shawnessy had disappeared. I laid the creeping indifference I felt to shortcomings of my own.

Shawnessy's return, in maturity, to Raintree County restored him to life. There were three women: a good, if intimidated wife, an attractive feminist, and an enchanting daughter. Even better, there was the devilish Prof. Jerusalem Webster Stiles, the other side of the Shawnessy coin and the perfect Shawnessy foil. In the Socratic dialogues between the two, Lockridge was wrapping up his story and, he hoped, the human experience.

Turning the last of the 1066 pages I was staggered at what Lockridge had set out to do. Far from home, groping toward a first novel of my own, I could scarcely believe it. He was my own age. Where did he get the brass and courage, to say nothing of the knowledge, for so heroic an undertaking?

Now, a few years later, I had joined Lockridge's publisher and I still knew little about him. The Book-of-the-Month Club bulletin which announced *Raintree County* told club members he was a native of Bloomington, Indiana, the seat of Indiana University, and was the son of an authority on local history. He had been outstanding as both scholar and athlete and he had married his high school sweetheart. This was Vernice Baker, a girl described as "lovely, rather than pretty, with very fair hair, very fair skin and a completely tranquil disposition." She had typed the final manuscript and at the same time kept peace among their four small children.

At Houghton, the people who had known Lockridge best recalled his exuberance. He was of medium size, with curly, dark-brown hair and a striking handsomeness, but the unusual thing about him was his energy. It glowed and crackled. It was very much a part of his attractiveness and, at the same time, was wearying. They found it exhausting to be with him for more than a few minutes.

He had an accountant's eye for the small change, even after his book had made him rich. And yet he was still naïve. Although he had spent a year in Paris as a student, done graduate work at Harvard and lived in Boston for several years, he gave the impression of someone fresh from Indiana.

Although he had often talked of doing so, Ross had never brought his wife to meet his friends at Houghton Mifflin. Not one had ever met her and after Ross's death Vernice was notably cool to them, letting the firm know she felt it had, in its own interest, brought pressures to bear on Ross and these had contributed to his suicide.

During the next fifteen years, in which I published some novels of my own and moved to New York to work at Harper's, I asked anyone who might know for news of the Lockridge family and learned that Vernice continued her strong, custodial feelings about her husband. Obviously a private sort of person, she was bringing up her children with great care and an awareness of their father's accomplishment. The two older boys were taking on the Lockridge pattern of academic brilliance and an interest in writing.

When I met Vernice it was January 1967. We had agreed to meet for dinner at the Student Union on the Indiana University campus. Her children were grown now, all away and busy with writing and teaching careers of their own. She had married again, but only recently. Her husband was Russell Noyes, a professor of English at Indiana under whom Ross had studied.

Cautiously, with an emotion clearly painful, Vernice told me that her first glimpse of Ross had been at a meeting of the Epworth League, the youth organization of the Methodist Church. Most of the sanctioned fraternizing between Bloomington's boys and girls took place at these sessions and although there was some praying they were not at all grave.

She had known his name from headlines in their high school paper, *The Optimist*: "Ross Lockridge Heads Honor Roll," "Ross Lockridge Elected Class President," always telling about some new honor for him. So she was surprised to find him this slight, dark-haired boy with blue-gray eyes that shone in joy.

After one Epworth meeting, at which Ross, as secretary, wrote hilarious minutes, he asked her to come along on a search for a forest fire reported in Brown County. Malcolm Correll, his closest friend, drove and joined with Ross in telling stores about "F'" Sharp, their violin teacher, one picking up the narrative as the other choked on his laughter.

They did not find the fire but Vernice was not disappointed, for on the way home Ross sat beside her in the back seat and recited the whole of "The Raven."

This was not much to go on but it was enough for Vernice, though only a junior, to come to Ross's graduation exercises. He was valedictorian and had barely begun the address when a freight train was heard approaching. It was an infinite one. Car after car thumped across the tracks just outside the gymnasium, drowning him out, but Ross did not even consider surrender. He continued to speak, smiling and gesturing as though he could be heard perfectly, right into the teeth of the thunderstorm which broke the moment the train had passed. Seeing him under attack from both the Monon Railroad and the heavens themselves, Vernice decided he was dauntless.

Ross was the youngest, by a decade, of a family fervently loyal to Indiana University. His father, mother, brother and sister were graduates. It was as natural as breathing that he should follow them, but in entering college, Ross was lost to Vernice. He was immediately caught up in campus life, on the run from fraternity to class to field house to armory. He seemed to belong to everything, and Vernice realized he was moving in many directions, all away from the path of their adolescence and surely into the path of other girls. She felt that Ross, with his good looks, would have his pick of them.

The following year she entered the university herself but beaus and dates were not on her program. She had to have a job to pay her thirty-five-dollar-a-term tuition and rarely had enough on hand for more than a five-dollar installment to the bursar. There was little play and no luxury in her life.

While Vernice lacked the leisure and clothes other coeds enjoyed, she made good friends among them and was habitually optimistic. Even though she did not see him, she still thought about Ross—the exuberance in his voice, the way he carried his head slightly forward, as though he were really going places, the shy modesty which never quite contained the belief he could do anything.

She was sure that college would bring them together again, but then in the spring of her freshman year she learned that Ross had won a scholarship and was going away to the Sorbonne in France.

In the midst of her despair, a friend urged her to come along to an Epworth meeting, one which was to plan the Rivervale Retreat. This was a week-long holiday at the church camp, famous for its romantic possibilities, and one of the vacation joys she felt denied. She weighed the idea of begging off, but then agreed to go.

Ross was at the meeting and when she congratulated him on his French year, he sat beside her. When she told him she could not go to Rivervale because of her job, he suggested she come for the weekend. She agreed.

That weekend she discovered that during the week Ross had taken an interest in Mary Eloise Humphrey, a girl from Bloomfield whose lustrous red hair swung in long braids down her back by day, and by night made a coronet for her handsome head.

Later, Ross had his own turn with jealousy over the track team's star half-miler, Charlie Hornbostel, but he continued to ask Vernice for dates and he found that the more they were together the more he disliked being apart.

By summer's end he had fallen in love with her with all the seriousness of a first time and of a boy who always had been shy of girls. Still, his seriousness did not outweigh the uncertainty and adventure of the year ahead, not enough for a promise—and none was made, except that they would write each other often. . . .

[Write they did, and after Ross returned to Bloomington from his junior year abroad, at the Sorbonne, they reached an understanding that led to marriage and, eventually, four children. While teaching at Simmons College, Ross completed his long novel, *Raintree County*, but with a drain on his health, a condition aggravated by quarrels with his publishers. In Bloomington, on March 6, 1948, when he was only 34, he committed suicide.—A.L.]

There is no longer need to bury Ross properly, only to clear away the mystery he left us—that astonishing, still tantalizing gesture of rejecting what he had sought so single-mindedly.

It is hard to dismiss the notion of the bitch-goddess success, shaped like a Circe, who with her potions of money, flattery and celebrity transforms the private poet into a pig for the public roast.

But success was not thrust upon Ross. He sought it. It was young Lockridge, dreaming of *Life*'s pages, Book-of-the-Month Club announcements and Hollywood, who rounded up Houghton's startled flock and sent it flying along the promotion trail. And in any case, I am convinced that success was not in itself a spoiling force for him but rather the warm, propagating culture for a vulnerableness he might otherwise have carried safely.

There were so many optional situations in Ross's life that there is an illusion of accidental pattern to it. *If only* he had left the promotion of *Raintree County* to his publisher and gone on to another book. *If only* he had not been offered that monstrous prize, or had refused it. *If only* Elsie[1] had been less sure of the human spirit's capacity for miracles. *If only* Frank Lockridge[2] had heeded his doctor friend's warning, placed less stock in the soundness of Ross's mind and exercise as its restorative. *If only* Vernice had been spared that searing experience with her sister Imogen. *If only* all the family had been less alive to appearances and faced up to his real illness. *If only* Ross had finished his course in electroshock therapy.

And underlying all this seeming bad luck, *if only* the rise of *Raintree County* had been less spectacular. *If only* his progress as a writer had been more gradual. There is a temptation to put it, *if only* it hadn't been America where overnight success is both a legend and

1. Elsie—Ross's mother.
2. Frank—Ross's father.

a major industry. One of the arresting features of Ross's story is its Americanness—the native dream of conquest and triumphant home-coming, turned nightmare.

Of course there was nothing accidental about Ross's life. It is true tragedy, the end inevitable, carefully prepared in the beginnings—in Elsie's will to fulfill her father's dream of literary accomplishment, then in the promise and death of her first son, then in vague disap-pointments by her husband, a second son and daughter, and, finally, in Ross's acceptance of her challenge.

As a child, Ross's acceptance was mere wish, a stage for his fanta-sies, but as he matured and saw the shape his energies might take, the will to write a book for his mother became more elaborate and more focused. The force grew. He had no doubt about what force it was. He even wrote about it in his first bid for publication. Without any attempt at disguise, he built *The Dream of the Flesh of Iron* around the protean family triangle and the energy generated by its perpetual conflict—the fair, love-bestowing woman being tyran-nized by the old, powerful man while she is adored by the young narrator.

Ross made his purpose as explicit in *Raintree County*. He put himself into the composite character of his mother's true love, her own father. "It's your book, Mother," he told her when she came up to Manistee to read it. "You'll notice I haven't dedicated it to you—it's written *for* you." Elsie Lockridge's challenge to Ross had become the necessary will, with all the emotion and energy he would need to fire it.

A book is often revealing of the caves of its author's soul. It blows up out of primary tensions, out of anxiousness rooted in childhood, out of his original need for love.

Nearly always, good writing is an act of love—a plea, an offer, a demand for love, but somewhere along the line the author must acknowledge that he is in fact making art, not love. This is a disengag-ing, a maturing, a tempering act and in essence it is the discovery that he must write only to please himself, that a genuine egoism is a writer's only defense against the enemies of indifference, dispar-agement, flattery, that are surely awaiting him. This was a discovery Ross had yet to make.

When he said, "Mother, sometimes it seems to me as if I wrote my book in a vacuum—that nobody would ever read it but us," he had been seized by a foreboding that his innocent wish for attention had released a torrent of it. He could hear it, tumbling their way, and was frightened. But he certainly had not intended *Raintree County* as a private affair between them. The good opinion of others, *fame*, was the essence of *The Great Stone Face* and, at least in Ross's mind, of the American dream itself.

Success was an essential part of the gift he had intended but he had not anticipated this would attract moral and literary criticism and show up such flaws in his gift for his mother.

But *Raintree County*'s success plunged on. It was even accelerated by the controversies. It fulfilled to the letter Ross's reveries. He had rebelled, left his father's workshop to set up one of his own, and there he had fashioned a gift so wealth-and-fame-producing, so much more glorious than anything his father had ever done, and all of it such a public spectacle that there was no denying it. To his own astonished eyes, Ross had demolished his father.

Nor was that all. In toppling him he had broken the relationship, snapped the circuit of love and jealousy which joined his mother, his father and himself. Finally, it was his own disaster, for that triangle was the source of his creative stream.

While Ross's patricidal act was a symbolic one and all three could, in their affection for each other, cover it over with gestures of congratulation and assurance, the damage was real. For Ross the result was guilt—lonely, paralyzing and, in the end, unendurable.

WILBUR SHAW

(b. Shelbyville, 1902–d. 1954) was educated in the Greensburg public schools and at Arsenal Technical High School (alma mater, also, of the celebrated playwright Joseph Hayes). A race driver since 1923, Shaw had won the "Indy 500" races in 1937, 1939, and 1940. From 1945 until his death in a plane crash in 1954, he served as President of the Indianapolis Motor Speedway. Had he lived he probably would be surprised to hear the inevitable change from "Gentlemen" to "Ladies and Gentlemen, Start Your Engines!"

Gentlemen, Start Your Engines

This was the "big show" and I was a part of it.

To me it was a world's series, a heavyweight championship fight, a National Open, a Rose Bowl game and a Kentucky Derby all rolled into one tremendous spectacle—with a touch of the pomp and ceremony of a coronation.

Eight years earlier, when I was only sixteen, the original Howdy Wilcox had given Indianapolis its first hometown winner of the annual 500-mile automobile race. On that occasion I had vowed that some day I would drive in the International Classic, too, and win it.

Now, a few minutes before ten o'clock on the morning of May 30, 1927, I was about to start an automobile on the world's greatest race course where all of the motor sport immortals of the last eighteen years had performed. I was about to get my first chance to join that exclusive list of "500" victors, which is the ultimate goal of racing men all over the world.

To the ears of a race driver, I'm sure, there are no sweeter words in the English language than the traditional command at the Indianapolis Motor Speedway: "Gentlemen, start your engines."

But until you actually hear your own engine roar into life on the starting line, you worry about each of the hundreds of mechanical parts which might fail you. . . .

The car everyone was talking about that year [1952] was the Cummins Diesel Special. The Cummins Engine Company of Columbus, Indiana, had decided to use the Speedway as an outdoor laboratory and proving ground for its product, as many of the pioneer automobile manufacturers had done during the early years of the track's existence. Don Cummins, the company's vice president in charge of engineering, was directing the project. He had chosen Freddie Agabashian as the driver of the heavy car, which weighed several hundred pounds more than the conventional entries. A speed in excess of 134 miles an hour probably would be necessary to qualify for a starting position and there was considerable speculation concerning whether or not the Cummins car would be fast enough.

On the first day of time trials, Agabashian climbed into the cockpit for the supreme test. He took two quick warm-up laps and signaled for the green flag. Clockers could hardly believe their eyes as their watches revealed an average of more than 139 miles an hour on the first official trip around the course. Three more first laps followed and Agabashian had set the car on the pole for the race with a 10-mile average of 138.010 for a new track record. Bill Vukovich and Chet Miller raised the mark still higher on subsequent days. But the car I was itching to drive was the Cummins Diesel and a few days later I did. Even though I didn't put as much pressure on the throttle as Freddie had applied, it was a perfectly wonderful feeling to be back on the track and running at high speed.

Race day dawned with hardly a cloud in the sky. The pre-race ceremonies moved along on split-second schedule. Such former race drivers as Tom Milton, Harry McQuinn and Earl Cooper headed the capable staff of AAA officials. The Purdue University Band swung through its sixty-minute program. With all cars in position, Morton Downey climbed on top of the concrete wall in front of the judges stand and sang "Back Home Again in Indiana." Then it was my turn.

As I had done in 1946, and every year since, I stepped to the microphone and took a deep breath to make sure I was in full control of my emotions. A little more than nine months earlier I wouldn't have given a plugged nickel for my chances of being on the starting line when the 1952 race got under way. But I'd won my fight and no longer was there any doubt in my mind concerning the future. I was in the groove again, with the green flag flying and a clear course ahead.

Out of the corner of my eye, I could see P. O. Peterson at the wheel of the Studebaker convertible, which had been chosen as the pace car because of that company's many important contributions to land transportation over a period of a hundred years. Alongside the car, with a smile on his face to reassure me that everything was all right, stood Carl Stockholm.

Thirty-three impatient drivers and 175,000 spectators were waiting for me to say the magic words. But I took another second or two to look down the track toward the spot where Boots and Bill were sitting in a box near the first turn. Even though I couldn't actually see them among the restless mass of humanity on hand for the big event, I waved in their general direction. Something inside me recorded their instant reply.

Facing the starting field again I suddenly realized that the feeling of envy, which I'd always experienced in former years at this particular moment on every May 30th, was gone. I was completely happy. I had my family—and my health*—and my home—and my exciting job of building the annual 500-mile race into an even greater attraction each succeeding year.

With a feeling of sincere gratitude to God, I lifted the mike to my lips and gave the traditional command:

"Gentlemen, start your engines!"

*He was at this time recovering from a heart attack. Two years later, on October 30, 1954, he was killed in a private plane crash.—A.L.

DAN WAKEFIELD

(b. Indianapolis, 1932–) was educated at Shortridge High School and at Harvard, among other universities. He has taught at the Bread Loaf Workshop of Creative Writing, in Vermont, and is now a Contributing Editor on the *Atlantic Monthly*. His books include *Island in the City* (1959), *Between the Lines* (1966), and *Going All the Way* (1970).

KURT VONNEGUT, JR.

(b. Indianapolis, 1922–) is another graduate of Shortridge High School. For biographical notes see "The Euphio Question," page 250.

In Vonnegut's Karass

The first time I read anything by Kurt Vonnegut, I was sitting in a barbershop in Indianapolis, leafing through a dog-eared copy of *The Saturday Evening Post* while waiting to have my favorite barber give me one of those kind of haircuts that prompted jocular fellows to quip, "Hey, I see you got your ears set out!" Har, har, har. (People said "Har, har, har" then to let you know something was funny; it was one of those doldrum years like 1953 when people seemed especially self-conscious and wanted to be what was called "One of the boys.")

To return to Vonnegut's story: I hardly remember it, but vaguely recall that it was about a little boy who played a large musical instrument, a tuba I think. It was not so much the story itself that impressed me as the fact that it was written by Kurt Vonnegut, Jr. The impressive thing about *that* was that Vonnegut, like me, was born and raised in Indianapolis, and also like me had gone to Shortridge High School and written for the Shortridge *Daily Echo*, the first high-school daily paper in the entire United States of America!

The word *karass* is defined and explained in the biographical sketch above.—A.L.

Vonnegut had graduated from Shortridge ten years before me, but his name was known to all of us aspiring writers who worked on the *Echo*. He, like us, had first been published in those pages, no doubt starting out like all other neophytes by covering meetings of the Stamp Club or freshman wrestling matches or the appointment of new officers of the ROTC. And, from such humble beginnings, he had gone on to be a professional writer, a writer whose stories were published in the Big Magazines, meccas of literary success like *Collier's* and *The Saturday Evening Post!* And if *he* could do it, maybe it meant—well, there was just the hope that perhaps we too could aspire to such glory. (As a matter of fact, glorious or no, a remarkable number of former writers for the Shortridge *Daily Echo* have gone on to make a career as authors of some sort or other, including Vonnegut, me, the novelist Jeremy Larner, the sportswriter Bill Libby, *Newsweek* correspondent and political author Richard T. Stout, *Life* staff writer Wally Terry, former *Life* staff writer and now editor-publisher of *Earth* magazine, Jim Goode, journalist John Bartlow Martin; and I'm sure there are others.)

If, as a young man in Indianapolis, you were so bold and reckless as to let anyone know that you hoped to become a writer when you grew up, it was usually regarded with the same seriousness as a little kid's expressed desire for a career in the Fire Department. Of course, there *had* been writers who came from Indianapolis, Famous Men like James Whitcomb Riley and Booth Tarkington. But they were dead. Sometimes, though, if you spoke of the dream of authordom, a knowing citizen would stroke his chin and say, "Well, I understand the Vonnegut boy does some writing. Even gets paid for it sometimes."

It was not known, however—to me or my Indianapolis informants, anyway—whether he got paid enough to live on. I heard somewhere that he worked for one of those big corporations, like Western Electric or General Electric, one of those corporations that everyone seemed to work for in the fifties. It was said that he worked in their public-relations department, and wrote his stories and things for magazines at night. It was said that he was married and had a lot of children to support. At odd moments, looking out of train windows, or drinking a beer, or studying for a test in my cubicle at Columbia in New York City, I would think of this guy Kurt Vonnegut, Jr., and wonder how he was making out. I was rooting for him, in my own mind, mostly from selfish motives; in some superstitious way it seemed to me that if *one* guy who came from Indianapolis and had

172]   THE INDIANA EXPERIENCE

gone to Shortridge High School could make a living as a writer, then
another guy could too (the other guy being me).

Sometime during that hazy period—I think we are still in the early
fifties—I heard he had published a novel, and somehow I got ahold
of it. The novel was called *Player Piano,* and was set in the future.
It was about this fictional town of Ilium, New York, where the corporation owned everything, and people were divided along very strati-
fied lines of work and leisure, all of which was planned out by the
corporation. It expressed the way a lot of people felt in the fifties
about the way things were going; about the kind of life we were all
going to end up with, a sort of American version of *1984,* with the
corporation as Big Brother. None of us could foresee then that
though the corporations would remain powerful, a time would come
when great masses of young people would refuse to go to work for
them anymore, would simply pretend that they didn't exist, and
would invent other styles of life that they found more suitable. In this
sense, *Player Piano* is the only one of Vonnegut's books that I think
seems a little "dated" when read in the seventies; it was so accurately
and spiritually a vision borne of the frustration of the fifties. But it
was, and is, a good book—it was believable and sad and also very
funny.

I was cheered not only because I liked the book but because this
Indianapolis guy had written and published it. I thought that meant
he had it made. Like many people, I assumed if you got a book
published that meant you were an established writer and you lived
off your royalties. Little did I know that in the vast majority of cases
the publication of a book meant that you got a couple of reviews here
and there and a thousand-dollar advance. (I didn't learn that till 1959,
when I had my own first book published.)

It was difficult then to "follow Vonnegut's career," because nobody
in the literary world mentioned him. Your best bet was to get a lot
of haircuts and see if you could find any new stories he had written
in the copies of *Collier's* and *The Saturday Evening Post* that were
lying around the barbershops.

The next word I got about Vonnegut's career came from my
mother. My mother had met his mother-in-law. There must be a
special bond between mothers of writers, as well as mothers of girls
who are married to writers. These mothers are long-suffering ladies
whom fate has dealt an unkind blow. The mother just wants her child
to be happy, and have a nice life, a good income, and be in good
health. It is possible for a writer to turn out that way, but not likely.
Their incomes are unsteady, at best. They tend to drink more than

other people, which is bound to affect their health. (A psychologist's recent study showed that of the seven Americans who won the Nobel prize for literature, five were alcoholics and one "drank heavily"; the other was Pearl Buck.) My mother accepted her (or my) fate with courage and a spirit of helpfulness. She was always managing to meet the relatives of writers, to find out whatever tips they might have for me (and her). During my years in college, my mother managed to meet Kurt Vonnegut's mother-in-law, journalist John Bartlow Martin's mother, and Ralph McGill's sister.

But the news from Vonnegut's mother-in-law was dire. According to what Vonnegut's mother-in-law told my mother, who told me, Vonnegut might decide to give up writing altogether. His stories at that time weren't selling, and he was very discouraged, according to this third-hand account.

Sometime later, when I was living the wine-and-spaghetti life in Greenwich Village and managing to eke out an existence writing pieces for *The Nation* magazine, I heard from someone that Vonnegut had become a "science-fiction writer." That seemed dire to me also, science fiction then being a category that was very unfashionable, and smacked of "commercialism," whatever that might mean in terms of writing.

In 1963 I escaped New York for a period in Boston and New Hampshire, and around those environs I heard that Vonnegut was living on Cape Cod and teaching English at a grammar school. I don't know if that is true, as I never asked him, but that was "the word" then on Vonnegut. There was also a more cheering word, in the form of a novel he had written called *Cat's Cradle,* that a lot of people were talking about. They said it was quite wonderful. I read it, and agreed. In the book, Vonnegut invented a new religion (he is always inventing new religions) called Bokononism, with a prophet named Bokonon. One of the concepts Bokonon gave the world was the *karass,* which Vonnegut explained like this:

> Humanity is organized into teams, teams that do God's Will without ever discovering what they are doing. Such a team is called a *karass* by Bokonon.... "If you find your life tangled up with somebody else's life for no very logical reasons," writes Bokonon, "that person may be a member of your *karass.*"

Not long after reading about that, I met Kurt Vonnegut, Jr., for the first time in my life. It was at a very nice dinner at the home of some friends in Cambridge, Massachusetts, in 1964. There were eight people at the dinner, and I didn't get to say much to Vonnegut, nor he to me, as everyone there had a lot of things to say to everyone else. There were only two things I remember him saying. One was that during the treacherous period when he quit his corporation job and devoted full time to writing, there came a particular year that seemed to him like a "magic year" when all his stories sold and his writing went very well and he figured he could really do it. The other thing was private, and I won't tell you that, but I liked both things I remember him saying, and I liked *him*. He laughed a lot, and was kind to everyone.

The following year I finished writing a book called *Between the Lines,* and I asked the publisher to send a set of galleys to Vonnegut in case he would be so kind as to want to make a comment about it. The book was essentially a collection of magazine articles and essays, but I added a personal, autobiographical narrative to it that explained something of what was happening to me when I was writing those things. The introductory part was all about how I grew up in Indianapolis, and how my dreams of athletic stardom were smashed when I found that I could not break the seven-minute mile. I got back a wonderful letter from Vonnegut about the book. He confessed that he, too, had been unable to break the seven-minute mile, and that we had had so many of the same teachers and same experiences as I described that, as he put it, "I almost feel that there shouldn't be two of us."

I was grateful for his nice letter, and elated by it. I began to feel guilty that I had not read all of his works, so I set about trying to find the ones I had missed, which were the ones in between *Player Piano* and *Cat's Cradle.* It wasn't easy, in those days, to just walk into a bookstore and get any book you wanted by Kurt Vonnegut. *Cat's Cradle* was a growing "underground" success, "underground" meaning that the publisher never told the public much about it, but that a lot of people who read it urged it upon their friends as an experience not to be missed. I was able to get *Mother Night* in a paperback edition, but *The Sirens of Titan* was out of print, and I finally was able to borrow a private copy of one from an editor of the house that had published it.

I liked these very different books very much. Now, you may think this was due to dumb prejudice because Vonnegut had liked *my* book, but I assure you that I am perfectly capable of not liking books written by the dearest of friends, or books by reviewers who have said nice things about books of mine. If I don't like a book written by a friend, I don't lie and pretend I like it; I just don't say anything at all. And, in turn, I have friends who do the same for me. Silence, in this area, is indeed golden. If you know a friend has read your book, and he hasn't commented to you about it, just don't ask. Stay friends.

Vonnegut is the sort of writer whom you either like a lot or dislike a lot; if you like one of his books, you are likely to enjoy the others. If you read one or two and don't like them, you might as well stop and accept the fact he's not for you. But even if you like them all, you have favorites. One of my favorites turned out to be *The Sirens of Titan,* and that surprised me, because it was supposed to be the most "science-fiction" type of all his books, and I don't like science fiction. By that I mean I don't like books that have green monsters with five arms, and lost tribes that are ruled by electronic lizards.

But Vonnegut's "science fiction" wasn't like that at all. It was about people, doing things that people might do if things had just turned out a little differently; or maybe if we *knew* more of what was really going on. One of my favorite lines is in *The Sirens of Titan.* (I have quoted it to explain many things that have little or nothing to do with science or fiction.) In this book, as in others, Vonnegut has invented another religion; in it, a man is supposed to fall from space and say a particular holy piece of scripture that will mark him as the long-awaited prophet. Well, this man falls out of the sky, and the believers gather around, and he knows he is expected to say something of great import, but he doesn't know what it is, so he just says the truth: "I was a victim of a series of accidents, as are we all." The believers cheer; that is indeed the exact thing he was supposed to say. So I wrote Vonnegut telling him of my pleasure in these books of his, and another just out called *God Bless You, Mr. Rosewater.* A lot of that one takes place in Indianapolis. In all of Vonnegut's books there is at least one person who is from Indianapolis; it is like Alfred Hitchcock always making a walk-on appearance in each of his movies.

I heard in a year or so that Vonnegut had gone out to Iowa to teach at the Iowa Writers Workshop. Then I heard he was back at Cape Cod. We kept in touch by means of our books, which we sent to each other, and wrote friendly letters about. In 1968 I went out to California to try to write a novel I had been trying to write for most of my adult life. That winter, maybe over into 1969, his novel *Slaughter-house-Five* came out. He didn't send me a copy, probably because he didn't know where I was, but I eagerly bought one, and thought it a marvel of a book. I wrote him about it, saying that in some strange way that had nothing to do with the subject matter, it reminded me of *Walden;* that it was the first book I had read since I read *Walden* while living in New Hampshire in 1964 that gave me the feeling of "lights coming on" in my head as I read it. He wrote back saying he thought I had overestimated the book, but thanked me anyway. He mentioned he had gone to Indianapolis for an autographing party at the bookstore of the L. S. Ayres department store. "I was there for three hours," he reported, "and sold eleven copies. All of them to relatives, I swear to God."

By that time Vonnegut was a hero on most college campuses in America, his book was a best seller, he was being written up in every magazine under the eye of God, he was asked to give graduation addresses, launch ships, and bless babies, but in good old Indianapolis, his hometown, his personal appearance drew only a handful of relatives. A third-string astronaut's wife from Hackensack, New Jersey, would have been a bigger draw. I guess it figures. The old "prophet-in-his-own-country" routine. So it goes.

But I see I have gotten ahead of the story, have jumped an important part of the plot. Which is, when Vonnegut left the Iowa Writers Workshop, and went back to Cape Cod to work on *Slaughterhouse*, the book that finally "hit" for him, how did he support himself? Vonnegut himself tells us, in *Slaughterhouse:*

> And somewhere in there a nice man named Seymour Lawrence gave me a three-book contract, and I said, "O.K., the first of the three will be my famous book about Dresden."

The way I heard it—not from Vonnegut himself or from Sam Lawrence, but the way writers hear these things about other writers and publishers' advances and so on—I heard that when Sam Lawrence first met Vonnegut he said to him, "How much money do you need to live on for the time it will take you to write your book?" And Vonnegut figured out the sum, and told Sam, and Sam gave him the sum, in advance of royalties. Which is something like a gamble or an act of faith, or both, on the part of Sam as the publisher. It turned out to be a good gamble and an intelligent act of faith.

I *do* know how Sam Lawrence happened to meet Vonnegut, because Sam told me the story himself. It was like this. Sam, who had been the director of the Atlantic Monthly Press and published *Ship of Fools* and the first J. P. Donleavy books and many other distinguished writers, had set up his own company in Boston, in conjunction with Dell Publishing, in New York. Sam was of course looking for authors. One day he read a review in *The New York Times* of the new Random House dictionary by Kurt Vonnegut. It was an astute and humorous review about dictionaries, and Sam liked it a lot and wrote to Vonnegut saying he liked it and if Vonnegut were ever in Boston, why didn't he drop in to Sam's office. And one day, without previous plan or announcement, Vonnegut dropped in. And it all began, the very nice relationship of Vonnegut as author and Sam as his publisher.

When I finally finished my own lifetime-in-progress novel, I had my agent submit it to ten publishers, one of whom was Sam Lawrence. I was living in Boston at the time, and I was nervous as hell wondering who, if anyone, would like my novel. Early reports came in: some people loved it and some people hated it. I heard early on from Sam that he was reading it and liking it. One night, pacing my fabulous book-lined study on Beacon Hill and trying not to jump out of my skin with nervous dread and anticipation, I did the very un-businesslike thing of calling up Sam at his home and asking if he would send a copy of the novel to Vonnegut and see what *he* thought of it. The novel was set in Indianapolis, and Vonnegut is a native of that place and he probably could give a good estimate of whether the novel was any good or full of crap. Sam said O.K., he'd do that if I got him an extra copy to send to Vonnegut on the Cape, and I found an extra and had another shot of bourbon and ran down the hill to deliver the damn thing to Sam, by hand. I honestly didn't know what in the world Vonnegut would think about my novel. I had, as you know now, met him once in my life and exchanged nice letters with him. He had liked my journalistic books, but a novel is of course a different and more delicate kettle of fish.

The next thing was I got a telegram from Vonnegut that congratulated me on "your very important novel." Then Sam showed me a letter Vonnegut sent him, saying of my very own book that it was "the truest and funniest sex novel any American will ever write."

Wow. As it turned out, happily, Sam published my novel, and Vonnegut let him use that terrific quote on the jacket, and I couldn't have been more pleased. Also, before publication, Sam asked Vonnegut if he would make any editorial suggestions or criticisms of the book, and Vonnegut wrote a very intelligent two-page letter about it, making about seven suggestions of minor changes or possible additions, and I think I did about four of them.

Sam also asked Vonnegut if he could help us think up a good title for the book. My working title had been *Sons and Mothers,* and Sam pointed out that this was too confusing, there being so many other books that sounded like that, such as *Sons and Lovers, Mothers and Sons,* just plain *Sons,* and so on. So we all tried to think of titles, and Vonnegut sent in a long list of potential titles. . . . We finally ended up with *Going All the Way,* which I felt was faithful to the fifties tone and spirit of the book. Titles are very hard.

A month or so after all that, Vonnegut said he was coming up to Boston for the day and perhaps we could have lunch. I looked forward to that, because I had never really had a chance to sit down and talk to Vonnegut alone. We met at Jake Wirth's, which is Vonnegut's favorite restaurant in Boston. It is an old authentic German place, very plain, with lots of wurst and potato salad and thick honest sandwiches and steins of beer. The lunch was very pleasant, and like Vonnegut himself, low-keyed and kind of ironically amusing. The only thing I really remember him saying was, when he first saw me as I came in: "That's quite a head of hair you've got."

I had let my hair get long, all right, down over my ears. His comment didn't seem critical, just observational. I think we talked some about Indianapolis, and some people we knew in common there. Writers rarely, if ever, talk about writing. Maybe we did just a little, concerning some of his suggestions about my novel.

Later that spring I heard that *Life* magazine asked Vonnegut if he would like to review my novel. He said he would, but insisted on saying in the review that he was a friend of mine. This was a revolutionary thing to do—I mean, to *say* that. Most reviews are written either by friends of the author or enemies of the author, but they never admit it in the review, they pretend they just came upon this book out of the clear blue sky and are making a wholly objective judgment on it. But Vonnegut wouldn't make that pretense. He started his review by saying: "Dan Wakefield is a friend of mine. We both went to Shortridge High School in Indianapolis. . . . His publisher is my publisher. He has boomed my books. So I would praise his first novel, even if it were putrid. But I wouldn't give my Word of Honor that it was good." He went on to give his Word of Honor that it really was good.

So then everyone knew I was a friend of Vonnegut, which was fine with me, I am proud to be so counted; the only trouble was a lot of people started asking me for his address or his phone number or an introduction to him and all I would say was I knew he lived on Cape Cod, which was public knowledge from various articles about him. I knew he was being bombarded with requests and letters and queries about his life and work, and people just showing up on his doorstep, and wanting him to go ZAP or something and tell them the secret of the universe.

What was happening, especially with his adoption of the youth cult, reminded me of a story I had heard in New York about another writer who in my day was popular with children. That was the marvelous sports writer John R. Tunis, who wrote terrific sports books for boys, like *The Iron Duke, The Duke Decides,* and *A City for Lincoln.* Anyway, this friend in New York told about a kid from his hometown who, around the age of twelve, ran away from home. And where did he go? He went to the home of John R. Tunis, hoping to live there. Mr. Tunis of course had to call the boy's parents and send him back home.

Today the same kid probably wouldn't be reading sports books, and if he were precocious, he might have read Vonnegut and run away from home in hopes of living at *his* house. Anyway, a lot of kids showed up at his house, till it got to the point where he said publicly something to the effect that he really didn't *like* kids. It was similar in a way to the plight of Eugene McCarthy; Vonnegut didn't go looking for the kids, they adopted *him.*

I was especially uneasy when some very nice young friends of mine who lived on communes in Vermont and Massachusetts told me they wanted to go visit Vonnegut. I liked them, and I figured Vonnegut would like them too, but I said they would have to do whatever they wanted on their own, as I just didn't feel I could aid in what he might well construe as an invasion of his privacy.

They went ahead anyway, and it turned out O.K. One of them, Steve Diamond, gave me an account of what happened. There was Steve, a young writer, and his writer buddy Ray Mungo, and their friend Verandah Porche, "Queen of the Bay State Poets for Peace," and a few others. They went to Vonnegut's house, and he came to the door and said, "What can I do for you people?" Steve said they didn't want him to "do anything" for them, and they feared he thought they wanted some favor. Anyway, Vonnegut suggested they take a walk, and he led them out to a very beautiful spot near his house, and they all sat down on the ground. They talked, with some uneasiness, and then Steve suddenly said to Vonnegut, "Actually, there is a real reason we have come here. We are forming an organization called 'The Old Farts.' To belong, you have to smoke a lot of Pall Malls, and you have to have a porch to sit on. We would like you to be President."

All that was an allusion to Vonnegut's self-description in *Slaughterhouse-Five,* and he laughed and they laughed, and everything was O.K. They invited him, Sam Lawrence, and me to come to the May Day Festival that they and their neighboring communes were holding in 1970. We all went up, and it was a pleasant but rather restrained day, less festive than I had expected.

The main thing I remember was Vonnegut talking to Ray Mungo, who had founded the commune where the event was being held. Ray was explaining their future plans, and said that they had lived on that farm for three years now, had learned how to survive on it, and they felt they should pass it on to some of the throngs of younger kids who were coming up that way in escape from the cities; and they, as pioneers, should go farther north, where it would be more difficult, and they would learn how to survive under more primitive conditions. "You see," Ray explained, "we would like to be the last people on Earth."

Vonnegut pondered that for a moment and then asked, "Isn't that kind of a stuck-up thing to want to be?"

I don't think I had heard the term "stuck-up" since high school, but it seemed to apply quite nicely to the situation. Ray is no phony— he is in fact a remarkable young man and a very gifted writer—but he does have a real "prophetic" streak in him. Vonnegut does not, though some people assume it from his work.

Some friends of mine out here in Los Angeles, where I am living at the moment, were a little surprised about that very thing when they had dinner with Vonnegut on a trip he made out here in the spring of 1971. Both of them are writers, and mutual friends got them together for this dinner with Vonnegut. The next day my friends called me up and said how terrific Vonnegut was, and how frankly they had been afraid they wouldn't like him and were so glad they did.

"Why," I asked, "were you afraid you wouldn't like him?"

There was a silence, and then my friend said, "We were afraid he would be—'prophetic.' "

"But he's not," I said.

"Not at all," said my friend. "He's really a listener—he listened very closely to what everyone else was saying, and every once in a while he would make some wry, very funny, and pertinent comment."

No, he is not the prophetic type, and it is just another one of the ironies he finds in our weird existence that he should have been adopted as a kind of prophet by so many people, in so many places.

Excepting, of course, Indianapolis.

Short Stories and
Other Fiction

❖❖❖❖❖❖❖❖❖❖❖❖❖❖❖❖❖❖❖❖❖❖❖

GEORGE ADE

(b. Kentland, 1886–d. 1944) was educated in the Newton County schools and at Purdue University. After working on several newspapers in Lafayette and Chicago, he turned to free-lance writing. His humorous columns reached a wide audience through syndication and were collected as *Fables in Slang* (1900), later reprinted in several editions. A wealthy bachelor, he built a large home—"Hazeldon"—near Brook, Indiana. Here he entertained his many friends, when he was not traveling around the world. Here, too, he did most of his writing. Several of his stories and plays, including *The College Widow* (1924), were re-created as motion pictures. Of his sixty-five books the most memorable, besides those mentioned above, remain *Stories of the Streets and of the Town: Eighth Series* (1900) and *In Babel* (1903), from which comes this story.

The Set of Poe

Mr. Waterby remarked to his wife: "I'm still tempted by that set of Poe. I saw it in the window to-day, marked down to fifteen dollars."

"Yes?" said Mrs. Waterby, with a sudden gasp of emotion, it seemed to him.

"Yes—I believe I'll have to get it."

"I wouldn't if I were you, Alfred," she said. "You have so many books now."

"I know I have, my dear, but I haven't any set of Poe, and that's what I've been wanting for a long time. This edition I was telling you about is beautifully gotten up."

"Oh, I wouldn't buy it, Alfred," she repeated, and there was a note of pleading earnestness in her voice. "It's so much money to spend for a few books."

"Well, I know, but—" and then he paused, for lack of words to express his mortified surprise.

Mr. Waterby had tried to be an indulgent husband. He took a selfish pleasure in giving, and found it more blessed than receiving. Every salary day he turned over to Mrs. Waterby a fixed sum for household expenses. He added to this an allowance for her spending money. He set aside a small amount for his personal expenses and deposited the remainder in the bank.

He flattered himself that he approximated the model husband.

Mr. Waterby had no costly habits and no prevailing appetite for anything expensive. Like every other man, he had one or two hobbies, and one of his particular hobbies was Edgar Allan Poe. He believed that Poe, of all American writers, was the one unmistakable "genius."

The word "genius" has been bandied around the country until it has come to be applied to a long-haired man out of work or a stout lady who writes poetry for the rural press. In the case of Poe, Mr. Waterby maintained that "genius" meant one who was not governed by the common mental processes, but "who spoke from inspiration, his mind involuntarily taking superhuman flight into the realm of pure imagination," or something of that sort. At any rate, Mr. Waterby liked Poe and he wanted a set of Poe. He allowed himself not more than one luxury a year, and he determined that this year the luxury should be a set of Poe.

Therefore, imagine the hurt to his feelings when his wife objected to his expending fifteen dollars for that which he coveted above anything else in the world.

As he went to his work that day he reflected on Mrs. Waterby's conduct. Did she not have her allowance of spending money? Did he ever find fault with her extravagance? Was he an unreasonable husband in asking that he be allowed to spend this small sum for that which would give him many hours of pleasure, and which would belong to Mrs. Waterby as much as to him?

He told himself that many a husband would have bought the books without consulting his wife. But he (Waterby) had deferred to his wife in all matters touching family finances, and he said to himself, with a tincture of bitterness in his thoughts, that probably he had put himself into the attitude of a mere dependent.

For had she not forbidden him to buy a few books for himself? Well, no, she had not forbidden him, but it amounted to the same thing. She had declared that she was firmly opposed to the purchase of Poe.

Mr. Waterby wondered if it were possible that he was just beginning to know his wife. Was she a selfish woman at heart? Was she complacent and good-natured and kind only while she was having her own way? Wouldn't she prove to be an entirely different sort of woman if he should do as many husbands do—spend his income on clubs and cigars and private amusement, and gave her the pickings of small change?

Nothing in Mr. Waterby's whole experience as a married man had so wrenched his sensibilities and disturbed his faith as Mrs. Waterby's objection to the purchase of the set of Poe. There was but one way to account for it. She wanted all the money for herself, or else she wanted him to put it into the bank so that she could come into it after he—but this was too monstrous.

However, Mrs. Waterby's conduct helped to give strength to Mr. Waterby's meanest suspicions.

Two or three days after the first conversation she asked: "You didn't buy that set of Poe, did you, Alfred?"

"No, I didn't buy it," he answered, as coldly and with as much hauteur as possible.

He hoped to hear her say: "Well, why don't you go and get it? I'm sure that you want it, and I'd like to see you buy something for yourself once in a while."

That would have shown the spirit of a loving and unselfish wife.

But she merely said, "That's right; don't buy it," and he was utterly unhappy, for he realised that he had married a woman who did not love him and who simply desired to use him as a pack-horse for all household burdens.

As soon as Mr. Waterby had learned the horrible truth about his wife he began to recall little episodes dating back years, and now he pieced them together to convince himself that he was a deeply wronged person.

Small at the time and almost unnoticed, they now accumulated to prove that Mrs. Waterby had no real anxiety for her husband's happiness. Also, Mr. Waterby began to observe her more closely, and he believed that he found new evidences of her unworthiness. For one thing, while he was in gloom over his discovery and harassed by doubts of what the future might reveal to him, she was content and even-tempered.

The holiday season approached and Mr. Waterby made a resolution. He decided that if she would not permit him to spend a little money on himself he would not buy the customary Christmas present for her.

"Selfishness is a game at which two can play," he said.

Furthermore, he determined that if she asked him for any extra money for Christmas he would say: "I'm sorry, my dear, but I can't spare any. I am so hard up that I can't even afford to buy a few books I've been wanting a long time. Don't you remember that you told me that I couldn't afford to buy that set of Poe?"

Could anything be more biting as to sarcasm or more crushing as to logic?

He rehearsed this speech and had it all ready for her, and he pictured to himself her humiliation and surprise at discovering that he had some spirit after all and a considerable say-so whenever money was involved.

Unfortunately for his plan, she did not ask for any extra spending money, and so he had to rely on the other mode of punishment. He would withhold the expected Christmas present. In order that she might fully understand his purpose, he would give presents to both of the children.

It was a harsh measure, he admitted, but perhaps it would teach her to have some consideration for the wishes of others.

It must be said that Mr. Waterby was not wholly proud of his revenge when he arose on Christmas morning. He felt that he had accomplished his purpose, and he told himself that his motives had been good and pure, but still he was not satisfied with himself.

He went to the dining-room, and there on the table in front of his plate was a long paper box, containing ten books, each marked "Poe." It was the edition he had coveted.

"What's this?" he asked, winking slowly, for his mind could not grasp in one moment the fact of his awful shame.

"I should think you ought to know, Alfred," said Mrs. Waterby, flushed, and giggling like a schoolgirl.

"Oh, it was you—"

"My goodness, you've had me *so* frightened! That first day, when you spoke of buying them and I told you not to, I was just sure that you suspected something. I bought them a week before that."

"Yes—yes," said Mr. Waterby, feeling the saltwater in his eyes. At that moment he had the soul of a wretch being whipped at the stake.

"I was determined not to ask you for any money to pay for your own presents," Mrs. Waterby continued. "Do you know I had to save for you and the children out of my regular allowance. Why, last week I nearly starved you, and you never noticed it at all. I was afraid you would."

"No, I—didn't notice it," said Mr. Waterby, brokenly, for he was confused and giddy.

This self-sacrificing angel—and he had bought no Christmas present for her!

It was a fearful situation, and he lied his way out of it.

"How did you like *your* present?" he asked.

"Why, I haven't seen it yet," she said, looking across at him in surprise.

"You haven't? I told them to send it up yesterday."

The children were shouting and laughing over their gifts in the next room, and he felt it his duty to lie for their sake.

"Well, don't tell me what it is," interrupted Mrs. Waterby. "Wait until it comes."

"I'll go after it."

He did go after it, although he had to drag a jeweller away from his home on Christmas-day and have him open his great safe. The ring which he selected was beyond his means, it is true, but when a man has to buy back his self-respect, the price is never too high.

❖ ❖ ❖ ❖ ❖

GEORGE BARR McCUTCHEON

(b. Tippecanoe County, 1866–d. 1928). For biographical notes, see *The Double Doctor,* page 299. The short story below appeared in the June, 1912 issue of *Good Housekeeping* Magazine.

When Girl Meets Girl

At a glance one would have said that they were desperadoes—the two of them. The one who stood outside the shadow of the black, low-lying wall was a brawny, sinister-looking woman whose age might have been fifty, or it might have been thirty, so deceptive was the countenance she bore. Her companion, a short, heavily built creature, slunk farther back into the protecting shadows and betrayed unmistakable signs of nervousness, not to say fear. At the corner below, a shuddering automobile purred its ugly song, the driver sitting far back in the shelter of the top, her eyes fixed steadily upon the two who lurked in the shadow of the wall that surrounded the almost deserted clubhouse. The woman who drove the car was manifestly of a station in life far removed from those who stood watch near the opening in the hedge-topped wall that gave entrance to the grounds of the Faraway Country Club. Muffled and goggled as she was, it was easily to be seen that she was of a more delicate, aristocratic mold than the others, and yet they were all of a single mind. They were engaged in a joint adventure, the character of which could not be mistaken.

The taller of the two women suddenly darted into the shadow, gripping the arm of her companion with a hand of iron:

"Sh! Here he comes. Remember now, Brown; no faltering. He's alone. Don't lose your nerve, woman."

"I'm new at this sort of thing, Quinlan," whispered the other, nervously. "I don't like it."

"You're not supposed to like it, but you've got to see it through just the same. Stand ready, and do what I told you. I'll take care of the rest."

A young man, tall and graceful, came swinging down the shrub-lined walk, whistling a gay little air, far from suspecting the peril that awaited him at the gate below. His cheery farewell shout to friends on the clubhouse veranda had been answered by joyous voices. It was midnight.

"Better wait a while, old man," someone had called after him. "It's bound to rain cats and dogs before you get to the trolley."

"A little water won't hurt me," he had shouted back. "So long, fellows."

Then he passed through the gate, under the single electric light that shadowed the way, and turned swiftly into the dark lane. Threatening rolls of thunder already smote the air and faint flashes of lightning shot through the black, starless sky. A gust of wind blew a great swirl of dust from the roadway, filling his eyes and half blinding him. As he bent his half-turned body against the growing hurricane, a pair of strong arms seized him from behind; almost simultaneously a thick blanket from which arose the odor of chloroform was thrown over his head and drawn tight. Shrill, sibilant whispers came to his ears, as he struggled vainly to free himself from those who held him.

Someone hissed: "Don't hit him, you fool! Don't spoil his face!"

He remembered kicking viciously, and that his foot struck against something resisting. A suppressed screech of pain and rage rewarded this final conscious effort on his part. Very hazily he realized that he was being dragged swiftly over the ground, for miles it seemed to him. Then came what appeared to be a fall from a great height, after which his senses left him.

The automobile leaped forward, swerved perilously at the sharp curve below the club gate and rushed off into the very teeth of the storm, guided by the firm, resolute hand of the woman at the wheel.

Once, when they had traversed a mile or more of the now drenched and slippery road, the woman who drove the car in its mad flight—unmistakably the master mind in this enterprise—called back over her shoulder to the twain who held watch over the captive in the tonneau:

"Is he regaining consciousness? Don't let him go too long."

"He's all right, ma'am," said the taller of the two ruffians, bending her ear to the captive's breast. "Fit as a fiddle."

"Say, we'll get twenty years for this if we're nabbed," growled the burly one called Brown. "Kidnaping is a serious business"—

"Hold your tongue!" cried the woman at the wheel.

"Well, I'm only telling you," grumbled Brown, nervously straightening her black sailor.

"It isn't necessary to tell me," said the driver. Her voice, high and shrill in battle with the storm, was that of a person of breeding and refinement, in marked contrast to the rough, coarse tones of her companions.

Mile after mile the big machine raced along the rain-swept highway, back from the Hudson and into the hills. Not once did the firm hand on the wheel relax, not once did the heart of the leader in this daring plot lose courage. Few are the men who would have undertaken this hazardous trip through the storm, few men with the courage or the recklessness.

At last, the car whirled into a narrow, almost unseen lane, and, going more cautiously over the treacherous ruts and stones, made its way through the forest for the matter of a mile or two, coming to a stop finally in front of a low, rambling house in which lights gleamed from two windows on the ground floor.

The two strong-armed hirelings dragged their still inert prisoner from the car, and, without a word, carried him up the walk to the house, following close upon the heels of their mistress. A gaunt old woman opened the door to admit the party, then closed it behind them.

The Disappearance of Cuthbert Reynolds

Two days passed before Cuthbert Reynolds, one of the most popular and one of the wealthiest young men in New York, was missed from his usual haunts, and then the city rang with the news that he had disappeared as completely as if the earth had opened to swallow him in a hungry, capacious maw.

Heir to a vast estate, unusually clever for one so markedly hand-some, beloved by half the marriageable young women in the smart-est circles, he was a figure whose every movement was likely to be observed by those who affected his society and who profited by his position. When he failed to appear at his rooms in Madison Avenue —he had no business occupation and therefore no office down-town —his valet, after waiting for twenty-four hours, called up several of his friends on the telephone to make inquiries. Later on, the police were brought into the case. Then the newspapers took up the mys-tery, and by nightfall of the third day the whole city was talking about the astounding case.

Those whilom friends who had shouted good-by to him from the country club veranda were questioned with rigid firmness by the authorities. They could throw no light upon the mystery. The un-usual circumstance of his returning to town by trolley instead of by motor was easily explained. His automobile had been tampered with in the club garage and rendered unfit for use. The other men were not going into town that night, but offered him the use of their cars. He preferred the trolley, which made connections with the subway, and they permitted him to go as he elected.

Naturally the police undertook to question his friends of an oppo-site sex. It was known that many of them were avowedly interested in him and that he had had numerous offers of marriage during the spring months of the year, all of which, so far as could be learned, he had declined to consider. As for possessing evil associates among women, there was no one who could charge him with being aught but a man of the most spotless character. No one, man or woman, had ever spoken ill of him in that respect. The police, to whom nothing is sacred, strove for several days to discover some secret *liaison* that might have escaped the notice of his devoted friends (and the more devoted one's friends are, the more they love to speculate on his misdemeanors) but without avail. His record was as clear as a blank page. There was not a red spot on it.

Gradually it dawned upon everyone that there was something really tragic in his disappearance. Those who at first scoffed at the idea of foul play, choosing to believe that he was merely keeping himself in seclusion in order that he might escape for the while from the notably fatiguing attentions of certain persistent admirers, came at last to regard the situation in the nature of a calamity. Eligible young men took alarm, and were seldom seen in the streets except in pairs or trios, each fearing the same mysterious and as yet unex-plained fate of the incomparable Reynolds. Few went about unattended after nightfall. Most of them were rigidly guarded by devoted admirers of an opposite sex. It was no uncommon thing to see a young man in the company of three or four resolute protectors.

In the meantime, Reynolds' relatives had the reservoir dredged, the Hudson raked, the Harlem scooped, and all of the sinister byways of the metropolis searched as with a fine-tooth comb. A vast reward was offered for the return of the young man, dead, alive or maimed. The posters said that $100,000 would be paid to anyone giving information which might lead to the apprehension of those who had made away with him. The Young Women's Society for the Prevention of Manslaughter drafted resolutions excoriating the police department, and advocated a wholesale rewriting of the law.

The lowliest of Cuthbert's admirers was Linda Blake, and the most unheralded. No one regarded her as a possible rival, for no one took the slightest notice of her. The daughter of a merchant princess, she was somewhat beyond the pale, according to custom, and while she was an extremely pretty young woman she was still shy and lamentably modest. As third corresponding secretary of the Spinsters' League she was put upon dreadfully by four-fifths of the members, and seldom had a moment of her own in which to declare herself to be anything more than a drudge in the movement to establish equality among God's images. She had little time for social achievements and but little opportunity to escape from the Spinsters' League by the means looked upon as most efficacious. She loved Cuthbert Reynolds, but she was denied the privilege of declaring her love to him because she seldom got near enough to be seen by the popular bachelor, much less to speak to him except to pass the time of day or to hear him reply that his program was full or that his mother was feeling better.

She had but three automobiles, whereas her haughty rivals possessed a dozen or more.

And yet it was Linda Blake who took the right and proper way to solve the mystery attending the disappearance of Cuthbert Reynolds, the pet of all the ladies.

The Mysterious House in the Hills

Let us now return to Reynolds, whom we left on the threshold of that mysterious house in the hills back of Tarrytown. When he regained his senses—he knew not how long he had been unconscious —he found himself in a small, ill-furnished bedchamber. The bed on which he was lying stood over against a window in which there were strong iron bars. For a long time he lay there wondering where he could be and how he came to be in this unfamiliar place. There was a racking pain in his head, a weakness in his limbs that alarmed him. Once, in his callow days, he had been intoxicated. He recalled feeling pretty much the same as he felt now, the day after that ribald supper party. Moreover, he had a vague recollection of iron bars, but no such bed as this.

As he lay there racking his brain for a solution to the mystery, a key rasped in the door across the room. He turned his head. A gas jet above the wretched little washstand lighted the room but poorly. The door opened slowly. A tall, ungainly woman entered the room —a creature with a sallow, weather-beaten face and a perpetual leer.

"Where am I?" demanded he.

The woman stared at him for a moment and then turned away. The door closed swiftly behind her, and the key grated in the lock. He floundered from the bed and staggered to the door, grasping the knob in his eager, shaking hand.

"Open up, confound you!" he cried out. The only response was the fast-diminishing tread of heavy footsteps on a stairway outside. He tried the window bars. The night was black outside; a cool drizzle blew against his face as he peered into the Stygian darkness. Baffled in his attempt to wrench the bars away, he shouted at the top of his voice, hoping that some passer-by—some good Samaritan—would hear his cry and come to his relief. Someone laughed out there in the night: a low, coarse laugh that chilled him to the bone.

He looked at his watch. The hour was three. With his watch in his hand, he came to realize that robbery had not been the motive of those who held him here. His purse and its contents were in his pocket; his scarf pin and his gold cigarette case were not missing. Lighting a cigarette, he sat down upon the edge of the bed to ruminate.

Suddenly his ear caught the sound of soft footsteps outside the door. They ceased abruptly. He had the uncanny feeling that someone was peeping through the keyhole. He smiled at the thought of how embarrassing it might have been.

"Get away from there!" he shouted, loudly. There came the unmistakable sound of someone catching breath sharply, and the creaking of a loose board in the floor. "A woman," he reflected with a smile.

"If this is a joke, I don't appreciate it," he said to himself, looking at himself in the mirror. After adjusting his disarranged necktie and brushing his hair, he sat down in the low rocker to await developments.

He had not long to wait. A resolute tread sounded on the stairway, and a moment afterward the door was thrown open to admit the tall, athletic figure of a very handsome young woman. Reynolds leaped to his feet in amazement.

"Miss Crouch!" he cried, clutching the back of the chair. A slow flush of anger mounted to his brow. "Are you responsible for this beastly trick?" he asked.

She smiled. "I expected to hear you call it an outrage," she said quietly.

"Well, outrage, if it pleases you. What does it mean?"

She crossed the room and stood directly in front of him, still smiling. He did not flinch, but the light in her eyes was most disquieting.

"It means, my dear Cuthbert, that you are in my power at last. You'll not leave this house alive, unless you go forth as my husband."

He stared at her in utter amazement. "Your husband? Woman, have you no pride?"

"Bushels of it," she said.

"But, I have refused to marry you at least a half dozen times. That ought to be ample proof that I don't love you. To be perfectly brutal about it, I despise you."

"Thanks for the confidence, but it will do you no good. I am not the sort of woman to be thwarted, once my mind and heart are fixed on a thing. Whether you like it or not, you shall be my husband before you're a day older."

"Never!" he exclaimed, his eyes flashing.

Before he could make a move to defend himself, she clasped him in her strong, young arms and was raining passionate kisses upon his lips, his brow, his cheek.

Weak from the effects of the chloroform, his struggles were futile. He would have struck her had there been a weapon handy.

"I'll die before I'll marry you, Elinor Crouch," he shouted, freeing himself at last.

"We'll see about that," she said, standing off to survey him the better. "I'll give you until tomorrow night to submit to my demands, peaceably and sensibly. Then, if you are still obdurate, we'll see what starvation will do to—"

"You wouldn't starve me, you wretch!" he cried in horror.

"It's a most efficacious way of bringing a man to terms," said Miss Crouch, fixing him with glittering eyes.

"By Jove," said he, shaking his head in despair, "I knew we'd come to this sort of thing if we passed that infernal law giving you women the upper hand of us men."

"We only ask for equal rights, my friend," she said. "This is the sort of thing you men used to do and no one made a fuss about it. Now it's our turn to apply the whip."

"I'm blessed if I'll ever vote for another woman, if I live to be a million," he growled.

"Oh, yes, you will. You'll vote just as your wife tells you to vote, and there's the end to that. But I can't stand here discussing politics with you. I give you until tomorrow night to think it over. A justice of the peace will be here to perform the ceremony. You know I love you. You know I'll make you a good wife—a devoted, adoring wife. I am fair to look upon. I am rich, I am of good family. Half the men in town would give their boots to be in yours. You have but to say the word and we set sail this week on my yacht for a honeymoon trip to the ends of the earth. Everything that love and money can procure for you shall be—"

"Stop! I will hear no more. Leave the room! No! Wait! Where am I?"

She laughed softly. "You are where no one will ever think of looking for you. Good night!"

She turned and went swiftly through the door. With an execration on his lips, he sprang after her, only to find himself confronted by two vicious-looking women with pistols in their hands. With a groan, he drew back into the room. The door closed with a bang, the key turned in the lock, and he was alone to reflect upon the horrors of the fate ahead of him.

Elinor Crouch was a beautiful girl, and an alluring one. Even though he hated her, he was forced to admit to himself that she was the most beautiful creature he had ever seen. Not once, but a hundred times, had he passed judgment upon her physical charms from a point of view obtained in his club window, but always there had been in his mind the reservation that she was not the sort of woman he would care to marry. Now he was beginning to know her for what she really was: a scheming Amazon who would sacrifice anything to appease a pride that had been wounded by his frequent and disdainful refusals to become her husband.

Would she carry out her threat and starve him if he persisted in his determination to defy her? Could she be so cruel, so inhuman as that?

He was considerably relieved, after the few hours of sleep that followed his interview with the fair Miss Crouch, to find a bountiful and wholesome breakfast awaiting him. True, it was served by an evil-appearing woman who looked as though she could have slit his throat and relished the job, but he paid little heed to her after the first fruitless attempts to engage her in conversation. She was a sour creature and given to monosyllables, this Quinlan woman.

Reynolds had been brought up to respect the adage concerning "a woman scorned." He knew that women in these days are not to be trifled with. If Elinor Crouch set about to conquer, the chance for mercy at her hands would be slim. There was absolutely no means of escape from his prison. Daylight revealed a most unpleasant prospect. The barred window through which he peered was fifty or sixty feet from the ground, which was covered with jagged boulders. On all sides was the dark, impenetrable forest which covers the hills along the Hudson. After a few minutes' speculation he decided that he was confined in an upper chamber of the pump house connected with the estate. Investigation showed him that the bars in the window had been placed there but recently.

In considerable agitation he awaited the coming of night, fully determined that if the worst came to the worst he would accept starvation and torture rather than submit to the cruel demands of Elinor Crouch. He would die before he would consent to become her husband.

The Attempted Ceremony

She came at nine o'clock, accompanied by a fat little woman in black, who was introduced as a justice of the peace.

"Well?" said his captor, with her most enticing smile. "Have you decided, Cuthbert?"

"I have," said he resolutely. "I want to warn you, Elinor, that you shall pay dearly for this outrage. I shall—"

"Then you consent?" she cried, her face aglow.

"No! A thousand times no! I mean—"

"You are wasting your breath, Cuthbert Reynolds," she interrupted, a steely glitter in her eyes. "Justice Snow, will you proceed at once with the ceremony? I will not—"

Reynolds sprang past her with the agility of a cat and hurled himself through the half-open door, hoping to find the way momentarily clear for a dash to liberty. Even as hope leaped up in his breast it was destroyed.

Two brawny figures fell upon him at the landing, and he was borne to earth with a fierceness that stunned him into insensibility.

When he regained consciousness a few moments later, he was lying bound on the bed. The grim figure of the redoubtable Quinlan sat in the rocker over against the door, and there was a scornful leer on her thin lips.

"Bread and water for you, my laddiebuck," said she, with a broad wink. "What a blithering fool you are! The finest lady in the land wants to make you her husband, and you kick up a row about it. You —"

"You go to thunder," said Reynolds, savagely.

Quinlan laughed.

For four days and nights he remained in the small, bare room. Each day brought his persecutor to his side, and on each occasion she went away baffled but hopeful. She pleaded, stormed, and threatened, but he held steadfast to his resolve.

"I'll die a thousand times, you fiend, before I'll consent to this ceremony. Go on starving me, as you've set out to do. What will you have gained in the end?"

"At least the consolation of knowing that no other woman shall call you husband," she said vindictively.

He was thin, emaciated, and hollow-eyed from lack of proper sustenance. His captors gave him barely enough food and drink to keep body and soul together. Once a day the gaunt Quinlan brought bread and water to his room, and once the beautiful Elinor forgot her cigarettes and a bonbon box on leaving him in a rage. He hid the boxes after emptying them, cunningly realizing that if he ever escaped her clutches the articles would serve as incontrovertible evidence against her. But Quinlan and Brown, strong and vigorous, were more than a match for him in his weakened condition. They choked him until he revealed the hiding place of the two gold boxes. Then they beat him cruelly.

"If you tell the boss that we beat you up, young feller, you'll get your come-uppin's good and plenty," said Quinlan savagely, as he fell back exhausted in the corner. "You keep your mouth closed, if you don't want it closed forever."

"If you have a spark of humanity in your body, woman, you'll give me food," he cried. "I'm dying. Have you no heart, either of you? See here, I'll give each of you enough money to keep you in comfort for the rest of your lives, if you'll—"

"None o' that, Mr. Reynolds," snapped Quinlan. "What do you take us for? Men?"

"Gad, I wish you were," he exclaimed. "I'd thrash you within an inch of your lives if you were."

"Well, don't go to offering us money, that's all. We're women, and we don't sell out a friend. Say, ain't you about ready to give in to her?

You'd better say the word. She'll make you the happiest man on earth. What's more, you'll get a good square meal the minute you say you'll marry her."

"I wouldn't marry her if she were the last woman in the world," he cried. "Listen to me! Haven't you two women husbands who are dear to you? Haven't you husbands—"

"They're both in the penitentiary, curse 'em," snarled Brown, clenching and unclenching her hands. "I wish I could get my hooks on that man of mine, that's all."

"Lucky dog!" said Reynolds.

"You bet he's a lucky dog. I believe he got sent up deliberately."

"Well, he's only got eight more years to serve, Brown," said Quinlan. "He'll come back to you for food and clothes. Then you can make up for all this lost time."

"I'll do it, all right," said Brown, smiting the windowsill with her huge fist. Quinlan chuckled.

That night Reynolds made his last stand. When Miss Crouch left him, he was almost ready to submit. Had she but known it, another five minutes of argument would have brought him to terms. Starvation had conquered him.

"If I live till morning," he kept repeating to himself in the solitude of his cell, "I'll give in. I can't stand it any longer. I shall go mad."

He fell back on the bed and lay staring at the ceiling, a beaten wreck. Delirium was at hand.

Some time during the night he was aroused from a fitful slumber by a sound at his window. The night was very dark. He could see nothing, and yet he knew that someone was there—someone who would help him in his final hour of despair. Struggling weakly from the bed, he dragged himself to the bars. Reaching between them, his hand encountered the topmost round of a ladder. Someone was ascending from below. He could feel the supports quiver, he could hear the ladder creak beneath the weight of a living, moving body.

A moment later, the dull outlines of a head and shoulders appeared in the black frame—the head of a woman! With a groan of despair he shrank back, thinking that the visitor was one who had come to torment him in some new fashion.

"Cuthbert!" whispered the woman on the outside. "Cuthbert, dear, are you there? Speak!"

He staggered to the window once more. Hope buoyed him up. The voice was not that of one of his inquisitors. It was low, sweet, gentle, yet quivering with anxiety.

"Yes, yes!" he whispered. "Who are you? For God's sake, get me out of this place. I am dying here."

"Thank God, you are alive," came the tense whisper from the woman. "I am not too late."

"Who are you?" He had discovered that her features were rendered unrecognizable by an ugly pair of motor goggles. A thick veil held her panama motor hat in place.

She laughed nervously, even shyly.

"Never mind, Mr. Reynolds," she said. "Enough to say that I am here to release you if it is in the power of woman to do so."

"You call me Mr. Reynolds now," he protested. "A moment ago it was 'Cuthbert, dear.' Who are you, oh, my deliverer?"

"You shall know in good time. How long have you been here?"

"Ages, it seems. In truth, but five days. She is starving me to death."

"The fiend! Tell me, are you married to her?"

"No!"

"Then I shall do my best to save you."

He reflected. Perhaps it would be leaping from the frying pan into the fire.

"Just a moment, please. How am I to know that I am bettering my position by accepting liberty at your hands?"

"O-ho! You fear that I may want to marry you against your will? Is that it? Well, the instant you are free you shall be at liberty to go whither you please and to marry whomsoever it pleases you. Is that fair enough?"

"Forgive me for doubting you. But how are you to effect a rescue? I am guarded by powerful women who would make short work of you in combat. I can see that you are slight. They are huge, well-armed creatures. Are you—"

"Don't worry about me," she whispered eagerly. "I can take care of myself. And now be patient. I must leave you. I'll be back in a jiffy. Don't lose heart."

She went rapidly down the ladder.

Vastly excited and strangely revived, he awaited her return, praying that she might not be intercepted by the minions of Elinor Crouch. An hour passed. He was about to give up in despair, confident that she had been summarily dealt with by the eagle-eyed Quinlan, when stealthy sounds came to his ears from the landing outside his door.

A key was gently inserted in the lock.

The door opened a few inches, then swung wide. Instead of Elinor Crouch or her hirelings on the threshold stood the lithe, graceful figure of a girl in a gray motoring suit. She sprang into the room. The goggles were no longer in evidence, but the green veil hid her features quite completely.

"Quick! Follow me! I have accounted for the tall woman who stood guard on the stairway. We must get away before the others discover her body."

"Good heavens! Have you killed her?"

"I hope not. Just a little tap on the head with this wrench, that's all. She'll come out of it all right. Hurry! I've got a couple of friends watching outside. They'll give the alarm if we fail to appear at once."

"Men? Thank heaven!"

"No! Women! What good are men at a time like this? Merciful— Are you going to faint?"

He sank to the floor with a groan, and the chair clattered against the wall with a noise that must have been heard throughout the house.

When he opened his eyes again, his head was pillowed on her knees and she was wildly whispering words of love and encouragement to him.

"My darling, speak to me. I am here to save you! Oh, thank heaven! You are alive!"

He looked up into the now uncovered face and an expression of utter bewilderment grew in his eyes.

"Linda Blake!" he murmured. "Can it be possible?" His fingers tightened on her arm and a glad light leaped into his eyes.

She pulled down her veil in confusion.

"Don't look at me," she whispered. "I hope you didn't hear what I said to you."

"I heard every word, love of my life. I— Listen! What's that?" He sat bolt upright.

"Someone's coming!" she cried, springing to her feet and placing herself between him and the door. He saw a glistening revolver in her small white hand.

"It's Elinor Crouch," he whispered. "Heavens, how I have come to hate those footsteps of hers."

Elinor Crouch, her face pale with anger and apprehension, dashed into the room an instant later.

Her dark eyes scarcely took in the slight figure of Linda Blake. They were for the man on the floor, and for him alone.

"Thank heaven, you are here!" she cried, in a voice thrilling with relief. "I was afraid you might have—"

"Stand back, Miss Crouch," interrupted Linda firmly.

"Who—who are you?" gasped Elinor, for the first time granting the girl a look of surprise, but not of fear. "Why, on my life, it's that Blake girl. So-ho! This is your work, is it? May I inquire, Miss Blake, what you are doing in my house at this time of night?"

"I am not here to parley with you, Miss Crouch. Stand aside, please. If you attempt to stop us, I shall shoot you like a dog."

"Oh, you think you can take him away from me, do you? Well, we shall soon make short shrift of you, my excellent heroine. Brown! Quinlan! Here, at once!" She called angrily down the stairs.

Linda smiled. "I think you'll find that my friends have taken care of Brown and Quinlan."

As if to prove the declaration, a ringing voice came up the stairway from far below:

"Are you all right, Linda?" It was a woman's voice and it was full of triumph. "We've fixed these two wretches down here. Shall we come up?"

"Stay where you are, girls. I can manage nicely by myself, thank you," called Linda. Then she turned to the infuriated Elinor, who had shrunk back against the wall, panting with rage and disappointment. "You'd better come with us peaceably, my woman," she said coldly, still keeping the revolver leveled at the person of her rival. "Don't make any trouble for us. If you show fight we'll be obliged to — Here!"

The Fight for Cuthbert

Elinor Crouch suddenly threw herself forward. The movement was so unexpected that she was upon Linda before the girl could fire. Twice the revolver was discharged in a vain attempt to end the struggle at its beginning, and both bullets came so near to hitting Reynolds that he hastily rolled under the bed, from which position he watched the contest in some security but with a great deal of interest.

The combatants swayed back and forth across the narrow room, locked in a tight embrace. The Crouch woman was the larger and stronger, but her adversary was lithe and sinewy and as cool as a veteran in the line of battle. She succeeded in tripping the heavier woman, resorting to a new trick in wrestling that had just come into practice among athletic women, and they went to the floor with a crash, Reynolds' rescuer on top.

He crawled forth to assist her, keeping his eye on the pistol all the while. Weak as he was, he succeeded in sitting upon Miss Crouch's head while Linda attempted to secure her arms with the thick veil she had torn from her hat.

Just as Elinor Crouch relaxed with a groan of despair, two eager young women dashed into the room. In a jiffy, the late mistress of the situation was bound securely, hand and foot, and Linda Blake stood triumphant and lovely over her foe.

"We'll turn you over to the police," she said, smiling down upon the ghastly face of Elinor Crouch.

"For heaven's sake, spare me," groaned the unhappy captive. "It was all for love, Cuthbert. I—"

But Cuthbert Reynolds had already passed from the room, leaning feebly on the arm of his deliverer.

"How did you trace me here, dear?" he asked as they slowly descended the stairs.

"I found out that she was having her mail forwarded to the village over yonder, and I knew that she owned this place in the woods. I only had to put two and two together, Cuthbert. You—you don't mind if I call you Cuthbert, do you?"

He pressed her arm closer to his side. "You are a darling, Linda. I'll marry you tomorrow if you say the word."

She kissed him rapturously.

"It's too good to be true," she sighed.

BOOTH TARKINGTON

(b. Indianapolis, 1869–d. 1946), of 4270 North Meridian Street, Indianapolis, was educated at Phillips Exeter Academy and at Purdue and Princeton. His Purdue classmates George Ade and the McCutcheon brothers (George and John) became his lifelong friends. His first wife, Laurel, was the daughter of the well-known Fletcher Bank president. Despite his high connections Tarkington struggled almost in vain during the first five years of his writing career—he sold only one story ("Cherry") for $22.00. But during the next five years his writing earned him over $22,000, and he was destined to win two Pulitzer Prizes (1919 and 1922). Of his seventy books (novels, plays, short-story collections) the most memorable remain *The Gentleman From Indiana* (1899), *Monsieur Beaucaire*

(1900), *Penrod* (1914), *Penrod and Sam* (1916), *The Magnificent Ambersons* (1918), and *Alice Adams* (1921). The following selection comes from *The Arena and Other Stories* (1905).

Great Men's Sons

Mme. Bernhardt and M. Coquelin were playing "L'Aiglon."* Toward the end of the second act people began to slide down in their seats, shift their elbows, or casually rub their eyes; by the close of the third, most of the taller gentlemen were sitting on the small of their backs with their knees as high as decorum permitted, and many were openly coughing; but when the fourth came to an end, active resistance ceased, hopelessness prevailed, the attitudes were those of the stricken field, and the over-crowded house was like a college chapel during an interminable compulsory lecture. Here and there—but most rarely—one saw an eager woman with bright eyes, head bent forward and body spellbound, still enchantedly following the course of the play. Between the acts the orchestra pattered ragtime and inanities from the new comic operas, while the audience in general took some heart. When the play was over, we were all enthusiastic; though our admiration, however vehement in the words employed to express it, was somewhat subdued as to the accompanying manner, which consisted, mainly, of sighs and resigned murmurs. In the lobby a thin old man with a grizzled chin-beard dropped his hand lightly on my shoulder, and greeted me in a tone of plaintive inquiry:
"Well, son?"
Turning I recognized a patron of my early youth, in whose woodshed I had smoked my first cigar, an old friend whom I had not seen for years; and to find him there, with his long, dust-coloured coat, his black string tie and rusty hat, brushed on every side by opera cloaks and feathers, was a rich surprise, warming the cockles of my heart. His name is Tom Martin; he lives in a small country town, where he commands the trade in Dry Goods and Men's Clothing; his speech is pitched in a high key, is very slow, sometimes whines faintly; and he always calls me "Son."
"What in the world!" I exclaimed, as we shook hands.

*"L'Aiglon"—Edmond Rostand's play about Napoleon's son "the Eagle" (so nicknamed by Victor Hugo).—A. L.

"Well," he drawled, "I dunno why I shouldn't be as meetropolitan as anybody. I come over on the afternoon accommodation for the show. Let's you and me make a night of it. What say, son?"

"What did you think of the play?" I asked, as we turned up the street toward the club.

"I think they done it about as well as they could."

"That all?"

"Well," he rejoined with solemnity, "there was a heap *of* it, wasn't there!"

We talked of other things, then, until such time as we found our-selves seated by a small table at the club, old Tom somewhat uneasily regarding a twisted cigar he was smoking and plainly confounded by the "carbonated" syphon, for which, indeed, he had no use in the world. We had been joined by little Fiderson, the youngest member of the club, whose whole nervous person jerkily sparkled "L'Aiglon" enthusiasm.

"Such an evening!" he cried, in his little spiky voice. "Mr. Martin, it does one good to realize that our country towns are sending repre-sentatives to us when we have such things; that they wish to get in touch with what is greatest in Art. They should do it often. To think that a journey of only seventy miles brings into your life the magnifi-cence of Rostand's point of view made living fire by the genius of a Bernhardt and a Coquelin!"

"Yes," said Mr. Martin, with a curious helplessness, after an ensu-ing pause, which I refused to break, "yes, sir, they seemed to be doing it about as well as they could."

Fiderson gasped slightly. "It was magnificent! Those two great artists! But over all the play—the play! Romance new-born; poesy marching with victorious banners; a great spirit breathing! Like 'Cyrano'—the birth-mark of immortality on this work!"

There was another pause, after which old Tom turned slowly to me, and said: "Homer Tibbs's opened up a cigar-stand at the deepo. Carries a line of candy, magazines, and fruit, too. Home's a hustler."

Fiderson passed his hand through his hair.

"That death scene!" he exclaimed at me, giving Martin up as a log accidentally rolled in from the woods. "I thought that after 'Wagram' I could feel nothing more; emotion was exhausted; but then came that magnificent death! It was tragedy made ecstatic; pathos made into music; the grandeur of a gentle spirit, conquered physically but morally unconquerable! Goethe's 'More Light' outshone!"

Old Tom's eyes followed the smoke of his perplexing cigar along its heavy strata in the still air of the room, as he inquired if I remembered Orlando T. Bickner's boy, Mel. I had never heard of him, and said so.

"No, I expect not," rejoined Martin. "Prob'ly you wouldn't; Bickner was governor along in *my* early days, and I reckon he ain't hardly more than jest a name to you two. But *we* kind of thought he was the biggest man this country had ever seen, or was goin' to see, and he *was* a big man. He made one president, and could have been it himself, instead, if he'd be'n willing to do a kind of underhand trick, but I expect without it he was about as big a man as anybody'd care to be; governor, senator, secretary of state—and just owned his party! And, my law!—the whole earth bowin' down to him; torchlight processions and sky-rockets when he come home in the night; bands and cannon if his train got in, daytime; home-folks so proud of him they couldn't see; everybody's hat off; and all the most important men in the country following at his heels—a country, too, that'd put up consider'ble of a comparison with everything Napoleon had when he'd licked 'em all, over there.

"Of course he had enemies, and, of course, year by year, they got to be more of 'em, and they finally downed him for good; and like other public men so fixed, he didn't live long after that. He had a son, Melville, mighty likable young fellow, studyin' law when his paw died. I was livin' in their town then, and I knowed Mel Bickner pretty well; he was consider'ble of a man.

"I don't know as I ever heard him speak of that's bein' the reason, but I expect it may've be'n partly in the hope of carryin' out some of his paw's notions, Mel tried hard to git into politics; but the old man's local enemies jumped on every move he made, and his friends wouldn't help any; you can't tell why, except that it generally *is* thataway. Folks always like to laugh at a great man's son and say *he* can't amount to anything. Of course that comes partly from fellows like that ornery little cuss we saw to-night, thinkin' they're a good deal because somebody else done something, and the somebody else happened to be their paw; and the women run after 'em, and they git lowdown like he was, and so on."

"Mr. Martin," interrupted Fiderson, with indignation, "will you kindly inform me in what way 'L'Aiglon' was 'low-down'?"

"Well, sir, didn't that huntin'-lodge appointment kind of put you in mind of a camp-meetin' scandal?" returned old Tom quietly. "It did me."

"But—"

"Well, sir, I can't say as I understood the French of it, but I read the book in English before I come up, and it seemed to me he was pretty much of a low-down boy; yet I wanted to see how they'd make him out; hearin' it was thought, the country over, to be such a great *play;* though to tell the truth all I could tell about *that* was that every line seemed to end in 'awze'; and 't they all talked in rhyme, and it did strike me as kind of enervatin' to be expected to believe that people could keep it up that long; and that it wasn't only the boy that never quit on the subject of himself and his folks, but pretty near any of 'em, if he'd git the chanst, did the same thing, so't almost I sort of wondered if Rostand wasn't that kind."

"Go on with Melville Bickner," said I.

"What do you expect," retorted Mr. Martin with a vindictive gleam in his eye, "when you give a man one of these here spiral staircase cigars? Old Peter himself couldn't keep straight along one subject if he tackled a cigar like this. Well, sir, I always thought Mel had a mighty mean time of it. He had to take care of his mother and two sisters, his little brother and an aunt that lived with them; and there was mighty little to do it on; big men don't usually leave much but debts, and in this country, of course, a man can't eat and spend long on his paw's reputation, like that little Dook of Reishtod—"

"I beg to tell you, Mr. Martin—" Fiderson began hotly.

Martin waved his bony hand soothingly.

"Oh, I know; they was money in his mother's family, and they give him his vit'als and clothes, and plenty, too. *His* paw didn't leave much either—though he'd stole more than Boss Tweed. I suppose— and, just lookin' at things from the point of what they'd *earned,* his maw's folks had stole a good deal, too; or else you can say they were a kind of public charity; old Metternich, by what I can learn, bein' the only one in the whole possetucky of 'em that really *did* anything to deserve his salary—" Mr. Martin broke off suddenly, observing that I was about to speak, and continued:

"Mel didn't git much law practice, jest about enough to keep the house goin' and pay taxes. He kept workin' for the party jest the same and jest as cheerfully as if it didn't turn him down hard every time he tried to git anything for himself. They lived some ways out from town; and he sold the horses to keep the little brother in school, one winter, and used to walk in to his office and out again, twice a day, over the worst roads in the State, rain or shine, snow, sleet, or wind, without any overcoat; and he got kind of a skimpy, froze-up look to him that lasted clean through summer. He worked like a mule, that boy did, jest barely makin' ends meet. He had to quit runnin' with the girls and goin' to parties and everything like that; and I expect it may have been some hard to do; for if they ever *was* a boy loved to dance and be gay, and up to anything in the line of fun and junketin' round, it was Mel Bickner. He had a laugh I can hear yet —made you feel friendly to everybody you saw; feel like stoppin' the next man you met and shakin' hands and havin' a joke with him.

"Mel was engaged to Jane Grandis when Governor Bickner died. He had to go and tell her to take somebody else—it was the only thing to do. He couldn't give Jane anything but his poverty, and she wasn't used to it. They say she offered to come to him anyway, but he wouldn't hear of it, and no more would he let her wait for him; told her she mustn't grow into an old maid, lonely, and still waitin' for the lightning to strike him—that is, his luck to come; and actually advised her to take 'Gene Callender, who'd be'n pressin' pretty close to Mel for her before the engagement. The boy didn't talk to her this way with tears in his eyes and mourning and groaning. No, sir! It was done *cheerful;* and so much so that Jane never *was* quite sure after *werds* whether Mel wasn't kind of glad to git rid of her or not. Fact is, they say she quit speakin' to him. Mel *knowed;* a state of puzzlement or even a good *mad's* a mighty sight better than bein' all harrowed up and grief-stricken. And he never give her—nor any one else—a chanst to be sorry for him. His maw was the only one heard him walk the floor nights, and after he found out she could hear him he walked in his socks.

"Yes, sir! Meet that boy on the street, or go up in his office, you'd think that he was the gayest feller in town. I tell you there wasn't anything pathetic about Mel Bickner! He didn't believe in it. And at home he had a funny story every evening of the world, about something 'd happened during the day; and 'd whistle to the guitar, or git his maw into a game of cards with his aunt and the girls. La! that boy didn't believe in no house of mourning. He'd be up at four in the morning, hoein' up their old garden; raised garden-truck for their table, sparrowgrass and sweet corn—yes, and roses, too; always had the house full of roses in June-time; never *was* a house sweeter-smellin' to go into.

"Mel was what I call a useful citizen. As I said, I knowed him well. I don't recollect I ever heard him speak of himself, nor yet of his father but once—for *that,* I reckon, he jest couldn't; and for himself; I don't believe it ever occurred to him.

"And he was a *smart* boy. Now, you take it, all in all, a boy can't be as smart as Mel was, and work as hard as he did, and not *git* somewhere—in this State, anyway! And so, about the fifth year, things took a sudden change for him; his father's enemies and his own friends, both, had to jest about own they was beat. The crowd that had been running the conventions and keepin' their own men in all the offices, had got to be pretty unpopular, and they had the sense to see that they'd have to branch out and connect up with some mighty good men, jest to keep the party in power. Well, sir, Mel had got to be about the most popular and respected man in the county. Then one day I met him on the street; he was on his way to buy an overcoat, and he was lookin' skimpier and more froze-up and genialer than ever. It was March, and up to jest that time things had be'n hardest of all for Mel. I walked around to the store with him, and he was mighty happy; goin' to send his mother north in the summer, and the girls were goin' to have a party, and Bob, his little brother, could go to the best school in the country in the fall. Things had come his way at last, and that very morning the crowd had called him in and told him they were goin' to run him for county clerk.

"Well, sir, the next evening I heard Mel was sick. Seein' him only the day before on the street, out and well, I didn't think anything of it—thought prob'ly a cold or something like that; but in the morning I heard the doctor said he was likely to die. Of course I couldn't hardly believe it; thing like that never *does* seem possible, but they all said it was true, and there wasn't anybody on the street that day that didn't look blue or talked about anything else. Nobody seemed to know what was the matter with him exactly, and I reckon the doctor did jest the wrong thing for it. Near as I can make out, it was what they call appendicitis nowadays, and had come on him in the night.

"Along in the afternoon I went out there to see if there was anything I could do. You know what a house in that condition is like. Old Fes Bainbridge, who was some sort of a relation, and me sat on the stairs together outside Mel's room. We could hear his voice, clear and strong and hearty as ever. He was out of pain; and he had to die with the full flush of health and strength on him, and he knowed it. Not *wantin'* to go, through the waste and wear of a long sickness, but with all the ties of life clinchin' him here, and success jest comin'. We heard him speak of us, amongst others, old Fes and me; wanted 'em to be sure not fergit to tell me to remember to vote fer Fillmore if the ground-hog saw his shadow election year, which was an old joke I always had with him. He was awful worried about his mother, though he tried not to show it, and when the minister wanted to pray fer him, we heard him say, 'No, sir, you pray fer my mamma!' That was the only thing that was different from his usual way of speakin'; he called his mother 'mamma,' and he wouldn't let 'em pray fer him neither; not once; all the time he could spare for their prayin' was put in fer her.

"He called in old Fes to tell him all about his life insurance. He'd carried a heavy load of it, and it was all paid up; and the sweat it must have took to do it you'd hardly like to think about. He give directions about everything as careful and painstaking as any day of his life. He asked to speak to Fes alone a minute, and later I helped Fes do what he told him. 'Cousin Fes,' he says, 'it's bad weather, but I expect mother'll want all the flowers taken out to the cemetery and you better let her have her way. But there wouldn't be any good of their stayin' there; snowed on, like as not. I wish you'd wait till after she's come away, and git a wagon and take 'em in to the hospital. You can fix up the anchors and so forth so they won't look like funeral flowers.'

"About an hour later his mother broke out with a scream, sobbin' and cryin', and he tried to quiet her by tellin' over one of their old-time family funny stories; it made her worse, so he quit. 'Oh, Mel,' she says, 'you'll be with your father—'

"I don't know as Mel had much of a belief in a hereafter; certainly he wasn't a great church-goer. 'Well,' he says, mightly slow, but hearty and smiling, too, 'if I see father, I—guess—I'll—be—pretty—well—fixed!' Then he jest lay still, tryin' to quiet her and pettin' her head. And so—that's the way he went."

Fiderson made one of his impatient little gestures, but Mr. Martin drowned his first words with a loud fit of coughing.

"Well, sir," he observed, "I read that 'Leglong' book down home; and I heard two or three countries, and especially ourn, had gone middling crazy over it; it seemed kind of funny that *we* should, too, so I thought I better come up and see it for myself, how it *was*, on the stage, where you could *look* at it; and—I expect they done it as well as they could. But when that little boy, that'd always had his board and clothes and education free, saw that he'd jest about talked himself to death, and called for the press notices about his christening to be read to him to soothe his last spasms—why, I wasn't overly put in mind of Melville Bickner."

Mr. Martin's train left for Plattsville at two in the morning. Little Fiderson and I escorted him to the station. As the old fellow waved us good-bye from within the gates, Fiderson turned and said:

"Just the type of sodden-headed old pioneer that you couldn't hope to make understand a beautiful thing like 'L'Aiglon' in a thousand years. I thought it better not to try, didn't you?"

THEODORE DREISER

(b. Terre Haute, 1871–d. 1948) was born into a large and economically depressed family, which he describes in his autobiographical *Hoosier Holiday* (1916). He was educated in at least three of Indiana's public school systems—those of Terre Haute, Sullivan, and Warsaw, reflecting his father's short-lived bouts with employment; in a parochial school in Evansville; and briefly at Indiana University. In 1891 his employment by the Chicago *Globe* initiated a long series of jobs on newspapers and magazines, including *Harper's* and *Cosmopolitan.* Meanwhile he made use of every spare moment, trying his hand at writing novels and short stories. With the help of such friendly critics as H. L. Mencken and George Jean Nathan, Dreiser persevered against much more hostile critics and eventually vindicated Mencken's and Nathan's confidence in him. Dreiser's best known novels remain *Sister Carrie* (1900), *The Financier* (1912), *The Titan* (1914), *The Genius* (1917), and *The American Tragedy* (1926). His collection of short fiction, *Free and Other Stories* (1918), won praise from Sherwood Anderson; and in that collection, the story "The Lost Phoebe" was hailed "a poetic triumph" by Harvard Professor F. O. Matthiessen, and it is cited by Robert Penn Warren in *Homage to Theodore Dreiser* (1971).

The Lost Phoebe

They lived together in a part of the country which was not so prosperous as it had once been, about three miles from one of those small towns that, instead of increasing in population, is steadily decreasing. The territory was not very thickly settled; perhaps a house every other mile or so, with large areas of corn- and wheat-land and fallow fields that at odd seasons had been sown to timothy and clover. Their particular house was part log and part frame, the log portion being the old original home of Henry's grandfather. The new portion, of now rain-beaten, time-worn slabs, through which the wind squeaked in the chinks at times, and which several overshadowing elms and a butternut-tree made picturesque and reminiscently pathetic, but a little damp, was erected by Henry when he was twenty-one and just married.

That was forty-eight years before. The furniture inside, like the house outside, was old and mildewy and reminiscent of an earlier day. You have seen the what-not of cherry wood, perhaps, with spiral legs and fluted top. It was there. The old-fashioned four poster bed, with its ball-like protuberances and deep curving incisions, was there also, a sadly alienated descendant of an early Jacobean ancestor. The bureau of cherry was also high and wide and solidly built, but faded-looking, and with a musty odor. The rag carpet that underlay all these sturdy examples of enduring furniture was a weak, faded, lead-and-pink-colored affair woven by Phœbe Ann's own hands, when she was fifteen years younger than she was when she died. The creaky wooden loom on which it had been done now stood like a dusty, bony skeleton, along with a broken rocking-chair, a worm-eaten clothes-press—Heaven knows how old—a lime-stained bench that had once been used to keep flowers on outside the door, and other decrepit factors of household utility, in an east room that was a lean-to against this so-called main portion. All sorts of other broken-down furniture were about this place; an antiquated clotheshorse, cracked in two of its ribs; a broken mirror in an old cherry frame, which had fallen from a nail and cracked itself three days before their youngest son, Jerry, died; an extension hat-rack, which once had had porcelain knobs on the ends of its pegs; and a sewing-machine, long since outdone in its clumsy mechanism by rivals of a newer generation.

The orchard to the east of the house was full of gnarled old apple-trees, worm-eaten as to trunks and branches, and fully ornamented with green and white lichens, so that it had a sad, greenish-white, silvery effect in moonlight. The low outhouses, which had once housed chickens, a horse or two, a cow, and several pigs, were covered with patches of moss as to their roof, and the sides had been free of paint for so long that they were blackish gray as to color, and a little spongy. The picket-fence in front, with its gate squeaky and askew, and the side fences of the stake-and-rider type were in an equally run-down condition. As a matter of fact, they had aged synchronously with the persons who lived here, old Henry Reifsneider and his wife Phœbe Ann.

They had lived here, these two, ever since their marriage, forty-eight years before, and Henry had lived here before that from his childhood up. His father and mother, well along in years when he was a boy, had invited him to bring his wife here when he had first fallen in love and decided to marry; and he had done so. His father and mother were the companions of himself and his wife for ten years after they were married, when both died; and then Henry and Phœbe were left with their five children growing lustily apace. But all sorts of things had happened since then. Of the seven children, all told, that had been born to them, three had died; one girl had gone to Kansas; one boy had gone to Sioux Falls, never even to be heard of after; another boy had gone to Washington; and the last girl lived five counties away in the same State, but was so burdened with cares of her own that she rarely gave them a thought. Time and a commonplace home life that had never been attractive had weaned them thoroughly, so that, wherever they were, they gave little thought as to how it might be with their father and mother.

Old Henry Reifsneider and his wife Phœbe were a loving couple. You perhaps know how it is with simple natures that fasten themselves like lichens on the stones of circumstance and weather their days to a crumbling conclusion. The great world sounds widely, but it has no call for them. They have no soaring intellect. The orchard, the meadow, the cornfield, the pig-pen, and the chicken-lot measure the range of their human activities. When the wheat is headed it is reaped and threshed; when the corn is browned and frosted it is cut and shocked; when the timothy is in full head it is cut, and the hay-cock erected. After that comes winter, with the hauling of grain to market, the sawing and splitting of wood, the simple chores of fire-building, meal-getting, occasional repairing, and visiting. Beyond these and the changes of weather—the snows, the rains, and the fair days—there are no immediate, significant things. All the rest of life is a far-off, clamorous phantasmagoria, flickering like Northern lights in the night, and sounding as faintly as cow-bells tinkling in the distance.

Old Henry and his wife Phœbe were as fond of each other as it is possible for two old people to be who have nothing else in this life to be fond of. He was a thin old man, seventy when she died, a queer, crotchety person with coarse gray-black hair and beard, quite straggly and unkempt. He looked at you out of dull, fishy, watery eyes that had deep-brown crow's-feet at the sides. His clothes, like the clothes of many farmers, were aged and angular and baggy, standing out at the pockets, not fitting about the neck, protuberant and worn at elbow and knee. Phœbe Ann was thin and shapeless, a very umbrella of a woman, clad in shabby black, and with a black bonnet for her best wear. As time had passed, and they had only themselves to look after, their movements had become slower and slower, their activities fewer and fewer. The annual keep of pigs had been reduced from five to one grunting porker, and the single horse which Henry now retained was a sleepy animal, not over-nourished and not very clean. The chickens, of which formerly there was a large flock, had almost disappeared, owing to ferrets, foxes, and the lack of proper care, which produces disease. The former healthy garden was now a straggling memory of itself, and the vines and flower-beds that formerly ornamented the windows and dooryard had now become choking thickets. A will had been made which divided the small tax-eaten property equally among the remaining four, so that it was really of no interest to any of them. Yet these two lived together in peace and sympathy, only that now and then old Henry would become unduly cranky, complaining almost invariably that something had been neglected or mislaid which was of no importance at all.

"Phœbe, where's my corn-knife? You ain't never minded to let my things alone no more."

"Now you hush, Henry," his wife would caution him in a cracked and squeaky voice. "If you don't, I'll leave yuh. I'll git up and walk out of here some day, and then where would y' be? Y' ain't got anybody but me to look after yuh, so yuh just behave yourself. Your corn knife's on the mantel where it's allus been unless you've gone an' put it summers else."

Old Henry, who knew his wife would never leave him in any circumstances, used to speculate at times as to what he would do if she were to die. That was the one leaving that he really feared. As he climbed on the chair at night to wind the old, long-pendulumed, double-weighted clock, or went finally to the front and the back door to see that they were safely shut in, it was a comfort to know that Phœbe was there, properly ensconced on her side of the bed, and that if he stirred restlessly in the night, she would be there to ask what he wanted.

"Now, Henry, do lie still! You're as restless as a chicken."

"Well, I can't sleep, Phœbe."

"Well, yuh needn't roll so, anyhow. Yuh kin let me sleep."

This usually reduced him to a state of somnolent ease. If she wanted a pail of water, it was a grumbling pleasure for him to get it; and if she did rise first to build the fires, he saw that the wood was cut and placed within easy reach. They divided this simple world nicely between them.

As the years had gone on, however, fewer and fewer people had called. They were well-known for a distance of as much as ten square miles as old Mr. and Mrs. Reifsneider, honest, moderately Christian, but too old to be really interesting any longer. The writing of letters had become an almost impossible burden too difficult to continue or even negotiate via others, although an occasional letter still did arrive from the daughter in Pemberton County. Now and then some old friend stopped with a pie or cake or a roasted chicken or duck, or merely to see that they were well; but even these kindly minded visits were no longer frequent.

One day in the early spring of her sixty-fourth year Mrs. Reifsneider took sick, and from a low fever passed into some indefinable ailment which, because of her age, was no longer curable. Old Henry drove to Swinnerton, the neighboring town, and procured a doctor. Some friends called, and the immediate care of her was taken off his hands. Then one chill spring night she died, and old Henry, in a fog of sorrow and uncertainty, followed her body to the nearest graveyard, an unattractive space with a few pines growing in it. Although he might have gone to the daughter in Pemberton or sent for her, it was really too much trouble and he was too weary and fixed. It was suggested to him at once by one friend and another that he come to stay with them awhile, but he did not see fit. He was so old and so fixed in his notions and so accustomed to the exact surroundings he had known all his days, that he could not think of leaving. He wanted to remain near where they had put his Phœbe; and the fact that he would have to live alone did not trouble him in the least. The living children were notified and the care of him offered if he would leave, but he would not.

"I kin make a shift for myself," he continually announced to old Dr. Morrow, who had attended his wife in this case. "I kin cook a little, and, besides, it don't take much more'n coffee an' bread in the mornin's to satisfy me. I'll get along now well enough. Yuh just let me be." And after many pleadings and proffers of advice, with supplies of coffee and bacon and baked bread duly offered and accepted, he was left to himself. For a while he sat idly outside his door brooding in the spring sun. He tried to revive his interest in farming, and to keep himself busy and free from thought by looking after the fields, which of late had been much neglected. It was a gloomy thing to come in of an evening, however, or in the afternoon and find no shadow of Phœbe where everything suggested her. By degrees he put a few of her things away. At night he sat beside his lamp and read in the papers that were left him occasionally or in a Bible that he had neglected for years, but he could get little solace from these things. Mostly he held his hand over his mouth and looked at the floor as he sat and thought of what had become of her, and how soon he himself would die. He made a great business of making his coffee in the morning and frying himself a little bacon at night; but his appetite was gone. The shell in which he had been housed so long seemed vacant, and its shadows were suggestive of immedicable griefs. So he

lived quite dolefully for five long months, and then a change began.

It was one night, after he had looked after the front and the back
door, wound the clock, blown out the light, and gone through all the
selfsame motions that he had indulged in for years, that he went to
bed not so much to sleep as to think. It was a moonlight night. The
green-lichen-covered orchard just outside and to be seen from his
bed where he now lay was a silvery affair, sweetly spectral. The moon
shone through the east windows, throwing the pattern of the panes
on the wooden floor, and making the old furniture, to which he was
accustomed, stand out dimly in the room. As usual he had been
thinking of Phœbe and the years when they had been young together, and of the children who had gone, and the poor shift he was
making of his present days. The house was coming to be in a very bad
state indeed. The bed-clothes were in disorder and not clean, for he
made a wretched shift of washing. It was a terror to him. The roof
leaked, causing things, some of them, to remain damp for weeks at
a time, but he was getting into that brooding state where he would
accept anything rather than exert himself. He preferred to pace
slowly to and fro or to sit and think.

By twelve o'clock of this particular night he was asleep, however,
and by two had waked again. The moon by this time had shifted to
a position on the western side of the house, and it now shone in
through the windows of the living-room and those of the kitchen
beyond. A certain combination of furniture—a chair near a table,
with his coat on it, the half-open kitchen door casting a shadow, and
the position of a lamp near a paper—gave him an exact representa-
tion of Phoebe leaning over the table as he had often seen her do in
life. It gave him a great start. Could it be she—or her ghost? He had
scarcely ever believed in spirits; and still—— He looked at her fixedly
in the feeble half-light, his old hair tingling oddly at the roots, and
then sat up. The figure did not move. He put his thin legs out of the
bed and sat looking at her, wondering if this could really be Phœbe.
They had talked of ghosts often in their lifetime, of apparitions and
omens; but they had never agreed that such things could be. It had
never been a part of his wife's creed that she could have a spirit that
could return to walk the earth. Her after-world was quite a different
affair, a vague heaven, no less, from which the righteous did not
trouble to return. Yet here she was now, bending over the table in
her black skirt and gray shawl, her pale profile outlined against the
moonlight.

"Phœbe," he called, thrilling from head to toe and putting out one bony hand, "have yuh come back?"

The figure did not stir, and he arose and walked uncertainly to the door, looking at it fixedly the while. As he drew near, however, the apparition resolved itself into its primal content—his old coat over the highbacked chair, the lamp by the paper, the half-open door.

"Well," he said to himself, his mouth open, "I thought shore I saw her." And he ran his hand strangely and vaguely through his hair, the while his nervous tension relaxed. Vanished as it had, it gave him the idea that she might return.

Another night, because of this first illusion, and because his mind was now constantly on her and he was old, he looked out of the window that was nearest his bed and commanded a hen-coop and pig-pen and a part of the wagon-shed, and there, a faint mist exuding from the damp of the ground, he thought he saw her again. It was one of those little wisps of mist, one of those faint exhalations of the earth that rise in a cool night after a warm day, and flicker like small white cypresses of fog before they disappear. In life it had been a custom of hers to cross this lot from her kitchen door to the pig-pen to throw in any scrap that was left from her cooking, and here she was again. He sat up and watched it strangely, doubtfully, because of his previous experience, but inclined, because of the nervous titillation that passed over his body, to believe that spirits really were, and that Phœbe, who would be concerned because of his lonely state, must be thinking about him, and hence returning. What other way would she have? How otherwise could she express herself? It would be within the province of her charity so to do, and like her loving interest in him. He quivered and watched it eagerly; but, a faint breath of air stirring, it wound away toward the fence and disappeared.

A third night, as he was actually dreaming, some ten days later, she came to his bedside and put her hand on his head.

"Poor Henry!" she said. "It's too bad."

He roused out of his sleep, actually to see her, he thought, moving from his bed-room into the one living-room, her figure a shadowy mass of black. The weak straining of his eyes caused little points of light to flicker about the outlines of her form. He arose, greatly astonished, walked the floor in the cool room, convinced that Phœbe was coming back to him. If he only thought sufficiently, if he made it perfectly clear by his feeling that he needed her greatly, she would come back, this kindly wife, and tell him what to do. She would perhaps be with him much of the time, in the night, anyhow; and that would make him less lonely, this state more endurable.

In age and with the feeble it is not such a far cry from the subtleties of illusion to actual hallucination, and in due time this transition was made for Henry. Night after night he waited, expecting her return. Once in his weird mood he thought he saw a pale light moving about the room, and another time he thought he saw her walking in the orchard after dark. It was one morning when the details of his lonely state were virtually unendurable that he woke with the thought that she was not dead. How he had arrived at this conclusion it is hard to say. His mind had gone. In its place was a fixed illusion. He and Phœbe had had a senseless quarrel. He had reproached her for not leaving his pipe where he was accustomed to find it, and she had left. It was an aberrated fulfillment of her old jesting threat that if he did not behave himself she would leave him.

"I guess I could find yuh ag'in," he had always said. But her cackling threat had always been:

"Yuh'll not find me if I ever leave yuh. I guess I kin git some place where yuh can't find me."

This morning when he arose he did not think to build the fire in the customary way or to grind his coffee and cut his bread, as was his wont, but solely to meditate as to where he should search for her and how he should induce her to come back. Recently the one horse had been dispensed with because he found it cumbersome and beyond his needs. He took down his soft crush hat after he had dressed himself, a new glint of interest and determination in his eye, and taking his black crook cane from behind the door, where he had always placed it, started out briskly to look for her among the nearest neighbors. His old shoes clumped soundly in the dust as he walked, and his gray-black locks, now grown rather long, straggled out in a dramatic fringe or halo from under his hat. His short coat stirred busily as he walked, and his hands and face were peaked and pale.

"Why, hello, Henry! Where're yuh goin' this mornin'?" inquired Farmer Dodge, who, hauling a load of wheat to market, encountered him on the public road. He had not seen the aged farmer in months, not since his wife's death, and he wondered now, seeing him looking so spry.

"Yuh ain't seen Phœbe, have yuh?" inquired the old man, looking up quizzically.

"Phœbe who?" inquired Farmer Dodge, not for the moment connecting the name with Henry's dead wife.

"Why, my wife Phœbe, o' course. Who do yuh s'pose I mean?" He stared up with a pathetic sharpness of glance from under his shaggy, gray eyebrows.

"Wall, I'll swan, Henry, yuh ain't jokin', are yuh?" said the solid Dodge, a pursy man, with a smooth, hard, red face. "It can't be your wife yuh're talkin' about. She's dead."

"Dead! Shucks!" retorted the demented Reifsneider. "She left me early this mornin', while I was sleepin'. She allus got up to build the fire, but she's gone now. We had a little spat last night, an' I guess that's the reason. But I guess I kin find her. She's gone over to Matilda Race's; that's where she's gone."

He started briskly up the road, leaving the amazed Dodge to stare in wonder after him.

"Well, I'll be switched!" he said aloud to himself. "He's clean out'n his head. That poor old feller's been livin' down there till he's gone outen his mind. I'll have to notify the authorities." And he flicked his whip with great enthusiasm. "Geddap!" he said, and was off.

Reifsneider met no one else in this poorly populated region until he reached the whitewashed fence of Matilda Race and her husband three miles away. He had passed several other houses en route, but these not being within the range of his illusion were not considered. His wife, who had known Matilda well, must be here. He opened the picket-gate which guarded the walk, and stamped briskly up to the door.

"Why, Mr. Reifsneider," exclaimed old Matilda herself, a stout woman, looking out of the door in answer to his knock, "what brings yuh here this mornin'?"

"Is Phœbe here?" he demanded eagerly.

"Phœbe who? What Phœbe?" replied Mrs. Race, curious as to this sudden development of energy on his part.

"Why, my Phœbe, o' course. My wife Phœbe. Who do yuh s'pose? Ain't she here now?"

"Lawsy me!' exclaimed Mrs. Race, opening her mouth. "Yuh pore man! So you're clean out'n your mind now. Yuh come right in and sit down. I'll git yuh a cup o' coffee. O' course your wife ain't here; but yuh come in an' sit down. I'll find her fer yuh after a while. I know where she is."

The old farmer's eyes softened, and he entered. He was so thin and pale a specimen, pantalooned and patriarchal, that he aroused Mrs. Race's extremest sympathy as he took off his hat and laid it on his knees quite softly and mildly.

"We had a quarrel last night, an' she left me," he volunteered.

"Laws! Laws!" sighed Mrs. Race, there being no one present with whom to share her astonishment as she went to her kitchen. "The pore man! Now somebody's just got to look after him. He can't be allowed to run around the country this way lookin' for his dead wife. It's turrible."

She boiled him a pot of coffee and brought in some of her new-baked bread and fresh butter. She set out some of her best jam and put a couple of eggs to boil, lying whole-heartedly the while.

"Now yuh stay right there, Uncle Henry, till Jake comes in, an' I'll send him to look for Phœbe. I think it's more'n likely she's over to Swinnerton with some o' her friends. Anyhow, we'll find out. Now yuh just drink this coffee an' eat this bread. Yuh must be tired. Yuh've had a long walk this mornin'." Her idea was to take counsel with Jake, "her man," and perhaps have him notify the authorities.

She bustled about, meditating on the uncertainties of life, while old Reifsneider thrummed on the rim of his hat with his pale fingers and later ate abstractedly of what she offered. His mind was on his wife, however, and since she was not here, or did not appear, it wandered vaguely away to a family by the name of Murray, miles away in another direction. He decided after a time that he would not wait for Jake Race to hunt his wife but would seek her for himself. He must be on, and urge her to come back.

"Well, I'll be going'," he said, getting up and looking strangely about him. "I guess she didn't come here after all. She went over to the Murrays', I guess. I'll not wait any longer, Mis' Race. There's a lot to do over to the house to-day." And out he marched in the face of her protests taking to the dusty road again in the warm spring sun, his cane striking the earth as he went.

It was two hours later that this pale figure of a man appeared in the Murrays' doorway, dusty, perspiring, eager. He had tramped all of five miles, and it was noon. An amazed husband and wife of sixty heard his strange query, and realized also that he was mad. They begged him to stay to dinner, intending to notify the authorities later and see what could be done; but though he stayed to partake of a little something, he did not stay long, and was off again to another distant farmhouse, his idea of many things to do and his need of Phœbe impelling him. So it went for that day and the next and the next, the circle of his inquiry ever widening.

The process by which a character assumes the significance of being peculiar, his antics weird, yet harmless, in such a community is often involute and pathetic. This day, as has been said, saw Reifsneider at other doors, eagerly asking his unnatural question, and leaving a trail of amazement, sympathy, and pity in his wake. Although the authorities were informed—the county sheriff, no less—it was not deemed advisable to take him into custody; for when those who knew old Henry, and had for so long, reflected on the condition of the county insane asylum, a place which, because of the poverty of the district, was of staggering aberration and sickening environment, it was decided to let him remain at large; for, strange to relate, it was found on investigation that at night he returned peaceably enough to his lonesome domicile there to discover whether his wife had returned, and to brood in loneliness until the morning. Who would lock up a thin, eager, seeking old man with iron-gray hair and an attitude of kindly, innocent inquiry, particularly when he was well known for a past of only kindly servitude and reliability? Those who had known him best rather agreed that he should be allowed to roam at large. He could do no harm. There were many who were willing to help him as to food, old clothes, the odds and ends of his daily life—at least at first. His figure after a time became not so much a common-place as an accepted curiosity, and the replies, "Why, no, Henry; I ain't seen her," or "No, Henry; she ain't been here today," more customary.

For several years thereafter then he was an odd figure in the sun and rain, on dusty roads and muddy ones, encountered occasionally in strange and unexpected places, pursuing his endless search. Undernourishment, after a time, although the neighbors and those who knew his history gladly contributed from their store, affected his body; for he walked much and ate little. The longer he roamed the public highway in this manner, the deeper became his strange hallucination; and finding it harder and harder to return from his more and more distant pilgrimages, he finally began taking a few utensils with him from his home, making a small package of them, in order that he might not be compelled to return. In an old tin coffee-pot of large size he placed a small tin cup, a knife, fork, and spoon, some salt and pepper, and to the outside of it, by a string forced through a pierced hole, he fastened a plate, which could be released, and which was his woodland table. It was no trouble for him to secure the little food that he needed, and with a strange, almost religious dignity, he had no hesitation in asking for that much. By degrees his hair became longer and longer, his once black hat became an earthen brown, and his clothes threadbare and dusty.

For all of three years he walked, and none knew how wide were his perambulations, nor how he survived the storms and cold. They could not see him, with homely rural understanding and forethought, sheltering himself in hay-cocks, or by the sides of cattle, whose warm bodies protected him from the cold, and whose dull understandings were not opposed to his harmless presence. Over-hanging rocks and trees kept him at times from the rain, and a friendly hay-loft or corn-crib was not above his humble consideration.

The involute progression of hallucination is strange. From asking at doors and being constantly rebuffed or denied, he finally came to the conclusion that although his Phœbe might not be in any of the houses at the doors of which he inquired, she might nevertheless be within the sound of his voice. And so, from patient inquiry, he began to call sad, occasional cries, that ever and anon waked the quiet landscapes and ragged hill regions, and set to echoing his thin "O-o-o Phœbe! O-o-o Phœbe!" It had a pathetic, albeit insane, ring, and many a farmer or plowboy came to know it even from afar and say, "There goes old Reifsneider."

Another thing that puzzled him greatly after a time and after many hundreds of inquiries was, when he no longer had any particular dooryard in view and no special inquiry to make, which way to go. These cross-roads, which occasionally led in four or even six directions, came after a time to puzzle him. But to solve this knotty problem, which became more and more of a puzzle, there came to his aid another hallucination. Phœbe's spirit or some power of the air or wind or nature would tell him. If he stood at the center of the parting of the ways, closed his eyes, turned thrice about, and called "O-o-o Phœbe!" twice, and then threw his cane straight before him, that would surely indicate which way to go for Phœbe, or one of these mystic powers would surely govern its direction and fall! In which-ever direction it went, even though, as was not infrequently the case, it took him back along the path he had already come, or across fields, he was not so far gone in his mind but that he gave himself ample time to search before he called again. Also the hallucination seemed to persist that at some time he would surely find her. There were hours when his feet were sore, and his limbs weary, when he would stop in the heat to wipe his seamed brow, or in the cold to beat his arms. Sometimes, after throwing away his cane, and finding it in-dicating the direction from which he had just come, he would shake his head wearily and philosophically, as if contemplating the unbe-lievable or an untoward fate, and then start briskly off. His strange figure came finally to be known in the farthest reaches of three or four counties. Old Reifsneider was a pathetic character. His fame was wide.

Near a little town called Watersville, in Green County, perhaps four miles from that minor center of human activity, there was a place or precipice locally known as the Red Cliff, a sheer wall of red sandstone, perhaps a hundred feet high, which raised its sharp face for half a mile or more above the fruitful cornfields and orchards that lay beneath, and which was surmounted by a thick grove of trees. The slope that slowly led up to it from the opposite side was covered by a rank growth of beech, hickory, and ash, through which threaded a number of wagon-tracks crossing at various angles. In fair weather it had become old Reifsneider's habit, so inured was he by now to the open, to make his bed in some such patch of trees as this to fry his bacon or boil his eggs at the foot of some tree before laying himself down for the night. Occasionally, so light and inconsequential was his sleep, he would walk at night. More often, the moonlight or some sudden wind stirring in the trees or a reconnoitering animal arousing him, he would sit up and think, or pursue his quest in the moonlight or the dark, a strange, unnatural, half wild, half savage-looking but utterly harmless creature, calling at lonely road crossings, staring at dark and shuttered houses, and wondering where, where Phœbe could really be.

That particular lull that comes in the systole-diastole of this earthly ball at two o'clock in the morning invariably aroused him, and though he might not go any farther he would sit up and contemplate the darkness or the stars, wondering. Sometimes in the strange processes of his mind he would fancy that he saw moving among the trees the figure of his lost wife, and then he would get up to follow, taking his utensils, always on a string, and his cane. If she seemed to evade him too easily he would run, or plead, or, suddenly losing track of the fancied figure, stand awed or disappointed, grieving for the moment over the almost insurmountable difficulties of his search.

It was in the seventh year of these hopeless peregrinations, in the dawn of a similar springtime to that in which his wife had died, that he came at last one night to the vicinity of this self-same patch that crowned the rise to the Red Cliff. His far-flung cane, used as a divining-rod at the last cross-roads, had brought him hither. He had walked many, many miles. It was after ten o'clock at night, and he was very weary. Long wandering and little eating had left him but a shadow of his former self. It was a question now not so much of physical strength but of spiritual endurance which kept him up. He had barely eaten this day, and now exhausted he set himself down in the dark to rest and possibly to sleep.

Curiously on this occasion a strange suggestion of the presence of his wife surrounded him. It would not be long now, he counseled with himself, although the long months had brought him nothing until he should see her, talk to her. He fell asleep after a time, his head on his knees. At midnight the moon began to rise, and at two in the morning, his wakeful hour, was a large silver disk shining through the trees to the east. He opened his eyes when the radiance became strong, making a silver pattern at his feet and lighting the woods with strange lusters and silvery, shadowy forms. As usual, his old notion that his wife must be near occurred to him on this occasion, and he looked about him with a speculative, anticipatory eye. What was it that moved in the distant shadows along the path by which he had entered—a pale, flickering will-o'-the-wisp that bobbed gracefully among the trees and riveted his expectant gaze? Moonlight and shadows combined to give it a strange form and a stranger reality, this fluttering of bogfire or dancing of wandering fire-flies. Was it truly his lost Phœbe? By a circuitous route it passed about him, and in his fevered state he fancied that he could see the very eyes of her, not as she was when he last saw her in the black dress and shawl but now a strangely younger Phœbe, gayer, sweeter, the one whom he had known years before as a girl. Old Reifsneider got up. He had been expecting and dreaming of this hour all these years, and now as he saw the feeble light dancing lightly before him he peered at it questioningly, one thin hand in his gray hair.

Of a sudden there came to him now for the first time in many years the full charm of her girlish figure as he had known it in boyhood, the pleasing, sympathetic smile, the brown hair, the blue sash she had once worn about her waist at a picnic, her gay, graceful movements. He walked around the base of the tree, straining with his eyes, forgetting for once his cane and utensils, and following eagerly after. On she moved before him, a will-o'-the-wisp of the spring, a little flame above her head, and it seemed as though among the small saplings of ash and beech and the thick trunks of hickory and elm that she signaled with a young, a lightsome hand.

"O Phœbe! Phœbe!" he called. "Have yuh really come? Have yuh really answered me?" And hurrying faster, he fell once, scrambling lamely to his feet, only to see the light in the distance dancing illusively on. On and on he hurried until he was fairly running, brushing his ragged arms against the trees, striking his hands and face against impeding twigs. His hat was gone, his lungs were breathless, his reason quite astray, when coming to the edge of the cliff he saw her below among a silvery bed of apple-trees now blooming in the spring.

"O Phœbe!" he called. "O Phœbe! Oh, no, don't leave me!" And feeling the lure of a world where love was young and Phœbe as this vision presented her, a delightful epitome of their quondam youth, he gave a gay cry of "Oh, wait, Phœbe!" and leaped.

Some farmer-boys, reconnoitering this region of bounty and prospect some few days afterward, found first the tin utensils tied together under the tree where he had left them, and then later at the foot of the cliff, pale, broken, but elate, a molded smile of peace and delight upon his lips, his body. His old hat was discovered lying under some low-growing sapling the twigs of which had held it back. No one of all the simple population knew how eagerly and joyously he had found his lost mate.

REX STOUT

(b. Noblesville, 1886–d. 1975) was educated in the Noblesville schools and the U.S. Navy. Until his mystery stories and novelettes started selling to magazines like *Saturday Evening Post* and *The New Yorker,* he supported himself by working at all sorts of odd jobs, considering none too menial. Exemplifying the work-and-save ethic that characterized most of Indiana at the turn of the century, he devised the first school-children's "Thrift Savings" program in the United States. Most of his sixty books center around the exploits of detective Nero Wolfe, typically *Over My Dead Body* (1940) and *Three at Wolfe's Door* (1960). The following short story, sometimes reprinted with the title "Santa Claus Beat," is "the only story of less than 18,000 words I have ever written," said Stout.

Tough Cop's Gift

"Christmas Eve," Art Hipple was thinking to himself, "would be a good time for the murder."

The thought was both timely and characteristic. It was three o'clock in the afternoon of December 24th; and though the murder would have got an eager welcome from Art Hipple any day at all, his disdainful attitude toward the prolonged hurly-burly of Christmas sentiment and shopping made that the best possible date for it. He did not actually turn up his nose at Christmas, for that would have been un-American, but as a New York cop not yet out of his twenties who had recently been made a precinct dick and had hung his uniform in the back of the closet of his furnished room, it had to be made clear, especially to himself, that he was good and tough, and a cynical slant on Christmas was therefore imperative.

His hope of running across a murder had begun back in the days when his assignment had been tagging illegally parked cars, and was merely practical and professional. His dear ambition was promotion to Homicide, and the shortest cut would have been discovery of a beaut. It had not gone so far as obsession; as he strode down the sidewalk this December afternoon he was not sniffing for the scent of blood at each dingy entrance he passed; but when he reached the number he had been given and turned to enter, his hand darted inside his jacket to touch his gun.

None of the three people he found in the cluttered and smelly little room one flight up seemed to need shooting. Art identified himself and got their names down. The man at the battered old desk, who was twice Art's age and needed a shave, was Emil Duross, proprietor of the business conducted in that room—Duross Specialties, mail-order dealer in gimcrack jewelry. The younger man, small, dark, and neat, seated on a chair squeezed in between the desk and shelves stacked with cardboard boxes, was H. E. Koenig, adjuster, according to a card he had proffered, for the Apex Insurance Company. The girl, who had pale watery eyes and a stringy neck, stood backed up to a pile of cartons the height of her shoulder. She had on a dark brown felt hat and a lighter brown woolen coat that had lost a button. Her name was Helen Lauro, and it could have been not rheum in her eyes but the remains of tears.

Because Art was thorough it took him twenty minutes to get the story to his satisfaction. Then he returned his notebook to his pocket, looked at Duross, at Koenig, and last at the girl. He wanted to tell her to wipe her eyes, but what if she didn't have a handkerchief?

He spoke to Duross. "Stop me if I'm wrong," he said. "You bought the ring a week ago to give to your wife for Christmas and paid sixty-two dollars for it. You put it there in a desk drawer after showing it to Miss Lauro?"

Duross turned his palms up. "Just a natural thing. She works for me, she's a woman, it's a beautiful ring."

"Okay. Today you work with her filling orders, addressing packages, and putting postage on. You send her to the post office with a bag of the packages. Why didn't she take all of them?"

"She did."

"Then what are those?" Art pointed to a pile of little boxes, addressed and stamped, on the end of a table.

"Orders that came in the afternoon mail. I did them while she was gone to the post office."

Art nodded. "And also while she was gone you looked in the drawer to get the ring to take it home for Christmas, and it wasn't there. You know it was there this morning because Miss Lauro asked if she could look at it again, and you showed it to her and let her put it on her finger, and then you put it back in the drawer. But this afternoon it was gone, and you couldn't have taken it yourself because you haven't left this room. Miss Lauro went out and got sandwiches for your lunch. So you decided she took the ring, and you phoned the insurance company, and Mr. Koenig came and advised you to call the police, and you did so, and—"

"Only his stock is insured," Koenig put in. "The ring was not a stock item and was not covered."

"Just a legality," Duross declared scornfully. "Insurance companies can't hide behind legalities. It hurts their reputation."

Koenig smiled politely but noncommittally.

Art turned to the girl. "Why don't you sit down?" he asked her. "There's a chair we men are not using."

"I will never sit down in this room again," she declared in a thin tight voice.

"Okay." Art scowled at her. She was certainly not comely. "If you did take the ring you might—"

"I didn't!"

"Very well. But if you did you might as well tell me where it is because you won't ever dare to wear it or sell it."

"Of course I wouldn't. I knew I wouldn't. That's why I didn't take it."

"Oh? You thought of taking it?"

"Of course I did. It was a beautiful ring." She stopped to swallow. "Maybe my life isn't much, but what it is, I'd give it for a ring like that, and a girl like me, I could live a hundred years and I'll never have one. Of course I thought of taking it, but I knew I couldn't ever wear it."

"You see?" Duross appealed to the law. "She's foxy, that girl. She's slick."

Art downed an impulse to cut it short, get out, return to the station house, and write a report. Nobody here deserved anything, not even justice. Perhaps especially not justice. Writing a brief report was all it rated, and all, ninety-nine times out of a hundred, it would have got. But instead of breaking it off, Art sat and thought it over through a long silence, with the three pairs of eyes on him. Finally he spoke to Duross:

"Get me the orders that came in the afternoon mail."

Duross was startled. "Why?"

"I want to check them with that pile of boxes you addressed and stamped."

Duross shook his head. "I don't need a cop to check my orders and shipments. Is this a gag?"

"No. Get me the orders."

"I will not!"

"Then I'll have to open all the boxes." Art rose and headed for the table. Duross bounced up and got in front of him and they were chest to chest.

"You don't touch those boxes," Duross told him. "You got no search warrant. You don't touch anything."

"That's just a legality." Art backed off a foot to avoid contact. "And since I guessed right, what's a little legality? I'm going to open the boxes here and now, but I'll count ten first to give you a chance to pick it out and hand it to me and save both of us a lot of bother. One, two, three—"

"I'll phone the station house!"

"Go ahead. Four, five, six, seven, eight, nine—" Art stopped at nine because Duross had moved to the table and was fingering the boxes. As he drew away with one in his hand Art commanded him: "Gimme." He hesitated but passed it over, and after a glance at the address Art ripped the tape off, opened the flap of the box, took out a wad of tissue paper, and then a ring box. From that he removed a ring, yellow gold, with a large greenish stone. Helen Lauro made a noise in her throat. Koenig let out a grunt, evidently meant for applause. Duross made a grab, not for the ring but for the box on which he had put an address, and missed.

"It stuck out as plain as your nose," Art told him, "but of course my going for the boxes was just a good guess. Did you pay sixty-two bucks for this?"

Duross's lips parted, but no words came. Apparently he had none. He nodded, not vigorously. Then he looked down at the floor.

Art turned to the girl. "Look, Miss Lauro. You say you're through here. You ought to have something to remember it by. You could make some trouble for Mr. Duross for the dirty trick he tried to play on you, and if you lay off I expect he'd like to show his appreciation by giving you this ring. Wouldn't you, Mr. Duross?"

Duross managed to get it out. "Sure I would."

"Shall I give it to her for you?"

"Sure." Duross's jaw worked. "Go ahead."

Art extended a hand with the ring and the girl took it, but not looking at it because she was gazing incredulously at him. It was a gaze so intense as to disconcert him, and he covered by turning to Duross and proffering the box with an address on it.

"Here," he said, "you can have it. Next time you cook up a plan for getting credit with your wife for buying her a ring, and collecting from the insurance company for its cost, and sending the ring to a girl friend, all in one neat little operation, don't do it. And don't forget you gave Miss Lauro that ring before witnesses."

Duross gulped and nodded.

Koenig spoke. "Your name is not Hipple, officer, it's Santa Claus. You have given her the ring she would have given her life for, you have given him an out on a charge of attempted fraud, and you have given me a crossoff on a claim. That's the ticket! That's the old yuletide spirit! Merry Christmas!"

"Nuts," Art said contemptuously, and turned and marched from the room, down the stairs, and out to the sidewalk. As he headed in the direction of the station house he decided that he would tone it down a little in his report. Getting a name for being tough was okay, but not too damn tough. That insurance guy sure was dumb, calling him Santa Claus—him, Art Hipple, feeling as he did about Christmas.

Which reminded him, Christmas Eve would be a swell time for the murder.

JESSAMYN WEST

(b. Jennings County, 1907–) was educated in Quaker schools and at Whittier College. She has taught at several writers' institutes, especially at Indiana and Notre Dame Universities. Her twenty books and movie scripts include *The Friendly Persuasion* (1945), *Cress Delahanty* (1953), and *Massacre at Fall Creek* (1974).

Lead Her Like A Pigeon

It was deep in May. Fingers had lifted the green strawberry leaves and had found fruit beneath them. Wheat was heading up. Cherries, bright as Christmas candles, hung from the trees. The bees had swarmed twice. The wind was from the south and sent a drift of locust blossoms like summer snow—Mattie thought—through the air.

She left her churn on the back porch and stood for a minute by the spring-house with uplifted face to see how locust-snow felt; but the wind died down and no more blossoms fell, so she went back to her churning.

She counted slowly as she moved the dasher up and down. She was keeping track of the least and most strokes it took to bring butter. This at any rate was not going to be a least-time. "Eighty-eight, eighty-nine . . ." Little Jess was putting horsehairs in the rain barrel to turn into worms. Enoch stuck his head out of the barn door, saw her and directly pulled it in again.

"Mattie," called her mother, "get finished with thy churning and ride over to the Bents' with some rocks."

Mattie could smell the rocks baking: raisins and hickory nuts all bedded down together in sweet dough.

"Lavony Bent's as queer as Dick's hatband," her mother called above the slap and gurgle of the dasher, "half Indian and a new-comer. She needs a token to show she's welcome."

Listening, Mattie slowed her churning. "Bring that butter humping," her mother said. "Thee'll have to get a soon start or it'll get dark on thee." She came to the kitchen door, rosy from the oven's heat, bringing Mattie a new-baked rock. "Day fading so soon," she said.

Mattie looked at her mother because of the sadness in her voice, and felt uncertainty and sorrow herself.

"There'll be another to match it tomorrow," her mother promised. "Its equal or better, Mattie. That red sky's a sure sign."

The butter was slow coming, only five strokes short of the most she'd ever counted. "Thee'd best go as thee is, Mattie."

"In this?" said Mattie.

"Who's to see?" asked her mother. "None but Bents and hoot-owls at this hour."

Mattie wouldn't've named them together—hoot-owls and the black-haired, brown-faced boys she'd watched walking riverward with fishing poles over their shoulders.

"Once thee starts combing and changing it'll be nightfall."

So Mattie rode as she was to the Bents', barefooted and in her blue anchor print which had faded until the anchors were almost as pale as the sea that lapped about them.

She carried the rocks in a little wooden box her mother was fixing to make into a footstool. So far, it was only painted white, with cranes and cattails on each side. The brown cattails were set onto the box with so much paint that they curved up plump as real ones beneath Mattie's exploring thumb.

Old Polly walked like a horse in a dream ... slow ... slow ... with forever to arrive. Tonight, a short way on the pike and then across the wood lot. Mattie ate a rock, pulled down a limb to see it spring back in place ... remembered what she'd heard about the Bents ...

"Never seen a more comfortable sight in my life," her father called one day, and there on a padded chair was Jud Bent riding down the pike in his manure wagon sitting and reading like a man at ease in his parlor. "Wonderful emancipation," her father said. "Thee mark it, Mattie. The spirit of man's got no limitations."

Jud Bent read and farmed. His boys, all but Gardiner, fished and farmed. "Gardiner's a reader like his pa," said Mattie's father, "off to Normal studying to be a teacher. He figures on getting shut of the manure wagon and having just the book left."

But the day she rode through was more to Mattie than her destination. In the woods it was warm and sheltered and the sun, setting, lay like butter on the new green leaves.

At the far edge of the woods she stopped for a minute at the old Wright place. A little white tumbling-down house empty for years, stood there. A forgotten house, but flowers still came up about it in the patterns in which Mrs. Wright had planted them. It was a sad, beautiful sight, Mattie thought, to see flowers hands had planted, growing alone in the woods with not an eye to note whether they did well or not: the snowball bush where the front gate had been, spice pinks still keeping to their circle by the steps and white flags, gold-powered now at sunset, by the ruined upping-block. A pair of doves, as she watched, slid down from the deep shadows of the woods and wheeled about in the sunlit clearing as if coming home.

Mattie stretched a hand to them. "You don't act like wildings," she said.

She slipped down from fat old Polly and carrying her box of cookies went to pick some flags. These flowers and buildings have known people for too long, she thought, to be happy alone. They have grown

230] THE INDIANA EXPERIENCE

away from their own kind and forgotten the language of woods and doves and long to hear household words again. To hear at bedtime a woman coming to the door for a sight of stars and saying, "There'll be rain before morning. A circle round the moon and hark to that cock crowing. It's a sure sign."

Or a man at morning, scanning the sky as he hitches up his suspenders, "A weather breeder. Have to hustle the hay in."

Mattie talked for the house and flowers to hear as she gathered the flags and laid them across the top of the cookie-filled footstool.

"If it's a dry summer I'll bring you some water," she said. "I couldn't bear to lie abed a hot night, and you parching here. I'll carry buckets from the branch if the well's dry, and some night I'll come and light a candle in the house so it'll look like olden times. I'll sing a song in the house and it'll be like Mrs. Wright playing on her melodeon again."

"Sing now, why don't you?"

She was bending over the flags, but she wasn't frightened—the voice was so quiet. It was a young man's voice though and she dropped the flags in her hand onto her bare feet before she turned to face him.

"No human would enjoy my singing . . . only maybe an old house that can't be choosy."

"I'm not choosy, either."

"No, I'm on an errand to take some rocks to Lavony Bent. I only stopped to pick some flags."

"Well, I'm Gard Bent," the boy said, "and I'll walk along home with you. What's your name?"

"Martha Truth Birdwell. Only I'm mostly called Mattie."

"Martha Truth Birdwell. That's as pretty as any song. If he'd a known you," and Gardiner Bent held up the book he was carrying, "he'd written a poem called Martha Truth."

Mattie saw the name on the book. "He mostly writes of Jeans and Marys," she said. Now maybe this Bent boy wouldn't think she was a know-nothing, barefooted and talking to herself. "Thee take the rocks on to thy ma. I've dallied here so long it'll be dark going home through the wood lot."

"No, I'll walk back with you to the pike. Ma'd never forgive me if I let you go home with your box empty. The boys've been on the river this afternoon. They'll have a fine mess of catfish. Can I help you onto your horse?"

Mattie would dearly have liked being handed onto her horse had she been rightly dressed and old Polly saddled, but that would have to wait for another time. She would not be hoisted like a sack of meal, plopped barefooted onto a saddleless horse. She stood stock still, the flags covering her feet, and said nothing.

"I'll get the rest of my books," the boy said.

While he was gone Mattie led old Polly to the upping-block and settled herself as sedately as if she were riding sidesaddle, one bare foot curled daintily beneath her.

Old Polly stepped slowly along in the dusk down the back road that led to the Bents' and Gard walked beside her. There wasn't much Indian about him, Mattie thought, unless it was his black hair and his quiet, toed-in walk. But his hair wasn't Indian straight, and his eyes weren't black at all but the color of the sandstone in a go-to-meeting watch fob. It was a pleasing face, a face she did not tire of regarding. Her eyes searched its tenderness and boldness in the May dusk.

"I thought thee was away at Vernon, studying at the Normal."

"I was—but it's out. Now I'm studying to take the teacher's examinations. I've got the promise of the school at Rush Branch when I pass. That's why I come to Wrights'—to study where it's quiet. If it gets dark on you, you could see your way home by the fireflies, they're so thick," he finished, as if ashamed of telling so much of himself.

"Fireflies. Is that what thee calls lightning bugs?"

"Elsewhere they're known as fireflies."

It was full sunset before they reached the Bent place. Lavony Bent was cleaning fish on a stump at the edge of the yard. Jud Bent was on the back steps getting the last of the light on to the book he was reading. Two black-haired boys were rolling about on the ground wrestling; a third was trying to bring a tune from a homemade-looking horn. There weren't any flowers or grass about the Bents' house, but the yard was trodden flat and swept as clean as a palm.

Gard called out, "Ma, this is Martha Truth Birdwell come to bring you some cookies."

Mrs. Bent didn't stop her fish cleaning, but looked up kindly enough. "Light down, Martha Truth, light down. I knowed your folks years ago when we's all younger than you are now."

Jud Bent closed his book on his finger and walked over to Mattie. He was a little plump man with a big head of red hair and a silky red mustache. "If it isn't Spring," he said. "Spring riding a white horse and with flowers in her hands."

Mattie was too taken aback to answer, but Gard laughed. "She's got a box of cookies under the flowers, pa."

Mattie handed the box of cookies and the white flags to him. "Spring for looks and Summer for gifts," said Jud Bent and took a rock in two bites, shaking the crumbs from his mustache like a water-drenched dog.

Mattie was afraid to talk to this strange man who carried a book as if it had been a pipe or a jack-knife, and spoke of her as though she were absent, or a painted picture.

Mrs. Bent took the head from a still quivering catfish with a single, clean stroke. The boy with the horn started a tune she knew, but he couldn't get far with it. "Lead her like a pigeon . . . Lead her like a pigeon . . ." he played over and over. Mattie's ears ached to hear the next notes, have the piece played through to its ending, not left broken and unfinished. "Lead her like a pigeon . . ." Mattie's mind hummed the tune for him . . . "Bed her like a dove . . . Whisper when I'm near her . . . Be my only love . . ." but the horn could not follow. "Lead her like a pigeon," it said once more, then gave up.

The wrestlers groaned and strained. They turned up the earth beneath them like a plow. A catfish leaped from the stump and swam again, most pitifully, in the grass.

"I'll have to be turning homewards," Mattie spoke suddenly. "Could I have my box? Ma's fixing to make a footstool of it."

Mrs. Bent sent Gard into the house to empty the cookies, then she lined the footstool with leaves and filled it with fish.

"There's a mess of fish for your breakfast," she said. "Tell your ma she's so clever at sharing I can't hope to keep pace with her."

As they went out of the yard, Mattie once more on old Polly and Gard walking beside her, Jud Bent called after them, "Persephone and Pluto. Don't eat any pomegranate seeds, Martha Truth."

"What does he mean?" asked Mattie. What Mr. Bent had said didn't sound like English to her.

"Persephone was a girl," Gard said, "the goddess of Spring, and Pluto, another god, stole her away to live underground with him. And while she was gone it was winter on earth."

"She's back on earth now, isn't she?" Mattie asked, watching the fireflies light themselves like candles among the dark leaves.

"Yes, she's back again," Gard said.

They parted at the edge of the woods where Mattie could see the lights of home glimmering down the road. Supper was over when she brought her box of catfish into the kitchen, and the dishes half washed.

"Sit down, child," her mother said, "and have thy supper. What kept thee?"

"The Bents all talk a lot," said Mattie. "It didn't seem polite to go and leave them all talking."

"They'll not be hindered by thy leaving . . . never fear. Eat, eat. Thy food will lose its savor."

"I can't eat," Mattie said. "I don't seem to have any relish for victuals." She got the dishtowel from the rack and started drying.

"Was thee fanciful," asked her mother, who never attributed fright to aught but fancy, "crossing the wood lot?"

"No. Gardiner Bent came with me."

"The Normal School boy?"

"Yes," said Mattie. "He's learned. Flowers. Fireflies. Poetry. Gods and goddesses. It's all one to him," she declared ardently. "He can lay his tongue to anything and give thee a fact about it. Oh, he's full of facts. He's primed for an examination and knows more than he can hold in."

Mattie made the plates she dried fly through her hands like thistledown—as if they were weightless as thistles and as imperishable. Her hands were deft but they had not her mother's flashing grace, and they were silent; they could not play the tune she envied, the tinkling bell-like song of her mother's wedding ring against the china; the constant light clatter of gold against glass and silver that said, I'm a lady grown and mistress of dishes and cupboards.

Behind were the dark woods, shadows and bosky places and whatever might slide through them when the sun was set. Here, the kitchen, the stove still burning, sending a wash of light across the scrubbed floor boards, the known dishes in their rightful stacks, and ma's ring sounding its quick song of love.

Mattie hummed a little.

"What's thee humming?" her mother asked. "Seems like I've heard it."

" 'Lead Her Like a Pigeon,' " Mattie, smiling, said.

"Play-party tune." Her mother held her hands above the soapy water and looked far away. " 'Weevily Wheat.' Once I was tempted to lift my foot to that."

Lift her foot. . . . Mattie looked at her mother . . . the Quaker preacher, whose foot now never peeped from beneath her full and seemly skirts. Once tempted . . . the wedding-ring music began again, but Mattie was watching, not drying. A long time ago tempted, yet there was something in the way her mother'd bury her face in a cabbage rose, or run to the door when father's spring wagon turned off the pike that showed her the black-haired girl who once listened to that music.

"Who's the Bent boy favor, Mattie?"

"His mother, I reckon. But handsomer. He's got a face to remember," Mattie said earnestly. "A proud, learned face. He's got eyes the color of sandstones. When he walks there isn't any up and down. It's a pleasure to watch him walk."

Mattie's mother put a washed skillet on the still warm stove to dry. "After a good heart," she said, "the least a woman can do is pick a face she fancies. Men's so much alike and many so sorry, that's the very least. If a man's face pleasures thee, that doesn't change. That is something to bank on. Thy father," she said, "has always been a comely man."

She turned back to her dishpan. "Why, Mattie," she said, "what's thee crying about?"

Mattie would not say. Then she burst out. "Pushing me off. Pushing me out of my own home. Thee talking about men that way . . . as if I would marry one. Anxious to be shut of me." She cried into her already wet dishtowel. "My own mother," she sobbed.

"Why, lovey," her mother said and went to her, but Mattie buried her face more deeply in her dishtowel and stumbled up the back stairs. "My own mother," she wailed.

"What's the trouble? What's Mattie taking on about?" Mattie's mother looked up at her husband, filling the doorway from the sitting-room like a staunch timber.

"Well, Jess," she said. "I think Mattie got a sudden inkling of what leaving home'll be like."

"Leaving home?" asked Jess. "Getting married? Thee think that's a crying matter, Eliza?"

Eliza looked at the face that had always pleasured her. "Thee knows I don't, Jess," she said.

Jess smiled. "Seems like," he said, "I have a recollection of some few tears thee shed those first . . ." But Eliza would have none of that. "Tsk, tsk," she said, her wedding ring beating a lively tattoo against the last kettle, "tsk, tsk, Jess Birdwell."

"Thee happy now?" Jess asked, smiling.

Eliza wouldn't say, but she hummed a little raveling of a song.

"Seems as if I know that," Jess said. "A long time ago."

"Like as not," Eliza agreed and handed him the pan to empty.

Jess went out with it, trying the tune over. "Tum-te-tum-te-tum. I can't name it," he said when he came back, "but it runs in my mind I know it."

"Thee know it, Jess, never fear," Eliza said. She took the empty pan from him, her wedding ring making one more musical note.

WILL HAYS, JR.

(b. Indianapolis, 1915–) was educated in the Sullivan schools, Wabash College, and the Yale School of Law. He maintains offices in the Ben Hur Building, Crawfordsville, the city for which he served as Mayor from 1964 to 1972. His critically acclaimed novel *Dragon Watch,* which appeared in 1954, deserves to be read whole. Nevertheless, its second chapter (renamed below as "Harrisville" with the kind permission of the author) stands alone with remarkable integrity. The characters and scenes remain fictitious, of course, so that any resemblances to actual persons and places should be regarded as purely coincidental.

Harrisville

Except for certain physical and philosophical aspects peculiarly incident to coal mining Harrisville, seat of Harris County, Indiana, was a typical small Midwestern community with a courthouse in the center of the square, a genteel residential section in one end of town and a railroad station and its adjacent shanties in the other, surrounded by principally flat, occasionally rolling, sparsely wooded, creek-meandering corn and wheat fields.

Terre Haute, the nearest city, was about forty miles away. Indianapolis lay another sixty miles or so beyond that. And Chicago, with its suburban Indiana steel towns of Gary and Hammond and the rest, was a good two hundred miles to the north.

Harrisville had the usual complement of grocery, dry goods, drug and hardware stores, offices of doctors, dentists and lawyers, churches, utility plants, a hundred-bed hospital, a grain elevator near the railroad station and an old standpipe out in the East End that had been rendered obsolete by a concrete reservoir but still afforded the vicinity's most exciting adventure for juvenile climbers. Also there was a new high school building with an adjoining gymnasium, and a grade school for each quarter of the town.

Unlike many Pennsylvania and West Virginia mining communities but in common with most of those lying in southwestern Indiana's soft-coal belt, Harrisville was not dedicated exclusively to coal production. It was half mining and half agricultural. Its Saturday-night crowds were a composite of miners and farmers and other small-town occupational and social ingredients with no one group consciously outweighing another in local influence.

The miners constituted an inflection rather than a transfigurement of the usual Indiana rural scene.

Although perhaps set apart somewhat by the hazardous nature of their work and their taciturn acceptance of its dangers the miners looked about the same as everyone else standing on week-end evenings along the curbs in front of the You Name It Hardware and the Quality Notion Store and the flickering Bijou Theater, talking to acquaintances and spitting into the gutters and holding sacks of groceries while their harassed women returned to stores for more sacks to pile in the back seats of battered cars.

With slight surprise, as though the answer were obvious, Mike Capps would assure any inquirer that the miners' patronage of his Buckhorn Pool Room did not exceed their numerical proportion in the community. They came into his place or stayed away like everyone else and presumably for the same reasons. He would have to say, however, that their visits usually were confined to Saturdays except when a strike was on.

There were no hopeless little colonies of company houses clustered about the region's mine tipples. The miners lived either in the county's towns or on their own small acreages scattered across the countryside. And the countryside itself was normally green in the summer and white in the winter instead of gray all the year around as in some areas along the Monongahela River. That was not to say there were no large mines in the neighborhood; some of the Harris County operations were as large as the greatest in the anthracite states farther east. And the union locals were as strong and active. Coal production simply was not as self-conscious a business around Harris County perhaps as in other parts of the nation.

Men died as easily in it however.

Within the borders of the county there were eight or ten communities smaller than Harrisville, some composed merely of a crossroads grocery and a few houses but others being of appreciable size. Harrisville's population was about eight thousand. A couple of important highways and an interstate railroad passed through the county seat and one or two of the other towns. Spurs off this railroad served the shaft and slope mines and strip pits belonging to the Bancock Coal Company, the headquarters of which occupied the second floor of the Bancock Building. The other mines in the vicinity were mostly truck mines; as their name implied their relatively small tonnages were trucked to the railroad loading docks. The Bancock Company did not bother with that sort of thing. The company's largest operation, Indian Creek, of which David Tennessey was mine manager, employed six hundred men altogether and produced more coal in a week than most of the truck mines did in a year.

All in all Harrisville was quite a town. In fact a perpetual banner across the top of the daily *Journal* proclaimed it the "Biggest Little Town in the Wabash Valley." Claude Correll, the paper's editor, had thought that one up.

A few nights after the argument at supper in his home over the hell-shouting preacher, David Tennessey was deep in the chilly entrails of Indian Creek two miles east of town and three hundred feet below the level of its quiet streets, walking in the glow of his helmet lamp along the seventh east entry off the main north.

There was nothing quiet about the seventh east. But he hardly noticed the racket, not simply because he was used to it, but because he was thinking.

With the top half of his mind he was thinking about how to impress the miners—particularly the section bosses—with the importance of frequent roof checks and with the bottom half he was thinking about several more or less related subjects.

He was not supposed to be working nights. The safety engineer had called him out to the mine after supper to help settle a squabble just as he was about to light his pipe and sit down with a copy of the *Journal* before turning in. Not that it made a whole lot of difference about the hour of the day down where he earned his living. In that respect he sometimes thought he was like a mole. Or a night crawler the kids in the neighborhood dug up for bait. Darkness was his abode and the flickering shadows cast by electric lamps its decoration. But he was tired. And he had washed up once that afternoon and washing up was too much of a chore to be undertaken twice in twenty-four hours. . . .

The recent, slow-burning resentment against J. L. that Big Dave had sensed at Indian Creek, although reminiscent of earlier days, was not simply a renewal of former arguments. The question of union recognition was not involved now, nor was the matter of wages. This time it was based on safety. But it went deeper than that too. It found stimulus in an increasingly apparent indifference on J. L.'s part toward the lot and even, except as it benefited him, the existence of his employees.

Big Dave felt quite sure that his own consciousness of this undercurrent was not attributable merely to his current proximity to the Bancock Building or to the fact that Indian Creek was a more important element of the company's affairs than had been the pits near Mineville. It was not a question of a new view of an old problem. On the contrary he was convinced that some entirely new trouble was brewing, something upon which he had not been able quite to put his finger. It riled him.

And as though that were not enough he had his troubles at home. . . .

Pearl and her church, mostly!

His wife always had been a flighty woman, going off on some spree or other. The church business had started back in Mineville about the time Maggy was a baby but never really had got to the point where it bothered him until Pearl had run into this psalm singer in Harris-ville. Now the Tennessey house was commencing to sound like a tent meeting and it bored the hell out of him.

Pearl finally had got him to go to the church one night and darned if the preacher hadn't had the guts to make some remarks about Maggy. In front of everybody! Not exactly the kind of thing Big Dave could walk up front and kick him in the teeth about but something on the order of how a pretty girl like her had to watch her step and not be worldly or she might get in trouble. Pearl had seemed to agree with that even though the preacher had looked right at her daughter when he had said it.

Although Mark had laughed on the way home and had tried to kid Maggy out of being embarrassed over the thing it had made Big Dave mad. He might not fully understand his daughter and maybe, like Mark said, she was kind of an unusual girl with her peculiar, soft-spoken ways. But he sure loved her and was almighty proud of the way she looked. Mark said so too and Mark was a good boy, like a son.

She had better not be fooling her old man!

Big Dave sighed wearily. He wished all he had to do was to mine coal.

"Heads up, Dave, goddammit!"

David Tennessey jumped sidewise and plastered himself to the wall, his heart pounding against the back of his throat. A string of coal cars squealed past him, scraping the front of his denim jacket and spewing dust into his eyes. The violence was gone as quickly as it had arrived. Not gone actually, because it never left the mine. But retired temporarily.

"What you daydreaming about, Big Dave?" the trip rider yelled at him. "Your insurance policy?"

Soaring three hundred feet straight upward and then westward for two instantaneous miles, a phantom fragment of David's jeopardy darted into the brain of his daughter as she sat quietly in the public library. She frowned with the pain of her vision.

Across the room Henrietta Sinclair, librarian, wondered what thought abruptly had troubled the face of Magdalene Tennessey.

Henrietta had been watching the girl unobtrusively for half an hour. She enjoyed watching people even when they disgusted her and the fact that Maggy's aspect was far from disgusting had made the past half hour delightful.

By one of those happenstances of nature which would be termed freakish were she ugly Magdalene was extraordinarily beautiful. And she had no genealogical right to be, not with the great, lumbering, bovine Big Dave Tennessey and his neurotic little wife, her parents. But as unusual as was the girl's physiognomy her spirit intrigued the librarian even more. It fascinated her. And not much else in Harrisville did. At least pleasantly.

Miss Sinclair had been the public librarian for the past seven of her thirty-five years, which was a circumstance rather than the culmination of a design on her part. She did not hate her job. She found certain of its incidents, such as its convenient hours and its opportunities for reading and human observation, quite gratifying. But there were other things which she would have preferred to be doing.

She was an unhappy woman of marked artistic instincts and dexterity whose talents, by force of events and her secret vice of drinking too much, were very nearly buried in the conventionality of Harrisville. She never had married although she had suffered a passionate love affair with a young artist from Terre Haute who had died suddenly of cancer, leaving her only his paints, a dream, and a whiskey bottle to remember him by. The townspeople knew about neither the love affair nor the whiskey and tolerated her painting only because they did not know how good it was. And they had neither opinion nor, it must be confessed sadly, interest regarding her happiness.

She resided at Mrs. Brown's boardinghouse and when not at work in the library or attending a lonely movie she usually could be found in her room. What transpired there she so far had managed to keep pretty much to herself, largely because Mrs. Brown was stone deaf and almost blind. It was there that were articulated in oils on surprisingly powerful, discerning canvases her inner ragings against the neckbreathing society about her and there it was often that she drank herself into a stupor of forgetfulness.

Her problem, as she was fully aware, was one of discovering what

Harrisville might have to offer in the way of horizons and realizations for a commanding creative urge. And until recently the prospect of finding an answer had remained discouraging.

The recent, hopeful event had been her acquaintance with Maggy Tennessey.

She had met the girl for the first time through some papers left in the library one evening a couple of months ago: notebook pages enlivened in a scampering hand, full of colorful descriptions and vivid observations and sudden, shocking nuances which had rendered Miss Sinclair breathless for instants at a time as she had read them in the silence of the deserted stacks before turning off the lights for the night and walking to her room through the cool, dark streets.

After that evening she had watched the girl come and go in the library and sit beneath a low-hung lamp at one of the long tables, reading and writing occasionally and gazing off pensively at imaginary vistas, smiling now and then or perhaps frowning as she just had done. And it had not been long before they had begun talking quietly, after the girl had overcome her shyness about discussing her thoughts with a stranger, and the librarian's reckonings had been confirmed.

Here indeed, from the stagnant swamp of Harrisville, had emerged a vital, fastidious flower gleaming in its own spot of sunlight, happily unconscious of its vulnerability to the menacing slime about it.

Excitedly, a little desperately Miss Sinclair had realized that here was something she needed: an object for her guidance, a temporary outlet for her own creative instincts requiring protection from her own dreary fate. Maggy's was a spirit to defend from suffocation and perversion, a talent potentially grand and effective to nurture, a secret to keep inviolate. And she was a picture to paint as well.

And, working henceforth with the East End girl, Miss Sinclair felt, in addition to its own rewards, that she would have the worldly satisfaction of discrediting the smug Mr. Tilley, library board member, bank president, and thus both her and the girl's employer, because it appeared that he cherished a shallow estimation of Maggy's worth. That was typical of his attitude which acutely annoyed the librarian. To her mind the forty-year-old, wastefully handsome banker personified all of the stuffiness and conventionality of Harrisville which she so detested and vaguely feared, if too late for herself, at least for her young friend.

. . .

Wayne Tilley!

Damn him, why should his name keep cropping up in her thoughts, spoiling otherwise pleasantly reflective moments? Henrietta was giving him more consideration than he deserved. Perhaps the starkness of his emotional torpor intrigued her.

Reportedly a widower, he had come to town from Indianapolis five years ago. It was said that he had been assistant cashier of a large bank in the state capital at the time J. L. Bancock, as chairman of the local establishment, was looking about for a successor to old Mr. Babb, erstwhile Harrisville cashier, and that Tilley had been recommended for the job by some of the bankers over there. In any event he had been hired and since then had brought to the Harrisville State Bank some new administrative and financial theories which even Miss Sinclair had to admit begrudgingly were efficient and admirable. Subsequently he had been elected by its board to the presidency of the local institution.

All that seemed normal enough. Those things certainly did not comprise the basis of Miss Sinclair's distaste. It was his manner that annoyed her. And his evident philosophy of living. He seemed preoccupied and even slightly nervous most of the time, presumably about his job. He worked hard and appeared to enjoy his work in a close-mouthed sort of way. That was all right. But he never seemed to relax in it. He acted like it was the only job in the world. Certainly the most important one.

Aside from his election to the bank's presidency within a year after his arrival he had been constrained to join the Community Club and the Presbyterian Church and to serve on the library board, of which J. L. Bancock was chairman also. But he persisted in remaining peculiarly remote, not only from the town's society in general, but even from his associates and employees in the bank. And although undoubtedly he earned a decent salary he drove about in a disreputable old car and wore the same suit for weeks at a time. It was as though he were forcing himself to be extra-abstemious, colorless, and machinelike in order to conform precisely to the staid Harrisvillian's idea of proper and traditional bank presidency.

Some of the more exuberant and irreverent local spirits considered that he overdid this and Miss Sinclair particularly found herself possessed at times by an almost irresistible urge to prod him just to see him jump. But no one could deny that he was effective in his job in a robotlike way, and possibly no one but herself actually disliked him. They simply did not know him.

As soon as he had arrived in town nearly all of the unattached young women had taken note of him and breathed a communal sigh of satisfaction. But he had appeared not to notice them or at least to avoid intently the impression of doing so. He had been and remained a cold fish in that respect as in most others. The rebuffed females, giving lip service to the principle of decorous presidency, had not refrained from wondering aloud whether there was something wrong with such an unresponsive fellow. They even had smiled defensively at occasional male expressions of doubt about "this guy Tilley's" masculine normalcy.

Miss Sinclair did not believe in his inadequacy to that extent. But she did consider him a pompous ass. He was a peevish old maid in pants. Probably scared to death of a woman!

The librarian heard somebody ascend the carpet of yellow light that spread down the steps outside, and glanced toward the front door as it opened quietly. A teen-age, bespectacled girl entered, followed by a plump, red-cheeked boy. The latter allowed the door to fall shut as the girl stood looking about the room for an instant before her eyes alighted upon Maggy.

The newcomers were Elizabeth Walters, daughter of the Notion Store proprietor, and Orville Tuggles, presumably if somewhat apathetically her escort. The librarian smiled at them as they crossed the creaking floor in front of her desk and approached Maggy's table.

"Good evening," Orville murmured to Miss Sinclair.

But Elizabeth's gaze remained on the room's only other occupant. "Hello, Maggy."

Maggy looked up from her writing and smiled. "Hello, Betsy. Orville."

Betsy seemed to quiver like an adoring dog. Unbuttoning her coat, she slid into a chair across from Maggy. Orville sat down too and grinned ruddily.

"What you doing?" Betsy asked.

An infinitesimal breeze stirred by their approach had ruffled a sheet of paper lying on the table. Gently Maggy's fingers put the page into place, her hand resting on it for a moment white and naked in the light of the lamp. "Been to the movies?"

Betsy nodded disdainfully, dismissing the subject. She indicated the papers in front of Maggy. "Been writing stuff again?"

Maggy smiled as she pushed the pages aside, failing to notice that one of them fell to the floor. "What was it?"

"The show?" Betsy grimaced. "A Western. Orville likes Westerns."

"Nice night," Orville volunteered. He had not removed his eyes from Maggy since he had sat down. "Nice for walking."

Learning back with a sigh, Maggy uncurled her arms. Her red hair tumbled over the back of the chair. Orville looked at her white throat and swallowed. He pulled his eyes away and glanced at Betsy and then at the table, where an inkstand conveniently afforded a haven for their attention. Imperceptibly he exhaled.

"Thought you might be here," Betsy said. "Want to go to Johnson's for a Coke?"

Orville nodded hopefully, trusting his glance to abandon the inkstand.

"Yes. Thanks."

From across the room Miss Sinclair continued to consider the group. There was an example of what she had meant. The three of them were almost the same age in the matter of time. Maggy certainly was not more than a couple of years the others' senior. But in psychic terms Betsy and Orville were infants compared with the coal miner's daughter. The thought made Miss Sinclair feel warm and maternal.

Elizabeth Walters was an Elm Street girl with all the implicit material advantages of that condition. But she was not pretty. Her bent nose and furry eyebrows and blotchy complexion denied her that. And although neither of them probably realized it Miss Sinclair had sensed that the merchant's daughter envied the coal miner's, profoundly and lovingly envied the agonizing perfection of Maggy's nose, the patrician brows arching above her misty eyes, the satin of her cheek, the innate, chastely enslaved lasciviousness of her body and all of the emotions which those attributes inspired in young men far more desirable than Orville.

Despite the fact Betsy's father was well off and that both her parents undoubtedly loved their daughter the librarian was aware from past observation that the girl was lonely and perhaps throttled by a feeling of insecurity, unconvinced that her family fully appreciated the ravages of her physical appearance on her soul or seriously cared about helping her to overcome what she obviously considered to be a tragic problem. She struck Miss Sinclair as a kindly, affectionate, helpless individual who had surrendered to her instincts and to her desperate need for spiritual underpinning and developed a sort of crush on the East End girl. Maggy once had told Miss Sinclair that she felt sorry for Betsy. The librarian had not expressed her own appraisal of the dangers of feeling sorry for anyone, guessing that Maggy probably should look askance at such callousness and ignore the warning anyhow.

At the table Betsy glanced at the wrist watch that her parents had given her as a high school graduation present the previous spring. "We've just got time before it closes."

When Maggy had slipped into her coat and gathered up her sheaf of papers the three of them walked to the front door, Maggy calling good night to Miss Sinclair and the others nodding, and departed into the November evening.

After they had gone the librarian gazed thoughtfully for a while at the bronze eagle poised threateningly above the door. Then she crossed the vaulted room to switch off the reading lamps. As she reached over the table where Maggy had sat, her glance alighted upon a sheet of notebook paper on the floor.

Stepping around to it, she stooped and picked it up and stood quietly reading its penciled lines:

The Wind
By Maggy Tennessey

The grinding, express train-roar of the tornado
The subtle lover's caress of the breeze
Live together in the sky.
The slashing hurricane dwells with the whisperings of angels.
How can this be?
The wounding, healing, killing, saving, sightless movement
That engulfs humanity—
Morning, noon, afternoon, night—
With its sea-smell,
Its scent of sage, of gloaming hay, of icy-green pine forests.
Descending sunny slopes;
Its acrid, sooty, bloody, trash-halitosis of the city;
Its colliding wafts of afterbirth and death.
What is this mysterious, fumbling, whipping, groping
Presence?
This gusty nothingness?
This wind?

Is it the breath of the world, exhaled in prayer?
Is it life?

GEORGE P. ELLIOTT

(b. Knightstown, 1918–) was educated in the Knightstown schools and at the University of California. His fiction, poetry, and essays are widely published in distinguished periodicals and widely reprinted in books. One of these books, a collection of short stories called *Among the Dangs*, won an Indiana Authors Day Award in 1962. The short story "Miracle Play," below, is Mr. Elliott's own choice for *The Indiana Experience*.

Miracle Play

In my sixth year I learned to my wonder that there was an invisible world perfect with the one I saw.

I awoke on the morning of my sixth birthday, not to the strains of "Happy Birthday," not to my mother's kiss, not even as usual to the sound of my dad in the bathroom singing as he shaved, "Where is the child? for I am Herod thy king"; I awoke alone and late, hearing Granny's heavy foot in the hall and the clank of basins in the bathroom. When I came out, she told me in a cross voice to hurry with my dressing and then go outdoors to play. When I asked her why, she told me not to bother her, Mother was not well, and she gave me a whack on the bottom that wasn't for my birthday. All I had for breakfast was an apple. After breakfast I went out, and found tadpoles in a bucket. I took one up to Granny to see, but by the time I'd reached the first landing of the stairs she'd run down to me; she made a hissing noise when I showed her the tadpole, and cuffed my ears and said I was bad. A cuff is only a cuff, but I'd never been cuffed on the head before, or if I had been, it hadn't made much difference; I went into the parlor to be alone and lick my tears. I vowed not to go out till they came for me, and if they never came I'd die there of hunger on the horsehair sofa where I had no business being. I hadn't been bad, or good, or anything else. I'd just wanted to see my mother, and wanted to know what was the matter that I couldn't. I sat on the slick sofa quite straight; I thought for a time of putting my feet up to spite Granny, but I decided I wouldn't for fear the spite would hurt Mother more. The blinds were not quite down, and through the cracks I watched the sun go out and the heavens darken for a summer storm.

And then—I'm not sure when but a little before the storm broke —I heard Dad humming on the porch. When he opened the front door he was singing in his deep voice, "For I am Herod." Mother had told me he was practicing to be Herod in a Christmas pageant at church; but since I did not know what she meant by a pageant or by Herod I just listened to the songs he sang. He worked on the railroad at that time and would be gone for long stretches; he'd never been home so early in the day as this. I ran to the parlor door ready to jump to him in the hall, but then I heard Granny call from the kitchen, "Henry?" and I remembered where I was. I watched them, through a crack I made in the doorway, as Dad asked her in a low voice all sorts of questions I could not grasp. Granny was steaming and billowy, wisps of hair lay on her left cheek, she kept rolling her hands up in her apron. Dad was Dad.

"And where's the boy?" he said.

"I haven't been seeing him around for a while," she answered. "He was getting underfoot."

"We mustn't leave him out. He's afraid of thunder and lightning."

"Oh Lord, he is," she said impatiently.

"And besides," said Dad, "it's his birthday today."

She threw up her hands, sighed, "With all I've got to do," and went back to the kitchen.

What was there for me? As soon as she was gone I flung open the door and caught him with one foot on the stairs.

"Daddy!" I cried, "Daddy! I want to see Mother!"

His hands were raspy on the backs of my legs as he picked me up, and his beard hurt my cheek, and he smelled of sweat and pipe smoke. "Just let me go say hello to her, my boy, and see whether she can have you."

She couldn't. He told me she was dozing. But then, whatever Granny might say to the contrary, he carried me up to Mother's door and let me peek in at her with the white sheet up to her chin and her hair all loose on the pillow.

He held me during the storm, singing to me.

A doctor came while it was still hailing and stayed for a short time.

I thought two or three times I heard Mother cry out; Dad didn't seem worried enough. Then, once during a lull, I knew I'd heard her and began crying myself. He told me that she was not sorry to be in pain, so we must not cry. But I thought he was just comforting me, and as I lay in his arms crying, I gave myself over to hating Granny with all my heart. I was sure that she was responsible one way or another for Mother's hurting and that Dad simply did not understand. To myself I called Granny the Old Hag of the House, and I wished passionately that she would get locked up in the closet under the stairs till she was dead.

As soon as the storm had passed, Dad took me to the barbershop and for a birthday present had my hair cut for the first time by a barber; I was very proud. Then he took me to Aunt Rebecca's to stay till he should come for me; I couldn't go back home till a big surprise should be waiting for me; he winked as he said it; I wondered why. When he kissed me good-bye I told him I loved him.

Aunt Rebecca was Dad's older sister, very tall, and I'd heard people say she was afraid of men because she had a purple birthmark on her face and throat. Maybe she was, but that day a dandruffy, out-of-town man named Nathan, with whom she laughed, came by in a touring car and drove us into the country for a picnic. They were kind to me, but their real talk was only to each other. He kept saying what a character she was, and though I didn't know what he meant I knew she did not like being called it, and I loved her jealously. The grass was wet. They were stretched out on a blanket in the sun. I went off by a brook to play. When I was squatting behind some bushes, they kissed. I was astonished to see them do it, for Nathan's feet didn't go much farther down than Aunt Rebecca's knees. I stood up to watch but they kept on kissing and laughing away. I was ashamed of their rudeness and went off by myself. Yet, on the ride home, Aunt Rebecca held me in her lap and talked only to me, or sang under her breath a song I'd been hearing her practice, "This babe a crown doth wear"; when she said good-bye to Nathan, she did not shake his hand or even look at him, but thanked him "for the nice time" in the way you don't mean it.

After a while she took me home. On the front steps we met the doctor again.

"Well, Harvey," he said, "how do you like the idea of a twelve-pound baby brother?"

He smelled of medicine. I didn't know what he was talking about.

"How is everything going?" Aunt Rebecca asked.

"Fine, everything's fine and dandy." And he pushed a lemon drop into my mouth.

There was a baby in the house all right; I could hear that squeaky noise babies make. When Granny said so, Dad carried me up to Mother's room. Mother was very pale but she smiled at me and held out her hand; Dad leaned me over and she kissed me on the forehead and patted my hair.

The baby was asleep, tucked under her arm. His name was Jimmy. I thought it particularly outrageous that he should already have a name. Granny said I must get out and leave Mother in peace with the baby.

Some time later I was again sent off to stay with Aunt Rebecca, this time because Granny was sick. Next morning Dad came for me, took me on his knee, and told me that Granny had passed away to a better world and that I must be very careful with Mother. Aunt Rebecca said she would bake a spice cake for our dinner, she had to do something. As soon as Dad and I walked in the door of our house, Mother grabbed me and burst into sobs that alarmed me into tears.

Next afternoon I was told to go alone into the parlor to look at my grandmother for the last time. In the parlor, it felt chilly on the hottest day; the casket was sleek as a piano and lined with pink satin; the air was dripping with the odor of flowers; I was very solemn. Her face was not the same: broader, smoother, pinker on the cheeks. I would not have known her but for the mole on the side of her nose. I touched her hand, and nothing happened.

It occurred to me that, if this was really Granny, though she looked so changed, then Jimmy might be changed too from what he really was. Maybe he was really a little pig; he looked as much like a pig as this Granny looked like the Granny I had always known. Mother had said that God had given us Jimmy and now she said that God had taken Granny; yet here Granny was; so where had Jimmy been before God had given him to us? Probably in a pigpen. Mother and Dad had both told me that Granny was happier now than she had been in life, in this vale of tears, Dad called it; but neither of them acted as though they believed what they'd said, especially Mother, and the expression on Granny's face was very stern. I tried to make my face as stern as hers, but as I stood there stiff as a soldier I began to feel my heart beating in my neck, and I was seized by the fear I might blow up if I didn't start breathing again. I panted till I was dizzy.

Only one thing was I clear about: I felt the opposite of what everyone else was feeling; just as I was sorry Jimmy had been born, I was glad Granny had died. I felt neither proud nor guilty about this, but only wondering; to be sure, I hid signs of my contrary, imprudent emotions.

Aunt Rebecca sang at Granny's funeral. She wore a long black dress with a white lace collar, and she sang "Nearer My God to Thee" and "The End of a Perfect Day." She stood facing the casket as though she was singing to Granny; but I knew that Granny was in heaven listening to the angels' music; perhaps the angels sounded like Aunt Rebecca. Afterward, everyone said how beautifully Aunt Rebecca had sung and how lovely she looked. The way she was standing we could see only the right side of her face, the unafflicted side. I hardly knew her.

By December life seemed to be getting satisfactory again. It's true Mother paid me much less attention than before, most of the time, and often she looked sad, when she was thinking of Granny; but since I was off at school a lot, it wasn't so bad; besides, Dad had taught me to read already, and I often read Bible stories while she was ironing. Jimmy improved; he was fun to play with once in a while; he laughed at me and liked to grab my nose; he began to look less like a pig and more like Mother. Dad was Dad.

Then the Sunday before Christmas Dad went off right after supper, and Mother took Jimmy next door to stay with old Mrs. Shipley, and she and I bundled up and went off to church. I had never before been to church in the evening; the only light was from candles; where the pulpit had been stood a tall plush chair; on the other side, in front of the choir seats, was an old-fashioned cradle and a stool. The piano was not in sight, but from behind a curtain of sheets on a wire came piano music. Nathan was sitting in front of us, by himself; he didn't notice me and I didn't tell Mother I knew him. The church was full.

The three wise men came out and sang how far they had come to see the child that was to be born. Someone came and told them the king wanted to see them. I was very excited because these wise men were really members of the church whom I saw every Sunday and often around town during the week; the thin one was our mailman. Yet they seemed taller than usual, larger in every way, and their beards astonished me. The next thing I knew they had gone to see the king on his throne, the tall chair, and the king was my dad. "Herod!" they sang. I gasped. I leaned against Mother, who put a finger to my lips and said it was only Daddy. It was as much as I could do to keep from crying out to tell him to become my dad again, but Mother's hand was right on my shoulder ready to clap over my mouth; I made no noise.

For he wasn't only my dad, he was Herod too. His voice was deep, he wore king's robes, he was taller than all the rest, his eyes were dark and fierce. Dad was trusting and warm, but Herod was full of suspiciousness and hate. Dad was kind to any dog or cat, but Herod said with a dreadful sneer, "Thou cur," to a servant. Dad loved me, and spanked me only when there was nothing else to be done, but Herod ordered all the first-born men-children to be put to the sword. After he had sung this order to his soldiers, there was a thunderous drum roll from behind the curtain.

I was used to the thought that everyone had a soul, and I was used to God as I was used to loving and being loved; I had always more or less assumed that, though I'd never seen a soul or God, in heaven souls and God would all see one another. Nothing unimaginable was.

For several minutes I was a jelly of terror. Mother knew nothing of it, for she only patted me idly from time to time, watching the play.

The next thing I knew, Aunt Rebecca in a long white gown and with sparkling jewels in her hair was singing to Mary that her babe should be crowned the Savior of the world. The robe, as I knew, was really a double-bed sheet which Mother had been helping her sew on the day before, but when she stretched her arms out to Mary on the stool, I was sure this was how the angels appeared. I heard Nathan sigh; he shook his head a little; I liked him better; he didn't think she was a character now. There was an invisible violin playing the melody along with her as she sang.

Yet, though she was standing so we could see her whole face, birthmark and all, she was—everything was—so beautiful I had a falling-away feeling in the stomach.

My terror awoke while the shepherds and wise men were adoring the blessed doll, for I remembered that Herod's soldiers were at that very moment looking for this first-born to kill him. Then, at the end as I listened to the invisible angel, visible Aunt Rebecca, warn Mary and Joseph to flee to Egypt where the child would be safe, I realized that it was far more important that these people had done what they had done, and that God had wished it so, than that actually they were church members and my family. The beauty was as great as the terror. All of us sang "Noël."

KURT VONNEGUT, JR.

(b. Indianapolis, 1922–) is a graduate of Shortridge High School. He also attended Cornell, Carnegie Institute, and the University of Chicago. After serving overseas in World War II, he worked in Chicago as a police reporter and as a public relations writer for the General Electric Company. Since 1950 he has devoted full time to free-lance writing. His best known works include the novels *Cat's Cradle* (1963), *Slaughter House Five* (1969), *Breakfast of Champions* (1973), and *Slapstick* (1976); the collection of short stories *Welcome to the Monkey House* (1968); and the play *Happy Birthday, Wanda June* (1971).

The Euphio Question

Ladies and gentlemen of the Federal Communications Commission, I appreciate this opportunity to testify on the subject before you.

I'm sorry—or maybe "heartsick" is the word—that news has leaked out about it. But now the word is getting around and coming to your official notice, I might as well tell the story straight and pray to God that I can convince you that America doesn't want what we discovered.

I won't deny that all three of us—Lew Harrison, the radio announcer, Dr. Fred Bockman, the physicist, and myself, a sociology professor—found peace of mind. We did. And I won't say it's wrong for people to seek peace of mind. But if somebody thinks he wants peace of mind the way we found it, he'd be well advised to seek coronary thrombosis instead.

Lew, Fred, and I found peace of mind by sitting in easy chairs and turning on a gadget the size of a table-model television set. No herbs, no golden rule, no muscle control, no sticking our noses in other people's troubles to forget our own; no hobbies, Taoism, push-ups or contemplation of a lotus. The gadget is, I think, what a lot of people vaguely foresaw as the crowning achievement of civilization: an electronic something-or-other, cheap, easily mass-produced, that can, at the flick of a switch, provide tranquillity. I see you have one here.

My first brush with synthetic peace of mind was six months ago. It was also then that I got to know Lew Harrison, I'm sorry to say. Lew is chief announcer of our town's only radio station. He makes his living with his loud mouth, and I'd be surprised if it were anyone but he who brought this matter to your attention.

Lew has, along with about thirty other shows, a weekly science program. Every week he gets some professor from Wyandotte College and interviews him about his particular field. Well, six months ago Lew worked up a program around a young dreamer and faculty friend of mine, Dr. Fred Bockman. I gave Fred a lift to the radio station, and he invited me to come on in and watch. For the heck of it, I did.

Fred Bockman is thirty and looks eighteen. Life has left no marks on him, because he hasn't paid much attention to it. What he pays most of his attention to, and what Lew Harrison wanted to interview him about, is this eight-ton umbrella of his that he listens to the stars with. It's a big radio antenna rigged up on a telescope mount. The

way I understand it, instead of looking at the stars through a telescope, he aims this thing out in space and picks up radio signals
coming from different heavenly bodies.

Of course, there aren't people running radio stations out there. It's
just that many of the heavenly bodies pour out a lot of energy and
some of it can be picked up in the radio-frequency band. One good
thing Fred's rig does is to spot stars hidden from telescopes by big
clouds of cosmic dust. Radio signals from them get through the clouds
to Fred's antenna.

That isn't all the outfit can do, and, in his interview with Fred, Lew
Harrison saved the most exciting part until the end of the program.
"That's very interesting, Dr. Bockman," Lew said. "Tell me, has your
radio telescope turned up anything else about the universe that
hasn't been revealed by ordinary light telescopes?"

This was the snapper. "Yes, it has," Fred said. "We've found about
fifty spots in space, *not hidden by cosmic dust,* that give off powerful
radio signals. Yet no heavenly bodies at all seem to be there."

"Well!" Lew said in mock surprise. "I should say that *is* something!
Ladies and gentlemen, for the first time in radio history, we bring
you the noise from Dr. Bockman's mysterious voids." They had
strung a line out to Fred's antenna on the campus. Lew waved to the
engineer to switch in the signals coming from it. "Ladies and gentlemen, the voice of nothingness!"

The noise wasn't much to hear—a wavering hiss, more like a leaking tire than anything else. It was supposed to be on the air for five
seconds. When the engineer switched it off, Fred and I were inexpli-
cably grinning like idiots. I felt relaxed and tingling. Lew Harrison
looked as though he'd stumbled into the dressing room at the
Copacabana. He glanced at the studio clock, appalled. The monoto-
nous hiss had been on the air for five minutes! If the engineer's cuff
hadn't accidentally caught on the switch, it might be on yet.

Fred laughed nervously, and Lew hunted for his place in the
script. "The hiss from nowhere," Lew said. "Dr. Bockman, has anyone proposed a name for these interesting voids?"

"No," Fred said. "At the present time they have neither a name
nor an explanation."

The voids the hiss came from have still to be explained, but I've
suggested a name for them that shows signs of sticking: "Bockman's
Euphoria." We may not know what the spots are, but we know what
they do, so the name's a good cne. Euphoria, since it means a sense
of buoyancy and well-being, is really the only word that will do.

After the broadcast, Fred, Lew and I were cordial to one another to the point of being maudlin.

"I can't remember when a broadcast has been such a pleasure," Lew said. Sincerity is not his forte, yet he meant it.

"It's been one of the most memorable experiences of my life," Fred said, looking puzzled. "Extraordinarily pleasant."

We were all embarrassed by the emotion we felt, and parted company in bafflement and haste. I hurried home for a drink, only to walk into the middle of another unsettling experience.

The house was quiet, and I made two trips through it before discovering that I was not alone. My wife, Susan, a good and lovable woman who prides herself on feeding her family well and on time, was lying on the couch, staring dreamily at the ceiling. "Honey," I said tentatively, "I'm home. It's suppertime."

"Fred Bockman was on the radio today," she said in a faraway voice.

"I know. I was with him in the studio."

"He was out of this world," she sighed. "Simply out of this world. That noise from space—when he turned that on, everything just seemed to drop away from me. I've been lying here, just trying to get over it."

"Uh-huh," I said, biting my lip. "Well, guess I'd better round up Eddie." Eddie is my ten-year-old son, and captain of an apparently invincible neighborhood baseball team.

"Save your strength, Pop," said a small voice from the shadows.

"You home? What's the matter? Game called off on account of atomic attack?"

"Nope. We finished eight innings."

"Beating 'em so bad they didn't want to go on, eh?"

"Oh, they were doing pretty good. Score was tied, and they had two men on and two outs." He talked as though he were recounting a dream. "And then," he said, his eyes widening, "everybody kind of lost interest, just wandered off. I came home and found the old lady curled up here, so I lay down on the floor."

"Why?" I asked incredulously.

"Pop," Eddie said thoughtfully, "I'm damned if I know."

"Eddie!" his mother said.

"Mom," Eddie said, "I'm damned if *you* know either."

I was damned if anybody could explain it, but I had a nagging hunch. I dialed Fred Bockman's number. "Fred, am I getting you up from dinner?"

"I wish you were," Fred said. "Not a scrap to eat in the house, and I let Marion have the car today so she could do the marketing. Now she's trying to find a grocery open."

"Couldn't get the car started, eh?"

"Sure she got the car started," said Fred. "She even got to the market. Then she felt so good she walked right out of the place again." Fred sounded depressed. "I guess it's a woman's privilege to change her mind, but it's the lying that hurts."

"Marion lied? I don't believe it."

"She tried to tell me everybody wandered out of the market with her—clerks and all."

"Fred," I said, "I've got news for you. Can I drive out right after supper?"

When I arrived at Fred Bockman's farm, he was staring, dumbfounded, at the evening paper.

"The whole town went nuts!" Fred said. "For no reason at all, all the cars pulled up to the curb like there was a hook and ladder going by. Says here people shut up in the middle of sentences and stayed that way for five minutes. Hundreds wandered around in the cold in their shirtsleeves, grinning like toothpaste ads." He rattled the paper. "This *is* what you wanted to talk to me about?"

I nodded. "It all happened when that noise was being broadcast, and I thought maybe—"

"The odds are about one in a million that there's any maybe about it," said Fred. "The time checks to the second."

"But most people weren't listening to the program."

"They didn't have to listen, if my theory's right. We took those faint signals from space, amplified them about a thousand times, and rebroadcast them. Anybody within reach of the transmitter would get a good dose of the stepped-up radiations, whether he wanted to or not." He shrugged. "Apparently that's like walking past a field of burning marijuana."

"How come you never felt the effect at work?"

"Because I never amplified and rebroadcast the signals. The radio station's transmitter is what really put the sock into them."

"So what're you going to do next?"

Fred looked surprised. "Do? What is there to do but report it in some suitable journal?"

Without a preliminary knock, the front door burst open and Lew Harrison, florid and panting, swept into the room and removed his great polo coat with a bullfighter-like flourish. "You're cutting him in on it, too?" he demanded, pointing at me.

Fred blinked at him. "In on what?"

"The millions," Lew said. "The billions."

"Wonderful," Fred said. "What are you talking about?"

"The noise from the stars!" Lew said. "They love it. It drives 'em nuts. Didja see the papers?" He sobered for an instant. "It *was* the noise that did it, wasn't it, Doc?"

"We think so," Fred said. He looked worried. "How, exactly, do you propose we get our hands on these millions or billions?"

"Real estate!" Lew said raptly. " 'Lew,' I said to myself, 'Lew, how can you cash in on this gimmick if you can't get a monopoly on the universe? And, Lew,' I asked myself, 'how can you sell the stuff when anybody can get it free while you're broadcasting it?' "

"Maybe it's the kind of thing that shouldn't be cashed in on," I suggested. "I mean, we don't know a great deal about—"

"Is happiness bad?" Lew interrupted.

"No," I admitted.

"Okay, and what we'd do with this stuff from the stars is make people happy. Now I suppose you're going to tell me that's bad?"

"People ought to be happy," Fred said.

"Okay, okay," Lew said loftily. "That's what we're going to do for the people. And the way the people can show their gratitude is in real estate." He looked out the window. "Good—a barn. We can start right there. We set up a transmitter in the barn, run a line out to your antenna, Doc, and we've got a real-estate development."

"Sorry," Fred said. "I don't follow you. This place wouldn't do for a development. The roads are poor, no bus service or shopping center, the view is lousy and the ground is full of rocks."

Lew nudged Fred several times with his elbow. "Doc, Doc, Doc —sure it's got drawbacks, but with that transmitter in the barn, you can give them the most precious thing in all creation—happiness."

"Euphoria Heights," I said.

"That's great!" said Lew. "I'd get the prospects, Doc, and you'd sit up there in the barn with your hand on the switch. Once a prospect set foot on Euphoria Heights, and you shot the happiness to him, there's nothing he wouldn't pay for a lot."

"Every house a home, as long as the power doesn't fail," I said.

"Then," Lew said, his eyes shining, "when we sell all the lots here, we move the transmitter and start another development. Maybe we'd get a fleet of transmitters going." He snapped his fingers. "Sure! Mount 'em on wheels."

"I somehow don't think the police would think highly of us," Fred said.

"Okay, so when they come to investigate, you throw the old switch and give *them* a jolt of happiness." He shrugged. "Hell, I might even get bighearted and let them have a corner lot."

"No," Fred said quietly. "If I ever joined a church, I couldn't face the minister."

"So we give *him* a jolt," Lew said brightly.

"No," Fred said. "Sorry."

"Okay," Lew said, rising and pacing the floor. "I was prepared for that. I've got an alternative, and this one's strictly legitimate. We'll make a little amplifier with a transmitter and an aerial on it. Shouldn't cost over fifty bucks to make, so we'd price it in the range of the common man—five hundred bucks, say. We make arrangements with the phone company to pipe signals from your antenna right into the homes of people with these sets. The sets take the signal from the phone line, amplify it, and broadcast it through the houses to make everybody in them happy. See? Instead of turning on the radio or television, everybody's going to want to turn on the happiness. No casts, no stage sets, no expensive cameras—no nothing but that hiss."

"We could call it the euphoriaphone," I suggested, "or 'euphio' for short."

"That's great, that's great!" Lew said. "What do you say, Doc?"

"I don't know." Fred looked worried. "This sort of thing is out of my line."

"We all have to recognize our limitations, Doc," Lew said expansively. "I'll handle the business end, and you handle the technical end." He made a motion as though to put on his coat. "Or maybe you don't want to be a millionaire?"

"Oh, yes, yes indeed I do," Fred said quickly. "Yes indeed."

"All righty," Lew said, dusting his palms, "the first thing we've gotta do is build one of the sets and test her."

This part of it *was* down Fred's alley, and I could see the problem interested him. "It's really a pretty simple gadget," he said. "I suppose we could throw one together and run a test out here next week."

The first test of the euphoriaphone, or euphio, took place in Fred Bockman's living room on a Saturday afternoon, five days after Fred's and Lew's sensational radio broadcast.

There were six guinea pigs—Lew, Fred and his wife Marion, myself, my wife Susan, and my son Eddie. The Bockmans had arranged chairs in a circle around a card table, on which rested a gray steel box.

Protruding from the box was a long buggy whip aerial that scraped the ceiling. While Fred fussed with the box, the rest of us made nervous small talk over sandwiches and beer. Eddie, of course, wasn't drinking beer, though he was badly in need of a sedative. He was annoyed at having been brought out to the farm instead of to a ball game, and was threatening to take it out on the Bockmans' Early American furnishings. He was playing a spirited game of flies and grounders with himself near the French doors, using a dead tennis ball and a poker.

"Eddie," Susan said for the tenth time, "please stop."

"It's under control, under control," Eddie said disdainfully, playing the ball off four walls and catching it with one hand.

Marion, who vents her maternal instincts on her immaculate furnishings, couldn't hide her distress at Eddie's turning the place into a gymnasium. Lew, in his way, was trying to calm her. "Let him wreck the dump," Lew said. "You'll be moving into a palace one of these days."

"It's ready," Fred said softly.

We looked at him with queasy bravery. Fred plugged two jacks from the phone line into the gray box. This was the direct line to his antenna on the campus, and clockwork would keep the antenna fixed on one of the mysterious voids in the sky—the most potent of Bockman's Euphoria. He plugged a cord from the box into an electrical outlet in the baseboard, and rested his hand on a switch. "Ready?"

"Don't, Fred!" I said. I was scared stiff.

"Turn it on, turn it on," Lew said. "We wouldn't have the telephone today if Bell hadn't had the guts to call somebody up."

"I'll stand right here by the switch, ready to flick her off if something goes sour," Fred said reassuringly. There was a click, a hum, and the euphio was on.

A deep, unanimous sigh filled the room. The poker slipped from Eddie's hands. He moved across the room in a stately sort of waltz, knelt by his mother, and laid his head in her lap. Fred drifted away from his post, humming, his eyes half closed.

Lew Harrison was the first to speak, continuing his conversation with Marion. "But who cares for material wealth?" he asked earnestly. He turned to Susan for confirmation.

"Uh-uh," said Susan, shaking her head dreamily. She put her arms around Lew, and kissed him for about five minutes.

"Say," I said, patting Susan on the back, "you kids get along swell, don't you? Isn't that nice, Fred?"

"Eddie," Marion said solicitously, "I think there's a real baseball in the hall closet. A *hard* ball. Wouldn't that be more fun than that old tennis ball?" Eddie didn't stir.

Fred was still prowling around the room, smiling, his eyes now closed all the way. His heel caught in a lamp cord, and he went sprawling on the hearth, his head in the ashes. "Hi-ho, everybody," he said, his eyes still closed. "Bunged my head on an andiron." He stayed there, giggling occasionally.

"The doorbell's been ringing for a while," Susan said. "I don't suppose it means anything."

"Come in, come in," I shouted. This somehow struck everyone as terribly funny. We all laughed uproariously, including Fred, whose guffaws blew up little gray clouds from the ashpit.

A small, very serious old man in white had let himself in, and was now standing in the vestibule, looking at us with alarm. "Milkman," he said uncertainly. He held out a slip of paper to Marion. "I can't read the last line in your note," he said. "What's that say about cottage cheese, cheese, cheese, cheese, cheese . . ." His voice trailed off as he settled, tailor-fashion, to the floor beside Marion. After he'd been silent for perhaps three quarters of an hour, a look of concern crossed his face. "Well," he said apathetically, "I can only stay for a minute. My truck's parked out on the shoulder, kind of blocking things." He started to stand. Lew gave the volume knob on the euphio a twist. The milkman wilted to the floor.

"Aaaaaaaaaaah," said everybody.

"Good day to be indoors," the milkman said. "Radio says we'll catch the tail end of the Atlantic hurricane."

"Let 'er come," I said. "I've got my car parked under a big, dead tree." It seemed to make sense. Nobody took exception to it. I lapsed back into a warm fog of silence and thought of nothing whatsoever. These lapses seemed to last for a matter of seconds before they were interrupted by conversation of newcomers. Looking back, I see now that the lapses were rarely less than six hours.

I was snapped out of one, I recall, by a repetition of the doorbell's ringing. "I said come in," I mumbled.

"And I did," the milkman mumbled.

The door swung open, and a state trooper glared in at us. "Who the hell's got his milk truck out there blocking the road?" he demanded. He spotted the milkman. "Aha! Don't you know somebody could get killed, coming around a blind curve into that thing?" He yawned, and his ferocious expression gave way to an affectionate smile. "It's so damn' unlikely," he said, "I don't know why I ever brought it up."

He sat down by Eddie. "Hey, kid—like guns?" He took his revolver from its holster. "Look—just like Hoppy's."

Eddie took the gun, aimed it at Marion's bottle collection and fired. A large blue bottle popped to dust and the window behind the collection splintered. Cold air roared in through the opening.

"He'll make a cop yet," Marion chortled.

"God, I'm happy," I said, feeling a little like crying. "I got the swellest little kid and the swellest bunch of friends and the swellest old wife in the world." I heard the gun go off twice more, and then dropped into heavenly oblivion.

Again the doorbell roused me. "How many times do I have to tell you—for Heaven's sake, come in," I said, without opening my eyes.

"I *did*," the milkman said.

I heard the tramping of many feet, but had no curiosity about them. A little later, I noticed that I was having difficulty breathing. Investigation revealed that I had slipped to the floor, and that several Boy Scouts had bivouacked on my chest and abdomen.

"You want something?" I asked the tenderfoot whose hot, measured breathing was in my face.

"Beaver Patrol wanted old newspapers, but forget it," he said. "We'd just have to carry 'em somewhere."

"And do your parents know where you are?"

"Oh, sure. They got worried and came after us." He jerked his thumb at several couples lined up against the baseboard, smiling into the teeth of the wind and rain lashing in at them through the broken window.

"Mom, I'm kinda hungry," Eddie said.

"Oh, Eddie—you're not going to make your mother cook just when we're having such a wonderful time," Susan said.

Lew Harrison gave the euphio's volume knob another twist. "There, kid, how's that?"

"Aaaaaaaaaaah," said everybody.

When awareness intruded on oblivion again, I felt around for the Beaver Patrol, and found them missing. I opened my eyes to see that they and Eddie and the milkman and Lew and the trooper were standing by a picture window, cheering. The wind outside was roaring and slashing savagely and driving raindrops through the broken window as though they'd been fired from air rifles. I shook Susan gently, and together we went to the window to see what might be so entertaining.

"She's going, she's going, she's going," the milkman cried ecstatically.

Susan and I arrived just in time to join in the cheering as a big elm crashed down on our sedan.

"Kee-*runch!*" said Susan, and I laughed until my stomach hurt.

"Get Fred," Lew said urgently. "He's gonna miss seeing the barn go!"

"H'mm?" Fred said from the fireplace.

"Aw, Fred, you missed it," Marion said.

"Now we're really gonna see something," Eddie yelled. "The power line's going to get it this time. Look at that poplar lean!"

The poplar leaned closer, closer, closer to the power line; and then a gust brought it down in a hail of sparks and a tangle of wires. The lights in the house went off.

Now there was only the sound of the wind. "How come nobody cheered?" Lew said faintly. "The euphio—it's off!"

A horrible groan came from the fireplace. "God, I think I've got a concussion."

Marion knelt by her husband and wailed. "Darling, my poor darling—what happened to you?"

I looked at the woman I had my arms around—a dreadful, dirty old hag, with red eyes sunk deep in her head, and hair like Medusa's. "Ugh," I said, and turned away in disgust.

"Honey," wept the witch, "it's me—Susan."

Moans filled the air, and pitiful cries for food and water. Suddenly the room had become terribly cold. Only a moment before I had imagined I was in the tropics.

"Who's got my damn' pistol?" the trooper said bleakly.

A Western Union boy I hadn't noticed before was sitting in a corner, miserably leafing through a pile of telegrams and making clucking noises.

I shuddered. "I'll bet it's Sunday morning," I said. "We've been here twelve hours!" It was Monday morning.

The Western Union boy was thunderstruck. "Sunday morning? I walked in here on a Sunday night." He stared around the room. "Looks like them newsreels of Buchenwald, don't it?"

The chief of the Beaver Patrol, with the incredible stamina of the young, was the hero of the day. He fell in his men in two ranks, haranguing them like an old Army top-kick. While the rest of us lay draped around the room, whimpering about hunger, cold, and thirst, the patrol started the furnace again, brought blankets, applied compresses to Fred's head and countless barked shins, blocked off the broken window, and made buckets of cocoa and coffee.

Within two hours of the time that the power and the euphio went off, the house was warm and we had eaten. The serious respiratory cases—the parents who had sat near the broken window for twenty-four hours—had been pumped full of penicillin and hauled off to the hospital. The milkman, the Western Union boy, and the trooper had refused treatment and gone home. The Beaver Patrol had saluted smartly and left. Outside, repairmen were working on the power line. Only the original group remained—Lew, Fred, and Marion, Susan and myself, and Eddie. Fred, it turned out, had some pretty important-looking contusions and abrasions, but no concussion.

Susan had fallen asleep right after eating. Now she stirred. "What happened?"

"Happiness," I told her. "Incomparable, continuous happiness—happiness by the kilowatt."

Lew Harrison, who looked like an anarchist with his red eyes and fierce black beard, had been writing furiously in one corner of the room. "That's good—happiness by the kilowatt," he said. "Buy your happiness the way you buy light."

"Contract happiness the way you contract influenza," Fred said. He sneezed.

Lew ignored him. "It's a campaign, see? The first ad is for the long-hairs: 'The price of one book, which may be a disappointment, will buy you sixty hours of euphio. Euphio never disappoints.' Then we'd hit the middle class with the next one—"

"In the groin?" Fred said.

"What's the matter with you people?" Lew said. "You act as though the experiment had failed."

"Pneumonia and malnutrition are what we'd *hoped* for?" Marion said.

"We had a cross section of America in this room, and we made every last person happy," Lew said. "Not for just an hour, not for just a day, but for two days without a break." He arose reverently from his chair. "So what we do to keep it from killing the euphio fans is to have the thing turned on and off with clockwork, see? The owner sets it so it'll go on just as he comes home from work, then it'll go off again while he eats supper; then it goes on after supper, off again when it's bedtime; on again after breakfast, off when it's time to go to work, then on again for the wife and kids."

He ran his hands through his hair and rolled his eyes. "And the selling points—my God, the selling points! No expensive toys for the kids. For the price of a trip to the movies, people can buy thirty hours of euphio. For the price of a fifth of whisky, they can buy sixty hours of euphio!"

"Or a big family bottle of potassium cyanide," Fred said.

"Don't you see it?" Lew said incredulously. "It'll bring families together again, save the American home. No more fights over what TV or radio program to listen to. Euphio pleases one and all—we proved that. And there is no such thing as a dull euphio program."

A knock on the door interrupted him. A repairman stuck his head in to announce that the power would be on again in about two minutes.

"Look, Lew," Fred said, "this little monster could kill civilization in less time than it took to burn down Rome. We're not going into the mind-numbing business, and that's that."

"You're kidding!" Lew said, aghast. He turned to Marion. "Don't you want your husband to make a million?"

"Not by operating an electronic opium den," Marion said coldly.

Lew slapped his forehead. "It's what the public wants. This is like Louis Pasteur refusing to pasteurize milk."

"It'll be good to have the electricity again," Marion said, changing the subject. "Lights, hot-water heater, the pump, the—oh, Lord!"

The lights came on the instant she said it, but Fred and I were already in mid-air, descending on the gray box. We crashed down on it together. The card table buckled, and the plug was jerked from the wall socket. The euphio's tubes glowed red for a moment, then died.

Expressionlessly, Fred took a screwdriver from his pocket and removed the top of the box.

"Would you enjoy doing battle with progress?" he said, offering me the poker Eddie had dropped.

In a frenzy, I stabbed and smashed at the euphio's glass and wire vitals. With my left hand, and with Fred's help, I kept Lew from throwing himself between the poker and the works.

"I thought you were on my side," Lew said.

"If you breathe one word about euphio to anyone," I said, "what I just did to euphio I will gladly do to you."

And there, ladies and gentlemen of the Federal Communications Commission, I thought the matter had ended. It deserved to end there. Now, through the medium of Lew Harrison's big mouth, word has leaked out. He has petitioned you for permission to start commercial exploitation of euphio. He and his backers have built a radio-telescope of their own.

Let me say again that all of Lew's claims are true. Euphio will do everything he says it will. The happiness it gives is perfect and unflagging in the face of incredible adversity. Near tragedies, such as the first experiment, can no doubt be avoided with clockwork to turn the sets on and off. I see that this set on the table before you is, in fact, equipped with clockwork.

The question is not whether euphio works. It does. The question is, rather, whether or not America is to enter a new and distressing phase of history where men no longer pursue happiness but buy it. This is no time for oblivion to become a national craze. The only benefit we could get from euphio would be if we could somehow lay down a peace-of-mind barrage on our enemies while protecting our own people from it.

In closing, I'd like to point out that Lew Harrison, the would-be czar of euphio, is an unscrupulous person, unworthy of public trust. It wouldn't surprise me, for instance, if he had set the clockwork on this sample euphio set so that its radiations would addle your judgments when you are trying to make a decision. In fact, it seems to be whirring suspiciously at this very moment, and I'm so happy I could cry. I've got the swellest little kid and the swellest bunch of friends and the swellest old wife in the world. And good old Lew Harrison is the salt of the earth, believe me. I sure wish him a lot of good luck with his new enterprise.

HARRY MARK PETRAKIS

(b. 1923–) a native of St. Louis, lives on the Chesterton dunes. A prolific writer, he also contributes much time to Indiana community schools and workshops. In 1965 he won an O. Henry Award. Two of his collections of short stories, *Pericles on 31st Street* (1965) and *A Dream of Kings* (1966) were nominated for National Book Awards.

The Song of Rhodanthe

I was twenty-seven years old that spring. Papa had still not given up hope that a man would be found to marry me. My brothers, Kostas and Marko and Niko, were married and had numerous children of their own. They were all concerned about me.

It was true that I wanted to be married. Papa had presented a number of men to me for my approval. I was not beautiful but neither was I so homely that I had to accept one of them. They were either too old or too loud or red-faced from drinking too much beer and wine. I think Papa grieved most about me when wine made him tearful. His only daughter, twenty-seven, and still unmarried. Friends who were bachelors drank and grieved with him. In the end they offered themselves as suitors to ease Papa's despair.

After an evening with one of them Papa waited for my decision. I told him I refused to accept such a man.

"You are twenty-seven years old!" he cried. "A daughter still unmarried at twenty-seven is a plague on a man's spirit. I cannot sleep for worrying about you. My health is breaking down. At the market everyone asks me, Panfelio, is your daughter married yet? Is she even engaged? I cannot bear much more."

"Yes, Papa."

"What was the matter with Gerontis?" he asked.

"He is too old," I said, "and his false teeth whistle when he speaks."

"You are too choosy!" Papa shouted. "Remember you are twenty-seven years old."

"Yes, Papa."

"What was the matter with Makris?" he asked. "He is a younger man than Gerontis."

"He is younger," I said. "But he greases his hair until it drips oil down his cheeks and he spent all evening telling me how he can crack open a crate with his bare hands."

"I can still crack open a crate with my bare hands," Papa shouted. "Your poor Mama was never the worse for it. You forget, my girl, you are twenty-seven years old."

"Yes, Papa."

One evening a week, my brothers brought their wives and children to our house to eat supper. The wives were redcheeked with great bosoms and ate like contented mares. The house became a bedlam with children hanging from the lamps and chairs collapsing with a sound of thunder. We assembled at the table and bowed our heads and Papa said grace.

"We are grateful, O Lord, that we are well and together and for the food upon this table. Bring us together again next week and let there be a man for Rhodanthe among us. Amen."

When dinner was over and it was time to leave, each of the wives of my brothers kissed me benevolently on the cheek. One after the other my big brothers embraced me sadly and kissed me somberly. Every parting was a festival of grief. Poor Rhodanthe.

I told Papa goodnight and kissed him tenderly because I loved him very much. He was foolish sometimes and shouted a great deal but I knew how much he loved me too.

I went to my room and prepared for bed. I sat before the mirror and brushed my long hair. In those moments I fiercely felt a wish to be married and raise children of my own. Sometimes I thought I wanted that as much for Papa and Kostas and Marko and Niko as for myself.

The last cold months of winter passed. The winds grew gentle. The rain fell during the night and in the daylight the earth smelled fresh as if it were awakened from a long sleep. One morning I saw a robin sitting on a branch of the cherry tree in our yard and I knew the spring had really come.

Each morning Kostas and Marko and Niko drove up in their trucks to have a cup of coffee while Papa ate breakfast. I knew they did that for me so that I would not feel too lonely during the day.

They sat around the kitchen table, big strong men that made the kitchen seem smaller than it really was. The cups looked tiny and fragile in their massive hands. They smoked cigars and spoke in loud gruff voices to each other. But they were soft and gentle when they spoke to me.

When they had left with Papa for the market, I washed the dishes and cleaned the house. I worked quickly and felt a glow in my cheeks.

Because that day was so beautiful I decided to take the bedding outside to air. I carried the sheets and blankets to the back yard and draped them across a line. When I finished hanging them up I was a little out of breath.

There was the sound of whistling in the alley in back of the yard and a young man appeared. He was striding along with his hands in his pockets and his head flung back and a wild jubilant whistling ringing from his lips. I had heard whistling before, even the strong bass whistling of my brothers, but never a sound like he made. It was as if the spring had burst into song. As if the first slim green buds and the blades of new grass and the soft fresh wind had suddenly found a voice. And I felt a strange wild tremor through my heart.

When he saw me standing there he paused. For a quick tight moment the whistling ceased. His hair was thick and dark and an untamed and errant curl glittered across his forehead. He smiled then and his smile was as reckless and daring as his whistle. Then he walked on quickly and the wild whistling rang out again. As the sound faded a terrible loneliness overcame me. I went quickly into the house.

That night at supper I broke a cup and spilled soup from the pot while pouring it into a bowl.

"What is the matter with you?" Papa said. "You are nervous as a cat tonight."

"Nothing is the matter, Papa," I said and felt a quick flame in my cheeks.

He cleared his throat and sighed heavily.

"It is not normal," he said somberly. "Twenty-seven years old and still unmarried. You will become sick."

"I will not become sick, Papa," I said. "Do not worry about me."

"How can I help worrying?" he said. "What kind of father would I be if I did not worry about my daughter, still unmarried at twenty-seven?" His lips quivered and he wiped a stray tear from his eye.

"Yes, Papa."

"You are too choosy!" he shouted. "You have not that right at your age. Gastis passed the market today. He asked how you were. He was taken with you. What in God's name was the matter with Gastis?"

"I have told you before, Papa," I said.

"Tell me again!" he shouted.

"His face is like one of his grapefruit," I said. "He never smiles. Whatever time of day you are with him always appears to be night."

Papa threw up his hands in despair.

"One is too young," he said. "And one is too old. One laughs like an idiot and one does not laugh enough. One is a banana and one is a grapefruit. I am telling you, my girl, I am losing patience!"

"Yes, Papa."

"What kind of man do you want?" he shouted again. "Tell me what kind of man you want?"

I paused for a moment in the doorway of the kitchen. A reckless excitement swept my tongue.

"I want a young man with dark hair," I said boldly. "And a wild dark curl across his forehead. A man who whistles and makes the earth burst into song."

Papa made his cross.

"What I have feared has come to pass," he said sadly. "You have become unbalanced."

"Yes, Papa," I said, and I ran back to him and kissed him gently. "Good night, Papa."

In the morning I could not wait for all of them to leave. They sat over their coffee for what seemed to be an eternity. Yet each time I looked at the clock I saw they were no later than they usually were.

When they had gone I ran to my room and carefully brushed my hair and tied it with my brightest ribbon. I touched my lips with a light red stain and pinched my cheeks. I went quickly downstairs and out the back door. A moment of panic seized me when I realized I could not just stand there waiting. I hurried back into the house and pulled the blankets from my bed and ran with them down the stairs. I had just finished hanging them across the line when I heard the sound of the whistling again.

He came down the alley just as he had the morning before. His head flung back and his legs walking with great strong strides and that wonderful wild whistle singing on his lips. My heart beat suddenly as if it were going to burst apart.

When he saw me he stopped. He smiled again, a perfect and riotous smile. I could not help myself and smiled back. He walked slowly to the fence and carelessly and with a supple grace leaned his elbows upon it and put his face in his hands.

"You live here?" he asked. And he had a deep man's voice but not nearly as harsh a voice as Papa had, and with revelry in it, unlike the voices of Marko and Kostas and Niko.

"Yes," I said.

"With your husband?" he asked slyly.

"With my father," I said quickly. "I am not married."

"Good," he said, and he smiled again and threw back his head and laughed a festival of tuneful laughter from his throat. "Good," he said again and then he waved goodby and started striding down the alley.

There were a dozen questions I wanted to call after him, a dozen things I wanted to say. I was ashamed because I had answered and yet I felt strange and alive for the first time in my life. I looked at the budding leaves and at the first blades of grass and at the early tulips and felt a fervent kinship with them.

The next morning it rained and I was in despair. I could not stand in the rain waiting for him to pass, or hang blankets on a line in the downpour. After a while I gave up hoping it would stop in time and consoled myself that the following morning the sun might shine again.

I finished the kitchen and wiped the last breakfast cups without spirit. I hung the dish towel upon the rack, and heard a light tapping at the window.

My heart leaped to my throat because he was there. He waved to me through the rain-smeared glass. I ran to the door and flung it open. He came in dripping from the rain and the dark curly hair matted upon his head.

"You are soaked!" I said. "You'll catch cold! I'll get a towel."

He took the clean towel from my hands and began briskly to dry his hair. He rubbed his cheeks with vigor and smiled and shook his head.

"You weren't in the yard," he said.

I looked at him helplessly.

"It was raining so hard," I said. "I wasn't sure you would come."

When I realized what I had said I put my hand quickly to my mouth. But he only laughed softly.

"The rain is nothing," he said. "I missed you."

We looked at each other and there was taunting merriment in his dark eyes. I tried to think of something to say but all my senses seemed to have fled.

"I've got to go in a minute," he said. "I'll be late for work."

"A cup of coffee," I said. "It's still hot. It will warm you."

He came to the table and he was not as tall as any of my brothers and not as broad in the shoulders as my father, but there was grace and strength in the way he moved.

I brought the pot of coffee to the table and filled his cup. I could sense him watching me and I spilled some into the saucer.

"Weren't you afraid to let me in?" he said.

I turned away quickly and shook my head.

"What's your name?" he said.

"Rhodanthe," I said. I put the pot back on the stove and then turned to face him.

"A pretty name," he said. "A name for a flower."

I looked down at the floor because I was sure the frantic beating of my heart would show in my cheeks.

"I know a great deal about you," he said and when I looked up he winked slyly. "I know more about you than you realize."

"You do?" I said.

"I know you are sometimes sad," he said, "because you do not smile. I know you are sometimes lonely because you do not laugh."

We were both silent for a moment and I marveled at how quickly he understood. And how natural it seemed that he should be sitting at my table drinking coffee.

He pushed back his cup and rose from the table and walked to the door. I followed him there and he turned and paused with his hand on the knob. He bent a little and kissed me. A quick impulsive kiss that brushed my lips with the grace of the spring wind.

I stepped back shocked.

"You had no right!" I said. "You should not have done that."

"I wanted to kiss you," he said and smiled wickedly. "I do what I want."

Then he was walking swiftly with long strong strides through the rain. My heart flew after him.

That night the family gathered again. All the rosy-cheeked wives and the multitude of children. I worked with a jubilation I found hard to conceal. I even sang a little to myself and several times noticed one of my brothers watching me strangely.

At the end of the meal the children scrambled from the table to resume playing in another room. The wives picked up the plates and carried them to the kitchen. Niko, the youngest of my brothers, caught my arm.

"What makes you sparkle tonight?" he said. "I have never seen you like this before." He gestured at Papa. "What has happened to this girl?"

I tried to shake off his hand but he laughed and held me tight. All of them watched me and I felt my cheeks flaming.

"She is blushing," Marko cried. "Blushing like a schoolgirl."

"Let me go," I said to Niko, "or I will bring this plate of bones across your head."

"She is in love!" Kostas roared. "The girl's in love!"

A reverent quiet descended upon the room. The wives came from the kitchen to stand in the doorway with their eyes open to great bursting cups. Niko let me go slowly. All of them watched me in some kind of awe.

"Rhodanthe," Papa said and there was a great joy stirring in his voice. "Is this true?"

My heart went out to him. He was growing old and loved me so much. I looked at each of my brothers and felt a great wave of affection for them. I could even forgive their smug wives, secure in marriage to good men, who listened in the doorway.

"Yes," I said. "Yes."

"Thunder and lightning!" Kostas roared. He beat with his big fist upon the table. The dishes rattled and jumped.

"Hurrah!" Niko cried.

"I'll be damned!" Marko shouted.

Everybody looked at Papa. He silently made his cross and looked as if he were about to cry.

"God be praised," he said and his voice trembled. "I knew you must come to your senses. I have brought you some good men. Which one of them have you reconsidered?"

"Five bucks to a buck it's Makris!" Niko shouted.

"That grease pot?" Kostas cried. "She wouldn't touch him with a yardstick."

"It must be Gastis!" Marko said. "It has to be Gastis!"

"Silence!" Papa roared. "Silence!"

The room went quiet. No sound except for the shrieking children in the parlor.

"Silence those little monsters!" Papa roared again. One of the wives went quickly to the parlor and a moment later silence fell in every part of the house. She came back and softly closed the door.

"Which one is it?" Papa spoke to me gently.

I stood at the foot of the table and folded my hands. I took a deep breath and for one brief moment closed my eyes and then opened them again.

"It is none of the men you have brought home," I said.

They all looked shocked. A rumbling began around the table. Papa waved his hand fiercely for silence.

"I do not understand," he said slowly. "It is not Gastis or Makris or Sarantis or Gerontis or any of those other good men?"

"No, Papa," I said.

"Who the devil is it then?" Marko said angrily.

A flare of panic seized me but I had gone too far to turn back.

"A young man who passes on his way to work in the morning," I said. "He has dark and curly hair and he whistles in a way I have never heard anyone whistle before."

For a long startled moment no one spoke.

"She has gone nuts!" Kostas cried. He looked around for confirmation.

"Who is this guy?" Marko shouted. "I'll teach him to whistle at my sister!"

"Dirty hoodlum!" Niko spit between his teeth.

Papa beat with his fist upon the table. Everyone became quiet again.

"You are joking?" Papa said and he made an effort to laugh and one of the wives began to laugh with him. Papa stopped laughing and glared at her and she almost choked closing her mouth.

"I am not joking," I said. "He is a young man that I have spoken to a number of times. This morning we had coffee together."

"He had coffee with you this morning?" Marko shouted angrily. "In this house alone with you?"

"We'll have his teeth hot from his mouth!" Kostas cried.

"Dirty hoodlum!" Niko shouted. "Sneaking behind our backs."

"Who is he?" Papa cried. "Who is he?"

"I don't know his name," I said. I knew how that sounded but I flung at them because I was becoming angry too.

Papa exploded for all of them. Shock and anger ripping his face. The wives cowered in the doorway.

"You don't know his name!" Papa thundered. "You don't know his name!"

They all began roaring at once. I bit my lips hard trying to stop the tears that burned to break from my eyes.

"I don't know his name!" I cried angrily."I don't know his name! I know I love him! I heard him whistling and saw him and everything changed. This morning it rained and I could have cried because I would not see him and then he knocked on the window." They all sat staring at me and I struggled furiously to find words to overwhelm them. "There were other men I might have loved years ago," I said. "Men who were frightened off by your shouts and your fists. But you will not take this man from me. He told me he knew I was sad because I did not smile and that I was lonely because I did not laugh and then he kissed me!" I felt a tremor shake my body and my voice rose fiercely. "I don't know his name! I only know I love him!"

They were sorry afterwards. Papa came to my room and kissed me and cried a little. Then Marko and Niko and Kostas came and touched my hair gently with their big hands and tried to speak with their eyes. I forgave them because I knew how much they cared for me. And I consented to let Niko wait with me in the morning to see the young man.

But he did not come the next morning. I thought perhaps he knew about Niko and the following day I waited alone. I waited in the yard with the spring wild and tangled about my head and the blossoms breaking on the branches of the trees and the earth flowing and alive.

He did not come. And the spring passed into summer and the leaves grew long and green on the trees and the sunflowers bloomed among the stones and the birds were everywhere. The speckled robins and the gray starlings and the brownish redwings.

After a while I knew Papa and the others thought I had made it all up. That I had grown weary of the procession of sad suitors and made the story up to keep others away.

They do not understand that someday he will come back. On a morning when the green hearts of the lilac bushes tremble awake in the wind. When the first slim green buds break upon the branches of the maples and the catalpas.

He will come striding along with his hands in his pockets and his reckless head flung back and the wild jubilant whistle ringing from his lips. And I will feel once again that the early green buds and the first fragile flowers and the soft new winds have suddenly burst into song.

❖ ❖ ❖ ❖ ❖

WILLIAM GASS

(b. 1924–), although a native of North Dakota, lived for several years in Brookston and taught in the Philosophy Department at Purdue. He now teaches at Washington University and is a contributing editor to the *New York Review.* His novel *Omensetter's Luck* (1966) and his literary criticism, especially *Fiction and the Figures of Life* (1970), have won international acclaim. His experimental novel *In the Heart of the Heart of the Country* (1968) represents fiction written in the form of a journal. From that book the excerpts below (approved by Mr. Gass) share as their setting an Indiana town called B. Although B does stand for Brookston, not Yeats's Byzantium, you should keep in mind that what you are reading is primarily fiction and that the characters, even the narrator, are not actual persons but rather the creatures of Mr. Gass's imagination.

In the Heart of the Heart of the Country

A Place

So I have sailed the seas and come . . .
　　　　　　　　　　　　　　　　to B . . .
a small town fastened to a field in Indiana. Twice there have been twelve hundred people here to answer to the census. The town is outstandingly neat and shady, and always puts its best side to the highway. On one lawn there's even a wood or plastic iron deer.

You can reach us by crossing a creek. In the spring the lawns are green, the forsythia is singing, and even the railroad that guts the town has straight bright rails which hum when the train is coming, and the train itself has a welcome horning sound.

Down the back streets the asphalt crumbles into gravel. There's Westbrook's, with the geraniums, Horsefall's, Mott's. The sidewalk shatters. Gravel dust rises like breath behind the wagons. And I am in retirement from love.

Weather

In the Midwest, around the lower Lakes, the sky in the winter is heavy and close, and it is a rare day, a day to remark on, when the sky lifts and allows the heart up. I am keeping count, and as I write this page, it is eleven days since I have seen the sun.

My House

There's a row of headless maples behind my house, cut to free the passage of electric wires. High stumps, ten feet tall, remain, and I climb these like a boy to watch the country sail away from me. They are ordinary fields, a little more uneven than they should be, since in the spring they puddle. The topsoil's thin, but only moderately stony. Corn is grown one year, soybeans another. At dusk starlings darken the single tree—a larch—which stands in the middle. When the sky moves, fields move under it. I feel, on my perch, that I've lost my years. It's as though I were living at last in my eyes, as I have always dreamed of doing, and I think then I know why I've come here: to see, and so to go out against new things—oh god how easily —like air in a breeze. It's true there are moments—foolish moments, ecstasy on a tree stump—when I'm all but gone, scattered I like to think like seed, for I'm the sort now in the fool's position of having love left over which I'd like to lose; what good is it now to me, candy ungiven after Halloween?

A Person

There are vacant lots on either side of Billy Holsclaw's house. As the weather improves, they fill with hollyhocks. From spring through fall, Billy collects coal and wood and puts the lumps and pieces in piles near his door, for keeping warm is his one work. I see him most often on mild days sitting on his doorsill in the sun. I notice he's squinting a little, which is perhaps the reason he doesn't cackle as I pass. His house is the size of a single garage, and very old. It shed its paint with its youth, and its boards are a warped and weathered gray. So is Billy. He wears a short lumpy faded black coat when it's cold, otherwise he always goes about in the same loose, grease-spotted shirt and trousers. I suspect his galluses were yellow once, when they were new.

Wires

These wires offend me. Three trees were maimed on their account, and now these wires deface the sky. They cross like a fence in front of me, enclosing the crows with the clouds. I can't reach in, but like a stick, I throw my feelings over. What is it that offends me? I am on my stump, I've built a platform there and the wires prevent my going out. The cut trees, the black wires, all the beyond birds therefore anger me. When I've wormed through a fence to reach a meadow, do I ever feel the same about the field? . . .

My House

Leaves move in the windows. I cannot tell you yet how beautiful it is, what it means. But they do move. They move in the glass.

People

Their hair in curlers and their heads wrapped in loud scarves, young mothers, fattish in trousers, lounge about in the speedwash, smoking cigarettes, eating candy, drinking pop, thumbing magazines, and screaming at their children above the whir and rumble of the machines.

At the bank a young man freshly pressed is letting himself in with a key. Along the street, delicately teetering, many grandfathers move in a dream. During the murderous heat of summer, they perch on window ledges, their feet dangling just inside the narrow shelf of shade the store has made, staring steadily into the street. Where their consciousness has gone I can't say. It's not in the eyes. Perhaps it's diffuse, all temperature and skin, like an infant's, though more mild. Near the corner there are several large overalled men employed in standing. A truck turns to be weighed on the scales at the Feed and Grain. Images drift on the drugstore window. The wind has blown the smell of cattle into town. Our eyes have been driven in like the eyes of the old men. And there's no one to have mercy on us.

Vital Data

There are two restaurants here and a tearoom, two bars, one bank, three barbers, one with a green shade with which he blinds his window, two groceries, a dealer in Fords, one drug, one hardware, and one appliance store, several that sell feed, grain, and farm equipment, an antique shop, a poolroom, a laundromat, three doctors, a dentist, a plumber, a vet, a funeral home in elegant repair the color of a buttercup, numerous beauty parlors which open and shut like night-blooming plants, a tiny dime and department store of no width but several floors, a hutch, homemade, where you can order, after lying down or squirming in, furniture that's been fashioned from bent lengths of stainless tubing, glowing plastic, metallic thread, and clear shellac, an American Legion Post and a root beer stand, little agencies for this and that: cosmetics, brushes, insurance, greeting cards and garden produce—anything—sample shoes—which do their business out of hats and satchels, over coffee cups and dissolving sugar, a factory for making paper sacks and pasteboard boxes that's lodged in an old brick building bearing the legend OPERA HOUSE, still faintly golden, on its roof, a library given by Carnegie, a post office, a school, a railroad station, fire station, lumberyard, telephone company, welding shop, garage . . . and spotted through the town from one end to the other in a line along the highway, gas stations to the number five.

My House, This Place and Body

I have met with some mischance, wings withering, as Plato says obscurely, and across the breadth of Ohio, like heaven on a table, I've fallen as far as the poet, to the sixth sort of body, this house in B, in Indiana, with its blue and gray bewitching windows, holy magical insides. Great thick evergreens protect its entry. And I live *in*.

Lost in the corn rows, I remember feeling just another stalk, and thus this country takes me over in the way I occupy myself when I am well . . . completely—to the edge of both my house and body. No one notices, when they walk by, that I am brimming in the doorways. My house, this place and body, I've come in mourning to be born in. To anybody else it's pretty silly: love. Why should I feel a loss? How am I bereft? She was never mine; she was a fiction, always a golden tomgirl, barefoot, with an adolescent's slouch and a boy's taste for sports and fishing, a figure out of Twain, or worse, in Riley. Age cannot be kind.

There's little hand-in-hand here . . . not in B. No one touches ex-

cept in rage. Occasionally girls will twine their arms about each other
and lurch along, school out, toward home and play. I dreamed my lips
would drift down your back like a skiff on a river. I'd follow a vein
with the point of my finger, hold your bare feet in my naked hands.

My House, My Cat, My Company

I must organize myself. I must, as they say, pull myself together,
dump this cat from my lap, stir—yes, resolve, move, do. But do what?
My will is like the rosy dustlike light in this room: soft, diffuse, and
gently comforting. It lets me do . . . anything . . . nothing. My ears
hear what they happen to; I eat what's put before me; my eyes see
what blunders into them; my thoughts are not thoughts, they are
dreams. I'm empty or I'm full . . . depending; and I cannot choose.
I sink my claws in Tick's fur and scratch the bones of his back until
his rear rises amorously. Mr. Tick, I murmur, I must organize myself.
I must pull myself together. And Mr. Tick rolls over on his belly, all
ooze.

I spill Mr. Tick when I've rubbed his stomach. Shoo. He steps away
slowly, his long tail rhyming with his paws. How beautifully he
moves, I think; how beautifully, like you, he commands his loving,
how beautifully he accepts. So I rise and wander from room to room,
up and down, gazing through most of my forty-one windows. How
well this house receives its loving too. Let out like Mr. Tick, my eyes
sink in the shrubbery. I am not here; I've passed the glass, passed
second-story spaces, flown by branches, brilliant berries, to the
ground, grass high in seed and leafage every season; and it is the same
as when I passed above you in my aged, ardent body; it's, in short,
a kind of love; and I am learning to restore myself, my house, my
body, by paying court to gardens, cats, and running water, and with
neighbors keeping company.

Mrs. Desmond is my right-hand friend; she's eighty-five. A thin
white mist of hair, fine and tangled, manifests the climate of her
mind. She is habitually suspicious, fretful, nervous. Burglars break in
at noon. Children trespass. Even now they are shaking the pear tree,
stealing rhubarb, denting lawn. Flies caught in the screens and
numbed by frost awake in the heat to buzz and scrape the metal cloth
and frighten her, though she is deaf to me, and consequently cannot
hear them. Boards creak, the wind whistles across the chimney
mouth, drafts cruise like fish through the hollow rooms. It is herself
she hears, her own flesh failing, for only death will preserve her from
those daily chores she climbs like stairs, and all that anxious waiting.
Is it now, she wonders. No? Then: is it now?

We do not converse. She visits me to talk. My task to murmur. She talks about her grandsons, her daughter who lives in Delphi, her sister or her husband—both gone—obscure friends—dead—obscurer aunts and uncles—lost—ancient neighbors, members of her church or of her clubs—passed or passing on; and in this way she brings the ends of her life together with a terrifying rush: she is a girl, a wife, a mother, widow, all at once. . . . Her talk's a fence—a shade drawn, window fastened, door that's locked—for no one dies taking tea in a kitchen; and as her years compress and begin to jumble, I really believe in the brevity of life; I sweat in my wonder; death is the dog down the street, the angry gander, bedroom spider, goblin who's come to get her; and it occurs to me that in my listening posture I'm the boy who suffered the winds of my grandfather with an exactly similar politeness, that I am, right now, all my ages, out in elbows, as angular as badly stacked cards. Thus was I, when I loved you, every man I could be, youth and child—far from enough—and you, so strangely ambiguous a being, met me, heart for spade, play after play, the whole run of our suits.

Mr. Tick, you do me honor. You not only lie in my lap, but you remain alive there, coiled like a fetus. Through your deep nap, I feel you hum. You are, and are not, a machine. You are alive, alive exactly, and it means nothing to you—much to me. You are a cat—you cannot understand—you are a cat so easily. Your nature is not something you must rise to. You, not I, live in: in house, in skin, in shrubbery. Yes. I think I shall hat my head with a steeple; turn church; devour people. Mr. Tick, though, has a tail he can twitch, he need not fly his Fancy. Claws, not metrical schema, poetry his paws; while smoothing . . . smoothing . . . smoothing roughly, his tongue laps its neatness.

More Vital Data

The town is exactly fifty houses, trailers, stores, and miscellaneous buildings long, but in places no streets deep. It takes on width as you drive south, always adding to the east. Most of the dwellings are fairly spacious farm houses in the customary white, with wide wraparound porches and tall narrow windows, though there are many of the grander kind—fretted, scalloped, turreted, and decorated with clapboards set at angles or on end, with stained-glass windows at the stair landings and lots of wrought iron full of fancy curls—and a few of these look like castles in their rarer brick. Old stables serve as garages now, and the lots are large to contain them and the vegetable and flower gardens which, ultimately, widows plant and weed and then entirely disappear in. The shade is ample, the grass is good, the sky a glorious fall violet; the apple trees are heavy and red, the roads are calm and empty; corn has sifted from the chains of tractored wagons to speckle the streets with gold and with the russet fragments of the cob, and a man would be a fool who wanted, blessed with this, to live anywhere else in the world.

Wires

Where sparrows sit like fists. Doves fly the steeple. In mist the wires change perspective, rise and twist. If they led to you, I would know what they were. Thoughts passing often, like the starlings who flock these fields at evening to sleep in the trees beyond, would form a family of paths like this; they'd foot down the natural height of air to just about a bird's perch. But they do not lead to you.

> Of whose beauty it was sung
> She shall make the old man young.

They fasten me.

If I walked straight on, in my present mood, I would reach the Wabash. It's not a mood in which I'd choose to conjure you. Similes dangle like baubles from me. This time of year the river is slow and shallow, the clay banks crack in the sun, weeds surprise the sandbars. The air is moist and I am sweating. It's impossible to rhyme in this dust. Everything—sky, the cornfield, stump, wild daisies, my old clothes and pressless feelings—seems fabricated for installment purchase. Yes, Christ, I am suffering a summer Christmas; and I cannot walk under the wires. The sparrows scatter like handfuls of gravel. Really, wires are voices in thin strips. They are words wound in cables. Bars of connection.

Weather

I would rather it were the weather that was to blame for what I am and what my friends and neighbors are—we who live here in the heart of the country. Better the weather, the wind, the pale dying snow ... the snow—why not the snow? There's never much really, not around the lower Lakes anyway, not enough to boast about, not enough to be useful. ...

Place

I would rather it were the weather. It drives us in upon ourselves —an unlucky fate. Of course there is enough to stir our wonder anywhere; there's enough to love, anywhere, if one is strong enough, if one is diligent enough, if one is perceptive, patient, kind enough —whatever it takes; and surely it's better to live in the country, to live on a prairie by a drawing of rivers, in Iowa or Illinois or Indiana, say, than in any city....

People

Aunt Pet's still able to drive her car—a high square Ford—even though she walks with difficulty and a stout stick. She has a watery gaze, a smooth plump face despite her age, and jet black hair in a bun. She has the slowest smile of anyone I ever saw, but she hates dogs, and not very long ago cracked the back of one she cornered in her garden. To prove her vigor she will tell you this, her smile breaking gently while she raises the knob of her stick to the level of your eyes.

Final Vital Data

The Modern Homemakers' Demonstration Club. The Prairie Home Demonstration Club. The Night-outers' Home Demonstration Club. The IOOF, FFF, VFW, WCTU, WSCS, 4-H, 40 and 8, Psi Iota Chi, and PTA. The Boy and Girl Scouts, Rainbows, Masons, Indians and Rebekah Lodge. Also the Past Noble Grand Club of the Rebekah Lodge. As well as the Moose and the Ladies of the Moose. The Elks, the Eagles, the Jaynettes and the Eastern Star. The Women's Literary Club, the Hobby Club, the Art Club, the Sunshine Society, the Dorcas Society, the Pythian Sisters, the Pilgrim Youth Fellowship, the American Legion, the American Legion Auxiliary, the American Legion Junior Auxiliary, the Garden Club, the Bridge for Fun Club, the What-can-you-do? Club, the Get Together Club, the Coterie Club, the Worthwhile Club, the Let's Help Our Town Club, the No Name Club, the Forget-me-not Club, the Merry-go-round Club ...

[Elementary] Education

Has a quarter disappeared from Paula Frosty's pocket book? Imagine the landscape of that face: no crayon could engender it; soft wax is wrong; thin wire in trifling snips might do the trick. Paula Frosty and Christopher Roger accuse the pale and splotchy Cheryl Pipes. But Miss Jakes, I *saw* her. Miss Jakes is so extremely vexed she snaps her pencil. What else is missing? I appoint you a detective, John: search her desk. Gum, candy, paper, pencils, marble, round eraser —whose? A thief. I can't watch her all the time. I'm here to teach. . . .

Another Person

I was raking leaves when Uncle Halley introduced himself to me. He said his name came from the comet, and that his mother had borne him prematurely in her fright of it. I thought of Hobbes, whom fear of the Spanish Armada had hurried into birth, and so I believed Uncle Halley to honor the philosopher, though Uncle Halley is a liar, and neither the one hundred twenty-nine nor the fifty-three he ought to be. That fall the leaves had burned themselves out on the trees, the leaf lobes had curled, and now they flocked noisily down the street and were broken in the wires of my rake. Uncle Halley was himself (like Mrs. Desmond and history generally) both deaf and implacable, and he shooed me down his basement stairs to a room set aside there for stacks of newspapers reaching to the ceiling, boxes of leaflets and letters and programs, racks of photo albums, scrapbooks, bundles of rolled-up posters and maps, flags and pennants and slanting piles of dusty magazines devoted mostly to motoring and the Christian ethic. I saw a bird cage, a tray of butterflies, a bugle, a stiff straw boater, and all kinds of tassels tied to a coat tree. He still possessed and had on display the steering lever from his first car, a linen duster, driving gloves and goggles, photographs along the wall of himself, his friends, and his various machines, a shell from the first war, a record of "Ramona" nailed through its hole to a post, walking sticks and fanciful umbrellas, shoes of all sorts (his baby shoes, their counters broken, were held in sorrow beneath my nose—they had not been bronzed, but he might have them done someday before he died, he said), countless boxes of medals, pins, beads, trinkets, toys, and keys (I scarcely saw—they flowed like jewels from his palms), pictures of downtown when it was only a path by the railroad station, a brightly colored globe of the world with a dent in Poland, antique guns, belt buckles, buttons, souvenir plates and cups and saucers (I can't remember all of it—I won't), but I recall how shamefully, how rudely, how abruptly, I fled, a good story in my mouth but death in my nostrils; and how afterward I busily, righteously, burned my leaves as if I were purging the world of its years. I still wonder if this town—its life, and mine now—isn't really a record like the one of

"Ramona" that I used to crank around on my grandmother's mahogany Victrola through lonely rainy days as a kid.

[Basketball at] The Church [Gymnasium]

Friday night. Girls in dark skirts and white blouses sit in ranks and scream in concert. They carry funnels loosely stuffed with orange and black paper which they shake wildly, and small megaphones through which, as drilled, they direct and magnify their shouting. Their leaders, barely pubescent girls, prance and shake and whirl their skirts above their bloomers. The young men, leaping, extend their arms and race through puddles of amber light, their bodies glistening. In a lull, though it rarely occurs, you can hear the squeak of tennis shoes against the floor. Then the yelling begins again, and then continues; fathers, mothers, neighbors joining in to form a single pulsing ululation—a cry of the whole community—for in this gymnasium each body becomes the bodies beside it, pressed as they are together, thigh to thigh, and the same shudder runs through all of them, and runs toward the same release. Only the ball moves serenely through this dazzling din. Obedient to law it scarcely speaks but caroms quietly and lives at peace.

Business

It is the week of Christmas and the stores, to accommodate the rush they hope for, are remaining open in the evening. You can see snow falling in the cones of the street lamps. The roads are filling— undisturbed. Strings of red and green lights droop over the principal highway, and the water tower wears a star. The windows of the stores have been bedizened. Shamelessly they beckon. But I am alone, leaning against a pole—no . . . there is no one in sight. They're all at home, perhaps by their instruments, tuning in on their evenings, and like Ramona, tirelessly playing and replaying themselves. There's a speaker perched in the tower, and through the boughs of falling snow and over the vacant streets, it drapes the twisted and metallic strains of a tune that can barely be distinguished—yes, I believe it's one of the jolly ones, it's "Joy to the World." There's no one to hear the music but myself, and though I'm listening, I'm no longer certain. Perhaps the record's playing something else.

JEAN SHEPHERD

(b. 1929–) was brought up in Hammond and educated in its public schools. He also attended Indiana University during 1948–1949. His screen plays and telecasts have won critical acclaim. His books include *The America of George Ade* (1962), *In God We Trust: All Others Pay Cash* (1966), which won an Indiana Writers award that year, *Wanda Hickey's Night of Golden Memories* (1971), and *The Ferrari in the Bedroom* (1973). Mr. Shepherd wishes to stress that "Wilbur Duckworth" is purely fictional, "not in any way biographical or even autobiographical."

Wilbur Duckworth and His Magic Baton

When the bitter winds of dead winter howl out of the frozen North, making the ice-coated telephone wires creak and sigh like suffering live things, many an ex-B-flat sousaphone player feels an old familiar dull ache in his muscle-bound left shoulder, a pain never quite lost as the years spin on. Old aching numbnesses of the lips, permanently implanted by frozen German silver mouthpieces of the past. An instinctive hunching forward into the wind, tacking obliquely the better to keep that giant burnished Conn bell heading always into the waves. A lonely man, carrying unsharable wounds and memories to his grave. The butt of low, ribald humor; gaucheries beyond description, unapplauded by music lovers, the sousaphone player is among the loneliest of men. His dedication is almost monk-like in its fanaticism and solitude.

He is never asked to perform at parties. His fame is minute, even among fellow band members, being limited almost exclusively to fellow carriers of the Great Horn. Hence, his devotion is pure. When pressed for an explanation as to why he took up the difficult study and discipline of sousaphone playing, few can give a rational answer, usually mumbling something very much like the famed retort of the climbers of Mount Everest.

There is no Sousaphone category in the renowned jazz polls. It would be inconceivable to imagine an LP entitled:

HARRY SCHWARTZ AND HIS GOLDEN SOUSAPHONE BLOW
COLE PORTER
IN STEREO

And yet every sousaphone player, in his heart, knows that no instrument is more suited to Cole Porter than his beloved four-valver. Its rich, verdant mellowness, its loving, somber blues and grays in tonality are among the most sensual and thrilling of sounds to be heard in a man's time.

But it will never be. Forever and by definition those brave marchers under the flashing bells are irrevocably assigned to the rear rank.

Few men know the Facts of Life more truly than a player of this noble instrument. Twenty minutes in a good marching band teaches a kid more about How Things Really Are than five years at Mother's granite knee.

There are many misconceptions which at the outset must be cleared up before we proceed much further. Great confusion exists among the unwashed as to just what a sousaphone *is*. Few things are more continually irritating to a genuine sousaphone man than to have his instrument constantly called a "tuba." A tuba is a weak, puny thing fit only for mewling, puking babes and Guy Lombardo— the better to harass balding, middle-aged dancers. An upright instrument of startling ugliness and mooing, flatulent tone, the tuba has none of the grandeur, the scope or sweep of its massive, gentle, distant relation.

The sousaphone is worn proudly curled about the body, over the left shoulder, and mounting above the head is that brilliant, golden, gleaming disk—rivaling the sun in its glory. Its graceful curves clasp the body in a warm and crushing embrace, the right hand in position over its four massive mother-of-pearl capped valves. It is an instrument a man can literally get his teeth into, and often does. A sudden collision with another bell has, in many instances, produced interesting dental malformations which have provided oral surgeons with some of their happier moments.

A sousaphone is a worthy adversary which must be watched like a hawk and truly mastered 'ere it master *you*. Dangerous, unpredictable, difficult to play, it yet offers rich rewards. Each sousaphone individually, since it is such a massive creation, assumes a character of its own. There are bad-tempered instruments and there are friendly sousaphones; sousaphones that literally lead their players back and forth through beautiful countermarches on countless football fields. Then there are the treacherous, which buck and fight and must be held in tight rein 'ere disaster strike. Like horses or women, no two sousaphones are alike. Nor, like horses or women, will Man ever fully understand them.

Among other imponderables, a player must have as profound a knowledge of winds and weather as the skipper of a racing yawl. A cleanly aligned sousaphone section marching into the teeth of a spanking crosswind with mounting gusts, booming out the second chorus of *"Semper Fidelis,"* is a study of courage and control under difficult conditions. I myself once, in my Rookie days, got caught in a counter-clockwise wind with a clockwise instrument and spun violently for five minutes before I regained control, all the while playing one of the finest obbligatos that I ever blew on the "National Emblem March."

Sometimes, in a high wind a sousaphone will start playing *you.* It literally blows back, developing enough back pressure to produce a thin chorus of "Dixie" out of both ears of the unwary sousaphonist.

The high school marching band that I performed in was led by a maniacal zealot who had whipped us into a fine state of tune rivaling a crack unit of the Prussian Guards. We won prizes, cups, ribbons, and huzzahs wherever we performed; wheeling, countermarching, spinning; knees high, and all the while we played. "On the Mall," "The Double Eagle," "El Capitan," "The NC-4 March," *"Semper Fidelis"*—we had mastered all the classics.

Our 180-beat-to-the-minute cadence snapped and cracked and rolled on like the steady beating of an incessant surf. Sharp in itchy uniforms and high-peaked caps, we learned the bitter facts of life while working our spit valves and bringing pageantry and pomp into the world of the Blast Furnace and the Open Hearth, under the leaden wintry skies of the Indiana prairie land.

The central figure of the scene was our Drum Major. Ours was a Spartan organization. We had no Majorettes, Pom-Pom girls, or other such decadent signposts on the roadway of a declining civilization. In fact, it was an all-Male band that had no room for such grotesqueries as thin, flat-chested, broadbottomed female trombone players and billowy-bosomed clarinetists. A compact sixty-six man company of flat-stomached, hard-jawed Nehi drinkers, led by a solitary, heroic, high-kneed, arrogant baton twirler.

Drum majors are a peculiarly American institution, and Wilbur Duckworth was cast in the classic mold. Imperious, egotistical beyond belief, he was hated and feared by all of us down to the last lowly cymbal banger. Most drum majors of my acquaintance are not

All-American boys in the Jack Armstrong tradition. In fact, they lean more in the general direction of Captain Queeg, somehow tainted by the vanity of a Broadway musical dancer, plus the additional factor of High School Hero.

In spite of legend, many drum majors are notably unsuccessful with women. Wilbur was no exception, and his lonely frustration in this most essential of human pursuits had led him to incredible heights in Baton Twirling. He concentrated and practiced hour upon hour until he became a Ted Williams among the wearers of the Shako. His arched back, swinging shoulders, lightning-like chrome wands; the sharp, imperious bite of his whistled commands were legendary wherever bandsmen rested to swap tales over a Nehi orange. At a full, rolling, 180-beat-per-minute tempo, Duckworth's knees snapped as high as most men's shoulders. He would spin, marching backward, baton held at ready port, eyes gleaming beadily straight ahead in our direction. Two short blasts of his silver whistle, then a longer one, a quick snap up-and-down movement of the wand, and we would crash into "The Thunderer," which opened with a spectacular trombone, trumpet, and sousaphone flourish of vast medieval grandeur. Precisely as the last notes of the flourish ended and "The Thunderer" boomed out, Wilbur spun like a machine and began his act. Over the shoulder like a stiffened silver snake with a life of its own, under both legs, that live metal whip never lost a beat or faltered ever so slightly. Catching the sun, it spun a blur high into the Indiana skies and down again, Wilbur never deigning so much as to watch its flight. He knew where it was; it knew where he was. They were one, a spinning silver bird. Even as we roared into the coda, attacking the sixteenth notes crisply, with bite, we were always conscious of the steady swish of that baton, cutting the air like a blade, a hissing obbligato to John Philip Sousa.

Like all champion Drum Majors—and Wilbur had more medals at seventeen than General Patton garnered over a lifetime of combat —Wilbur's act was carefully programmed. Almost in the same way that an Olympic skater performs the classical School figures, Wilbur had mastered years before the basic baton maneuvers, the classical flips and spins, and performed them with razor-sharp, glittering precision. He would begin with a quick over-the-back roll, a comparatively simple basic move, and then, moment by moment, his work would grow increasingly complex as variation upon variation of spinning steel wove itself through the Winter air. And then finally, just as his audience, nervously awaiting disaster, to a man believed there was nothing more that could be done with a baton, Wilbur, pausing slightly to fake them out, making them believe his repertoire was over, would give them the Capper.

Every great baton twirler has one thing that he alone can perform, since he alone has created and honed and shaped his final statement. Midway in his repertoire, Wilbur would whip a second baton from a sheath held by a great brass clip to his wide white uniform belt. Using the dual batons, he worked upward and upward until the final eerie moment. As the last notes of "The Thunderer" died out, a drummer, on cue, beat out the rhythm of our march, using a single stick on the rim of his snare.

Tic tic tic tic tic tic tic

As we marched silently forward, Wilbur then, with great deliberation, holding both batons out before him, began to spin them in opposite directions.

Synchronized! Like the blades of a twin-engine plane, twin propellers interleaved before him, gaining speed. Faster and faster and faster, until the batons had all but disappeared into a faint silver film, the only sound the "tic tic tic" of Ray Janowski's snare and the steady, in-step beat of feet hitting the pavement.

His back arched taut as a bow, knees snapping waist-high, at the agonizingly right instant, with two imperceptible flips of the wrist, Wilbur would launch his twin rapiers straight up into the icy air, still in synchronization. Like some strange science fiction bat, some glittering metal bird, the batons, gaining momentum as they rose, would soar thirty or forty feet above the band. Then, gracefully, at the apex of the arc, spinning slower and slower, they would come floating down; Wilbur never even for an instant glancing upward, the band eyes-front. Down would come the batons, dropping faster and faster, and still Wilbur marched on. And then, incredibly, at the very last instant, just as they were about to crash into the street, in perfect rhythm both hands dart out and the batons, together, leap into life and become silver blurs. It was Duckworth's Capper!

The instant his batons picked up momentum and spun back to life, Janowski "tic'd" twice and the drum section rolled out our basic cadence, as the crowd roard. Unconcerned, unseeing, we marched on.

Wilbur rarely used the Capper more than once or twice in any given parade or performance. Like all great artists, Wilbur gave of his best sparingly. None of us realized that Duckworth had not yet shown us his greatest Capper.

The high point of our marching year traditionally came on the Thanksgiving Day Parade. And that fateful Thursday dawned dark and gloomy, full of evil portent. The last bleak week in November had been literally polar in its savagery. For weeks a bitter Canadian wind had droned steadily off Lake Michigan, blowing the blast-furnace dust into long rivers and eddies of red grime on the gray ice that bordered the curbs and coated the bus stops and rutted the streets. These are days that try a sousaphonist's soul to the utmost. That giant chunk of inert brass gathers cold into it like a thermic vacuum cleaner. Valves freeze at half-mast, mouthpieces stick to the tongue and lips in the way iron railings trap children, and the blown note itself seems thin and weak and lost in the knife-like air.

The assembly point for the parade was well out of the main section of town, back of Harrison Park. Any veteran parade marcher knows the scene, a sort of shambling, weaving confusion. The Croatian-American float, the Friends of Italy, the Moose, the Ladies of The Moose, the Children of The Moose, the Queen of The Moose, the Oddfellows' Whistling Brigade, the Red Men of America (in full headdress and buckskin), the Owls, the Eagles, the Wolves, the Imperial Katfish Klan, the Shriners (complete with Pasha and red fezzes), the A. F. of L., the C.I.O., Steelworkers Local 1010, all gathered to snake their way through the ambient Indiana-Sinclair Refinery air, for glory and to thank God that there is an America. Or maybe just to Parade, which seems to be a basic human urge.

This gathering point is always known as a "rendezvous" in parade-ese. On the bulletin board the week before, the usual notice:

THE BAND WILL RENDEZVOUS AT 0800 ON HOHMAN AVENUE
OPPOSITE HARRISON PARK. EACH UNIT WILL BE NUMBERED.
LOOK FOR THE NUMBER PAINTED ON THE CURB—TWELVE. WE
WILL STEP OFF *PROMPTLY* AND SMARTLY AT 0915.

Of course by twelve-thirty we are still milling around, noses running, and way off in the distance, always, the sound of some band or other playing something, and still we stood. The thin trickle of glockenspiel music came back to us through the frozen trees and bushes as the Musicians' Local Marching Band tuned up. Megaphones bellowing, cars racing back and forth over the disorganized line of march, until finally, slowly and painfully, we moved off. Wilbur Duckworth shot us aggressively into our assigned march position, and we were under way.

Rumors had gone from band to band, from drummer to drummer, that the Mayor up ahead on the reviewing stand was drunk, that we were delayed while they sobered him up, that he had chased a lady high school principal around the lectern. But these are just Parade rumors.

The Thanksgiving Day Parade is really a Christmas rite. Behind us on a huge white float rode Santa Claus, throwing confetti at the crowd as we moved through town.

It's hard to tell from a Marcher's standpoint just what Parade Watchers think, if anything: As we got closer to the center of town, the crowd grew thicker; muffled, hooded, mittened, earmuffed, gray staring faces of sheet metalworkers, iron puddlers; just standing in the dead zero air. This is where you begin to learn about Humanity. Their eyes look like old oysters. They just look. Once in a while you see a guy smoking a cigar; he spits, and from time to time a kid throws a penny or a Mary Jane or a Cherry Bomb into the bell of your sousaphone.

All the bands, of course, are marching to their own cadence. Up ahead the Ladies' Auxiliary of the Whales shuffles on. In the cold winter of the Midwest you can hear a girdle squeak for three blocks.

We march past the assembled multitude, Duckworth never glancing to right or left, straight ahead, brow high, paper-thin black kid gloves worn on his baton hands. Up ahead the flags and banners of all kinds are fluttering in the icy-cold breeze.

LITHUANIAN-AMERICAN CLUB. HOORAY FOR AMERICA!

GOD BLESS ALL OF US

The steelworkers just stand there silently, looking. From somewhere far behind a glockenspiel in the German-American Band tinkles briefly and stops, and all around the steady drumbeats roll. We were on the march.

Strung overhead from lamppost to lamppost across the main street were strings of red and green Christmas lights. Green plastic holly wreaths with imitation red berries hung from every other lamppost.

We are now right in the middle of town. This is the big moment. It's like Times Square in Hohman, Indiana. The crossroads. A streetcar line ran right down the middle of the main street, and I am straddling a track, trying to keep up the 180-beat-per-minute cadence; blow our own special version of "Jungle Bells" on my frozen sousaphone. Bitter frozen, sliding along the tracks with the ice packed in hard. I have lost all feeling. My ears, my nose, my horn are frozen; my hands are frozen.

We moved haltingly ahead. Slowly, slowly. We'd bump into the Italian ladies ahead, and the German plumbers behind would bump into us. Somewhere the Moose would swear, and the Eagles would yell. And then we were right at Ground Zero, the reviewing stand to our right, the assembled multitude cheering the National Champions on to further heights.

Wilbur spun and faced us with his old familiar stare and suddenly the cold was forgotten. We were On! Two sharp rips of the whistle, a sustained, long, rising note, baton at port: two quick flips of the wrist, and our great fanfare boomed out. The parade had come alive. The Champs were on the scene. The American Legion Junior Fife and Drum Corps faded into oblivion. The Firemen's Scottish Bagpipe Company disappeared into limbo. Wilbur Duckworth was in command.

Ray Janowski's beat was never sharper, leading his drum section to heights that rivaled our best performances. Duckworth aboutfaced and went into action. His great shako reaching up like a giant shaving brush with plume into the sullen gray sky. A magnificent figure, his gold epaulets glinting as we wove at half-tempo over the hard-caked ice, little realizing we were about to participate in an historic moment that has since become part of the folksongs and fireside legends of Northern Indiana.

"The Thunderer" echoed in that narrow street like a cannon volley being fired in a cave. Blowing a sousaphone at such a moment gives one a sense of power that is only rivaled, perhaps, by the feel of a Ferrari cockpit at Le Mans.

Spitzer, our bass drummer, six feet nine inches tall, caught fire. His sticks spinning into the air, his drum quivering, the worn gold and purple lettering on its head:

NATIONAL PRECISION MARCHING CHAMPIONS CLASS A

The crowd is subdued into a kind of tense silence. They were viewing greatness; the panoply of tradition and pomp, and they knew it. The fourteen-inch merchant mill and the coldstrip pickling department at the steel mill rarely see such glory. Children stopped crying; noses ceased to run, eyes sparkled, and blue plumes of exhaled breath hung like smoke wreaths in the air as we slammed into the coda.

Already I was beginning to wonder whether Duckworth would dare try his Capper on such a dangerously cold day as this, with those sneaky November crosswinds, and numbed fingers. His ramrod back gave no hint. One thing was sure, and everybody in the band knew it. Wilbur had never been sharper, cleaner, more dynamic.

By now he was three-quarters through his act. His figure eight and double-eagle had been spectacular. The trombones just ahead of me, usually a lethargic section, were blowing clean and hard. Wilbur's twin batons were alive. His timing was spectacular.

We arrived at the dead center of the intersection precisely as the last note of "The Thunderer" echoed from the plateglass windows of the big department store and died out against the gray, dirty façade of the drugstore on the opposite corner. For a moment the air rang with the kind of explosive silence that follows a train wreck, or the last note of "The Thunderer" played by a band with blood in its veins and juice in its glands. And then it began. Janowski "tic'd" his solitary beat. We marched forward almost marking time in place. The crowd sensed something was about to happen.

Duckworth towered ahead of us, weaving slightly left, right, left, right, as his twin batons, in uncanny synchronization, began to spin faster and faster.

Sound carries in cuttingly cold air, and even the Mayor up on the reviewing stand could hear the sound of those spinning chromium slivers:

zzzzzzzsssssstt zzzzsssssssssssst zzzzzzzzsssssttt

Wilbur held it longer than any of us had ever seen him do before, stretching the dramatic tension to the breaking point and beyond. Beside me, Dunker muttered:

"What the hell's he doing?"

Wilbur spun on. Janowski "tic'd" off the rhythm.

Tic tic tic tic tic . . .

We marched imperceptibly, like some great glacier, across the intersection. And then, like two interlocked birds of prey, Duckworth's batons rose majestically in the hard November gloom.

Higher and higher they spun, faster than even the day that Wilbur had won the National Championship. It was unquestionably his supreme effort. He was a senior, and knew that this was his last full-scale public appearance before the hometown rabble. His last majestic Capper.

Every eye in the band staring straight ahead followed the climbing arc of those two beautiful interleaved disks as they climbed smartly higher and higher above the street. Wilbur, true to his style, stared coldly ahead, knees snapping upward like pistons. He knew his trade and was at the peak of his powers.

And then it happened. Instinctively, every member of the Bass section scrunched lower in his sousaphone at the awesome sight.

Running parallel with our path and directly above Wilbur's shako, high over the street, hung a thin, curving copper band of wire. The streetcar high-tension line. Slightly below it and to the left was another thin wire of some nondescript origin. The two disks magically, in a single synchronous action, seemed to cut the high-tension wire in half as they rose above it, without so much as touching a single bit of copper. Then, ten or twelve feet above the high-tension wire, they reached their apex and in a style cleaner and more spectacular than any of us ever had suspected was in Duckworth, they slowed and began their downward swoop. We watched, the crowd watched, and Wilbur marched on, eyes straight ahead. My God, what a moment!

The Mayor leaned forward slightly on the reviewing stand and even the children sensed that History was about to be made.

For a fleeting instant it appeared as though the two batons would repeat their remarkable interleaving, dodging, weaving avoidance of that lethal wire on their way down. In fact, the one on the right did. But the left baton hovered for just an instant, spinning slower and slower above the copper band, and then, with a metallic "ting," it just ticked, barely *kissed* the current carrier with its chrome-silver ball. The other end fell across the other nondescript wire, gently. And for a split second nothing happened.

Janowski "tic tic tic'd" bravely on. Our cadence never varied as our feet sounded as one on that spiteful, filthy ice.

Then an eerie transparent, cerulean blue nimbus, a kind of expanding halo rippled outward from the suspended baton and from some far-off distant place, beyond the freight yards, past the Grasselli Chemical Plant, an inhuman, painful quickening shudder grew closer and closer, as though a wave were about to break over all of us.

BOOM BOOM BOOM!

Hanging over the intersection was a gigantic, unimaginably immense Fourth of July sparkler that threw a Vesuvius, a screaming shower of flame in a giant pinwheel down to the street and into the sky, over the crowd and onto the band. The air was alive with ozone. It seemed to flash with great thunderbolts, on and on. Time stood still. It could have been ten seconds, or an eternity. It just hung up there and burned and burned, ionizing before our eyes.

Janowski "tic'd" on. A few muffled screams came from the crowd. Fuses were blowing out over the entire county, as far away as Gary. High-tension poles were toppling somewhere miles away. Steel mills stopped; boats sank on the river. It was as though some ancient, thunderbolt-hurling God had laid one right down in the middle of Hohman on Thanksgiving Day. The ground shuddered. Generators as far south as Indianapolis were screaming. Duckworth had hit the main fuse. It was the greatest Capper of all time!

By now the second baton had descended. Without so much as an upward glance, Duckworth caught it neatly and spun on. The drum section picked up the cadence and we marched smartly through the intersection, leaving behind a scene that forms the core of several epic poems relating the incident.

Duckworth immediately signaled for "El Capitan," and as we attacked the intro the crowd burst into a great fantastic roar of applause and surging emotion. The aroma of burnt rubber, scorched copper, ionized chrome, and frozen ozone trailed us up the street. Santa Claus, in a window, sat mouth agape. Grumpy's hammer was held stiffly at half-mast. The Christmas trees had flickered out, and MERRY XMAS neon signs were dark.

We knew that the baton that had gone up in smoke had been one of Wilbur's awards—his Presentation set of matched wands, won at the State Championships. The other, the survivor, he held lightly in his gloved right hand, his arm shooting high over his head and down diagonally across his body, up and down, up and down. He spun as we finished "El Capitan." Three quick blasts, the signal for "Under the Double Eagle." His eyes as steely as ever; his jaw grim and square.

From all sides we could hear the sound of sirens approaching the scene we were leaving behind us. "Under the Double Eagle" with its massive crescendos, its unmatched sousaphone obbligato. As we played this great classic and Duckworth led us on into the gloom, every sousaphone player, every baritone man, the trombones, the clarinets, the piccolos and flutes, the snare drummers and Janowski, all of us thought one thing:

"Did he plan it!?"

You never can tell about Drum Majors. This was not the sort of mistake Wilbur Duckworth would make. Had he calculated this? Practiced, worked for this moment for four long years? Was this gigantic Capper, this unparalleled Capper his final statement to Hohman, Indiana, and the steel mills, the refineries, and the Sheet & Tube Works, those gray oyster eyes, and the Croatian Ladies' Aid Society?

Up ahead Duckworth's arched back, as taut as spring steel, said nothing. His shako reached for the sky, his great plume waved on. He blew a long, single, hanging blast, holding his remaining baton at a high oblique angle over his head. Two short blasts followed, and he smartly commanded a Column Right. The drums thundered as we moved into a side street and headed back toward school. The parade was over. The wind was rising and it seemed to be getting colder. A touch of snow was in the air. Christmas was on its way.

CHARLES TOOMBS

(b. Indianapolis, 1952–) was educated at Shortridge High School, where he was Editor of the *Daily Echo,* and at Purdue University. (Shortridge, incidentally, which has given us such writters as Claude Bowers, Kurt Vonnegut, and Dan Wakefield, was named for the Indianapolis Schools superintendent who became the first Purdue president to award degrees.) In 1976 Mr. Toombs won First Prize in Fiction and First Prize in Poetry in the Paul Robeson Literary Awards. The short story below is here published for the first time.

Master Timothy

The odors in this old, Meridian Street apartment, once occupied by more affluent tenants, struck Timothy Baker as both offensive and pleasant. Baby smells, mostly: urine, powder, pablum. He would carry these smells with him wherever he went—to school, to the park, to market, to bed.

Timothy was eleven, the oldest of five children. He took care of his two brothers (ages two and three) and his two sisters (the four-year-old and the nine months' baby) while his mother worked as assistant head maid at the downtown Hilton. Timothy fancied himself an athlete. He spent whatever precious free time he had, practicing to become a Master in Kung Fu. While other youngsters his age read comic books, he would study "the literature," actually some flyers he had picked up for free from the Martial Arts studio a few blocks south of the apartment on his way home from school. His secret ambition was to talk his way into that sanctum, first perhaps as floor sweeper or rug beater, ultimately as a trainee or "novice." Meanwhile with all the force and grunts he could muster he would make lethal kicks onto the cracked walls of the apartment, and one cockroach after another would fall dead. He also did battle with these cockroaches in more conventional ways simply because he didn't want them to harm his little sisters and brothers.

He remembered his father only vaguely—rarely thought about who that man was, or where he was. Timothy's mother, Mrs. Baker, must have made adequate wages, for he could never remember being without food. And even though he never had all the toys he would have liked, he felt that he did have his fair share. What bothered him, "at least sometimes," was having to babysit so much with his brothers and sisters. They were so much younger than he, and he loved them dearly, but he missed playing with kids his own age, kids who often teased him: "What a drag, man, you always playing Mommy!"

Since Mrs. Baker worked the late evening shift, Timothy had to babysit from the time he got home from school (in recent days a few minutes later and later as he lingered in front of Martial Arts) until his mother's return about midnight. Before she left for work she would cook dinner. Tim fed the children, played with them, scolded or comforted them as the need arose, and told them stories. Many a night, before his mother returned home, he would get up from a deep sleep and change a diaper or two. He was shouldering responsibilities not ordinarily assigned to eleven-year-olds, and he sometimes wondered if an emergency might arise which he couldn't handle. There had been incidents like the time his baby sister Janeil woke up, convulsing. He had phoned his mother first, and then picking his sister up in his arms, had carried her down the hall to Mrs. James, asking what he should do. The woman took one look at the baby and called the police, who soon afterwards rushed Janeil to the hospital.

Then there was the time he took the children to the park and saved one of his brothers from getting bitten by a German shepherd by risking his own flesh. Timmy always put himself last. He didn't like his existence, but he accepted the good with the bad and made the best of his lot in life. Sometimes he would think about leaving his brothers and sisters alone for an hour or two, but thinking about it was as far as it went. Yet when everybody was sound asleep, himself included, he dreamed about everything he was missing, especially the fun his school friends were having. He dreamed of learning side kicks, back kicks, foot blows, splitting wood with the side of one hand, and above all, having the title of "Master."

On his way home from school, as he stood at the store-front window of Martial Arts, he would observe the classical executions and jot down in his notebook what he thought the techniques must be. Once back home, he did not dare try any of these exercises with the siblings. *They* couldn't even play ball very well. And all of this upset him. Sometimes he felt frustrated enough to cry, although he told himself "That's only what babies do." When he felt he was going to cry anyway, he would slip into the pantry and count cans of beans. He didn't want his little brothers and sisters to see him cry ever. After all, wasn't he their big brother? And besides, such behavior would be unthinkable for a Master.

One day he asked his mother if she could somehow afford a babysitter so that he could take instruction in Kung Fu.

"Momma, you know Mrs. James down the hall—that nice old lady who helped with Janeil? I bet she'd babysit for not too much money. She told me yesterday how she wished they'd raise her social security or lower her food stamps. She seems real nice, Momma, and I think she likes children. Why don't you ask her? I'll even get a paper route —or a janitor job—if she wants that much money. Please, Momma, I want to get into that Kung Fu group so bad."

Mrs. Baker, with the worry mothers feel when they learn that their children are reaching out too far too soon, looked across the living room to the bay window and wrestled with the question put to her by "her little black man." She stared at the faded green curtains from the Methodist Thrift Shop and fished for words he might understand —words to the effect that while she couldn't afford a babysitter right now, she didn't wish to crush his ambitions. But there was no solution and she cried a little inside.

"Timmy," she said, "give it a little time. In a few more months I just might be able to afford a babysitter, especially when the head maid retires. You know I'm next in line for her job."

"That's okay, Momma."

And he really believed her. In her he constantly found his energy.

By the time summer rolled round, Timothy's ambition of getting at least part-time work as a janitor at the School of Martial Arts was fulfilled. Although his job of sweeping floors and beating mats paid only fifty cents an hour, it did afford him opportunities for watching the performers at close range. He was also befriended by Spencer Jones, a novice a few years his senior, who even taught him some of the fundamentals. These were, however, mostly by way of mitigating some of the battering Timmy had been taking, bruises he found hard to explain to the children.

"You can get yourself killed, kid," Spencer would say, "unless you learn how to defend yourself . . . Now, look! Discipline, man! You can do it! There! That's coming along, but—"

Summer slipped by all too fast. Timothy would now have to return to regular school. What with babysitting, he'd have next to no time at all for Kung Fu. The first and the second days of the semester he came home several minutes later than usual and received a scolding more for the tardiness than for the bruises, which his mother had failed to notice, so he said nothing about Martial Arts. On the third day he was over an hour late. By four-thirty Mrs. Baker grew frantic. If she were late for work again, she might be passed over for the position left by the retiring head maid. Five o'clock, and still no Timmy. Even the neighbors in the apartment expressed concern. At six Mrs. Baker phoned the Hilton night manager, explaining why she might not make it at all that night. She also phoned the police, reporting Timothy missing. She was assured they would do everything possible and would not wait the usual twenty-four hours.

Then she was suddenly overwhelmed by a paroxysm of guilt. She cursed herself for having failed to provide Timmy with the kind of life enjoyed by other boys his age. She also cursed Timmy's father ("that deserter") and a number of other "disaster areas" she regarded as bearing directly on her present plight. At eight she put the babies to bed and prepared for an all-night wait beside the telephone.

The call came in about ten-thirty. She picked up the receiver, her heart beating out of rhythm. "Hello?"

"Hello. Mrs. Baker? Timothy Baker's mother? There's been a very very serious accident here at the School of Martial Arts . . . Sorry to inform you that—"

"Oh, my God . . . My Timmy . . . "

The room smelled acrid with perspiration. It was a big room, almost the size of a gymnasium. On the walls between the windows stretched pictures of undulating green dragons. The windows, no longer store-fronts, were now arched and lofty, reaching almost to the ceiling, and all that one could see through them was the sky, a deep blue laced with wisps of clouds. On the north wall a door led to a storage room, its opening arched very much like cathedral windows. From that doorway there came—no, floated—a boy, or what seemed like a screen image of a boy about four-and-a-half feet tall. Or was he taller? He was dressed in a white jacket with padded lapels, loose trousers, and a belt wrapped around his waist twice. He was carrying an immaculately clean mat, and he was smiling.

❖ ❖ ❖ ❖ ❖

Plays

❖❖❖❖❖❖❖❖❖❖❖❖❖❖❖❖❖❖❖❖❖❖❖❖

GEORGE BARR McCUTCHEON

(b. 1866–d. 1928) was born near Lafayette, Indiana, where his father was Director of Purdue's first Experimental Farm. Almost as soon as George could read and write he composed and produced plays in collaboration with his brother "John T," who was to become a celebrated cartoonist. George ultimately won fame and fortune for his novels, however, among them *Graustark* (1901) and *Brewster's Millions* (1902). The latter was adapted by Winchell Smith into a Broadway play. Very few of McCutcheon's own plays were produced or published. In fact, *The Double Doctor* is published here for the first time. For over fifty years the manuscript —in longhand on foolscap—lay neglected in the Purdue University Library archives. McCutcheon had attended Purdue along with George Ade and Booth Tarkington.

The Double Doctor, somewhat irreverent for its time, remains an entertaining satire of the lifestyles of upper middle-class Middlewesterners at the turn of the century. While the play rarely attains to the wit of a Chekhov or a Molière (indeed, it sometimes descends to corniness), its caricature of manners and mores echoes Oscar Wilde and Max Beerbohm.

The setting is nominally a suburb of a large city a few miles to the northwest of Indiana, but McCutcheon's frame of reference was almost surely a fashionable section of Indianapolis. In fact, it works well to visualize the Murgatroyds' "drawing room" as if in a stately old Meridian Street mansion.

The cast consists of Jack Murgatroyd, a successful businessman; Gertrude, his wife; Annie, their housekeeper; Richard ("Dicky") Matternot, a friend of the Murgatroyds; Mamie Jerrold, Richard's fiancée; Bessie Farrington, a flirtatious widow; Dr. Thomas W. Brown, a physician and close friend of Jack's; and the Reverend Thomas W. Brown, a clergyman. Both the Browns and Jack Murgatroyd have attended Princeton—after the fashion of many a wealthy Hoosier of their times.

Whether or not you chuckle as you read, you may wish to decide which comes in for more ridicule—a certain type of clergyman or certain people's misguided attitudes toward clergymen. You may also enjoy recognizing the more universal kinds of hypocrisies the playwright pokes fun at.

The Double Doctor
A Farce

Scene: MRS. JACK MURGATROYD'S *drawing room.* MRS. MURGA-
TROYD *discovered asleep in a chair near the center table, a portfolio
of art engravings in her lap, some of them scattered on the floor. The
doorbell rings and she awakens sharply; begins to collect the pictures
nervously.*

MRS. M: Good heavens! If that *should* be the new minister! Jack
says he is a perfect saint and I'm sure these pictures would shock him.
That *would* be too bad at the outset. If Annie had shown him in while
I was napping I should have died with the awakening. These pictures
—this "Psyche"—oh, dear! They are coming and I haven't them half
picked up. *[With her feet she scrapes some of the pictures under the
table, tossing the others after them.]*

[Enter ANNIE, *followed by* MISS JERROLD *and* MR. MATTERNOT.*]*

MRS. M: *[Relieved]* Ooh! It's you, is it?

MISS J: *[Shaking hands]* Of course! Did you think it was Napoleon
Bonaparte? *[Exit* ANNIE.*]*

MATTERNOT: She evidently did, which can account for her be-
sieged appearance. What's up, Mrs. Murgatroyd?

MRS. M: I thought you were Dr. Brown.

MISS J: The new minister?

MATTERNOT: How flattering—to Brown.

MRS. M: I was dozing when the bell startled me. The minister is
coming and—and—by the way, Dicky, would you mind picking these
up and putting them under the piano—under that pile of music
there?

MISS J: How artless you are, Gertrude.

MATTERNOT: *[Picking up the pictures.]* Heartless, I'd say. You can
tell him when he comes that if he's a good boy he may look at the
picture books, so he may. But, have you seen the new shepherd?

MRS. M: No; have you?

MISS J: To be sure he has not. Dr. Brown does not belong to the
Club.

MATTERNOT: Well, how the Dickens do you suppose I'd know him
downtown, or anywhere else, for that matter. I'd know Henry Dixey,
or Nat Goodwin, or Jim Corbett, or any of the rest of 'em, but I have
no way of identifying an American angel. I've not seen his lithograph
or cigarette picture.

MRS. M: Well, you'll soon see him; Jack has invited him to dinner.

MATTERNOT: To dinner! Heaven help us; we were going to stay to dinner ourselves. This spoils everything! Foiled—ha! ha! Just imagine me forgetting myself so far as to try to blow the foam off of the coffee. I'd compromise you and Jack forever!

MISS J: You wouldn't if you were that plebeian. If you held your glass of water up to the light, looked through it and said abruptly "That's out of sight" or "Doesn't she sparkle" or "Always my favorite, old man!", you'd wreak disaster, but he'd never know what you meant if you blew at your coffee cup. He'd probably think it was hot.

MRS. M: Here's Jack's note to me; it came an hour or two ago. *[Reads* JACK's *note]* "Dearest, I find my old friend Tom Brown here —he's to be our new pastor—and I've asked him up to dinner this evening. Get everything ready for him; hide my pipes and those playing-cards—he's horribly sanctimonious. I won't be through at the office till late, so I'll send him up in the carriage beforehand.—Jack." Now, there it is! What time is it now?

MATTERNOT: 3:50. Time he was here, isn't it. Let's look around behind the chairs; he's probably of a retiring disposition.

MISS J: I guess I'll sit down again. He won't be here for some time. I'm sure Jack instructed Hawkins to drive the horses in a walk all the way out here.

MATTERNOT: But Hawkins is so confoundedly contrary that he'd gallop instead. I think we'd better go, Mamie. I'll put your pictures here, Gertrude, beneath this pile of music; the top piece is "The Gaiety Girl"—

MRS. M: Don't leave it there, stick it farther down in the pile and put another song on the top.

MATTERNOT: The next is "For She's a Daisy, Daisy, Daisy" and then comes "It's Easy, Dead Easy" and here's "My Pearl is a Bowery Girl"—

MRS. M: Just think of it! Put them all behind the piano, Dicky, do! I wouldn't have him see these for the world.

MISS J: And he will be sure to ask you to sing if he sees the music, too!

MATTERNOT: Ah, here is one! "Abide With Me"—let's see *[reads]*. "Come, live with me, my darling, In my cot down by the sea; There's room for two, my darling, But there is no room for three." *That* won't do! Here they all go! *[He places them behind the piano.]* I never saw such trash and I'm ashamed to learn that Jack Murgatroyd allows you to sing such stuff.

MRS. M: He buys it himself, sir, and absolutely compels me to sing it for him. It is the only kind of music he cares for.

MATTERNOT: Well, that's because they're familiar to him. He went wild at the Olympia last night when Jennie Nabob came out and sang—

MRS. M: Last night! Why, he attended a meeting of the directors!

MATTERNOT: I know it—they met at the Olympia and I bought the tickets. Had to meet there; couldn't get a box anywhere else.

MRS. M: Richard Matternot, I do not believe you.

MATTERNOT: I knew you wouldn't. Nobody believes the truth anymore. If I had said some other woman's husband had gone there you would swear it was true!

MISS J: Don't believe him on oath, Gertrude. He's getting worse every hour. When we were coming down here he told me he had not called on Bessie Farrington for over a week. I'm positive he has, though. We scarcely speak, you know, Mrs. Farrington and I. She's a mean little hypocrite.

MATTERNOT: Well, I *haven't* called on her. She's in Cincinnati.

MISS J: What!

MRS. M: Didn't you know that? She went down there a week ago yesterday.

MATTERNOT: I saw her off.

MISS J: There's no occasion to tell me that; I would have known it, anyhow. It must have been a touching good-bye.

MATTERNOT: Not as much so as it might have been if her confounded—I mean, if her mother had not been there. *[Aside to* MRS. MURGATROYD*]* Say, she's jealous, isn't she? Do you suppose she cares for me enough to be real jealous?

MRS. M: You foolish boy! Why don't you find out?

MATTERNOT: How the Dickens can I? I've tried a half dozen times to kiss her and got left every time. I don't know *what* to think about it.

MRS. M: *Ask* for your kisses; that's a woman's advice.

MATTERNOT: Well, I never thought of that. It's not the usual way, you see.

MISS J: Gertrude.

MRS. M: Well?

MISS J: You will find him like all the rest of them—a downright boor.

MATTERNOT: Well, that's refreshing. It's funny that I can't speak to Mrs. Murgatroyd without establishing myself a boor—

MISS J: I am speaking of the minister, Mr. Matternot. You were not in my mind, at all. And furthermore, I was addressing Mrs. Murga-troyd!

MATTERNOT: You talked in my direction, at any rate.

MISS J: Do you listen with your eyes?

MATTERNOT: *Have* to, sometimes. Couldn't see the point if I didn't.

MRS. M: Do stop quarreling and be witty. You may discuss all these things after dinner, for you are to remain.

MISS J: With a minister of the Gospel? I assure you—no! I can imagine my appetite flying already.

MATTERNOT: You don't need an appetite, Mamie. You are lucky if you haven't one when you're invited out. It's a waste of energy.

MRS. M: Or an energy of waist—which? But, I shall be offended if you do not stay. I need you—need you badly!

MATTERNOT: See here, Gertrude; I can't afford to meet that preacher. I belong to his church and it would be devilish awkward, you know.

MRS. M: You talk in riddles!

MATTERNOT: That's it, exactly! It would be an embarrassing riddle if he should happen to ask me how I liked his predecessor. How the Dickens could I tell him? I don't remember whether we had one before him or not. *[Bell rings sharply and all start, nervously.]* There! That's the parson. We don't belong here, Mamie, and we know it. I'll venture to say that not one of us knows whether Genesis comes before the Lord's Prayer or after the Ten Commandments. "Now I lay me down to sleep—" there, that's all I know of the Lord's Prayer—

MRS. M: Sit down, Dicky Matternot, and don't be a fool. You must be nice to Dr. Brown.

MATTERNOT: *[Perspiring]*. But he'll ask me to say grace! Good heaven! I don't know a word of it.

MISS J: You could say "amen," couldn't you? "As it was in the beginning, is now and ever shall be," or something like that, couldn't you?

MRS. M: He'll not ask you. Jack will ask the Doctor to say grace.

MATTERNOT: Jack wouldn't even dream of such a thing.

MRS. M: I'll give Jack his instructions just as soon as I can get him alone. We'll arrange a code of signals. One wink means grace, two winks means—

MATTERNOT: You're mistaken; one wink means whiskey. Here they are!

[Enter MRS. BESSIE FARRINGTON, *airily.]*

ALL: "Bessie!" "Mrs. Farrington!" *etc.*

MISS J: [*Bowing stiffly, and aside*—"That widow!"]

MRS. F: How do you do, everybody! Are you surprised to see me?

MRS. M: Surprised and delighted. Sit down, Bessie. When did you return? Take off your things, dear.

MRS. F: I can't—I must go over to Mrs. Merrick's. I came in on the midnight express. Why were you not there to meet me, Dicky? Why, how sad you look. Been sick?

MATTERNOT: Not at all; had the blues, had 'em ever since you went away. [MISS JERROLD *draws herself up stiffly and* MRS. FARRINGTON *smiles ardently upon him.*]

MRS. F: I never have them; it makes people think one is in love. Dear me, Miss Jerrold, have you had them, too?

MISS J: [*Stiffly*] No, indeed—not even a symptom.

MRS. F: [*Aside*] Poor child! [*aloud*] I just dropped in to take dinner with you, Gertrude. I have been out calling with Sister Lou and I'm completely fagged out. You don't mind, do you, dear.

MATTERNOT: Not at all—glad to have you. Oh, I beg pardon.

MRS. M: I am delighted to echo Dicky's words. You will put life into the party; I'm so glad you've come.

MRS. F: Party!

MATTERNOT: No—parson! The parson's coming in to sup with 'em.

MRS. M: And Mamie and Dicky are to stay and help entertain him.

MISS J: I don't believe I can stay—

MATTERNOT: Oh, yes you can, Mamie—don't be afraid of a poor little minister.

MRS. F: Bravo, Dicky; you are a Daniel.

MISS J: [*Aside*]—I wouldn't stay for the world. The scheming thing; she knew that Dicky was here. But, no—I *shall* stay. I'll stay all night before I leave him alone with her; that is just what she is after. Oh, it's so disgusting! [*Aloud*] I *am* anxious to meet Dr. Brown. I ought not to stay, but I guess I will. Mamma won't care, I'm sure. [*Removes her hat, sweetly.*]

MRS. F: No, your indulgent mamma won't mind your being with a minister, I'm sure. But what sort of fellow is he? Is he cadaverously pious?

MRS. M: How do I know? I have never seen him; he arrived yesterday, I see by the *Record*. Do take off your things, Bessie.

MRS. F: I must run over to Mrs. Merrick's for a few minutes with a message for Mamma. I'll return in good time to take the parson in too; he shall be well groomed before we lead him up to the horn of plenty. It shall be my self-allotted duty to relieve you of the awful responsibility of entertaining him; it is not in your line, to begin with.

A minister is unruly, although it seems hard to believe. Most of them become so bigoted, so wrapt up in their own ideas and opinions that they are unapproachable from mere mortality's point of view. They must be dragged down from their heaven early in the day.

MATTERNOT: We'll trust you to bring heaven to earth, Mrs. Farrington.

MRS. M: But you must not shock him, Bess. Jack says he is a very tender plant.

MRS. F: One must treat tender plants considerately and—well, gradually; they improve under cultivation. I trust that he is young as well as tender.

MRS. M: He is fresh from the frocks of the Theological School at Princeton.

MRS. F: Then he has not had time to grow hard and knotty.

MATTERNOT: I shouldn't think you'd look for that condition in a preacher.

MRS. F: I said knotty, Dicky—k-n-o-t-t-y.

MRS. M: I have been racking my brain all day, trying to think what I have neglected. There is something, I am sure, that I have forgotten —something that is sure to create consternation at the last moment. I have secreted all the playing cards, the chessboard, "Trilby," Jack's horse journals and his pipes. Perkins has locked the billiard room, and the sideboard is decanterless. The cook has promised to use no brandy in the pudding sauce. I'm sure I know of nothing else, yet— I'm sure there is. *[During her remarks* MATTERNOT *carelessly arises and hangs his silk hat over a small statue of Venus which stands on the mantelpiece.]*

MRS. F: Gertrude, why haven't you put *Pilgrim's Progress, The Journey of the Soul* or *The Life of Luther* on the table, instead of Byron, Shakespeare and—what's this? Dante's *Inferno!* Dear me, it would seem more respectable.

MRS. M: But we haven't anything but *Pilgrim's Progress,* and I don't know whether the leaves have been cut in it or not.

MRS. F: Well, cut them and turn down the corner of a leaf somewhere. Get out your photograph albums, your stereoscopic views, and put a couple of hymn books on the music rack.

MRS. M: Good heaven! Do you suppose he is such a saint as all that? I'll die—positively die if he is. Oh, Bessie, this is such a new thing to me—to us, I mean. And it is all because he was in Jack's class at college.

MATTERNOT: Well, he's out of Jack's class now, I'll bet. We had better think up a few scriptural quotations, too.

MRS. M: Quotations! I can't remember a line.

MRS. F: You might run off the Ten Commandments incidentally during a lull—just as a matter of habit, you know—absentmindedly.

MRS. M: Oh, Bessie, you'll do it, won't you?

MRS. F: Do what, my dear?

MRS. M: Take him off my hands. I'm sure to be a fool.

MRS. F: If you are willing to risk me. Parsons have not been my customary diet, but I have a changeable appetite. I'll devour this one if we stay at table long enough. Now I'll run over to Mrs. Merrick's and be back in twenty minutes.

MRS. M: Don't dare to fail me.

MATTERNOT: Don't let her keep you. If you must gossip, come back here. We know a whole lot of fresh scandal.

MRS. F: Never fear—I am eager for the fray. A minister! A relief, a diversion, a saint! Do you want him to kiss me this evening, or shall I tempt him gradually? Well, good-bye, for a bit of a while. *[Exit* MRS. FARRINGTON, *looking laughingly at* MISS JERROLD, *who bows, freezingly.]*

MATTERNOT: I am determined to study for the ministry. What lucky dogs they are! I wonder why it is that a woman takes so much delight in undoing a divine.

MISS J: It would be more competent if you asked why Mrs. Farrington delights in undoing anything that looks like a man.

MATTERNOT: I don't see how she can help liking a man if he acts like a man. We're not so bad if you'll only look at us in the right way.

MISS J: It would be impossible for me to look at you as Mrs. Farrington does; I cannot squint and smirk and wink and—and—do all those things, you know. Mrs. Farrington is a flirt and she would flirt with anything from a minister to you!

MRS. M: Oh, you shouldn't say that, Mamie—that was too strong. Bessie is lively—refreshingly so—but she is only so because she enjoys life and all of its conditions. I think that is quite a happy state.

MISS J: The conditions have certainly changed since her husband died. She used to wear the longest face in town.

MATTERNOT: Do you blame her? He was two years in dying—the longer the suspense, the longer the face. It puzzles me to explain how she even got her face back at all.

MISS J: She certainly deserves credit for the face she has prepared; it is most exquisitely done. I wonder what she uses, Gertrude.

MRS. M: That is a mystery which she will allow no one to solve, but she shows her secret in her face.

MATTERNOT: Smart woman. Therein lies her store of roses, peaches and cream, honey—yum, yum!— *[The door bell rings and all start.]*

MRS. M: That's Dr. Brown!

MATTERNOT: I guess I'll go—

MRS. M: No, indeed;—sit down, both of you.

MISS J: Do I look sanctimonious enough, Gertie, in this no-waist and with these feathers?

MATTERNOT: You look like an angel—with parrot's feathers. *[Enter* ANNIE *with a card, which* MRS. MURGATROYD *takes with dignity.]*

MRS. M: *[Reading]* "Thomas W. Brown." Sh—show him in, Annie. *[Exit* ANNIE, *leaving the trio sitting stiffly in their chairs.] [Enter* DR. THOMAS W. BROWN *at Center Door. Pauses for a moment up-stage.* MRS. MURGATROYD *goes up to greet him.]*

MRS. M: Dr. Brown, I am so delighted to meet you. I—I—

DR. BROWN: I can readily guess that you are Jack's wife. He told me that he married an angel and I am overjoyed to meet one of your kind, Mrs. Murgatroyd. They are so woefully scarce, you know.

MRS. M: *[Slightly confused]* That foolish boy. The idea—an angel!

DR. BROWN: He's uncommonly discriminating, I should say, for one who displayed such utter disregard for that sort of research in the past. His must have been an unconscious taste or good luck personified.

MRS. M: Ahem! Dr. Brown, let me introduce you to Miss Matternot —or Mrs. Jerrold—I mean—*Miss* Jerrold and *Mr.* Matternot. *[Aside]* What a fool! *[After the acknowledgement of the introduction.]* Pray be seated, Doctor!

MATTERNOT: Take this one, Doctor; you'll find it the most comfortable in the whole shooting match—I mean, the house.

MRS. M: Oh, but this arm-chair is the favorite. Everybody likes it best.

DR. BROWN: Then I shall leave it to you—take it yourself, Mrs. Angel—Mrs. Murgatroyd. I'll drop into the first thing in sight. *[They all sit.]* Jack must be very busy today. Coachman came around to the hotel after me in a most surprisingly busy fashion; gave me a note from Jack in which he said he couldn't leave the office but ordered me to take the carriage and drive right out. Saw him this morning downtown and he didn't have time to take a—a bit of lunch with me. Jack has to be pretty busy to refuse lunch, you know. Said he'd see me later—ha—ha! He's a wonder, Jack is—a regular wonder. All hustle—all bustle. Same way at school—all bustle. By the way, how long have you been married, Mrs. Murgatroyd?

MRS. M: Nine years last month. I'm an old married woman, you see. *[Aside]* He's not a bit like what I thought he'd be.

MISS J: *[Aside to* MATTERNOT*]* He doesn't even wear a white cravat; and look at his shoes.

MATTERNOT: *[To* MISS JERROLD*]* He's got the marks of a sport. By George, he's not half a bad fellow.

MISS J: If he'll only keep it up and not get religion.

DR. BROWN: *[Aside, looking at* MISS JERROLD] By George, she's a beauty. *[Aloud]* I trust Jack notified you that I was coming; these surprise visits are not always pleasant.

MRS. M: On, yes; he told me you were to come to dinner.

DR. BROWN: *[Aside]* The devil he did! Well, that's more than he told *me!* Glad I'm to stay, though; I'll sit next to that pretty girl or die. *[Aloud]* Where are the youngsters?

MRS. M: The youngsters?

DR. BROWN: Yes—the kids—I mean, the children. Oh, I see! You haven't any little prattlers—Pshaw! How thoughtless of me! Well, they're just an annoyance, although I like 'em—I love babies. They are the gladsome life of a home, the projectors of trouble, yet the purloiners of care. Jack used to be so fond of children—even used to wish that he could be a child again. What he didn't like about childhood was the compulsory visit to the Sunday school every Sabbath morning; but in that he was like all boys. I never went to Sunday school in my life, except at Christmas time, that I didn't wish I could be out fishing or skating with Buster Lynch. Buster was the bad, bad boy in our ward and he was the idol of every lesson-deaf kid in that part of town. He is now a prize fighter; he's knocked out everything that has ever gone up against him, too. You have doubtless heard of him here. Musty—Mr. Matternot—Kid Lynch, the champion middleweight of the New England coast?

MATTERNOT: *[Aside]* What the Dickens shall I say—yes or no? *[Aloud]* Ahem! I—yes—I believe I have seen his name in print.

DR. BROWN: Well, he's a peach!

MATTERNOT: *[Aside]* A peach!

MRS. M: *[Aside]* A peach?

MISS J: *[Aside]* A *peach!*

DR. BROWN: But we outgrew all those Sunday school experiences and we should, for the sake of civilization, put aside the prizefighting era—relegate it to the fabulous past, as it were. The sport has degenerated abominably in the last few years—a man never knows who the best man is in the Hippodrome fights we have nowadays; there's no such a thing as a cinch on bets—but, I beg pardon, ladies! This conversation, through my thoughtlessness, has drifted away from your interests. We must change it, and I know of nothing better to discuss than Jack's ante-connubial days. Of course, you must not expect me to give away all that he did in those times. You'd want a divorce, Mrs. Murgatroyd! Well do I remember when you were Miss Galloway and he was getting love letters every day from you at college.

Mrs. M: *[Confusedly]* Why, Dr. Brown, you embarrass me! I never did such a thing in my life as to write to Jack every day.

Dr. Brown: Is it possible? Then it must have been some other girl. I know he got 'em every day. And they were frequently signed "Gertrude," sometimes plain "G." and once in awhile "Miss Galloway"—at which times I remember Jack had dreadful attacks of despondency. I am quite sure about the letters, you know; he allowed me to read some of them.

Mrs. M: *[Leaping to her feet]* He did? The wretch! Do you really mean—oh, Doctor, you are jesting.

Dr. Brown: *[Laughing]* Well, to keep peace in the family, I'll admit that I am somewhat of a liar myself; I never saw *one* of your letters. . . .

Mrs. M: But it is strange that you should know how I signed my name at different times.

Dr. Brown: *[Aside]* That's so; how did I know? *[Aloud]* Oh, we were such great friends that I always understood his moods, and as you made his moods it was easy to guess the rest. I was in love at the same time. Thirty-three of us were in love with Prof. Bromley's daughter, who, I hear, is still the college widow.

Matternot: *[Aside]* He's a corker! No more like a preacher than I am.

Mrs. M: *[Aside]* And Jack said he was a tender plant, as solemn as an owl. Why, he's just lovely!

Miss J: *[Aside]* He *will* suit the widow!

Dr. Brown: But Jack got her—for the time being, at least. He always was the wise one—more than wise, by the way. He was smooth!

Matternot: *[Aside]* Smooth! Ye Gads!

Mrs. M: Jack often speaks of you. You were his guide, his philosopher, his example, he holds.

Dr. Brown: *[Aside]* I was? What a liar Jack is! He has made her believe that *I* am an angel. *[Aloud]* Oh, no, my dear Mrs. Murgatroyd, I never felt that I did much for Jack, although I must confess I tried to keep him busy following my footsteps.

Mrs. M: He says you never drank, caroused around, played cards, or raised cain like the other boys. Oh, doctor, he looks upon you as a model, I assure you!

DR. BROWN: Ahem! He used to tell me that I was the next thing to an angel in his estimation. Poor fellow, he had an awkward and rather unrefined way of putting it, though. He called me a bird. Wasn't that angelic?

MRS. M: A bird? How odd! But I suppose it was his way of talking.

DR. BROWN: Dear old Jack; I couldn't break him of it.

MRS. M: It must have wounded you to be called a—a bird!

DR. BROWN: It did, to be sure, but I always forgave Jack everything. To make him feel that he did not offend me I went so far as to be as birdlike as possible—soar a little—take occasional fliers, as it were. But, alas, I was too slow to keep up with the flock.

MRS. M: And now you lead the flock. How funny! But you and Jack did not take the same course, did you?

DR. BROWN: [Absently] Generally—if I was swift enough. Oh, I beg pardon, I mean I took a different course, of course.

MRS. M: You were in the classical and he, the industrial school.

MISS J: [Enthusiastically] And Jack was on the football team, too.

DR. BROWN: Yes, and he was a star! I don't blame you, Mrs. Jack, for marrying him. Every woman in New York wanted to marry him that day when he tried to finish the game with all the ligaments torn from his left shoulder. Say! That was a game for you—and he was in it, too—with both feet! You've seen a football game, haven't you?

THE OTHERS: [Breathlessly] Oh, yes!

MISS J: I saw the game last week between Purdue and Stagg's team, and I am a crank all over.

DR. BROWN: Well, it's the caper east, you can bet; I didn't think they played it west. But that game in which Jack was hurt was the greatest ever played on Manhattan Field. That was the year the Tigers put it all over everything in sight. Everything we tackled got it in the neck—

MRS. M: [Amazed] In—the—neck!

DR. BROWN: [Enthusiastically] You're shouting, now;—where Nellie wore her beads.

MATTERNOT: [Excitedly] I remember reading an account of that Thanksgiving game. It must have been a dandy!

MISS J: [Reprovingly] Dicky! [Aside] Don't use slang before him!

DR. BROWN: Dandy? Why, it was a beaut! I won a cool seven hundred on it.

MRS. M: [Helplessly, as MATTERNOT removes the hat from the statue.] Why, I—I—Jack said you never did such a thing as bet.

DR. BROWN: *[Aside nervously]* What the devil has Jack been telling about me? This is getting warm. *[Aloud]* Did he say that? Well, the dear fellow never knew I made that bet—nobody knew it—and it was my only fall from the high pedestal which I see Jack has built for me. I am quite ashamed to admit it even now, and I lay awake two whole nights wondering whether my conscience would be eased if I took the money back to the fellows from whom I won it. Excitement caused it all, you see. It was during the forepart of the game and some Yale men were blowing off—doing a lot of talking around where we —where I was, and it finally became unbearable. I had $700 in my inside pocket—just happened to take that much along—

MRS. M: Wasn't that a large amount for a young man who was working his way through college? Jack says you deserved the greatest credit in the world for getting through as you did.

DR. BROWN: *[Aside]* What a great song-and-dance he must have given her! Ye Gads, I spent more money than any boy in college. *[Aloud]* True enough—it was a struggle, but you see, I was agent for a certain text-book—the—er—the "Philosophy of Life"—and I saved quite a good deal out of the business. That's how I happened to have the seven hundred plunkers—er, dollars—; the men all paid me that day. *[Aside]* Great brain! The idea of college men paying debts on such a day as that! By George, come to think of it, I owe Parson Tom Brown for one of those books yet. *[Aloud]* And as I was saying, I could not take a bluff—it was put up or shut up, and up went the seven hundred. Say, that game was one of the kind that hurts a man's heart, too. It was when the Tigers were making steady gains down the field that Jack's accident came. He had the ball and plowed through Yale's left tackle, clearing the line like a flash. Wow! You should have seen that boy sprint. I never yelled so loud in my life. It was immense. But you remember reading how Smith, a Yale substitute, tripped him near the side line, and how he fell with four or five big sons of Eli on top of him. That's how he got hurt—just when he was sure to score a touchdown. Oh, it was a damned shame. *[Realizes his slip and stops, blankly.]* I—I—beg pardon—I always get pretty warm when I think about that miserable trick.

MRS. M: *[To* MISS J*]* The swine!

MISS J: Don't you suppose I heard him?

MATTERNOT: *[Aside]* Say! He'll be the most popular preacher in town!

DR. BROWN: If I could have found Smith after the game I'd have punched his head, that's all. But, you see, I had to administer to Jack; we thought he'd die for a while.

MRS. M: Oh, dear! I never knew that. Did you have to pray for him?

DR. BROWN: Pray? Good heaven, no! It was not a time to pray. I had to rub—rub—rub! He fainted as they carried him from the field. By the way, I just heard today that Smith has turned preacher—got a little charge up in Pennsylvania somewhere. He's a nice object to do the gospel act, isn't he?

MRS. M: *[Surpressing a smile as she walks upstage]* I only hope he proves as much of a stumbling block for them as he did for Jack. *[Aside]* I see very plainly that it will require no exertion to entertain him. He can do it all.

MATTERNOT: *[Cautiously]* Doctor, who do you think will win the game this Thanksgiving?

DR. BROWN: Do you want a safe bet?

MATTERNOT: I—I—well, I wouldn't mind.

DR. BROWN: Bet on Princeton—all you can raise. It will be dead easy. I'm a stranger here, but, if you get more bets than you can take care of, I'll be glad to take 'em off your hands. I'll bet my clothes on the Tigers.

MATTERNOT: You? How?

DR. BROWN: Certainly—why not? Do I look like a man without any sand in my neck?

MATTERNOT: But, what will the people say?

DR. BROWN: I don't expect to have it shouted from the house-tops. If you think the people will kick, I'll let you put up the stuff for me.

MATTERNOT: *[Grasping his hand]* Well, say, old man, you *are* a brick, every inch of you.

DR. BROWN: Thanks; that's a compliment. Ah, Miss Jerrold, may I ask what you are reading? *[Goes over to the sofa on which she sits.]* I am something of a bookworm and therefore inclined to turn to all that's new.

MISS J: *[Handing him* Pilgrim's Progress] This is Bunyan's book. I like it so much; it is so deep, so spiritual.

DR. BROWN: *[Laying it aside carelessly]* Ah, I presume so; I've never read it; heard some one speak of it, seems to me, however. *[Picks up another book]* "The Dangers of Skepticism"—umph! pretty dry, I should say. Have you ever read *Trilby? [They engage in conversation.]*

MRS. M: *[To MATTERNOT]* What do you think of the Parson now, Dicky?

MATTERNOT: He's a wonder. Say! I like that fellow. There's nothing sanctimonious about him—not a particle.

MRS. M: He *is* charming; I'm half in love with him! And we were so afraid he would be a bore—a piece of unendurable piety.

MATTERNOT: I'm going to church every Sunday, now.

MISS J: *[To* DR. BROWN*]* You will have to miss the game next month, won't you?

DR. BROWN: Not for a thousand dollars!

MATTERNOT: But how can you leave with all the special work on hand?

DR. BROWN: I won't have anything to do here unless some of the local players get hurt, and I guess you have doctors enough to save their lives. If not, there'll have to be a funeral. This town seems perfectly able to do anything. I like it here.

MISS J: I am so glad; you will find the church people ever ready to assist you in your good work. *[Aside]* I hope that sounded well.

DR. BROWN: The—ahem—yes I hope so. *[Aside]* What the deuce does she mean?

MISS J: I am quite sure you will like your charge.

DR. BROWN: Beg pardon?

MISS J: You will like the people here and it will be a pleasure to minister to us.

DR. BROWN: Thank you. I shall have to have patients, of course.

MISS J: Oh, yes—patience is the greatest of virtues.

MATTERNOT: *[To* MRS. M*]* And Jack says he is an angel, does he? He must be wearing a disguise today.

*[*DR. BROWN *accidentally rings the table call bell]*

DR. BROWN: Hello! I've rung this bell.

MISS J: And the servant is prompt in answering. What will you say to her? *[Laughingly]*

DR. BROWN: Order up the drinks! *[Laughs heartily]*

[Enter ANNIE, *who is sent away by* MRS. MURGATROYD.*]*

MISS J: You are such a funny man, Doctor. Everything you say is so happy.

DR. BROWN: *[Drawing close to her]* How can I help being happy when I am near one who inspires happiness?

MISS J: *[Giddily]* Oh, Dr. Brown!

DR. BROWN: *[Softly, causing* MATTERNOT *to exhibit unmistakable signs of jealousy]* I'll have to admit that I like to talk to a pretty girl. They cause me to think of dark nooks beneath the grand staircase, the seclusion of the conservatory, moonlight drives—but you know how it is....

MISS J: Why, Doctor, how *can* you?

DR. BROWN: I don't know whether I can or not; I'm only experimenting. Pardon my impatience.

MATTERNOT: *[To* MRS. M, *savagely]* He's a hypocrite, that's what he is. No good preacher would talk football, *bet, swear* and *spoon* like *he* does!

MRS. M: Oh, that's pure jealousy in you, Dicky! If you are alarmed I'll call him away from her. Dr. Brown! Dr. Brown! Oh, Doctor!

MATTERNOT: Call him away? You can't *drag* him away. But, *I'll* get him!

MRS. M: Be quiet! Doctor!

MISS J: Mrs. Murgatroyd is speaking to you.

DR. BROWN: Excuse me, please. What is it, Mrs. Jack?

MRS. M: Have you called on any of the ministers in town?

DR. BROWN: Ministers? Well, hardly. If they need me, *they* can call on *me*. *[Aside]* I hope Jack hasn't gone and married a crank on religion. Is it possible that Christianity has got a foothold out here?

MRS. M: They are so very agreeable and they will surely make it pleasant for you.

DR. BROWN: I'll turn my hopeless cases over to them as an exchange of courtesy. I may be able to keep up friendly relations in that way, you know. But there's a divinity that shapes our ends, eh, Mr. Matternot?

MATTERNOT: *[Confusedly]* Yes—er—that's from the Book of John, isn't it?

DR. BROWN: *[Bewildered]* Yes—that's one of John's best.

MISS J: Why, that is from *Hamlet!*

DR. BROWN: *[Promptly]* To be sure it is—John Hamlet. I didn't understand you, Mr. Matternot; John was the Dane's Christian name, you know. But I don't think I'll have any trouble with the preachers; we go hand in hand. Religion is on the boom.

MISS J: On the boom!

MRS. M: *[Aside]* I never heard such amazing language in my life.

DR. BROWN: *[Aside]* They seem to like religion. I'll have to remember that. *[Aloud]* Mrs. Murgatroyd, I see a piano. Who is the performer? Whose play is it—I mean, who plays it? Let us have a tune or two; I'm passionately fond of music. Oh, songs! *[Goes to piano, discovering the stack of music behind it. To the consternation of the others, he goes down on his knees and looks over the music.]*

MRS. M: *[Rushes over frantically]* Oh, Doctor, no one plays or sings —not *now* at least. Please don't mind the music. I—I—

MATTERNOT: *[Frantically]* Say, Doctor—say—look here—have you ever met Rev. David Swing? Here's his picture.

DR. BROWN: I've seen it a hundred times. But here are some I haven't. Do you mind if I look them over, Mrs. Jack? I'm so fond of pictures—

MRS. M: *[Snatching the folio away rudely]* Yes—no—some other time, some other time, Doctor. Do you play, Doctor?

DR. BROWN: *[Arising, very much bewildered]* Oh, I—I play a little. I'm always willing to show how little, however. *[Sits at the piano and rattles off "After the Ball"]* Want to waltz? *[Plays a waltz, and* MATTERNOT *forces* MRS. MURGATROYD *to waltz a few turns]* Say! If Jack was only here! He'd enjoy this.

MRS. M: *[Aside]* He wouldn't do anything of the kind. He'd faint. *[Aloud]* I wonder why he does not come. I am beginning to feel a little bit worried. If you will excuse me I'll run down to the drug store and telephone to the office. *Our* phone is being repaired.

[All exit.]

[Enter JACK MURGATROYD *and the* REV. THOMAS W. BROWN, *the former barely able to conceal his nervousness.]*

JACK: *[Anxiously]* Wonder where Gertrude is! Sit down, Tom; make yourself at home. She'll be down presently.

REV. BROWN: Oh, thank you. John, you have a delightful home here; I should think you would be happy.

JACK: I am—it's out of sight, old man; nothing like married life to straighten a fellow out and make him feel like he has something to live for. I don't see why the devil—why *you* don't get married.

REV. BROWN: *[Sitting]* But, my dear John, there is something far more worth living for than the earthly joys of matrimony.

JACK: I don't know about that; we've both had a limited experience. By the way, I've got some real news for you.

REV. BROWN: What is it, John?

JACK: Old Tom Brown is in town and he's going to practice medicine here. I saw him downtown this forenoon. He's the same old boy.

REV. BROWN: I trust that he has mended his ways, however.

JACK: It's rather funny, isn't it, that we should all locate in this city.

REV. BROWN: It is, indeed. What I chiefly remember of my association with Tom was through the unlucky demands I used to make on him for $7.50, the price of a *Philosophy of Life* book which I sold him in his third year. He has not paid me to this day.

JACK: I'd tackle him for it again.

REV. BROWN: What say?

JACK: I say, I'd ask him for it. He's got a barrel of money now—an uncle died.

REV. BROWN: *I* shall never ask him for it. If I took *one* cent from him my conscience would never spare me. It would be cheating him, for I know that he never found his money's worth in that truly good publication.

JACK: He never read it.

REV. BROWN: Never read it?

JACK: *[Hastily]* Until I told him what sort of a book it was. Then he read it and—and felt just as I did about it.

REV. BROWN: I see you have some good books here, John; does your wife like this kind of literature?

JACK: Yes; we read to each other almost every evening.

REV. BROWN: The little prayer book is very pretty. *[He picks up and opens one of those deceptive playing-card holders and out drops half of the deck.* JACK *is covered with dismay as he assists in collecting them.]*

JACK: *[Laughing disjointedly]* Ha—ha! Those are—ha—ha—Dicky Matternot's; he—he left them here yesterday. Ha ha! Pretty good joke on Dicky, isn't it?

REV. BROWN: What odd designs—quite original. And what does he do with these extraordinary pictures, John?

JACK: Why *[aside]* Good heaven! He doesn't know what a playing card is! *[Aloud—staggered]* Those? Why—he—he has them for the children to play with. Neat, aren't they? I thought perhaps you had seen some before—er—on Christmas trees, you know.

REV. BROWN: I do not recall them. I shall have to suggest them to our Sunday School superintendent. Once, at school, I saw some fellows playing that nefarious game of seven-out—or seven-in, and their cards were something like these.

JACK: That's so—I never noticed it before; they are quite familiar —I mean, *similar.* By the way, will you excuse me a few minutes, old fellow? I'll run upstairs and see what has become of Gertrude. Make yourself at home. There's the library; go in and help yourself. *[Exit]*

REV. BROWN: *[Picking up* Pilgrim's Progress] I am glad to see that John Murgatroyd has gone to reading such books as this. *[Reads]*

[Enter MRS. FARRINGTON, *hastily; stops up stage to remove her hat]*

MRS. F: That you, Dicky, old boy?

REV. BROWN: *[Answering in amazement]* I beg your pardon.

MRS. F: *[Astonished]* Oh, I beg *yours!*

REV. BROWN: We've been waiting—that is, your husband has just gone up to find you.

MRS. F: My husband! Well, I'm glad he has gone *up.* This is Dr. Brown? Well, I am Mrs. Farrington and my husband is—has passed away.

REV. BROWN: I beg a thousand pardons; I thought you were Mrs. Murgatroyd. We are total strangers. If you will just take a seat, Mrs. Har—Har—

MRS. F: Farrington, Doctor, Farrington with an F . . . Thank you; *[sits]* I am to stay to dinner, too. We will soon know each other well for our strange introduction. Mrs. Murgatroyd and I are old, old chums, and Jack, too, for that matter.

REV. BROWN: *[Aside]* I always thought of widows as old women. *[Aloud]* This is the first time I have visited her—er—Jack—since his marriage. We were classmates at college.

MRS. F: He never tires talking of Tom Brown! *[Aside]* Not Parson Tom Brown, but *my* Tom Brown. Ah, how I should like to see my Tom Brown!

REV. BROWN: I beg pardon?

MRS. F: I was just thinking of the nice things he has said of Tom Brown. *[Aside]* And of the nice things I should like to say to *him*.

REV. BROWN: There was another Tom Brown in our class.

MRS. F: *[Innocently]* Another? I have heard him speak of but one.

REV. BROWN: I must say, though not unkindly, that he was the worst scapegoat in the class. He was always in a scrape of some kind.

MRS. F: Oh, I adore college stories! Won't you tell me of some of his scrapes—his worst ones, say. What did he do that particularly stirred up the monkeys?

REV. BROWN: I never heard of his doing such a thing as that, but he did keep the faculty in a state of turmoil.

MRS. F: That's what I meant. I've heard Jack say it was fun to make monkeys of the professors. But what *did* this bad boy do, doctor?

REV. BROWN: Just now I cannot recall. As—oh—well, his chief fault was his popularity. We all admired him, not withstanding his evil ways. When he wooed Prof. Bromley's daughter from thirty-odd rivals, he became the lion of the whole school. Had he given more attention to study and less to thoughts of love he would have progressed more admirably, I think.

MRS. F: He was a great fellow to fall in love, then?

REV. BROWN: It was his constant condition. Furthermore, he wrote love letters to a dozen different girls at the same time.

MRS. F: *[Sharply]* How do *you* know, Dr. Brown?

REV. BROWN: Possessing precisely the same name, we used to get each other's mail. A glance always convinced me that *his* were not *mine*. No one ever wrote a letter to me and signed such names as "Ducky," "Birdie," or "Dovey."

MRS. F: *[Rather unhappily]* You say he received many such letters? But could they not all have been from the same person who might have forgotten how she signed them at different times?

REV. BROWN: She would scarcely forget herself so far as to write

three or four letters in one day, each in a different style of chirography, and above all, forget whether she was a duck, a dove, or—or—

MRS. F: *[Morbidly]* Just an ordinary bird! Yes, I suppose he must
have had several.

REV. BROWN: Which was not at all to his credit.

MRS. F: *[Energetically]* Which was not at all to his credit.

REV. BROWN: Mr. Murgatroyd has just informed me that he is in
town.

MRS. F: *[Starting to her feet]* What! In town? Impossible!

REV. BROWN: Why, you seem surprised.

MRS. F: I *am* surprised. Are you *sure* it is *that* Tom Brown?

REV. BROWN: It is Thomas Walter Brown, M.D. He is to locate here.

MRS. F: *[Joyously]* Locate here? Oh, it cannot be true!

REV. BROWN: Mrs. Farrington, if it is not true, do not accredit me
with the falsehood. John Murgatroyd first informed me; accuse *him.*

MRS. F: *[Aside]* Tom to locate here? Oh, the dear, dear fellow. He
expects to surprise me! *[Aloud]* If you will excuse me, Doctor, I shall
see what detains Mr. and Mrs. Murgatroyd. *[Exits unceremoniously]*

REV. BROWN: She is an amazingly pretty woman. I never thought
it of a widow. I think I shall see what John's library contains. *[Exit]*

[Enter DR. BROWN *(the physician) and* MATTERNOT*]*

MRS. M: *[Outside]* We will be down in a moment, doctor.

DR. BROWN: *[Looking off]* Take an hour—that's what a moment
means to a woman. *[To* MATTERNOT*]* Jack must be almost home by
this time.

MATTERNOT: He drives like the dev—very fast, I should say.

DR. BROWN: That old mare of his has a wonderful knee action; she
ought to go in a three minute clip.

MATTERNOT: *[Aside]* He's a racehorse preacher, too. I've a notion
to ask him if he plays pool. *[Aloud]* You seem to know something
about horses.

DR. BROWN: I have thought, on various occasions, that I knew, and
the assumption proved my misfortune. A man doesn't know much
about a horse until he has backed him against the field and then sees
the field win. Have a cigarette? Wonder if Mrs. Murgatroyd will care
if we smoke here? *[They light their cigarettes.]*

MATTERNOT: Not at all, I *know*. But, say, Doc, I didn't think *you*
could smoke.

DR. BROWN: I don't see why. I make it a rule to smoke a cigarette
every time I want a drink. In that way, I have become quite a fiend.

MATTERNOT: Would you like a drink now?

DR. BROWN: *[Throwing the cigarette into the grate]* That is the only way in which I ever hope to break this terrible cigarette habit. *[MATTERNOT procures a glass of water for him and he takes it disgustedly. After drinking a sip or two he lights another cigarette.]*

MATTERNOT: *[Aside]* There's the signal again. He must be a tank. *[Aloud, going to the window.]* Hello! I see Hawkins down there with the carriage. Jack must be home. I'll go and hurry him up. *[Exit]*

DR. BROWN: These are the most damnably inexplicable people I have ever met. Hello! Here comes one of them.

[Enter MRS. FARRINGTON; both look at each other in amazement and then he rushes toward her.]

MRS. F: Why, Tom Brown!

DR. BROWN: Bess! What—the—deuce—are—you—doing here! *[He attempts to kiss her but is repulsed.]*

MRS. F: Stop! You shan't do that!

DR. BROWN: Shan't? Well, I just will! *[Makes another fruitless effort.]* Why, what's the matter, Bess, dear? We haven't seen each other for a year—do you forget that? You can't have forgotten me in four days, either. See this! *[Triumphantly pulls a letter from his coat pocket.]* Here's your last letter, written on Friday last, and you close with "I send you a million kisses—"

MRS. F: How ridiculous and how impossible! You know I couldn't get a million kisses on that sheet of paper in a life time. But what name do I sign there—Ducky, Dovey, or Birdie?

DR. BROWN: Neither! Look here! *[As she peers over his shoulder he kisses her.]* "Darling"!

MRS. F: That *is* what I signed, isn't it? But I didn't mean it. Come over here, sir, and kneel before me. I have a crow to pick with you. *[They sit on the sofa.]* In the beginning, why are you here?

DR. BROWN: Because Jack invited me. There's no crime in that, I reckon.

MRS. F: Are you sure he invited you?

DR. BROWN: I haven't tasted liquor since—yesterday. What do you mean?

MRS. F: That he invited the Rev. Thomas W. Brown here to dinner today, but there hasn't been a word said about a pill peddler, sir. There's a mistake out, my boy.

DR. BROWN: There can't be any on my part or his; he sent a note to the hotel, directed plainly. I don't believe an intelligent hotel clerk would send into the billiard room to deliver a note to a preacher, do you?

MRS. F: Mrs. Murgatroyd expects the preacher, just the same.

DR. BROWN: You are mistaken. I have seen her.

MRS. F: And she knows?

DR. BROWN: She does unless she is crazy. By George, though! I wonder if she *does* take me for another fellow. She has conducted herself mighty queerly and so have the others. Say, Bess, this is a devil —pardon me, I must say it—a devil of a note. I guess I'm not the man. What shall I do?

MRS. F: *[Aside]* It is quite evident that there are two Richmonds in the field. *[Aloud]* You say *Jack* wrote you a note; why not let *him* explain the situation. Be discreetly dumb and you'll fare better. Now I want to ask another question of you, and a serious one. Do you still love me?

DR. BROWN: A thousand times more than ever! *[As he attempts to put his arm about her waist she arises coldly.]*

MRS. F: Then why are you here and not where a devoted lover should be—at *my* house? Do you call this love? Answer me!

DR. BROWN: But you are in Cincinnati.

MRS. F: I am not in Cincinnati.

DR. BROWN: But you *are* in Cincinnati. Jack *said* so this morning. I was on my way to your house when I met him. So help me Moses, Bess, he said you'd gone away.

MRS. F: Did he? And are you sure you were on your way to see me?

DR. BROWN: You know I was. I have been half mad with the desire to see you again—to kiss you—to hold you—to talk to you as I did in that happy year ago. When I came here it was with the hope that I could surprise you and then kiss the surprise away. You were gone —and now what am I getting for my pains? Here I am, ready to practice and kill medicine, and all because I didn't want to take you away from your old home, your friends, dear.

MRS. F: Take me away? What do you mean by that?

DR. BROWN: That I am going to marry you.

MRS. F: You take my breath. Have you my consent?

DR. BROWN: It isn't necessary, I guess. You have kissed me, you have sworn you love me and I have done the same by you. I, at least, am conscientious; Bess Farrington, I am not the kind of a man to deceive a woman! *[Heroically—with a prodigious smile]*

MRS. F: *[Smilingly, as she places her hand in his]* Well, I shan't let you deceive me, Tom. *[He draws her to him and kisses her. Enter MRS. MURGATORYD, unheard. She stops in the doorway as if petrified.]*

DR. BROWN: *[Seated on the sofa with MRS. FARRINGTON, his arm about her]* Bess, dear, how soon can I call you all my own?

MRS. F: *[Modestly]* I have been a widow almost four years; I had been one almost three when I met you; I don't believe I care to draw the period out *over* four years, all told.

DR. BROWN: *[Kisses her ecstatically]* Well, you shan't, bless you!

MRS. M: *[Comes down, blazing]* What does this mean? What does it mean, I say? *[They separate confusedly.]* You—you—Bessie Farrington—you vile, unwomanly creature! And *you*—oh, you wretch!

DR. BROWN: My dear Mrs. Murga—

MRS. M: Don't "dear" me! Mrs. Farrington, you will leave this house instantly! And you, sir, though you be the minister of all the churches in Christendom, you are beneath my contempt—bah! *[They both laugh unrestrainedly.]* And you treat it as a laughing matter! Vile—oh wretches! Dr. Brown, my husband shall see that you never preach one sermon in the pulpit which you seek to disgrace with your presence.

DR. BROWN: *[Laughing]* Let me explain—listen! Oh, this is too good! Ha! Ha!

MRS. M: You scoundrel! Oh, if I could only see Jack; he would kick you into the street like a dog. Bessie Farrington, you asked if you should kiss the preacher tonight. Well, you have and now—go!

DR. BROWN: Oh, ho, Bess—you wanted to kiss the parson, eh?

MRS. F: Gertrude, you *know* I was only jesting.

MRS. M: Do you call this a jest?

JACK: *[Outside]* Gertrude! Where are you?

MRS. M: *[Rushing to the door]* Here—here, Jack! Oh, do come to me! *[Weeps]*

[Enter JACK and REV. BROWN from the library.]

JACK: *[Seeing DR. BROWN]* Tom Brown!

REV. BROWN: Is it possible? *[The two shake hands vigorously, exclaiming "How do!" "Old man," "Glad to see you," etc.,* MRS. MURGATROYD *looking on in blank amazement.]*

MRS. F: *[Leading REV. BROWN to her]* Mrs. Murgatroyd, *this* is Rev. Thomas Brown—our new pastor.

MRS. M: *[Faintly]* Then who is—is—

DR. BROWN: Dr. Thomas W. Brown, M.D., at your service.

MRS. F: —and who is soon to be my husband!

DR. BROWN: Number two.

MRS. M: Oh, Bess, forgive me! I—I didn't know! What a horrible—horrible mistake. I knew I'd never get through without one, too! *[Puts her penitent head on MRS. FARRINGTON's shoulder]*

[Enter MATTERNOT and MISS JERROLD, her hair somewhat disarranged.]

MATTERNOT: *[Going to DR. BROWN, in an excited aside]* Say, doctor, I've got a job for you. Ha! Ha! I'm going to be married during the holidays.

DR. BROWN: Let me congratulate you. So am I.

MATTERNOT: The dev—deuce! But we want you to marry us.

DR. BROWN: *[Aside to him]* Mr. Matternot, that would be a fatal error. I am perfectly willing to become your family physician but I fear that I would be seriously interfering in family matters if I tried to marry you. If you will allow me, I should like to introduce the Rev. Thomas Brown. He will look after your case for the present. *[Leads him over to the minister.]*

CURTAIN

DAVID GRAHAM PHILLIPS

(b. 1867–d. 1911) grew up in Madison, Indiana, in a home that was, as Eric Goldman puts it,

> filled with books and an atmosphere that encouraged reading them. Before David was twelve he had romped through all of Victor Hugo, Walter Scott, and Charles Dickens; he went over and over the Bible, which rested on the mantelpiece when it was not having its regular reading before meals.*

Such an atmosphere did much to shape Phillips' mind and character. He attended Asbury College (now De Pauw University) before finishing at Princeton. He worked on newspapers in Cincinnati and New York, ultimately writing editorials for Pulitzer's newspaper *The World.* In many editorials and in articles for popular magazines Phillips criticized abuses in certain industries. And under the pen-name of "John Graham" he carried his muckraking into such novels as *The Great God Success* (1901), *The Light-Fingered Gentry* (1907) and *The Conflict* (1911).

But through all of his articles, novels, and plays, he kept gravitating toward "the problems of women." And it was as a feminist that he culminated his career—notably in his play *The Worth of a Woman* (New York: D. Appleton & Co., 1908) and in his posthu-

---

*From Goldman's biographical essay "David Graham Phillips, Victorian Critic of Victorianism."

mously published novel *Susan Lennox* (1917). In "Before the Curtain," notes on the program for the Madison Square Theater production of *The Worth of a Woman*, Phillips wrote: "*The Worth of a Woman* is not a problem; it is a love story—an agitated day in the lives of two young Americans. Don't look on woman as mere female, but as human being. Remember that she has a mind and a heart as well as a body."

In 1911, when Phillips was at the height of his career, he was murdered by one Fitzhugh Goldsborough, a fanatical chauvinist who believed that Phillips was "trying to destroy the whole ideal of womanhood." See whether you agree or disagree with Goldsborough!

The Worth of a Woman

PERSONS OF THE PLAY:

HUBERT MERIVALE . . . . Of Clifty Farm
DIANA MERIVALE   His younger daughter, manager of the farm
PHYLLIS DAGMAR . . . . His elder daughter
LUCIUS DAGMAR . . . . Husband of Phyllis
JULIAN BURROUGHS . . . . A young lawyer from the East
THE REV. EBEN WOODRUFF, D.D. . . . Merivale's life-long friend
MAGGIE SALYERS . . . . Housekeeper
BILLY . . . . Man-of-all-work

Scene: Clifty Farm, Indiana, in the valley of the Ohio River
Time: A day in July, early 1900s

ACT I

The library at Clifty Farm. The walls are filled bookshelves, the furniture old-fashioned mahogany. A large table desk with cigars, cigarettes, writing materials; a smaller table to the right with books and magazines. In the rear wall, great French windows thrown wide and revealing a railed and columned veranda; it views from an eminence a harvest-time landscape of gentle hills and valleys with a broad river in the distance. On the veranda, in a wicker chair under an awning umbrella, white, with green lining, sits HUBERT MERI-

VALE, *owner of the farm—white hair, smooth-shaven, deeply wrinkled face, strong, rather stern, intellectual. He is dressed in white linen and a Panama; an ebony cane with a gold knob leans against his chair. He is reading and making notes at a book-strewn wicker table beside him. The door to the right opens and* MAGGIE SALYERS, *the housekeeper, crosses toward the left, carrying an armful of cut flowers. At sight of* MR. MERIVALE *she halts.*

MAGGIE. If I was to ask him what day it is, he wouldn't know. My, what a thinker! Always at big serious books that it makes a body headachy to look at. But always with the gay band on his Panama, and the tie to match—Miss Diana looks out for that. *[Sees a telegram on the large table.]* "Miss Diana Merivale." Probably the one she's so eager about. Mr. Merivale! *[*MERIVALE *does not hear.]*

MAGGIE. Mr. Merivale!

*[*MERIVALE *frowns, mutters, sighs like a disturbed sleeper, resumes his work.]*

MAGGIE. Mr. Merivale!

MERIVALE. Eh? . . . Ah? . . . What? . . . You, Maggie? Oh, yes. Um —where was I? *[Returns to his work, saying abstractedly,]* My dear child, the first law of human intercourse is, "Don't interrupt!" *[With a kindly, absent smile.]* Your interruption has perhaps slain an immortal thought. *[Quite absorbed again.]* Whether or no the soul is immortal, certain it is there are immortal thoughts. Perhaps Milton and Hugo were right, and some souls, like some thoughts, are immortal, others not.

MAGGIE. *[Holding up the telegram.]* Isn't this telegram on the table here the one Miss Diana wanted as soon as it came?

MERIVALE. *[Staring at her dazedly.]* Yes? . . . Eh? . . . Telegram? . . . How came it there? . . . Ah! *[He rises, confused and ashamed.]* Inexcusable! Diana particularly enjoined me!

MAGGIE. Yes, sir—she asked us all to be on the lookout.

MERIVALE. *[Self-reproachfully.]* And Peter brought it to me, to know what to do about it—

MAGGIE. Peter ought to have come to me.

MERIVALE. No—no—it was my fault—entirely my fault. I vaguely recall he asked me some question, and I—I must have been—not listening. I'm not usually so preoccupied. *[*MAGGIE *smiles.]* But this morning—I've come to a most important chapter. The telegram must go to her at once. *[*MAGGIE *presses an electric button to the left of the closet fireplace.]*

MERIVALE. *[Walking up and down the veranda.]* It's the first time I remember Diana's asking me to do anything for her—and I neglect it! She who does everything for me, and neglects nothing! *[Enter by door to left* BILLY, *the man-of-all-work, in shirt sleeves and collarless, his trousers held up by a broad leather belt. He has plainly been toiling and is in no very good humor.]*

BILLY. *[Crossly.]* Yes, Mr. Merivale.

[MERIVALE, *walking up and down the veranda, muttering to himself, does not hear.]*

MAGGIE. Billy, saddle a horse and take this to Miss Diana—down to the creek farm.

BILLY. I'm busy with the rooms next to Miss Diana's—those for this here preacher that's coming.

MAGGIE. I'll have Lizzie look after them.

[She holds out the telegram, waving it impatiently. BILLY *advances with reluctant, hesitating step.]*

BILLY. Then, there's the hall floor to be polished, and—

MERIVALE. *[Pausing, notes* BILLY.] Ah—Billy! Diana wants that telegram immediately.

BILLY. *[With complete change of manner and tone.]* Oh, if Miss *Diana* wants it—

[He takes the telegram and hastens out by door to right.]

MERIVALE. Inexcusable! Inexcusable!

MAGGIE. I shouldn't worry, sir. If it's good news, it'll be the better to her for the delay. If it's bad news, she oughtn't to have it at all.

MERIVALE. She didn't tell me what it was, but—*[smiles]*—I suspect.

MAGGIE. *[With a nod and knowing smile.]* No doubt it's from—*him.* What a lovely young gentleman Mr. Burroughs is! So democratic!

MERIVALE. When you've said gentleman, you've implied democratic.

MAGGIE. It ought to be, sir, but somehow it isn't, any more.

[She puts the flowers on the table and busies herself at rearranging small articles and polishing with her apron.]

MERIVALE. Not in the East, where he comes from. But, thank God, out here we are still Americans.

MAGGIE. Not all of us. Those that go East to school usually come back quite different.

MERIVALE. The power of a bad example over the weak-minded! . . . *[Notes the flowers as she takes them up.]* Delightful!

MAGGIE. For Dr. Woodruff's room. Miss Diana told me to have them cut fresh about the time he was due, and to put them there to welcome him, if she wasn't back to attend to it herself.

MERIVALE. She thinks of everything.

MAGGIE. Everything but herself, as Peter often says to me and me to Peter.

MERIVALE. Everything but herself. And hers is the usual reward of self-sacrifice. Those for whom she does all take her for granted.

MAGGIE. As Peter and I often say, what will become of us when she's married to Mr. Burroughs and off to that East? Of course, Miss Phyllis and her husband will be living here. But nobody could take *her* place.

MERIVALE. I don't let myself think of it. *[Sighs.]* And January will soon be here. *[Sighs again.]* But, Maggie, we mustn't let her see how we feel. The least we can do is not to shadow her happiness. She *is* happy, don't you think?

MAGGIE. As happy as could be expected, with Mr. Burroughs gone back home nearly five weeks now.

MERIVALE. Five weeks! I should have said a few days.

MAGGIE. Naturally you don't miss him as much as she does. We all miss him. He's a fine young man, if ever there was one. I never thought I'd like an Easterner. I didn't altogether like him at first. All those Easterners seem to think that, of course, their ways are just right, and that because our ways are different, we're wrong and queer.

MERIVALE. It shouldn't irritate us, Maggie. It's only amusing. We are broader than they, and that should make us more tolerant.

MAGGIE. That's true, Mr. Merivale. I soon saw it wasn't he, but his bringing up, that was to blame.

MERIVALE. Precisely. He had been what we out here'd call badly brought up—more like an Englishman than an American. But after he'd been among us a while—out here in God's country—he showed he was one of us beneath.

MAGGIE. Indeed he is! Of course, he ain't good enough for Miss Diana. But she's blind to his faults. That's always the way with us women.

MERIVALE. Fortunately for us men.

MAGGIE. Oh, I don't know, Mr. Merivale. There's another side to that. The men have to overlook a great deal, don't they now?

MERIVALE. *[Smiling.]* Not a *great* deal—but—something perhaps.

MAGGIE. I wouldn't admit it to Billy, but I have to laugh to myself when he says if a man wasn't a fool he'd never undertake to support a woman for life just for—for a little hugging and kissing and that, now and then.

MERIVALE. *[Absently.]* Six months until she goes—six swift months.

[MAGGIE *moves toward door to left. Enter there* LUCIUS DAGMAR, *fashionably dressed to the point of foppishness for morning in the country.* MERIVALE *eyes him and costume with tolerant, amused disapproval.]*

DAGMAR. *[To* MAGGIE.] I just picked up the auto with the telescope. It's climbing Cresson Hill. They'll be here in a few minutes.

MAGGIE. Oh, I must hurry.

[Exit MAGGIE *hastily by door to left.* DAGMAR *lights a cigarette.]*

DAGMAR. *[Speaking with a drawling nicety that seems to suit his manner and dress.]* How goes the great work this morning?

MERIVALE. *[Ignoring* DAGMAR'S *remark.]* Dr. Woodruff was in the auto with Phyllis?

DAGMAR. I've never seen him, you know. But I fancy it was he. White-haired, clerical-looking party—white whiskers—round collar —black clothes—all that. [MERIVALE *seats himself at his work again.]* What were Billy and Maggie shouting about?

MERIVALE. *[Absently.]* Telegram for Diana.

DAGMAR. Oh, *the* telegram.

MERIVALE. I don't *know* from whom, but—*[Smiles, leans back in his chair.]*

DAGMAR. So, he's taken to the telegraph, eh? The very frenzy of love. And he an Easterner—*and* Bostonian—*and* a Burroughs—of the *Boston* Burroughses.

MERIVALE. The description hardly suggests—Julian.

DAGMAR. Nevertheless, he does come of a family of icebergs stranded in Back Bay. If we knew him well, we'd find the chill all right, all right—you can gamble on that.

MERIVALE. *[Somewhat sharply.]* We do know him.

DAGMAR *[Soothingly.]* Not Phyllis and I. You'll remember we got back from Europe only two days before he left.

MERIVALE. He may have felt constrained with you. But I assure you he is frank—ardent—natural.

DAGMAR. *[Sitting at ease.]* He may have made himself seem all that, just to get solid with you and Diana. But—

MERIVALE. Julian is no hypocrite, Lucius.

DAGMAR. I didn't mean to say he is. At the same time, when a man's in love—he *believes* he believes a lot of things.

MERIVALE. Julian detests sham, and laughs at pretense.

DAGMAR. Bore into him—and you'll find a Burroughs of Boston. And why not? Where's the harm?

MERIVALE. You don't know the strength of his mind.

[DAGMAR *laughs, rises, lounges up and down.*]

DAGMAR. He may have honestly believed he'd been broadened. But I'm speaking of instincts—prejudices, if you please—that a man inherits—that begin to be nourished at his mother's breast. You've some of those prejudices yourself, sir.

MERIVALE. Not the kind that they have in the East.

DAGMAR. Perhaps not. . . . I confess I don't wildly fancy those fashionable Eastern upper-class people. They strike me as rather—funny—bunch of goldfish swimming round in their little tank and imagining it's the universe. However—I'm a bit of a snob—and as I don't have to associate with the Burroughses, this alliance with them—

MERIVALE. Eh? Still talking Burroughses? I don't know anything about them. I'm content with Julian, and that's sufficient. But here a man isn't a symbol of family or pocketbook.

WOODRUFF. *[Outside.]* Bertie!

[Enter DR. WOODRUFF *on veranda to left. He looks the successful, prosperous clergyman.* MERIVALE *rises, advances with boyish eagerness.]*

MERIVALE. Ben!

WOODRUFF. Hubert! Not the least changed by these eight years! Yes—the bright band on your hat, and the bright tie to show that your heart is young and gay.

[MERIVALE *and* WOODRUFF *shake hands again and again.]*

MERIVALE. *[Greatly moved.]* Ben—welcome! . . . My son-in-law, Dagmar—an acquisition of two years ago.

WOODRUFF. *[Shaking hands with* DAGMAR.] Of the Chicago Dagmars, I believe?

DAGMAR. Joel Dagmar was my father—but no doubt you and Phyllis talked all that over, on the way from the station. She's great on family trees. Did you have a pleasant journey from Louisville?

WOODRUFF. A rain providentially laid the dust.

[Enter from veranda PHYLLIS, *a fashionable, cynically good-humored woman of thirty.]*

MERIVALE. *[In raillery.]* Still imagining the Almighty looks after you especially.

WOODRUFF. *[Good-naturedly.]* Not a sparrow falls to the ground without His notice, says the Bible.

PHYLLIS. *[From the center of the room where* DAGMAR *is helping her off with her dust coat.]* But it doesn't say either that He causes the sparrow to fall or that He stops its falling.

WOODRUFF. *[Laughing heartily and shaking his head at her.]* I came to rest and to refresh myself in the friendship of my old pal here, not to engage in theological disputation. *[Looks out over the landscape.]* This superb place! Like the garden farms of the old world. What cultivation! What taste! Great changes here in eight years, my friend.

MERIVALE. In five years—less than five. At lunch you'll see the architect of it all.

WOODRUFF. Ah—that wonderful daughter—your Diana—*our* Diana, for I feel I have a share in her. Mrs. Dagmar tells me she's to be married. [MERIVALE *nods slowly, sighs.]* And only yesterday, it seems to me, I had her on my knee, teaching her to call me Uncle Ben. Married! Phyllis tells me the young man is of the Boston Burroughses—a fine family—in the front rank of our true aristocracy.

MERIVALE *[Dryly.]* That seems to have done him an unusually small amount of harm—though Dagmar here has just been protesting the contrary. But I trust Diana's judgment.

WOODRUFF. *[Surveying the landscape.]* That lake must be new. It doesn't look so, but I can't recall a lake.

MERIVALE. It was Diana's idea—one of her first big improvements. She changed the course of the creek, put a dam at the edge of the valley—

[The two link arms and go out on the veranda, MERIVALE *talking and using his cane to point out various features in the landscape. Exeunt left.* PHYLLIS *crosses to table desk at left, busies herself with contents of shopping bag.]*

PHYLLIS. *[Pausing abruptly.]* Did Di get her telegram?

DAGMAR. Billy took it to her. What's all this excitement about? What's in the telegram?

PHYLLIS. I wish I knew.

DAGMAR. No trouble between her and him?

PHYLLIS. None that *I* know of.

DAGMAR. I guess there isn't. Only this morning I saw a letter in the mail—for her—Boston postmark. A fat letter—three two-cent stamps. He's daft about her—if letters mean anything.

PHYLLIS. But they don't.

DAGMAR. That's a fact. The more a man—or a woman—protests—especially on paper—the less it means. Now I—

PHYLLIS. You never write at all.

DAGMAR. Exactly. And it's setting a good example, too. If I had my way, the cheapest stamp would cost a quarter. Then people wouldn't write unless they had at least a little something to say. . . . It's queer none of Julian's family has written—gad, *that's* what's been on your mind the last few weeks.

PHYLLIS. Really?

DAGMAR. But as long as your father doesn't mind—

PHYLLIS. *[Crossly.]* Conventionalities never enter his head.

DAGMAR. Or Di's.

PHYLLIS. Or Di's. *[Angrily.]* The way father's brought her up!

DAGMAR. Pretty good work, I say. She's made the whole place over —and it pays like a gold mine—mill, dairies, gardens, fancy chickens, horses, sheep, cattle—God knows what and what not. I never saw a woman like her. And so young, too. And always light-hearted. It'd be frightful if that chap . . . You know how it is with young fellows. And as long as the wedding is vague—

PHYLLIS. It's fixed for January.

DAGMAR. At his age January might look distant and hazy from June. And she's in love with him—really in love. It's rarely a woman's in love with the man she's marrying.

PHYLLIS. *Very* rarely.

DAGMAR. Nothing personal? [PHYLLIS *nods and laughs.]* No matter. You are, now . . . To resume— No, usually a woman—unless she's an out and out hard one—*likes* the man—more or less. But she's thinking about what he can do for her—substantial things—precious little about him.

PHYLLIS. I wish it were so with Di.

DAGMAR. Rubbish!

[WOODRUFF *and* MERIVALE *appear again on the veranda from left.]*

PHYLLIS. Take the old doctor away to his room. I've got something to say to father.

DAGMAR. What room's Di giving him?

PHYLLIS. The suite over the parlor.

DAGMAR. Oh, the rooms Burroughs had.

[WOODRUFF *and* MERIVALE *come into the room at window left center.]*

WOODRUFF. *[To* PHYLLIS.] I'm impatient to see Diana.

DAGMAR. *[Breaking in.]* She's the real thing. Her father there's brought her up—and a smashing good job he's made of it.

MERIVALE. I've brought her up like the Persian youth, Ben.

WOODRUFF. "To ride, to shoot, to speak the truth." You see I've not entirely forgotten my Xenophon. A *real* education—to ride, to shoot —to speak the truth!

DAGMAR. That's Di. Straight as a sapling.

PHYLLIS. Perhaps the doctor would like to go to his room.

DAGMAR. I'll show you, doctor—if you happen to want to trim up a bit before lunch.

WOODRUFF. Certainly, certainly.

MERIVALE. I'll go with him, Lucius.

PHYLLIS. Please stop here, father. You don't mind—do you, doctor?

WOODRUFF. Pray don't make a guest of me.

DAGMAR. Come, doctor.

WOODRUFF. You'll excuse me, Mrs. Dagmar?

PHYLLIS. Phyllis.

WOODRUFF. Phyllis! Thank you. I appreciate that.

[Exit WOODRUFF *and* DAGMAR *to right.]*

MERIVALE. Well, Phyllis?

PHYLLIS. Sit down, father, please. I want to talk with you about Julian.

MERIVALE. You're barking up the wrong tree. Go to Di. She's the authority on that subject.

PHYLLIS. When Lucius and I got back from Europe two days before Julian left—we found he'd been here, here in this house—nearly two months.

MERIVALE. Bless me—so long as that? . . . Yes, it must have been. But I saw little of him. He was occupied, and so was I. Do you know, Phyllis, until they came and told me, three days before he left, I *never* suspected?

PHYLLIS. *[Laughing.]* Incredible! . . . *[Serious and businesslike.]* Now, father, you'd know—if you weren't so busy with the past—love and marriage no longer go handcuffed together.

MERIVALE. Handcuffed! I'll never cease regretting that I was over-persuaded by your aunt into letting you go to that fashionable New York school. Ah, my daughter, bitter will be the afternoon and evening of your life if you let that veneer eat into you. It will destroy your heart. Handcuffed!

PHYLLIS. Linked then. Love is a sentiment—marriage a business.

Love's a personal matter. Marriage is a matter of family, position—prospects, pocketbook—pride, all sorts of things.

MERIVALE. Sordid. Sordid.

PHYLLIS. But highly important. Yet you've been treating this marriage as if it were a personal matter, only Diana's affair. And—you've been letting Julian treat it the same way.

MERIVALE. It *is* personal.

PHYLLIS. In a sense, yes. But how about Julian's family?

MERIVALE. *[Carelessly.]* I don't understand. Some of your muddy worldliness, I suppose.

PHYLLIS. Not at all, father. You've not heard from Julian's people.

MERIVALE. Well, what of that? They'll get round to it. Everybody isn't as energetic about trifles as you are, Phyllis. I can sympathize with anyone's not writing letters.

PHYLLIS. Don't you know why you haven't heard?

MERIVALE. *[Indifferent.]* No, and I don't care. Julian's family doesn't greatly interest me. I know him, and he's sound. That's enough.

PHYLLIS. *[Impatiently.]* How do you know he's sound? You met him—just happened to meet him—when he came out here about that railroad right of way. You knew nothing then of him, or his people. Yet you invited him to visit *here.*

MERIVALE. Why not?

PHYLLIS. But remember his people. What did *they* think when he went back home, and told them about his visit—In this house two months and Diana unchaperoned.

MERIVALE. *[Amused.]* Diana—chaperon.

PHYLLIS. Oh, I know Di needs no chaperon, still—

MERIVALE. *[Sternly.]* My dear Phyllis, nothing, *nothing* could be so bad as the spy system and its degradation of womanhood. I've brought Diana up with the only chaperon a *woman* could accept—the chaperon of her own self-respect.

PHYLLIS. That's true, father. I don't disagree with you. My own conventionality's only one skin deep. But with Julian here Di ought to have had a chaperon.

MERIVALE. If you want to make a spirited woman indiscreet, watch her.

PHYLLIS. A woman in love, or a man, either, for that matter, is a woman or man in need of watching. I've been there. I know.

MERIVALE. I'll concede *you* may have needed a chaperon. You were brought up by your Aunt Althea, and her idea of her sex is grossly physical. That a man has but one use for a woman.

PHYLLIS. Aunt Althea is a shrewd, sensible person.

MERIVALE. The men seeking to possess as cheaply as possible, the women striving to sell as dearly as possible.

PHYLLIS. Well, isn't it so? Isn't that the way of the world?

MERIVALE. I'll listen to no more of this. I'm glad to say Diana's been brought up to think and judge and decide for herself.

PHYLLIS. But I'm not talking of Diana. I'm talking of Julian's idea of her—Julian's and his people's.

MERIVALE. You're trailing the serpent of worldliness over your sister's idyll. Look at those fair reaches, Phyllis, and be ashamed. The girl who created that beauty and prosperity could not be misjudged by any man!

PHYLLIS. No, not while he was here. Not as far as he is capable of appreciating her—he bred in worldliness—in Boston upper-class snobbishness—a very young man too. Father, you don't know men —out in the world. And—

MERIVALE. No more, no more. [MERIVALE *moves to go.*]

PHYLLIS. He's been gone *five weeks* and not a word from his family. No explanation or apology from him—no explanation. *Five—weeks.* [MERIVALE *pauses.*] That can mean only one thing. His family at least, and possibly he too, now that he's back there with them—they misunderstand us, misunderstand our Di.

[MERIVALE *walks up and down, reflecting; then he turns abruptly upon* PHYLLIS.]

MERIVALE. I cannot be guilty of the impertinence of interfering.

PHYLLIS. I'm thinking of her; it's because I love her that I'm pleading with you. I like and admire him as much as you do—believe he can make Di happy. But—oh, father! A man brought up as he's been couldn't understand us. With the Easterners of his set, conventionality is god.

MERIVALE. Talk with her about it.

PHYLLIS. Of course I shall. But I want *you* to realize too—and *act.* Father, you owe it to her to guard her against her love-blindness. I'm thinking of her happiness. It's wrapped up in him.

[*A pause,* MERIVALE *reflecting.*]

MERIVALE. Perhaps our ways have tempted Julian into too great indifference to formalities.

PHYLLIS. And she so frank—so trusting—so in love—and *showing* it!

MERIVALE. Beautiful!

PHYLLIS. Yes—beautiful—but— Oh, if she only weren't in *love* with him! It's dangerous—terribly dangerous—when the woman's in love—*really* in love—with the man she wants to marry. It's so hard for her to see and do the prudent things that are necessary.

MERIVALE. How low!

PHYLLIS. But how true! Where's the man who isn't tempted to undervalue what's securely his? The safe rule for the woman is to keep the man guessing and grasping. Uncertainty!—charming uncertainty!

MERIVALE. For the shallow.

PHYLLIS. We were talking of the shallow—of human beings.

MERIVALE. We were talking of Diana.

PHYLLIS. Of Julian, rather. Julian and his family.

MERIVALE. *[Reflecting.]* His family—yes, perhaps. I'll see, I'll see. Diana's happiness— I'll see.

[Feels for his hat, looks helplessly round.]

PHYLLIS *[Laughing.]* Here it is. *[She gives him his Panama and a caress at the same time. Exit* MERIVALE, *left.* PHYLLIS *goes to table desk, sits preparing to write a note. Enter* DAGMAR, *right.]*

DAGMAR. Pleasant old parson, your friend Woodruff. Got a streak of fun in him. Well, how did you make out?

PHYLLIS. *[Carelessly.]* Oh, everything's all right.

DAGMAR. I thought so. Some day you'll learn there's nothing in this fretting like a hen on eggs. We mustn't take ourselves too seriously—we little nits on the whirling orange. When we do we're ridiculous. . . . Where *are* those cigarettes? *[Sees them on desk at left among small parcels put there by* PHYLLIS.*]* Oh, yes.

[Enter DIANA *from veranda, right. A slender, graceful girl, quick of eye and movement, with great physical charm, and irradiating open-air freedom and naturalness. She wears divided riding skirt, and is without hat.]*

DIANA. Hello, Phyl. 'Lo, Lucius.

DAGMAR. 'Lo, Di.

PHYLLIS. *[Without looking up.]* Get your telegram?

DIANA. Hours ago. I telephoned to town from the granaries and had it repeated to me. How long till lunch?

PHYLLIS. Half an hour, perhaps. [DAGMAR *groans.]*

DIANA. Heavens! I'm starved.

BILLY. *[Outside, right.]* Do you want your horse again to-day, Miss Diana?

DIANA. I'll let you know. Take him to the stable for me now, please.

BILLY. All right, Miss Diana.

[DIANA *goes to sofa, right, and flings herself carelessly upon it.*]

DIANA. My, but I'm tired. I've been in the saddle since six. Lucius, those creek bottoms are going to yield eighty bushels to the acre—eighty at least.

DAGMAR. *[Joining her.]* You don't say! Most exciting. Still, it doesn't begin to account for your spirits. There's a limit to the amount of joy over eighty bushels to the acre. You're miles beyond that limit.

DIANA. Really?

PHYLLIS. *[At desk, writing.]* You've even forgotten to ask after your beloved Dr. Woodruff—your Uncle Ben, as you call him.

DIANA. You caught me there. *[Radiantly.]* Well—Julian's coming!

[PHYLLIS *startles, shows delight.*]

DAGMAR. When?

DIANA. Was ever anybody so curious?

DAGMAR. Not many. I've no business of my own, so I give all my attention to other people's. . . . When? [DIANA *laughingly shakes her head.*] Don't tease me when I'm hungry. How you do hate to tell anything. You're most unfeminine. Close-mouthed—no affectations—truthful. Most unfeminine.

DIANA. *[Glancing at a book.]* I?

DAGMAR. No, to be honest. And you act so that one'd almost believe you really liked being a woman.

DIANA. I do.

DAGMAR. Unheard of!

DIANA. Glad and proud.

DAGMAR. What an eccentric! Full of surprises.

DIANA. Thanks. I'd hate to be—like this sort of book—large print—soon read and forgotten.

DAGMAR. You're an everlasting continued-in-our-next, with a surprise at the end of each chapter. People think they know you well, when all of a sudden—Bang!

DIANA. But I'm terribly *soft* where I care.

DAGMAR. Yes— *[After reflecting.]* and no. Well, be happy while you're young. Only— Let him do the loving—most of it. He's quite willing—quite. [PHYLLIS *pauses in writing.*]

DIANA. Equal shares—that's my idea.

DAGMAR. Generous, but not practical. Keep cool. Keep *sober.*

DIANA. And Julian?

DAGMAR. Oh, the man's a different matter.

DIANA. Not a bit of it.

PHYLLIS. It's the way of the world.

DIANA. *[Absently.]* Not my way—and not Julian's.

[PHYLLIS *makes an impatient gesture, resumes writing.*]

DAGMAR. What a lot of trouble's waiting for you when you find him out! *[Looks at her quizzically, affectionately, shakes his head.]* How are you going to stand it?

DIANA. Stand what?

DAGMAR. Being cooped up in a city—where nobody is ever truthful or natural. I can't think of you except as ranging freely—at a gallop —roads—fences—fields—like a—a—Valkyr. How'll you stand Boston?

DIANA. *[Inattentive.]* I don't know.

DAGMAR. And those iceberg relatives! He's the only person from his particular part of the Arctic regions I ever took to. I don't envy you your fashionable relatives.

[PHYLLIS *pauses in her writing, listens without turning.*]

DIANA. *[Half absently.]* I never think of them—*[Smiling.]* And I suppose they return the compliment.

DIANA. *[Dreamily.]* I never think of Julian as related to anybody —but as just—himself.

DAGMAR. *[Gently.]* Mysterious stranger—kind of Lohengrin—or fairy tale Knight-from-Nowhere.

DIANA. *[Laughing softly.]* Something like that.

DAGMAR. Um—Um—What a—what a *Di* you are!

[Flower pots falling from the balcony crash outside the veranda rail.]

DAGMAR. Jumping Jehoshaphat!

[DAGMAR *and* PHYLLIS *rise.* DIANA *rushes out to veranda rail and looks up.]*

DIANA. What is it? What's the matter?

BILLY. *[Above.]* I knocked 'em over, Miss Diana. I'm sorry.

DIANA. Oh! Father's pet heliotropes! You must get new pots at once.

BILLY. They ain't any.

DIANA. Yes, there are. I'll show you where. Come down—by the balcony stairs.

[Exit DIANA on veranda, right.]

DAGMAR. What a shock! I feel as if they'd fallen on my head.

PHYLLIS. Please leave—pretty soon. I want to be alone with Di.

DAGMAR. Take care, old girl. Go mighty easy with her. She's gentle and sweet, but—

[DIANA *reappears.]*

DIANA. *[To* BILLY, *outside.]* There you are—and please repot them right away. *[Reenters room.]* No damage.

DAGMAR. Any signs of lunch?

PHYLLIS. Why, you had a late breakfast. Don't you ever think of anything but eating?

DAGMAR. Not if I can help it. Of course, we're going to have chicken. They always do in this neck o' the woods when the preacher comes, don't they? Chicken with gravy—not sauce, but gravy.

DIANA. I'm starving, too. Do stop talking about it. Why not find out when lunch'll be ready?

DAGMAR. I don't dare go. I'd make a dash and tear it off the stove.

PHYLLIS. *[With a meaning look at* DAGMAR.*]* Lucius, please go and hurry things up. The doctor, too, must be hungry after his journey.

DAGMAR. All right, Phyl. *[Pauses at veranda, sniffing.]* Talk about your zephyrs from perfumed gardens—this one comes from the kitchen!

[Exit DAGMAR, *left.]*

DIANA. How's Uncle Ben looking?

PHYLLIS. *[Writing.]* About the same. I can't imagine what you and father see in him.

DIANA. A good heart.

PHYLLIS. The world's full of them. All well-fed people have good hearts.

DIANA. Not what I mean by a good heart. I used to admire brains more than anything. But latterly it seems to me a good heart is the finest thing in the world—and the rarest. And Uncle Ben has that. I'd trust him, next to father, as I'd trust no one else in the world.

PHYLLIS. *[Indifferently.]* And Julian?

DIANA. *[Absently.]* I wonder why it is, no matter how absolutely a woman trusts the man she loves, there's always the suggestion of a possibility of a shade of a—a—tiny misgiving.

PHYLLIS. *[Turns in chair, looks at* DIANA.*]* You distrust Julian?

DIANA. *[Smiling.]* Distrust? No, indeed! But I've too much at stake in him not to have a flutter now and then.

PHYLLIS. A woman, especially a woman who's physically attractive, does well to distrust the man who loves her. Before marriage his love's little more than passion. Real love doesn't begin to build till after the storm has calmed.

DIANA. And then maybe it'd build, and maybe it wouldn't. *[Reflectively.]* No—I'd not marry without being sure—sure my love was real —and his, too.

PHYLLIS. Then you'll never marry.

DIANA. How cheap you hold men and women!

PHYLLIS. It's a cheap world. So— Pretend to trust him—profess to trust him—but don't really trust till you've got him tied.

DIANA. Tied!

PHYLLIS. Tied. Then—if you don't like your bargain— There's nothing permanent in the marriage ceremony.

DIANA. Except the vows.

PHYLLIS. Mere form, mere convention.

DIANA. *[Dreamily.]* When I promise to "love, honor, and cherish until death do us part," I'll mean it, just as I mean any other promise I make. Yes, Julian and I'll mean it.

[PHYLLIS *gazes tenderly at her sister, then goes over and leans on the back of the sofa, toward her.]*

PHYLLIS. Di.

DIANA. Yes, dear.

PHYLLIS. Is Julian coming—soon?

DIANA. To-day—this afternoon.

PHYLLIS. I'm *so* glad! When he comes—*[A pause.]*

DIANA. Yes, Phyl?

PHYLLIS. *[Half laughing—half serious.]* You're *so* in love! What a pity! Really. I mean it. Di, he's very, *very* worth while—in every way. You must—*must*—be—a little sensible.

DIANA. *[Amused.]* In what way?

PHYLLIS. Don't be *too* frank. Don't make him so pleased with himself that he'll grow careless about pleasing you. Men are vain— easily spoiled. *[*DIANA *looks amused disdain.]* Remember, he has the weaknesses of men as well as the strength.

DIANA. Oh, he's not perfect, thank Heaven. I'd detest a man that was.

PHYLLIS. You resent interference in your affairs, and you're right. But, Di, you'll not take it wrong if I say something?

DIANA. Nothing against Julian.

PHYLLIS. It's not against him. It's— Isn't it strange his people don't write?

DIANA. I've not thought about it.

PHYLLIS. I understand that in you. But think! Five weeks, and neither of his parents, none of his people has written.

DIANA. No doubt there's some good reason. It amounts to nothing.

PHYLLIS. It means they don't approve.

DIANA. Perhaps. What of it?

PHYLLIS. His set there in the East—his people—they'd look on his engagement to an Indiana farmer's daughter as if it were to a bush-woman in the bush. If you were enormously rich—

DIANA. *[Interrupting.]* Granted they don't approve—still, what of it? That doesn't really concern Julian and me.

PHYLLIS. But it does, dear. Their not writing is the most—pointed —rudeness. His not apologizing—Isn't that—disrespectful—to you? — *[*DIANA *shrugs.]* —to father? *[*DIANA *looks serious.]*

DIANA. *[After reflecting.]* Not at all. If they're opposing, he's ashamed of them, ashamed to have father and me know about them.

PHYLLIS. *[Kissing her.]* What a loyal, generous girl you are! No wonder he loves you—and he does love you. But Di, it's as a man loves *before* marriage. *[*DIANA *makes emphatic protest.]* Listen, dear. His family's not writing and he's not apologizing—I'm afraid he's gotten away off there in his Eastern conventional home—with his mother subtly working on him—and his passion cooled by dis-tance and absence—and—

DIANA. *[Gentle but firm.]* It's useless for you to say those things to me, Phyl. Perfectly useless. We love each other, he and I.

PHYLLIS. I know. I know. But I don't want you to lose him. And when he comes, you must—

DIANA. *[Laughing.]* Lose him? Why, if he felt as you picture, I'd wish to lose him. I'd never have had his love, but only passion—only a passionate impulse.

PHYLLIS. Oh, Di! That "only"—that "passionate impulse" —it's the way we women get our husbands.

DIANA. Not I! The man I marry will not be trapped. He must want me—all of me. Not what any woman could give him—but what's really myself—what he could get from no other. The man I marry will want a woman, not merely a *female.*

PHYLLIS. Diana! Diana! You can't change human nature—*man* nature.

DIANA. *[Confidently.]* You're wrong, Phyl, you're wrong. It's not so with Julian. He loves me—*me,* I tell you . . . Why try to poison my heart? You can't. It's his—just as his is mine.

PHYLLIS. *[Heatedly.]* What I say is true of all men—true of Julian. And you couldn't blame him for being just human.

DIANA. *[Passionately.]* You can't understand *us.* We love. We trust. Love means trust.

PHYLLIS. *[Angrily.]* The love that means trust doesn't lead to mar-riage—not for women.

DIANA. Phyl! I'm ashamed of you!

PHYLLIS. *[Furious.]* Very well. But if you were to trust your Julian, he'd never make you his wife.

DIANA. *[Proudly.]* I do trust him. I *am* his wife!

PHYLLIS. *[Scornfully.]* Lover's talk! Why—*[She pauses, notes* DIANA'S *flushed, earnest face.]* You mean— *[Half pleased, half reproachful.]*—Oh, Di—you haven't gone and married him secretly? *[*DIANA *startles, betrays great confusion.]* No wonder you talked so confidently! *[Laughs.]* You impetuous, willful—

DIANA. *[Confused and with an effort.]* I—I—didn't mean—that.

PHYLLIS. *[Gazing at her with a slow change from wonder to alarm, to fear.]* Di! ... *[Breathlessly, in horror.]* You've—given yourself to him! Oh, Di!—*You!* ... It can't be! It can't. Not *you!*

DIANA. *[Haughtily.]* Keep off! My soul's my own!

PHYLLIS. My *poor* Diana! What have you done! What *have* you done! My poor—poor—

DIANA. *[Sharply.]* Phyllis!—

PHYLLIS. *[Rushing toward her.]* You infatuated girl! Come to your senses! Can't you see— *[A musical bell is heard, left. Enter* WOODRUFF, *right.]*

DIANA. *[Intensely to* PHYLLIS.*]* It's *my* secret! Don't forget that! *Mine!*

WOODRUFF. A pleasant, cheerful sound—one of the cheerfulest in the world—that bell ... Ah, *this* is Diana! *[Takes both her hands.]* Do you realize it is eight years—eight—since I saw you? *[Holds her by her hands at arms' length, looks into her face.]* Still those honest, fearless eyes ... *[*DIANA *shrinks and trembles.]* I embarrass you.

PHYLLIS. *[To cover* DIANA'S *confusion.]* Such flattery would startle one far less shy than our Di, doctor.

WOODRUFF. Every promise of eight years ago redeemed, more than redeemed.

DIANA. *[Mistress of herself again, and smiling affectionately at him.]* You overwhelm me, Uncle Ben!—you see I've not forgotten my name for you in the eight years. I am glad—*so* glad—you're here. *[The bell rings again.]* But, I must go to my room a moment. *[To* PHYLLIS.*]* Please make my excuses to father for being late. And—remember what I said, Phyl. Remember!

[Exit DIANA *by door to right. Enter by veranda right and left* DAGMAR *and* MERIVALE. *A murmur of conversation as they move toward door to left. The bell heard again.]*

CURTAIN.

ACT II

The veranda. Two window doors of the house seen at left; several large columns and rail, at back; beautiful Indiana countryside, beyond. Wicker table, chairs and sofa. Discovered— Dr. WOODRUFF, looking at landscape through telescope; PHYLLIS, at left of table in center of veranda, absorbed in thought. Enter DAGMAR from extension of veranda to left.]

WOODRUFF. This magnificent view! I can scarcely takes my eyes off it. And through the telescope—
[He makes a gesture to indicate that he has no words to express it.]
DAGMAR. The telescope's all right, but you should see it through a highball. Oh, I beg pardon, I scandalize you.
WOODRUFF. *[With rather a strained smile.]* Not at all, not at all. My black clothes are not a mourning for a lost sense of humor.
DAGMAR. *[Looking for his watch]* Phyl—you, Phyl!
PHYLLIS. *[Springing up.]* I've done my half hour.
DAGMAR. Twelve minutes.
WOODRUFF. I don't understand.
PHYLLIS. Lucius and I have agreed to walk five miles a day, and not to sit for at least half an hour after each meal. He wants to keep his waist, and I want to avoid hips.
WOODRUFF. *[Sitting on sofa, right.]* Very sensible rules.
DAGMAR. Phyl's threatening to renege. She talks of getting a masseuse down from Chicago. If she does, I think I'll have the lady make a few passes at my scalp. The way I've been moulting lately is something fierce. What's the good of a waistline if I'm to get bald? *[PHYLLIS sits.]*
PHYLLIS. The doctor will think we live on a very low, material plane.
DAGMAR. Don't we? He might as well have the truth first as last. I always explain to people just what I am, at the outset. Then—no unpleasant surprises. *[DAGMAR sits.]*
WOODRUFF. Why, you're sitting, both of you. *[Both spring up, laughing.]*
DAGMAR. My waistline!
WOODRUFF. No, my young friends, you hardly do me justice. I try to avoid narrowness of every kind. The only thing I'm intolerant of is intolerance.
DAGMAR. That's the talk! My creed exactly. That's why I got after Phyl during the little discussion at lunch—when she jumped on Diana for expressing a few romantic notions about things in general

—love and life and all that. Let the young girls have their sentimental dreams, I say. They're soon over, and no harm done.

WOODRUFF. I must admit, Diana's views struck me as sensible, practical. I think she's altogether right about lies and shams.

PHYLLIS. Now, doctor! You know very well that this world was made for men. And Di should realize it. Why, we women *have* to be liars in order to live.

WOODRUFF. As Diana would say, in order to live among *liars;* not in order to—*live!*

PHYLLIS. One likes to be well thought of by the people the world thinks well of. That's what *I* call living.

DAGMAR. Damn it, Phyl—I beg pardon, doctor—Di's got a right to other views. She's even got a right to her own sort of life. It's *her* life, ain't it?

WOODRUFF. *[Gazing with enthusiasm at the view of the farm.]* And a fine, noble sort it is.

PHYLLIS. *[With energy.]* I say candidly, it's a crime to encourage a girl in any liberal ideas whatever until she's married. You can never tell where a liberal idea will lead—even one that's apparently harmless.

DAGMAR. Truthfulness—a liberal idea?

PHYLLIS. Indeed it is. Men—some of them—can perhaps afford to be themselves in this world. But not women. No woman. *[Crosses to WOODRUFF.]* Please don't forget that, doctor, in talking with my young sister.

WOODRUFF. *[Rising.]* My dear Phyllis, I see no crime in encouraging anyone to be frank—truthful—brave. Especially a girl about to be married. If you could know the miseries—the horrors—that often —too often—come through falsehoods in love and in marriage! At luncheon I had several instances on the tip of my tongue. But I refrained.

PHYLLIS. *[Dryly.]* I'm glad you did.

WOODRUFF. The longer I live the more I abhor concealments—lies of every kind. Oh, the slavery of lies!

PHYLLIS. Things have come to a pretty pass when the clergy—

DAGMAR. Oh, come now, Phyl, smooth down your feathers. Why, you act as if you were taking all this to heart.

PHYLLIS. Ridiculous . . . You'd better see if the auto's ready. You'll be late.

DAGMAR. *[Seating himself.]* Plenty of time.

PHYLLIS. *[To WOODRUFF.]* Lucius is going for Julian.

WOODRUFF. Julian?

PHYLLIS. Mr. Burroughs.

WOODRUFF. Ah, yes. I'm anxious to make sure with my own jealous eyes that Diana has chosen well.

PHYLLIS. Do be off, Lucius.

DAGMAR. Plenty of time. Auto's waiting.

WOODRUFF. It's amazing the way these autos eat up distance and save time.

DAGMAR. Save time—that's the mischief of it. What's a man to do with all the time he saves nowadays?

PHYLLIS. Lucius, *please!*

DAGMAR. You *are* nervous to-day. Well, here goes.

[Exit DAGMAR *by veranda, left.]*

WOODRUFF. And I think I'll settle my belongings—if you'll excuse me, Mrs. Dagmar.

PHYLLIS. Phyllis.

WOODRUFF. Phyllis—Phyllis.

[Exit WOODRUFF *into house.]*

DIANA. *[In house.]* Oh, Uncle Ben. Going to your room?

WOODRUFF. Yes, for a little while.

[Enter DIANA. *She is dressed as in Act I and is carrying a new hat band of blue and white silk for* MERIVALE'S *Panama.]*

DIANA. Where's father?

PHYLLIS. Still at his nap.

PHYLLIS. *[Appealingly.]* Di! *[*DIANA *hesitates, without turning.]*

PHYLLIS. Don't be cross with me. You're so secretive and Spartan that I sometimes forget how sensitive you are—how things affect you underneath. *[Puts her arms round her.]* You know I love you, Di?— that I'm not thinking harshly of you?

DIANA. Yes, I know. *[Kisses her shyly.]* . . . I suppose it's impossible for you to realize how it is with Julian and me. Believe me, Phyl— he *loves* me.

PHYLLIS. But if he doesn't? *[*DIANA *laughs at her gently.]*

DIANA. *[Carelessly.]* Why, then—of course—

[Shrugs.]

PHYLLIS. You wouldn't *release* him!

DIANA. *Release* him! Certainly I'd release him, as you call it, if he didn't love me. But he does.

PHYLLIS. He must marry you. He's no right to take your all and cast you off.

DIANA. My all! If that's a woman's all—if that's her sole claim—her chief claim—then we women *are* low—level with the beasts.

PHYLLIS. Women have to marry. *You* must marry *him*.

DIANA. If I were simply a woman-looking-for-a-husband, I suppose I might. But I'm not. I want love—to give love, to get it. I want him because I love him and because he loves me. I want his love—not anything else—not anything less. And I'd not kill it and my own self-respect by compelling him—in the least. He shall feel free—always free!

PHYLLIS. Oh, Diana! How can you hope to get on with the world!

DIANA. The world must get on with me.

PHYLLIS. Those ideas are fine, Di. We all profess them. But we don't—can't—*act* on them. You must remember this is a human world. *[DIANA makes a disdainful gesture.]* Suppose he should take you—your love for granted. Suppose he has no real intention of *marrying* you.

DIANA. *[Laughing frankly.]* Why, Phyl!

PHYLLIS. When a man's about to do a contemptible thing, he always covers up his purpose from himself—

DIANA. But it wouldn't be contemptible, if he no longer loved me.

PHYLLIS. *[Impatiently.]* Why discuss the ought-to-be! We're facing the thing-that-is!

DIANA. Nonsense! You're talking as if Julian didn't love me. It's disloyal of me to let you do it. I love and I trust him—and I *know* he loves me.

[Enter MERIVALE from house.]

DIANA. *[Holding up the hat band.]* Now, sir! I have it all ready to put on.

[PHYLLIS walks up to the veranda rail, stands there deep in thought.]

MERIVALE. *[Laughing and taking off his hat.]* I thought you were dressing.

DIANA. You first. *[Looks at the old band.]* How I've been neglecting you! *[Seats herself, MERIVALE standing erect and looking lovingly down at her.]* But we'll soon have you perfect. *[Glances up at him.]* Isn't he splendid, Phyl?

PHYLLIS. *[Absently.]* What is it?

MERIVALE. How happy you've made me. And before you came, your mother and I both hoped it would be a son!

[DIANA with the hat in her lap fits on the new band.]

DIANA. *[Rising.]* See! *[Holds out the hat in one hand, the old band in the other.]*

MERIVALE. *[Laughing.]* Now, I realize that you certainly have neglected me. *[She puts the hat on his head as he stoops to receive it.]* But I forgive you. *[With mock severity.]* Don't let it occur again.

DIANA. Dear! *[Kisses him.]* I must rush away. There are several things to be looked after, and I've got to dress. *[To* PHYLLIS.*]* Don't look so sad, Phyl!

[Exit, radiant, left. MERIVALE *gazes after her, touching and arranging his hat.]*

PHYLLIS. Father, you must have your talk with Julian before he sees Diana.

MERIVALE. *[Frowning, impatient, yet tolerant.]* I shall not meddle.

PHYLLIS. Meddle!

MERIVALE. In this household we respect one another's rights. If I should speak to Julian, Diana would be angry—justly angry. She loves him. He loves her. Let them alone. Meddlers are always muddlers.

PHYLLIS. You don't realize! He must be made to see he can't treat her as he'd not permit any man to treat one of his sisters. Father, don't tempt him to think we are not entitled to the respect his own people would demand. Don't tempt him to trifle.

MERIVALE. Julian's opinion of us is no more important than our opinion of him. Diana is what she is—*honest.* A woman out of ten thousand.

PHYLLIS. Indeed she is! That's why you—

MERIVALE. If he fails to appreciate his good fortune, the worse for him. Diana'd be well rid of him. Yes—I'll talk with him. I'll see just what there is in these suspicions of yours.

PHYLLIS. *[Agitated.]* Father! You mustn't take high ground with him. You must not! Don't let your false pride inflame his false pride. Remember, Diana's happiness or misery is at stake.

MERIVALE. Misery? Absurd!

PHYLLIS. I say, misery. You don't know how—*[hesitates—hurries on desperately]*—how utterly she has trusted him.

*[*PHYLLIS *stands breathless, fearing he has understood.]*

MERIVALE. True. Diana never is half-hearted. With her it's always all or nothing.

*[*PHYLLIS *draws a long breath of relief.]*

PHYLLIS. And you know how steadfast she is. If she lost him it'd break her heart.

MERIVALE. But if she got him, and he were unworthy, that too would break her heart—and blast her life, to boot. Hearts mend; but lives—not so easily.

PHYLLIS. He isn't unworthy—only careless, at most, I feel sure. *[Hurries to veranda rail, glances to left.]*

MERIVALE. *[Thoughtfully.]* Yes—yes. I'll speak to him.

PHYLLIS. I think I hear them . . . Yes . . . *[Going to* MERIVALE *and touching him affectionately.]* For *her* sake!

[Exit PHYLLIS *by window door, left.]*

DAGMAR. *[On veranda, outside.]* You know the way. They're on the south veranda.

[Enter JULIAN BURROUGHS *by veranda, left. He is dressed in a fashionable traveling suit. He is obviously from an Eastern city, a well-bred youth, ardent and attractive. He stands an instant—hesitates.]*

MERIVALE. *[With cordiality, yet with reserve.]* Ah—welcome!

[He advances with extended hand. BURROUGHS, *confused, hesitating, shakes hands.]*

BURROUGHS. Thank you, sir—thank you. I'm glad to see you so well.

MERIVALE. And you?

BURROUGHS. As always. *[With an effort.]* And glad to be here again.

MERIVALE. Diana will be in presently.

BURROUGHS. Ah—thank you—thanks.

MERIVALE. *[After a pause.]* And your father and mother?

BURROUGHS. *[Embarrassed.]* Father's abroad just now. Mother is—not very well—not ill, but—not very well.

MERIVALE. *[After an awkward pause, and speaking with nervous shyness.]* I've been rather expecting a—a—letter from her. *[With an attempt at a smile of raillery.]* You've told her of your—Western adventure?

BURROUGHS. *[Confused.]* The fact is—well—I—she— *[Pauses.]*

MERIVALE. *[With some sharpness.]* You have *not* told her?

BURROUGHS. Yes, sir, I have.

MERIVALE. Well, sir?

BURROUGHS. She's waiting until father returns.

MERIVALE. *[Stiffly, with a touch of haughtiness.]* I've no wish to interfere in what is Diana's business, but— Am I to understand that your mother is opposed to your marriage?

BURROUGHS. *[Embarrassed, but with engaging candor.]* The fact is, sir, my mother has had other ideas for me. You will appreciate how she might be reluctant to abandon them. She's not yet reconciled—hopes I'll change my mind. But—soon—I hope—I expect— *[Pauses, painfully embarrassed.]*

MERIVALE. *[Kindly, trying to put him at his ease.]* I understand. I knew there was some perfectly simple explanation.

BURROUGHS. You see, sir, mother is a woman of strong prejudices. One of them is Western people—just as one of yours is we of the East.

MERIVALE. *[Laughing.]* Yes. Yes. Exactly . . . She has only to see Diana. *[*BURROUGHS *turns away nervously.* MERIVALE *lays his hand reassuringly on his shoulder.]* I'm sure of it. Don't let that trouble you.

BURROUGHS. Of course, if my father should oppose, it might delay . . . It might make a very considerable difference in my income. But —in a few years—

MERIVALE. *[Eagerly relieved.]* No more, Julian. My interest is Diana's happiness—and yours—and that depends on you and herself, not on parents or fortune. *[*BURROUGHS, *unnoted by* MERIVALE, *hangs his head.]* Your father and mother have only to meet her. They'll welcome her. I appreciate their point of view. *[Shakes hands with* BURROUGHS.*]* I trust I'm broad enough for that. If I'd never seen the man my Diana was marrying, I'd feel precisely as they do. All is well—thank God! Where is Dagmar—Phyllis?

*[*MERIVALE *pauses as he sees* PHYLLIS *and* DR. WOODRUFF *entering by door to right.* PHYLLIS's *eyes seek her father's face, but she is not fully reassured by his air of a man with a weight happily off his mind. She and* BURROUGHS *shake hands, he embarrassed, she frank and cordial.]*

MERIVALE. Ben, this is the young man. *[*WOODRUFF *advances to* BURROUGHS, *takes him by the hand, scrutinizes his face.]*

WOODRUFF. I'm delighted to meet you, sir—delighted to meet you.

MERIVALE. *[In answer to an inquiring look from* BURROUGHS.*]* Dr. Woodruff.

BURROUGHS. I've often heard your name here.

WOODRUFF. Hubert and I celebrate next week the fiftieth anniversary of our friendship. A long time to keep on good terms with a quarrelsome old chap like him, eh?

MERIVALE. Come, now, Ben. Julian, I'll leave you here with Phyllis. *[Takes* WOODRUFF *by the arm and points with his cane out to the right.]* We'll go down the terrace to the granaries yonder. I'll show you a harvest sight that'll do your heart good. *[They go to the right along the veranda.]*

WOODRUFF. Diana's magic?

MERIVALE. Diana's magic—at work.
[Exeunt. Enter DAGMAR *by window door, left.]*

DAGMAR. A tall cold one, Burroughs?
BURROUGHS. No, thanks, Not just now.
DAGMAR. You're twenty minutes earlier than you were expected. That train was never on time before. Come on.
BURROUGHS. No, thanks. Later perhaps.
DAGMAR. They're ready and waiting.
PHYLLIS. Oh, you go and drink both, Lucius.
DAGMAR. I'll fill a drunkard's grave if I stay on here in the country. Always drinking alone, and always taking two, so as not to seem mean and unsociable. *[Exit* DAGMAR, *left, into the house.]*

PHYLLIS. That train deceived Diana. I'm afraid it'll be some time before she comes.
BURROUGHS. *[Embarrassed.]* I'm sorry.... I hope she'll not be long.... I've got to take the six o'clock express for the East.
PHYLLIS. *[Startling, then recovering her composure and speaking in a tone of polite regret.]* Six o'clock! ... A great journey for such a little stop.
BURROUGHS. You see, I'm arranging to go abroad.
PHYLLIS. When do you sail?
BURROUGHS. Next week—Wednesday.
PHYLLIS. So soon!
BURROUGHS. And I fear I'll be on the other side—longer than I had thought—perhaps until spring—possibly a year—though I hope not.
PHYLLIS. *[Constrainedly, almost absently.]* That'll be lonely.
BURROUGHS. *[With some awkwardness.]* Oh, I dare say Diana will pull through all right. She has her work.
PHYLLIS. I wasn't thinking of Diana. I was thinking of you—away off there in strange lands alone.
BURROUGHS. There's always a lot of people one knows in London and Paris. I've several relatives married there. Then ... mother's going with me. The doctor prescribed a winter on the Riviera for her.
PHYLLIS. Oh! ... Yes, of course.... That *will* be gay! Nice! Monte Carlo!
BURROUGHS. *[Confused and apologetic.]* I shan't be enjoying myself all the time. I'm going on business, too.
PHYLLIS. The business of amusing your mother?
BURROUGHS. That's the pleasure. We've always been chums. She looks like a sister rather than my mother, and she's great fun, when

she's with those she likes and doesn't feel distant with—or—that is —*[He becomes greatly embarrassed and* PHYLLIS *does not help him, but aggravates his discomfort by placidly eyeing him.]* . . . You and mother would like each other, I'm sure.

PHYLLIS. Yes? It's rather dangerous to predict what two women will think of each other.

BURROUGHS. *[Depressed.]* That's true, isn't it? I do hope she'll like Diana.

PHYLLIS. *[Dryly.]* It's important, too—I should say—whether Di will like her.

BURROUGHS. *[Confused.]* Of course—certainly. *[A constrained silence, then he, with a nervous attempt to make light conversation.]* I hope you'll do what you can to prevent Diana from forgetting me while I'm away.

PHYLLIS. I'll do my best. But you know Di—how busy she is. When one is busy, there's little time for anything except what absolutely forces itself on one's attention. She and father'll be going South this winter.

BURROUGHS. She works entirely too hard. A rest will be just the thing for her.

PHYLLIS. A change, rather than a rest. They'll go to Palm Beach. It's lively there, and she's been leading too secluded a life. Lucius and I are taking a house in Washington, and we'll have her visit us for February and March. She'll enjoy it, once she gets in the swing. I don't know any place so fascinating as Washington in the season. And what a hit Di will make!

BURROUGHS. *[Jealously.]* I hope so.

PHYLLIS. *[Sweetly.]* Lucius's aunt, Mrs. Throckmorton, has a big house there, and she'll give her the right sort of background.

BURROUGHS. *[Somewhat sourly.]* That'll be nice. . . . *[With an awkward laugh.]* I see there's small danger of my being missed.

PHYLLIS. You can't expect a girl like Di to play Mariana of the Moated Grange, and mix her fancies with the sallow rifted glooms, and moan, "He cometh not! He cometh not!"

BURROUGHS. *[Gruffly.]* Hardly. . . . *[Paces up and down restlessly.]* . . . Where is she?

PHYLLIS. *[With some embarrassment.]* She—she went to the Creek farm.

BURROUGHS. I think I'll go to meet her.

PHYLLIS. You can't miss her. There's only the one road.

BURROUGHS. I'll walk that way.

PHYLLIS. Yes. Your time here is so short. You'll meet her, no doubt, before you've gone far.

[Exit BURROUGHS *by veranda, left,* PHYLLIS *nodding and smiling friendlily at him. The instant he disappears, her face, her manner change to deep agitation.]*

PHYLLIS. Going for a year! A year!

[Enter DIANA *by door to left. She is dressed beautifully in a walking costume, with a very short skirt which makes her look extremely girlish, and is most becoming to her figure, which is graceful, alluring, free in line and in movement.]*

DIANA. Where's Julian?

PHYLLIS. *[Startled.]* Ah! . . .

DIANA. Lucius said he was here with you. Why didn't you tell me he'd come?

PHYLLIS. I sent him away because I must speak with you first. Di —he's—

DIANA. Interfering in my affairs! Phyllis—

PHYLLIS. Di, he's come to break his engagement!

DIANA. Oh, Phyl! *[Laughs.]*

PHYLLIS. I tell you he has. Of course, he's too thoroughly the man of honor to admit it to himself. But it's the truth. He and his mother are going abroad next week, to be gone a year—

DIANA. *[Sharply.]* A year!

PHYLLIS. Yes—a year. She's made him promise to sée whether a year's separation won't change him.

DIANA. *[Dazedly.]* A year. Promised his mother—

PHYLLIS. And of course it will—with her artfully poisoning him against you—you four thousand miles away.

DIANA. *[Dazedly.]* A year. *[Sharply to* PHYLLIS.*]* How do you know?

PHYLLIS. He told me himself. Here. Just now. *[*DIANA *turns away. A pause.]*

DIANA. *[Hoarsely.]* A year. . . . A promise. . . . When I telegraphed for him—*[She pauses, reflecting, oblivious of her sister.]*

PHYLLIS. *[Staring in amazement.]* You telegraphed for *him* . . . Then he didn't come of his own . . . Di! . . . You sent for him! . . . Disgrace! Disgrace! Disgrace! . . . *[Brokenly.]* Oh—Diana! Diana! . . . *[In a low, horrified voice.]* If he should refuse to marry you!

DIANA. *[Half absently.]* Don't say those things, Phyl! . . . *[Absorbed again.]* What shall I do?

PHYLLIS. But *if!—if!* Oh, my God!

DIANA. *[Calmly.]* There is no if.

PHYLLIS *[Distracted.]* He's surely a man of honor. He simply can't squirm out of it. When you tell him, he'll *have* to marry you.

DIANA. *[Strongly.]* I'll not tell him. He shall feel free. I'll not seem to be compelling him.

PHYLLIS. Mad! Mad! . . . But this is only talk. It can't be that you don't realize your position. When you see him—

DIANA. When I see him, I'll see a love like my own.

PHYLLIS. Love! Love! Let's hear no more about love till you've got a husband.

DIANA. And I'd hear nothing about a husband till I was *sure—sure* —about love.

PHYLLIS. *[Wildly.]* I tell you, Diana, Julian Burroughs has no intention of marrying you.

DIANA. You insult him!—you insult me!

PHYLLIS. Sh—father!

[Enter MERIVALE *on veranda, left.]*

MERIVALE. Is Julian there? I don't see him.

PHYLLIS. He'll be here in a moment, father.

MERIVALE. The sun got too hot for me. When Ben comes, tell him I'm in my study.

PHYLLIS. Very well, father.

MERIVALE. My eyes aren't what they once were. But I think I see how happy you are. Ah—youth—youth and love. It makes me feel old. But—happy—yes indeed, happy. I'm not altogether selfish—not altogether.

[Exit MERIVALE *into the house, left.]*

PHYLLIS. *[Softly, solemnly.]* Suppose you should be wrong about Julian—what of father? . . . He'd not reproach you . . . He'd cover his wound, smile—die. *[*DIANA *wavers, recovers herself.]*

DIANA. *[Strongly.]* He'd understand. It was he who taught me that self-respect is honor, lies shame. . . . Why, what are we talking about? You shan't tempt me into the disloyalty of doubt. I know Julian loves me as I love him. I know it!

BURROUGHS. *[Outside, on veranda.]* I went as far as Cresson Hill.

*[*DIANA *lifts her head exultantly, clasps her hands.* PHYLLIS *hastily exits, into house.]*

BURROUGHS *[Outside.]* Oh—

[Enter BURROUGHS. *He stands uncertainly an instant, distinctly shows embarrassment. As he gazes at her lithe figure and face aglow, his passion surges.]*

BURROUGHS. Diana! *[He extends his arms, rushes toward her, then with his hands upon her arms at the shoulders, pauses, and his eyes devour her face.]* Diana! *[Kisses her passionately. Her arms encircle his neck, and they cling together in a long embrace.]*

DIANA. My *dear* love! *[*BURROUGHS *holds her at arm's length, gazes into her face.]*

BURROUGHS. Your touch—*[kisses her passionately]*—it's like life in the glorious dawn of the world. *[Strains her in his arms.]* As soon as I got the first glimpse of this place, it all began to come back to me. And when I saw you— *[Gazes at her fervently.]* You!—it was as if love were racing through me with a torch, setting me on fire in every vein. *[Embraces her tightly.]* Cheek to cheek—breast to breast!

DIANA. Heart to heart! Oh, it has been so long—so long! But I've not been unhappy. I could always feel your love—strong—true!

BURROUGHS. *[Clasping her again.]* I do love you! *[Half to himself.]* I do! I could not—could not give you up.

*[*DIANA *slowly half releases herself, looks up at him laughingly.]*

DIANA. Give me up. Give up your wife! How absurd it sounds! As if *we* could be separated! *[Kisses him. Gazes at him again, notes his confused, nervous expression.]*—Ah!

BURROUGHS. *[Stammeringly.]* What is it, Di? *[Tries to draw her close to him again, but she gently resists.]* . . . Don't look at me like that . . . I didn't mean . . . that is—

DIANA. *[Drawing back slowly, wonderingly.]* Why do your eyes no longer meet mine? . . . Tell me, Julian! . . . Oh, Julian be frank—be frank!

BURROUGHS. It's nothing.

DIANA. Your mother—is it your mother?

BURROUGHS. I ought to have warned you. But, I didn't realize it myself—how she'd feel about—about my marrying.

DIANA. How do *you* feel about it?

BURROUGHS. Now that I see you again—feel your magic fingers—how my blood thrills!

DIANA. *[Sadly.]* Is that *all?*

BURROUGHS. All?

DIANA. What did you think when I was *not* with you?

BURROUGHS. *[Evasively.]* I don't understand.

DIANA. *[Sadly.]* Ah, yes—Julian. You understand.

BURROUGHS. My mother shall not come between us!

DIANA. She told you it was mere physical attraction? Was she right? If she was, be brave enough to say so, Julian. When you were clear of the spell over your sense, did you find you didn't care?—not as you believed?

BURROUGHS. Diana, I swear—

DIANA. You've a right to change your mind. You've not the right to hide it from me.

BURROUGHS Why should you think I changed?

DIANA. In all your letters, you said not one word about your mother's opposition.

BURROUGHS. I admit, that was not frank. But I didn't know what to do. Be just, Di. I love my mother. *[He takes her hand.]* We've always been the best friends in the world, as I've told you. You know you'd be the first to denounce me as a heartless cad if I showed no respect for her feelings. *[*DIANA *nods slowly.]* Put yourself in my place. I was in a frightful position—between my duty to her and my duty to you.

*[*DIANA *draws her hand away.]*

BURROUGHS. You'll understand, when you see her, why I speak as I do. There's a certain pride—a—a majesty— We've all been brought up to stand in awe of her—

DIANA. *[Coldly.]* The picture is not attractive.

BURROUGHS. *[Desperately.]* At any rate, she has promised that, as soon as we return, she'll withdraw her opposition, if— *[Checks himself.]*

DIANA. Go on!

BURROUGHS. That's all. What's the matter, Diana? You're not yourself.

DIANA. You were about to say she'd withdraw her opposition if you still wish to marry me.

BURROUGHS. *[Eagerly.]* I shall not change!

DIANA. And I?

*[*BURROUGHS *lowers his eyes.]*

DIANA. And I?

BURROUGHS. You *will* not understand me. You twist everything I say.

DIANA. You don't ask *me* to swear I'll not change. *[Laughs satirically.]* You feel I'm yours—to take or to cast aside, as you choose— as you shall choose, a year from now.

BURROUGHS. Diana, don't put it that way!

DIANA. It does look ugly—doesn't it—the naked truth?

BURROUGHS. *[Pleadingly.]* I didn't mean that.

DIANA. You mean, you didn't realize how your thoughts would sound until you spoke them. *[Laughs again; then with sudden anger.]* How dare you! How dare you think of me as a poor creature, at your mercy!

BURROUGHS. It isn't true. I never thought *that—never!*

DIANA. *[Facing him, suddenly.]* Then what did you think? *[His eyes sink before hers. A long pause.]*

BURROUGHS. I admit in a way and for a moment I may have faltered —*[He pauses.]*

DIANA. *[Mournfully.]* In love—such love as ours professed to be— to falter is to fail. *[She turns from him.]*

BURROUGHS. You wrong me, Diana. I admit I've been moved by my mother—more than I should. You can't understand—you who've always lived in this atmosphere of freedom—I was at home—and the home influence was strong about me. *[DIANA listens sympathetically.]* I did let my mother say more than I should. I did consent to wait. But, Di, I never wavered in my obligation to you.

DIANA. Obligation! *[Laughs wildly.]* Obligation! That word on the lips of a lover! . . . Obligation—duty—must . . . *[Her voice breaks.]* Oh, Julian, we've traveled far from love, you and I—haven't we?

BURROUGHS. *[Passionately seizing her.]* No! No! My words were unfortunate. And I've done things I ought not. But *now*—*now*—with you before my eyes—with my arms about you—I love you—love you as I always have. *[Tries to kiss her.]*

DIANA. *[Withholding her lips.]* You love me? *[Wistfully.]* You mean that?

BURROUGHS. I mean that. I—love—you. *[Embraces her sensuously.]* I love you. Diana! Diana! *[A long kiss; a close embrace.]*

DIANA. *[Releasing herself a little.]* Now, I can tell you. *[Kisses him, laughs softly.]* I didn't really doubt you—I couldn't. Only— When one loves, every little thing makes one tremble.

BURROUGHS. Dearest! . . . I *can't* go away so soon! I shan't go to-day.

DIANA. How would you like to take me with you?

BURROUGHS. *[Tenderly.]* Diana! *[Kisses her.]*

DIANA. *[Softly, shyly.]* Do you know why I telegraphed? I sent for you to marry me at once.

BURROUGHS. *[Releasing her, smiling uneasily.]* Marry? At once? *[Takes his arms away.]* I don't see how I can. *[Turns from her a little.]* My people—*[With a quick, nervous laugh]*—and yours, too, of course —they'd think it strange—wouldn't they? *[Looks at her, is fascinated by her expression.]* Di! . . . *[Low, intense.]* You telegraphed because — *[Falls back a step.]* This is—terrible! *[Faces her.]* Terrible! . . . *[Sees her expression of utter, dazed despair, pityingly.]* Poor girl! *[Advances toward her.]* Poor Di! *[Tries to take her in his arms.]*

DIANA. Don't—touch—me. *[BURROUGHS starts back, hangs his head. A pause.]*

BURROUGHS. *[Shamefacedly.]* Forget what I said. I—I didn't mean it.

DIANA. Quite unneccessary.

BURROUGHS. What do you mean, Diana?

DIANA. The hyprocrisy. Unnecessary. Most offensive.

BURROUGHS. *[With dignity.]* Surely you can't doubt my honor—that I'm willing to make reparation?

DIANA. Reparation! Reparation! . . . But I deserve it. Reparation! . . . *[To herself.]* I can't believe it! It's a dream!

BURROUGHS. What can I say to—

DIANA. Say? Nothing! . . . Look at me! . . . Do you love—*love* me?

BURROUGHS. I do—but—

DIANA. *[Wildly.]* Passion! Only a passionate impulse . . . It's a horrible dream—only a dream!

BURROUGHS. By all we've been to each other, I swear—

DIANA. "By all we've been to each other." And what was that? What was in your heart? Leave me! Go! I can't bear it . . . I can't realize it—I can't! I believed utterly—not a doubt! . . . Go! Go!

BURROUGHS. I'll not go. I must marry you. I'll see your father, say—

DIANA. *I? I—marry* a man whose heart is shrinking from me? *I?*

BURROUGHS. We must!

DIANA. *[Beside herself.]* Must! With love and trust dead—*[despairingly]*—dead! . . . *[Passionately.]* No!

BURROUGHS. *[Angrily.]* Yes—must . . . You—*forget!*

[A pause. DIANA stares at him, looks round wildly, sinks into a chair, gazes straight before her.]

DIANA. *[Breathlessly.]* Must! Must!

[BURROUGHS watches her uneasily, then exits by window door, left, into house.]

DIANA. I—must!

CURTAIN.

ACT III

Same as Act I.—The Library. At the table near the center MAGGIE *is arranging white flowers in vases;* BILLY *is carrying a large palm through the room.*

MAGGIE. *[Surveying the vase she has just filled.]* I'm afraid that looks stiff.

BILLY. *[Setting down the palm.]* What's the difference? There ain't going to be no outsiders in. Who'll notice?

MAGGIE. It ain't who'll notice; it's the inward satisfaction!

BILLY *[Contemptuously.]* In'ard satisfaction!

MAGGIE. That sniff explains why you'll always stay just a man-of-all-work.

BILLY. Be that as it may, I could 'a' had *you* for the asking.

MAGGIE. Not since the law allowed of my marrying. You'll have to court close to the cradle if you ever get a wife. A grown woman wants a somebody with something.

BILLY. Meaning a Peter? *[Laughs.]* Peter's a wonder, he is! . . . Dobbin—steady old Dobbin.

MAGGIE. Miss Diana has promised that from now on he's to share in the profits.

BILLY. *[Whistling.]* So that's it! I seen your airs before I seen you. Well, Peter's gettin' his pay for his bootlickin'.

MAGGIE. For his work, and you know it.

BILLY. *[After glancing round cautiously.]* Ain't it queer about this here wedding? I don't understand it, nohow.

MAGGIE. Of course you don't. As soon as anything happens out of the ordinary, you're all suspicion. Mr. Burroughs has to go to Europe on business. He wants to take her with him.

BILLY. But *is* she going—that's what I want to know. Is *she* going? Why hasn't she had the trunks up, to pack 'em?

MAGGIE. *[Lamely.]* It—it—ain't decided—yet.

BILLY. You don't know nothing about it!

MAGGIE. I mind my own business—and plenty to do it gives me.

BILLY. She looks strange. She acts strange.

MAGGIE. You think the whole world's rotten.

BILLY. *[Injured.]* Who said rotten? *[Excitedly.]* Do you think it's as bad as that?

MAGGIE. Now, did anybody *ever*! Trying to make me out as low as you are.

BILLY. Well, humans is humans, the high as human as the low—that's *my* experience. The high's got high names for it, and the low low, but there it is, just the same. All flesh is dust—and what's dust but dirt?

MAGGIE. Shame on you! Why are you hanging round here? Why ain't you attending to Mr. Julian?

BILLY. I did. I had to speak twice before he answered, and then he cut me off like a snapping turtle.

MAGGIE. I'd think you'd 'a' got used to being treated that way, and wouldn't notice it.

BILLY. *[Tauntingly.]* No, thank you! Peter's quite welcome—quite!
[Enter WOODRUFF *from the right.* BILLY *takes up the palm and exit by double doors, to the left, with a wag of the head and a wink at* MAGGIE *that infuriates her.]*

MAGGIE. *[Noting his depressed air.]* We shall miss her dreadful, doctor. If I gave way, I'd not be able to do anything for crying.

WOODRUFF. My friend Merivale is dazed—dazed. He's at his desk, staring at his books, seeing nothing, hearing nothing.

MAGGIE. What'll he be like when she's really gone, when he—we all—really miss her? It ain't the death or the separation so much—not right at the moment. It's the emptiness afterwards.

WOODRUFF. The emptiness afterwards. My wife—you remember her, Maggie?

MAGGIE. Yes, sir—yes, indeed.

WOODRUFF. It was more than a month after—after God took her, when the real heartache began. And it's never left me . . . and never shall . . . until I see her again. *[Enter* PHYLLIS *from left. She is in fashionable afternoon dress. Her air is excited and gay.]*

PHYLLIS. Why, doctor! One'd think you were about to conduct a funeral. And you, too, Maggie. This won't do! Doctor, go cheer up father. Maggie, bring me more flowers—help Billy with them.
[Exit MAGGIE *by veranda, left.* PHYLLIS *inspects the vases on the table.]*

WOODRUFF. It's true, we're not losing Diana but gaining Julian.

PHYLLIS. That's the way to look at it! *[As* WOODRUFF *turns to leave.]* First, go into the parlor and see what you think of things—And the hall and dining room, too.

WOODRUFF. Delighted!
[Exit WOODRUFF *by double doors.* PHYLLIS, *humming, busies herself rearranging flowers in the vases. Enter* DAGMAR *from right, smoking cigarette and moving leisurely, as usual.]*

PHYLLIS. Oh, I thought it was Billy. But he couldn't be back yet. I sent him for more flowers. These ridiculous country bouquets of Maggie's! But she did her best.

DAGMAR. Why the rush? You'll give yourself prickly heat. Take it easy. You've more than an hour before the wedding, and only the one room left to fix up. *[Stands at parlor door.]* Why, it's practically ready. Very smart. Very smart.

PHYLLIS. I thought you were looking after Julian.

DAGMAR. He endured me half an hour, then said flatly that he preferred to be alone. Of course marriage is a joke—a joke on the man. But Julian ought to buck up—be a sport—have a sense of humor.

PHYLLIS. *[Pausing abruptly, and gazing at* DAGMAR.*]* Where is he?

DAGMAR. Calm yourself. He hasn't fled.

PHYLLIS. *[Resuming her work.]* Don't be an idiot.

DAGMAR. He's terribly restless. He'll wear himself out before the party begins. I understand, though. I was in a frightful stew on our wedding day, myself.

PHYLLIS. Really!

DAGMAR. But then, I had more excuse than he has. Our day was fixed months beforehand. That's bad business. His way's the best. All the difference between dating a dentist months ahead and just popping in off the street to have it out. Yes, Burroughs is wise. . . . I don't wonder he's nervous. If we men weren't such cowards, the first strains of the wedding march'd be the signal for the flight of many a bridegroom.

PHYLLIS. I see no fun in cheap comic-paper humor about marriage.

DAGMAR. Humor? I was philosophizing. Julian's face set me thinking. It's a true wedding face. You know, nobody but the bride's father and mother ever looks cheerful at a wedding. *[Seriously.]* But— Julian's face is unusually—*[Hesitates.]*

PHYLLIS. Unusually what?

DAGMAR. Joking aside, Phyl, there's *sure* something queer about this wedding—now, isn't there? *[*PHYLLIS *ignores him.]* If the man I drove over from the station—the man with no change suit—if he was on his way to marry—I'll eat my hand. Ain't I right?

PHYLLIS. *[With cheerful sarcasm.]* We've lived together two years, and you haven't yet learned that I—never—answer—questions.

DAGMAR. Oh, yes, I have, but I like to ask questions. Besides, I'm hopeful. . . . Of course, I know he's in love with her—*[Walks up and down smoking.* PHYLLIS *hums gayly.]* You *are* in a good humor!

PHYLLIS. Rather. *Rather.* A great weight off my mind—getting Di married safely—

DAGMAR. And so well.

PHYLLIS. And so well. A young sister—impulsive—with noble, silly notions about the equality of men and women—with a belief everyone's as honest and high-minded as herself—What a dangerous character to be at large!

DAGMAR. Appalling!

[Enter MAGGIE *with apron full of flowers.]*

PHYLLIS. *[To* MAGGIE.*]* I find I've enough after all, Maggie. Take them into the parlor and put them with those already banked on the mantel.

MAGGIE. Yes, Miss Phyllis.

[Exit MAGGIE.*]*

PHYLLIS. *[To* DAGMAR.*]* Carry in these vases. I've got to go up and look Diana over and smooth myself out a bit. You know you and father aren't to change, as Julian has only his traveling suit. And see that Maggie doesn't ruin the mantel. She's so heavy handed—so countrified. . . . No, I'd better go myself.

[As she is about to exit with a vase, enter WOODRUFF, *almost bumping into her. He is beaming and rubbing his hands.]*

WOODRUFF. Pardon—I beg your pardon! . . . The parlor and hall are exquisite. And the dining room, too.

PHYLLIS. Aren't they! And we'd really no time at all.

[Exit PHYLLIS *with vase.]*

DAGMAR. You'll excuse us, doctor?

WOODRUFF. Don't mind me. I'm one of the family.

[Exit DAGMAR *with vase, whistling the wedding march as he goes. Enter* MAGGIE *presently, to take up the remaining vase from the table.]*

WOODRUFF. These delicious flowers! The Lord is indeed good to give them to us.

MAGGIE. *[Indignantly.]* Oh, my, these didn't grow wild, sir. Miss Diana, she developed them. No, indeed—they're anything but wild.

*[*WOODRUFF *looks disconcerted, starts to explain, shrugs and smiles. In lifting the vase* MAGGIE *drops several flowers, sets it down to pick them up. Enter* BURROUGHS *from veranda, right. He is somber, restless.]*

BURROUGHS. I'm looking for Mrs. Dagmar. I thought I'd find her here.

MAGGIE. She *was* in the parlor. But I reckon she's gone up by now. Shall I send her?

BURROUGHS. No—no, thanks. It was nothing.

MAGGIE. You haven't given us much time, Mr. Julian.

WOODRUFF. But time enough, after all. When everything's ready for the voyage, why fuss and dawdle over the mere embarking?

BURROUGHS. Why, indeed.

[Enter BILLY *by door to left, front.]*

WOODRUFF. It's a pity your parents couldn't be here.

BURROUGHS. *[Curtly.]* It was impossible. *[Somewhat less abruptly.]* Father's in Europe, and mother not well enough to travel.

[MAGGIE glances at BILLY with a nod and smile of triumph. BURROUGHS is moving restlessly about.]

WOODRUFF. I'm sorry to hear that. Nothing serious, I trust?

BURROUGHS. No—oh, no.

WOODRUFF. I'm sure the sight of your bride will cure her.

BURROUGHS. *[Awkwardly.]* Thank you.

BILLY. *[To WOODRUFF.]* Mr. Merivale'd like to see you, if you can come.

WOODRUFF. Certainly. You'll excuse me?

BURROUGHS. I'll wait for Mrs. Dagmar.

[Exit WOODRUFF by door to left, front, BILLY following. BURROUGHS strolls uneasily about the room.]

MAGGIE. I'll go tell her.

BURROUGHS. No—not the least hurry. Don't let me interrupt your work.

MAGGIE. I've just finished. How do you like the looks of the room?

BURROUGHS. *[Absently.]* Charming—charming.

[Enter PHYLLIS by the door left, front.]

PHYLLIS. How quickly you've worked—and how well!

MAGGIE. I'm glad you're pleased.

PHYLLIS. You'd better go up to Miss Diana and see if she wants anything. *[Glances at the clock.]* Still nearly an hour before the wedding.

MAGGIE. So it is. Who'd a thought it? It's surprising how much a body can do when they've no time.

[MAGGIE takes the vase and moves toward parlor doors. PHYLLIS watches BURROUGHS uneasily. As MAGGIE reaches the door, enter MERIVALE and WOODRUFF. She stands aside for them to pass, then exits.]

MERIVALE. *[Gravely, to BURROUGHS.]* I was in search of you.

[BURROUGHS looks disconcerted, PHYLLIS uneasy.]

BURROUGHS. Of me, sir?

[WOODRUFF and PHYLLIS go to the veranda, talk at extreme left rear of scene, she watchful of her father and BURROUGHS.]

MERIVALE. A moment ago—only a moment ago—I suddenly remembered our conversation about the opposition of your parents.

BURROUGHS. *[Showing great relief.]* I hope I did not give you the impression, sir, that their opposition was—serious?

MERIVALE. No—oh, no. But— When you came to me a while ago
—told me you wished to take her now, I—I—I thought only of my
own distress, over giving her up so soon. *[*MERIVALE *with an effort
steadies himself.]* But now— Have you told *her* about your parents?

BURROUGHS. *[With constraint.]* She understands the situation.

MERIVALE. *[Hesitatingly.]* I suppose, then, I've no right to interfere. It has always been my idea that the most that can be wisely done
by parents for children is to train them to be fearless and truthful.
The rest will take care of itself. They may—and—will—make mistakes, but they will certainly come out right, where children who
have been guarded and sheltered from experience never learn to
control themselves.

BURROUGHS. I assure you, sir, my parents would entirely approve,
were they here to be consulted.

MERIVALE. You are sure of this? Your own eagerness is not misleading you?

BURROUGHS. I am sure my eagerness is not misleading me.

MERIVALE. *[After a brief pause, turning suddenly and appealingly
to* BURROUGHS.*]* Love her, Julian! Her nature is a vein of gold—the
deeper, the richer. *Love* her.

*[*BURROUGHS *lowers his eyes, then his head. His lips move, but he
is inaudible.* MERIVALE *lays one hand affectionately on his shoulder
for an instant.]*

MERIVALE. Love! Youth! *[Sighs, with an effort at cheerfulness.]* I
am selfish—selfish. *[Approaches* WOODRUFF *and* PHYLLIS. *To*
WOODRUFF.*]* You and Phyllis will take care of my son, here. And
Phyllis, will you send Diana to me?

PHYLLIS. She is very busy.

MERIVALE. But not too busy to give her father a few minutes alone
before the wedding.

PHYLLIS. Very well, father.

[Exit WOODRUFF, BURROUGHS, *and* PHYLLIS *by veranda, to left.*
MERIVALE *sits on the sofa to left, reflecting. He rises, takes a framed
photograph of* DIANA *from the top of the cabinet to right, gazes long
at it, kisses it. He returns it to its place, reseats himself on the sofa
to the left with a heavy sigh. Enter* DIANA *from the right, in a white
embroidered batiste that reveals her throat. She is very pale. She halts
at the threshold.]*

MERIVALE. Diana—my daughter.

*[*DIANA *crosses to him, seats herself upon his knee, looks into his
face. He strokes her hair and kisses her brow.]*

MERIVALE. Diana, are you *sure* you love Julian?

DIANA. Yes, father. I—love—him.

MERIVALE. Are you *sure* he loves you?

[DIANA lowers her eyes, evades an answer by pressing her head against his.]

MERIVALE. You have always been good—what I call good—truthful, honest, unafraid, splendidly willful.

DIANA. *[Absently.]* Willful—willful!

MERIVALE. Thank God, I never had a docile child. As the great American poet said, "Resist much, obey little." I've tried to teach you that no one is up to the full human stature who isn't master, and sole master, within himself.

DIANA. I thank you for having taught me that. That's why I'm able to look at you and say: "Father, I've made mistakes—grave mistakes —one that has cost me dear—dear! But never anything you'd frown on me for, if you knew *all* about it."

MERIVALE. One that has cost you dear?

DIANA. One that has cost me dear. *[As he begins to speak, lays her fingers on his lips.]* But you've taught me to act for myself, to learn from my mistakes, and to bear consequences without shirking—and in silence.

MERIVALE. Can't I help you?

DIANA. Not this time—thanks, daddy. *[Cheerfully.]* I'll come out all right.

MERIVALE. Indeed you will. And your happiness is secure, with Julian. *[DIANA'S face clouds and she turns away to hide it from him.]*

DIANA. I shall make my own life, as you have taught me.

MERIVALE. Thanks to the great and good God whom creeds caricature, I've a daughter fit to be the wife of a *man*, the mother of children!

DIANA. I shall make many, many mistakes, father, but—*[She lifts her eyes to his.]* I'll do nothing of which I shall be ashamed.

MERIVALE. And from you that means, nothing of which your father would be less than proud.

DIANA. *[Suddenly clinging to him.]* I want to believe so, father. *[She embraces him.]* I feel I could count on you, no matter what might come. How strong that makes me!

MERIVALE. What is it, child? Why do you speak so sadly?

DIANA. Not sadly. No—not sadly—only earnestly.

MERIVALE. I see the years—long, yet short, stretching away before you—years of sun and storm, but after every storm, the sun; beyond every shadow, the sun; and you strong and fearless, beside your husband, with your children about you—children like yourself.

DIANA. *[Painfully moved.]* Father!

MERIVALE. You are founding your life solidly upon love and truth. Love and truth!

*[*DIANA *draws away sharply, gazes into the distance.]*

DIANA. *[Slowly and in a strange voice.]* Love and truth—Love—and—truth. *[Looks at him gravely.]* That is the *only* foundation?

MERIVALE. There is no other. Against it, storms rage in vain. Without it, the fairest house tumbles to ruin.

*[*DIANA *rises, walks slowly up and down, her head bent, her hands clasped tightly behind her.]*

DIANA. Love—and—truth.

[Enter from the left WOODRUFF. *She pauses, gazes at him. He returns her look with a fatherly smile.]*

WOODRUFF. Mrs. Dagmar—Phyllis—sent me to—*[Pauses.]*

MERIVALE. You're not interrupting, Ben.

DIANA. *[Aside.]* Love—and—truth. *[To* MERIVALE.*]* Daddy, leave me with Uncle Ben.

*[*MERIVALE, *still preoccupied, rises, kisses her, looks long into her face, kisses her again.]*

MERIVALE. A wedding is very solemn, Ben—far more solemn than a funeral. Death is a conclusion, a finality, while marriage is a beginning, full of possibilities and perplexities. *[Releases* DIANA *lingeringly.]* Thank God, our girl here sets sail in a stout ship. I am selfish—selfish.

[Exit MERIVALE *to the left.]*

WOODRUFF. Well, little girl, what is it?

DIANA. *[Earnestly studying his face.]* Yes, I can trust you.

WOODRUFF. I have loved you very especially, child, since you were a baby in long dresses, in the arms of your dear mother. . . . I see in your eyes that you are greatly troubled.

DIANA. Uncle Ben, suppose I knew Julian does not love me as he should—does not respect me as a man must respect his *wife*—

WOODRUFF. Does not respect you! Why, child—why, Diana—that's impossible.

DIANA. It is true.

WOODRUFF. You are deluding yourself. The excitement—the strain—

DIANA. He does not respect me because I have been to him what he thinks of as his—his mistress.

WOODRUFF. *[Springing to his feet.]* Diana!

DIANA. You see how it affects you. Well—that's the way he feels.

WOODRUFF. *[Sitting and taking her hand.]* My poor, poor Diana.

DIANA. *[With bitterness.]* Precisely! Just what *he* thinks—pity and contempt.

WOODRUFF. No! No! I'll not believe it.

DIANA. Believe or not, as you please. It is true. And, since it is so —since he does look down on me—since he would not marry me, had he choice—ought I to marry him?

WOODRUFF. He must realize that, if you did such a thing, it was in a moment of passing weakness—an impulse you were not responsible for. He must realize that he is to blame.

DIANA. But that is not true. It never is. Women plead it, and men, liking to think woman the weaker vessel, believe them. But it isn't so. *[Impatiently.]* Let's not discuss that. What I wish to know is, ought I to marry him? Would it be right?

WOODRUFF. Why not? He has—*[Rises, paces up and down.]* . . . Who'd have believed it of him? He looks an honorable man.

DIANA. And so he is. A dishonorable man would have twisted his conscience to his inclination. He's quite willing to "make reparation" —I believe that's the classical term. It's the term he used. Oh, his attitude is correct, I assure you. He looks down on me, and that is most manlike, most conventional. He is willing to marry me, and that is most honorable.

WOODRUFF. *[Bursting out again.]* To insinuate himself into this beautiful, this ideal home, to poison—

DIANA. Don't, please! You know better. *[Faces him.]* Am *I* the woman a man could entrap?

WOODRUFF. You tell me he has.

DIANA. I did not say that. Uncle Ben, you've lived many years. You've dealt with human nature in the confessional. You know that in these cases the woman is the stronger. It's the woman who gives the man the courage to dare—or he does not dare.

WOODRUFF. Women are led by their emotions. *You* were.

DIANA. And what are men led by? But let's talk of what now is. I don't blame him—at least I try not to. I put him to too severe a test.

WOODRUFF. You did, indeed, Diana.

DIANA. He's been fighting against being influenced by his education—by his surroundings, by what all his world feels and says. But in spite of himself he *is* influenced.

WOODRUFF. Naturally—naturally.

DIANA. And when his mother was pleading with him to give me

up, I know now it was this that was her secret ally, that made him falter—and doubt himself—and doubt me. But the fact remains that he feels toward me as—as you'd feel toward a woman who had done what I have done. He feels *[with sad bitterness]* that he has got all I have to give—what you men always think. How contemptible women are in your eyes!

WOODRUFF. Contemptible?

DIANA. *[After a pause.]* Yes, contemptible. *[A pause, then slowly.]* What a man values in himself at less than nothing is in a woman *all* her worth. *[Silence.]*

WOODRUFF. God seems to have so ordained it.

DIANA. *[Springing up, rushing toward the windows.]* Not the God beyond these free skies! Not *my* God! *[Silence.]*

WOODRUFF. At least, this man isn't utterly depraved. He's not casting you off, as his sort usually do cast off their victims.

DIANA. Victims! I, a victim! Oh, Uncle Ben, why do you repeat these cant phrases? I am no victim. I stand here in strength, not in weakness. Victim! What a world! The love that trusts, that gives freely, is abased, while the love that doubts and calculates and first makes a bargain is exalted!

WOODRUFF. My poor child—

DIANA. *[Laying her hand on his arm entreatingly.]* Please, not that "my poor child" again. Call me anything you like—shameless, abandoned, but not an object of pity, a weak thing! Am I weeping? Am I maundering about my sin? Am I shirking or shifting consequences? I tell you, he has done *me* no wrong. He can't help being just man. . . . Either I must despise myself as what he thinks me, or despise him for thinking of me so.

WOODRUFF. Despise yourself—despise him. I—see. I—see.

DIANA. Then—ought I to marry him? Is it *right?*

*[*WOODRUFF *paces slowly up and down. A long pause.]*

WOODRUFF. I assume he would pass out of your life and leave—no trace.

DIANA. *[Passionately.]* *That* has nothing to do with it!

WOODRUFF. *[Throwing out his arms in a wild gesture.]* Diana! Diana! . . . Oh, God, why hast Thou permitted this crime against this good man and his noble daughter!

DIANA. Again I say, the crime is not yet. Not a crime; a mistake, a sorry mistake. But would it not become a crime if he and I, feeling as we do about each other, stood before God and took the marriage vows?

WOODRUFF. *[Starting violently.]* Ah!

DIANA. Can *you* marry us now?

*[*WOODRUFF *seats himself, his head resting upon his hands. A long pause. At length* WOODRUFF *rises.]*

WOODRUFF. *[Going toward her, and speaking solemnly.]* In this world, my child, we have not often choice between right and wrong. Almost always the choice is between the greater evil and the lesser.

*[*DIANA *draws her breath sharply; her fingers seek her throat as if she were stifling.]*

WOODRUFF. You will choose the lesser evil.

DIANA. The lesser evil! A reluctant husband—despising me—ashamed of me—suspecting me—doubting me, perhaps! Afraid my child will be like me!

WOODRUFF. There is your punishment.

DIANA. Yes—my punishment—my hell!—mine—and his—and— *[she pauses, gazes out in despair]*—and my child's.

WOODRUFF. *[Greatly agitated by her words and apparent hesitation.]* Hubert must never know. Never! What *agony* his would be! Diana, how could you—how could you!

DIANA. *[Stopping her ears with her palms.]* No! No! I will—I will! *[She rushes toward veranda exit to the right. In the left entrance from veranda appears* BURROUGHS.*]*

BURROUGHS. *[Commandingly.]* Diana—one moment.

*[*DIANA *motions him wildly aside with an inarticulate cry and rushes off. He gazes after her, shrugs his shoulders, elevates his head and advances.]*

BURROUGHS. *[Curtly.]* Ah, doctor.

*[*WOODRUFF *startles, wheels abruptly and frowns at* BURROUGHS, *who returns his gaze with open defiance.]*

BURROUGHS. They want me to wait here. The ceremony is to be in the parlor—in there. *[Indicates doors to left, seats himself on sofa to left, drums on it nervously.]* Make it brief as possible, please.

WOODRUFF. Sir!

BURROUGHS. Cut the ceremony short.

WOODRUFF. You are disrespectful.

BURROUGHS. *[Carelessly.]* Beg pardon. I meant no disrespect. *[Notes* WOODRUFF'S *steady gaze—grows still more restless—glares at him—springs up.]* By God!

WOODRUFF. Sir!

BURROUGHS. *[Advancing to him and looking him in the eyes.]* Why do you stare at me? Is it because—*[Laughs in angry scorn.]* So, she has told! A hell of a mess—

[Reënter DIANA *at right. She is cold, calm and stately.]*

BURROUGHS. You have told *him!*

DIANA. *[With contempt.]* The secret is mine. It's always the woman's, you know—the victim's.

BURROUGHS. *[Stung to fury.]* My position gives me the right to demand, and I do demand, that you shall not chatter about, to your own discredit.

DIANA. Discredit?

BURROUGHS. Discredit. You will remember that you are going to be my wife.

DIANA. *Going to be* your wife? Why, I thought I *was* your wife. Certainly, you said it often enough. It was your favorite phrase.

BURROUGHS. *[Beside himself.]* You would do well not to taunt me.

DIANA. Ah, true. The fallen creature must be politic. Forgive me. Be patient. I shall learn.

*[*BURROUGHS *gazes furiously at her.]*

WOODRUFF. *[In a low tone.]* Diana! I implore you!

DIANA. And marriage—real marriage—is founded on love and truth. Love and truth! *[She laughs scornfully.* BURROUGHS *hangs his head and turns away.]* Love—and—truth! ... *[To* WOODRUFF.*]* I want a last word with him before—before you—and *he*—purify me.

[Exit WOODRUFF *by door to left, with a parting look of entreaty at both.]*

DIANA. *[Contemptuously.]* And now, sir—

BURROUGHS. *[Turning on her.]* Do you wish me to hate you?

DIANA. I prefer it to the feeling you've been entertaining.

BURROUGHS. My God! Have I shirked my sin against your father and you? Am I not doing all I can to wipe it out, to—

DIANA. To restore me to the ranks of the respectable? Yes. Yes. And I am deeply grateful. I humble myself at your feet.

BURROUGHS. You can't move me. I've given my word. I'll keep it.

DIANA. Yes—you'll save yourself.

BURROUGHS. Myself! Do you think I fear for my life?

DIANA. Possibly. *[*BURROUGHS *clinches his teeth to restrain furious speech.]* But certainly you fear for your good name—your *[with intense sarcasm]*—your honor. Most men have your poor opinion of women's frailty under—*[with mocking irony]*—temptation. If this—

this—*escapade*—*[he winces]*—of yours—should become a scandal, what would men say of—*you*? . . . Even your mother—

BURROUGHS. Leave my mother out of this!

DIANA. Pardon. I must not take the name of a good woman upon my lips until I have been purified. *[With abrupt change to haughtiness.]* But, we waste time. I came to tell you what I purpose to do. I marry you because I must, just as you marry me because you must.

BURROUGHS. That is not true—not as you put it.

DIANA. Tell me—if you were entirely free, would you marry me to-day?

BURROUGHS. I've told you that—

DIANA. Yes or no?

BURROUGHS. I've explained to you—

DIANA. No. And, after you had been living in those sewers of conventional hypocrisy again for a year, breathing only their poisons, with never a breath of the fresh, pure air of sincerity—would you marry *me*? *[A brief pause.* BURROUGHS *looks down.]* Let's not lie—to ourselves, at least. You marry me only because you must. I marry you for the sake of—*[She falters, regains self-control.]* But I shall not go away with you. You have been my husband. The marriage is dissolved. This ceremony will be a form—nothing more. You will stop the night under this roof—that must be. But to-morrow you leave here alone, and I shall take care that I never see you again.

[She is facing him, erect, calm. At her last words BURROUGHS *starts back, then stands gazing at her, his shoulders heaving with passion.]*

BURROUGHS. Not so fast! Not so fast! It's true, when I went away from you to that cold, formal home of mine, I did begin to doubt my memory of you—

DIANA. *[Jeering.]* At last, at last—the truth.

BURROUGHS. Your anger sets me on fire. You are superb! I *never* wanted you so! Leave here alone? No! When you take my name I take you. *[*DIANA *shudders, shrinks.]* I've got to have you. You've been mine—*[Fiercely, triumphantly.]* Yes, mine! And you shall continue to be mine.

DIANA. Never!

BURROUGHS. You are mine! *[He seizes her in his arms.]* Mine! Do you hear? Mine! Do you understand?

[After a fierce struggle DIANA *releases herself, rushes to doors at left, flings them open.]*

DIANA. *[Panting and beside herself.]* Father!

[Enter from the left MERIVALE, PHYLLIS, DAGMAR, WOODRUFF. *They gaze in amazement from* BURROUGHS, *standing dazed at sofa*

to right, to DIANA, *at small table to left, with blazing eyes and surging bosom, pointing at* BURROUGHS.*]*

DIANA. Father, I will not marry this man!

BURROUGHS. *[Coming forward defiantly.]* I say she shall!

MERIVALE. Diana, what is it?

PHYLLIS. *[Seizing* DIANA *by the arm.]* Oh, Di—

DIANA. *[Releasing herself and approaching her father.]* I shall not marry him. I wish him to leave the house at once.

BURROUGHS. She *shall* marry me. She is mine!

DIANA. Yours? Not I. I am free!

MERIVALE. Diana, what's the meaning of this?

PHYLLIS. Don't listen to her! She—

DIANA. Enough! Father, hear me! Two months ago this man and I became husband and wife—in the sight of God. I took him—gave myself.

[Profound sensation. MERIVALE *starts, gazes from* DIANA *to* BURROUGHS, *to* DIANA *again.* PHYLLIS *clasps her hands despairingly.* DAGMAR *turns threateningly toward* BURROUGHS, *who sees only* DIANA.*]*

DIANA. I took him—I gave myself because I thought him a *man*— a man like you. And in the blindness and folly of my love, I felt as my dead mother felt when she lived in your arms.

*[*MERIVALE *staggers.* WOODRUFF *attempts to help him, but he pushes him aside, seats himself on the sofa to left, sitting rigidly erect.]*

MERIVALE. Go on, Diana.

DIANA. Father, I thought him like you. But, thank God, I found him out in time. And so I am saving myself from this man who said he loved me while in his heart he was despising me. I was about to marry him. But I see now my first instinct was right. I was wronging you —was false to all you taught me. Forgive me, and send him from our sight!

[A pause. Then MERIVALE *slowly rises and faces* BURROUGHS.*]*

MERIVALE. Begone!

WOODRUFF. Bertie!—

BURROUGHS. I shall not go without her.

PHYLLIS. Father—in a few months the world would know our dishonor.

DAGMAR. Good God!

*[*MERIVALE *looks round dazedly. Finally his eyes rest upon* DIANA, *standing with bowed head.]*

MERIVALE. *[Brokenly.]* Oh, Diana. My poor Diana!

DIANA. *[Straightening herself haughtily.]* You, too, father! You, too!

MERIVALE. *[Striking his cane sharply upon the floor.]* Woodruff! Marry them at once!

BURROUGHS. That is all I ask.

MERIVALE. Silence, sir!

DIANA. *[Calm and inflexible.]* I shall not marry him.

MERIVALE. *[Sternly.]* Either you marry him or he dies. *[To* DAGMAR.*]* What say you, my son?

DAGMAR. *[Quietly.]* Of course.

BURROUGHS. *[Snapping his fingers.]* That for threats! This woman belongs to me. I will have her.

DIANA. Do you hear, father?—do you hear? He calls *me* his *property!*

MERIVALE. Marry him, or he dies.

*[*DIANA *looks from face to face—at* WOODRUFF, *at* DAGMAR, *at* PHYLLIS, *finally at her father.]*

DIANA. I have no friends here—none. All—all, enemies. All, cowards. You pretend to love me; yet you would sacrifice me through fear of the sneers of strangers. You would force me to lie—to lie before God!

MERIVALE. *[Gentle but firm.]* You forget, Diana. You have brought this upon yourself.

DIANA. You ask me to atone for an error with a crime. . . . But I shall not do it. And you will not kill him—for, it was I who gave, not he who took, and it is I who refuse the "honorable reparation" he presses on us.

MERIVALE. You shall marry him!

DIANA. You do not ask it—not your real self—not the father who taught me to be fearless and truthful, to hold my own respect for myself dearer than the opinion of all the world beside. . . . No lie has soiled my lips or smirched my soul. I am a pure woman. What this man did not, could not do—what no man could do—you, my father, ask me to do. You ask your daughter to dishonor herself.

MERIVALE. Diana, it must be. For your own sake. I am thinking only of you.

*[*DIANA *draws herself slowly up, faces her father.]*

DIANA. Look at me, daddy! *[Their eyes meet.]* . . . If there were no one in the world but just you and me and that man—would you then demand that I marry him?

[A pause, all watching the father and daughter as they gaze at each other.]

DIANA. *[Very slowly.]* Was what you taught me—*false?* Do you tell *your daughter to—lie?*

[Silence, all watching MERIVALE, *except* BURROUGHS. *He is gazing at* DIANA *as if he were seeing a vision that dazed and dazzled him. At last* MERIVALE *stands tall and straight.]*

MERIVALE. You are right. *[Opens his arms toward* DIANA.*]* You are right—*[extends his arms toward her]*—my daughter!

[He encircles her with his arms. A pause.]

MERIVALE. *[To* BURROUGHS, *calmly and restrainedly.]* You see, sir, you have no place here.

*[*BURROUGHS *slowly, as if dazed and blinded, moves toward veranda, left. He turns, crushed and haggard.* MERIVALE *and* DIANA *look proudly at him and* MERIVALE *draws* DIANA *more closely into his arms. Exit* BURROUGHS.*]*

CURTAIN.

ACT IV

DIANA'S *sitting room, the same evening. To the right, double doors into her bedroom; to the left a door into the hall. At the rear, the wide balcony that encircles the second story of the house. Along its railing creepers, an edge of planted flowers, with potted plants on the pillars. The window doors opening upon the balcony are very wide. Instead of curtains there are broad light-green valences, matching the walls and upholstery. The background is the tops of the trees with fireflies winking among the branches, and the clear, starry night sky. In the room, to the left, near a desk, a great lamp on a tall, slender pedestal gives a sufficient but not brilliant light. The furniture is simple, comfortable, tasteful—including bookcases, racks of guns and fishing tackle.* PHYLLIS *in dinner dress enters by balcony window doors. As she is knocking at* DIANA'S *bedroom doors,* DAGMAR *appears from the balcony. He is dressed as before.*

DAGMAR. *[Softly yet sharply.]* Phyl! *[*PHYLLIS *turns.]* And you promised you'd keep away from her.

PHYLLIS. Did you find him?

DAGMAR. Not yet.

PHYLLIS. What *shall* we do?

DAGMAR. Don't get tragic. Be human and sensible. Stay on the ground. There's nothing in life that calls for stilts. . . . He didn't take the train. That means a lot.

PHYLLIS. Maybe we're mistaken. Maybe he did.

DAGMAR. With you watching it? A fly couldn't have got aboard without your seeing. What a stupid thing it was for us to do—dash to the station after him. It's perfectly obvious, if he were the sort that would have gone, he ought to have been let go, and good riddance. We'll make a mess of things, Phyl, with our meddling, if we don't look out.

PHYLLIS. Go away and let me talk to her. What a fool she is! What a fool!

DAGMAR. You didn't think so this afternoon.

PHYLLIS. Oh, for a moment. But I soon came to my senses. *[Goes toward* DIANA'S *door.]*

DAGMAR. Let her alone. You'll ruin any chance there may be to straighten things out.

PHYLLIS. I must bring her to her senses.

DAGMAR. Di's not such a fool after all—that's my opinion on second thought.

PHYLLIS. What *are* you talking about?

DAGMAR. You were right at first—though from a wrong reason— a sentimental reason. That's the way with you women. When you're right, it's always in the wrong way. It was so with Di. She did the sensible thing—though she didn't mean to.

PHYLLIS. Sensible!

DAGMAR. Sensible. And you'd see it, if you women weren't brought up without any real notion of personal pride, but simply for the matrimonial market. [PHYLLIS *turns impatiently away.* DAGMAR *detains her.]* Now, listen to me. Suppose she'd married him when he was thinking himself so grand and superior—what kind of a life would she have had? The worst possible—the *very* worst. No, he had to be brought up standing. And she did it—good and proper.

PHYLLIS. *[Somewhat calmed.]* That sounds well. But ... That scoundrel!

DAGMAR. There you go again! Not a scoundrel—just an everyday case of—

PHYLLIS. You men! You stick up for each other in the face of anything!

DAGMAR. As men go, Burroughs is—

[Enter by door, left, MERIVALE, *erect, vigorous.]*

PHYLLIS. *[Depressed by his evident cheerfulness.]* Father! Father!

MERIVALE. *[Shaking his head in good-humored rebuke.]* I suppose you'll never learn that worldliness isn't wisdom. Go away now. I wish to talk with your sister.

PHYLLIS. Father—I hope you at least won't—

MERIVALE. *[In a tone of finality.]* Enough.

DAGMAR. Come, Phyl. *[PHYLLIS hesitates.]* Come!

[Exit PHYLLIS followed by DAGMAR. MERIVALE looks hesitatingly at DIANA'S doors.]

WOODRUFF. *[Outside.]* Is your father in there, Phyllis?

PHYLLIS. *[Outside, her voice not yet under control.]* Yes, doctor. But he's—

MERIVALE. Come in, Ben.

[Enter WOODRUFF.]

WOODRUFF. I thought I heard your step in the hall. *[They shake hands affectionately.]* How is Diana?

MERIVALE. I haven't seen her. I've only just come up. *[WOODRUFF turns to leave.]* No, don't go yet.

WOODRUFF. I've been hoping she'd send for me.

MERIVALE. She hasn't even asked for me yet. I'm hesitating whether to disturb her. Ben, I've been dreaming the years away among my books—walking through the scenes of sorrow and suffering and failure called history. My girl has awakened me—my girl with her splendid, vivid sense of right.

WOODRUFF. Splendid, indeed. But—*[He shakes his head doubtfully.]*

MERIVALE. You were not convinced?

WOODRUFF. Convinced? It was impossible not to be. And yet— *[Shakes his head.]* What a pity the world didn't see what we saw this afternoon. Ah, Bertie, life isn't a matter of occasional great moments but of petty hours and days.

MERIVALE. *[Laying his hand cheerfully on WOODRUFF'S shoulder.]* If we let the light of the great moment illuminate those hours and days, they may not be so petty—eh, Ben?

WOODRUFF. They will not be! . . . What an inspiration courage is! . . . What a revelation of womanhood! . . . Bertie, I doubt not that young man has been awakened, too—awakened from the thoughtlessness of youth. *[MERIVALE clutches his cane, his face darkens, he half turns away.]* I'll say no more. Forgive me for saying so much. *[MERIVALE lays his hand affectionately on WOODRUFF'S shoulder. The two smile at each other.]* Why, Bertie, you look ten years younger than when I came this morning. And I feared—*[He pauses.]*

MERIVALE. *[Smiling.]* Feared I'd be broken? Because I find I've a daughter too proud and too brave to lie at any cost?

WOODRUFF. *[Smiling.]* What a man you are!

MERIVALE. And what a heart you've got!

WOODRUFF. God bless you! See Diana and talk with her.

MERIVALE. If I can without intruding.

WOODRUFF. Well, I'll take a turn round the garden before going to bed.

[WOODRUFF turns to go by door to left.]

MERIVALE. You can go this way. By the balcony stairs. It's shorter.

WOODRUFF. To be sure. *[At window door.]* What a wonderful night.

MERIVALE. The moon will soon be up.

WOODRUFF. Good night.

MERIVALE. Good night, Ben.

[Exit WOODRUFF. MERIVALE hesitates before DIANA'S doors, then taps softly on the floor several times with his cane.]

DIANA. *[Within.]* Yes, daddy.

[Enter DIANA, in a flowing white negligee, very simple, with graceful lines.]

MERIVALE. I'm not intruding?

DIANA. *You?* No, indeed. Why, father, how bright your face is!

MERIVALE. For the best of reasons.

DIANA. Really? ... *Really?*

MERIVALE. *[With his hands on her shoulders.]* I'm proud of my daughter—my grown-up daughter. I'd been thinking of you as still a child. And—this afternoon—I looked and—you are a woman—*what* a woman!

[DIANA shakes her head rather sadly.]

MERIVALE. It's easy, my daughter, to face shot and shell. Countless millions have done that. But all alone, to challenge hypocrisies the whole world worships, face in the dust—there's courage!

DIANA. I'm not brave. I'm even weak. Weak!

[He seats himself on the sofa, she walks slowly and aimlessly up and down.]

MERIVALE. No, no, my dear.

DIANA. Then why this—this desolation!

MERIVALE. You still love him?

DIANA. It *is* weak—isn't it?

[MERIVALE takes her hand tenderly. Then, his face grows stern. DIANA glances at him.]

DIANA. Daddy, you mustn't blame him—not altogether. It was the fault of your willful daughter, too—the *equal* fault.

MERIVALE. Generous. Brave.

DIANA. *[Shaking her head.]* No—neither. I didn't refuse this afternoon because I was brave, but—because I loved him.... Do you understand?

MERIVALE. *[After reflecting.]* Yes, dear—I understand.

DIANA. And that's why I haven't forgiven him.

*[*DIANA *struggles for self-control, then bursts into tears, burying her face in her father's arms.]*

MERIVALE. Diana—if—

DIANA. It's for the happiness that might have been—the happiness that could never be—unless love loved freely and loved *all. [She regains self-control.]* Oh, if he had only loved me!

MERIVALE. The shadow will pass.

DIANA. It all rests with me, father, doesn't it?

MERIVALE. You live in the real world, dear—the world that's called unreal—the world within. And you're at peace with that. But—*[He hesitates.]*

DIANA. Yes, father?

MERIVALE. My daughter mustn't forget she has to live in the other world, too—that the world beyond our hills will punish her.

DIANA. I know. I've thought of that—all of it. This afternoon Uncle Ben said to me: "There isn't often choice between absolute right and wrong. It's almost always choice between the greater evil and the lesser." ... I have chosen the lesser evil. *[*MERIVALE *nods emphatically.]* But—there's something else.

MERIVALE. You mean—

DIANA. Yes, father—my child. I chose the lesser evil for it, too. Nothing—*nothing*—could be so bad for it as a father who didn't respect its mother, a mother who had lost her self-respect. Nothing —nothing! But—*[A pause.]*

MERIVALE. Yes—dear?

DIANA. By and by—when it is old enough to judge—*[agitated]*— when it does judge—me ... will it justify me? ... That doubt will be my torment.

*[*MERIVALE *rises, moves to window door, gazes out. The moon rises, sharply lighting up his features.* DIANA *joins him, and they stand there together. A long silence.]*

DIANA. Good night, father.

[They go to the door, to left, and embrace.]

MERIVALE. Good night, dear.

DIANA. Good night—daddy.

[They embrace lingeringly. Exit MERIVALE. DIANA *slowly returns to window, pauses there in the moonlight, sighs heavily, goes to her desk, seats herself. She takes out of a drawer, reads and tears up several letters, with increasing anguish. She reads one that moves her beyond her power to control. She returns it to the drawer, closes the drawer. Then, with swift movements, she snatches it, tears it up, sends the fragments to join the others in the waste basket. She rises, gazes out into the moonlight, grows calmer. She goes toward her bedroom door, pauses to extinguish the lamp. As she turns away, a slight sound on the balcony startles her. She advances boldly toward the window doors, to see the cause.* BURROUGHS *appears, pauses just beyond the threshold. His dress shows some dishevelment and dust. He looks distinctly less the boy, more the man—subdued, humbled, but resolute.]*

BURROUGHS. Diana. *[He advances.]*

DIANA. *[Rigid, cold.]* You will not cross that threshold.

BURROUGHS. *[Firmly, quietly.]* Diana, I've come as you told me to come.

DIANA. I? I told you to go.

BURROUGHS. *[His manner subdued, respectful, yet insistent.]* Once, when we were very, very happy—it was on just such a night as this—you told me if ever anything—no matter what—should estrange us—you told me to come to you—to make you listen to me, no matter how you might try to prevent—you told me to come to you, face to face, and say "Diana, I love you." Do you remember?

DIANA. *[Self-controlled with an effort.]* I remember. Now, you will go.

BURROUGHS. Go? . . . Where? . . . Where in all this world *can* I go?

DIANA. *[Moving still farther from him.]* You dare come here—here of all places—

BURROUGHS. *[Interrupting.]* Yes—here where I learned what I now know was love's primer lesson. Remember, Diana—remember every moment of those wonderful hours together—recall my every look and word. Is there one—*one*—that does not cry out, "I love you."

DIANA. But in your heart—

BURROUGHS. No—no—not in my *heart*. My heart was yours—all yours. I loved you all the time—always—utterly. From the first instant I saw you, for me you stood apart from all the world—as the only woman—the one woman. Yes—I loved you. You know I loved you.

DIANA. No—no! You—

BURROUGHS. *[Solemnly.]* Yes. For better, for worse. You were mine, I yours. But I didn't—couldn't—realize what you were. I knew you were a treasure. My eyes told me that—all my senses. But I never thought to look farther—deeper—and find *you.*

*[*DIANA *trembles, but remains with her back to him, he several paces from her.]*

BURROUGHS. I valued you. But, oh, my God, how I undervalued! Why, not even my own mother ever made me realize that woman, womanhood—is not body, but mind and heart—soul! This afternoon you showed us all what woman can mean. Diana, I was dazed, crushed. I went away hopeless. In the woman I loved I had seen the woman I adored.

*[*DIANA *gives a faint suppressed cry, but does not turn. He advances a step, but only a step.]*

BURROUGHS. This afternoon your father said to me, "Love her, Julian. Her nature is a vein of gold." I thought I knew what he meant. But he didn't know himself. No one could have—until—I see you again as you stood there in all the glory of womanhood. Oh, Diana, if you were not so sweet, so tender, so human, I'd be afraid to venture to tell you of my love now. But you *are* tender. You *are* sweet and forgiving. Diana—forgive *me*—*believe* me!

DIANA. *[Turning and gazing earnestly, hesitatingly at him.]* Oh, I want to believe—I *want* to believe!

BURROUGHS. *[Extending his hands in manly appeal.]* Diana—forgive—believe. I love you—all of you—*you.*

[She advances a step toward him.]

DIANA. You are *sure?*

BURROUGHS. I am *sure.*

[She slowly gives him her hands. He puts them together, bends and respectfully kisses them. A brief pause.]

BURROUGHS. May I—may I come to-morrow?

DIANA. *[Softly.]* To-morrow.

[Holding hands, they go to the window door, pause on the threshold. He hesitatingly puts his arm round her, touches his lips to hers, releases her, except one hand.]

BURROUGHS. *[Going.]* Diana—my wife—I love you.

DIANA. You do—now—Julian.

CURTAIN.

Folk Songs and
Ballads of Indiana

❖❖❖❖❖❖❖❖❖❖❖❖❖❖❖❖❖❖❖❖❖❖❖❖❖❖❖❖

Folk songs and ballads are transmitted orally, for the most part, and those of Indiana are no exception. Still, such recorders and collectors as Paul Brewster, Editor of *Ballads and Songs of Indiana*, Clinton Huppert of Spencer County, and Phoebe Elliott of New Harmony have made it possible to reproduce in print certain versions of the most popular ballads. We are also indebted to Leora Harvey, Mrs. H. Vaughan, and Mrs. D. Strouse for versions more specifically identified below.

The Frozen Girl

"There's music in the sound of bells
    As o'er the hills we go;
What a squeaking noise the runners make
    As they leave the frozen snow!"

They rode to the door, and Charles jumped out
    And gave his hand to her:
"Why sit you there like a monument
    That has no power to stir?"

He tore the mantle from her brow,
    And the gold in her hair there shone;
She was a cold and frozen corpse
    As cold and stiff as stone.

He kissed her once, he kissed her twice;
    He kissed her frozen brow;
His thoughts ran back to where she said,
    "I'm growing warmer now."

Young Charlotte
(a variation of Fair Charlotte)

Young Charlotte lived on a   mountain side,

In a wild and   lonely spot; There was   no

dwelling for three miles round Except   her

father's cot. On many a   cold   and

wint'ry night Young swains were   gath'red

there, For   her   father   kept   a   social

board, And she was young   and   fair.

The Pretty Mohea

As I was out roving for pleasure one

day, With sweet recollection for to pass time a-

way, As I was amusing myself on the

grass, But whom did I spy but a

fair Indian lass?

She sat down beside me, took hold of my hand,
  Saying, "You look like a stranger, not one from our land;
And if you will follow, you're welcome to come,
  For I live all alone in a little wigwam."

The sun was fast setting across the wide lea
  As I wandered along with little Mauhee;
Together we rambled, together we roved,
  Till we came to a hut in a cocoanut grove.

She opened the door and invited me in,
  And treated me kindly to what was therein,
Saying, "Don't go a-roving out on the wide sea,
  And I'll learn you the language of little Mauhee."

"Mauhee, Mauhee, that never can be,
  For I have a sweetheart in my own country.
I've promised to wed her, the pride of the lea;
  Her heart beats as fondly as yours, Mauhee."

That last time I saw her she was out on the strand,
  And as I sailed by her she waved her hand,
Saying, "When you get home to the girl that you love,
  O think of Mauhee in the cocoanut grove."

So now I'm at home on my old native shore,
  My friends and connection crowd round me once more;
But of all that crowd round me not one do I see
  That I can compare with little Mauhee.

The girl that I trusted proved untrue to me;
  I'll turn my course backward across the wide sea.
I'll turn my course backward; from this land I'll flee,
  And go spend my days with little Mauhee.

Pretty Sairey

'Way down in some lone valley or in some other place
Where the small birds do whistle and their notes do increase,
I'll think on pretty Sairey, her ways so complete;
I love her, my Sairey, from her head to her feet.

My love she won't have me, as I understand;
She wants a freeholder, and I have no land.
Yet I could maintain her on silver and gold
And as many other fine things as my love's house could hold.

I went to my Sairey, my love to unfold,
To tell her my passion, so brave and so bold;
I said to her, "Sairey, will you be my bride,
And walk with me ever, right here at my side?

"I love you, my Sairey, as you can well see;
I'll take you a-travelling o'er land and o'er sea.
Silks, satins, and jewels I'll buy you to wear,
For there's no one, my true love, to me is more dear."

Then Sairey she held out her sweet little hand
And said, "I can't love you, for you have no land;
I've promised another to be his dear wife
And walk with him ever, for the rest of my life."

"Farewell, pretty Sairey, my true-love!" I said;
"I go from your presence; I wish I was dead.
Some other lover will kneel at your feet
And take the dear kisses I once thought so sweet."

Johnny Sands

A man whose name was Johnny Sands
    He married Betty Hague;
Although she brought him gold and lands,
    She proved a terrible plague.

For O she was a scolding wife,
    Full of caprice and whim;
He said that he was tired of life,
    And she was tired of him.

He said, "Then I will drown myself;
    The river runs below."
"Pray do," said she, "you silly elf;
    I wished it long ago."

Said he, "Upon the bank I'll stand,
  And you run down the hill,
And push me in with all your might";
  Said she, "My love, I will."

"For fear that I might courage lack
  And try to save my life,
Pray tie my hands behind my back";
  "I will," replied his wife.

She tied them fast, as you may think,
  And when securely done,
"Now stand," said she, "upon the brink
  While I prepare to run."

All down the hill his lovely bride
  Now ran with all her force
To push him—he stepped aside,
  And she fell in, of course.

Now splashing, dashing like a fish,
  "O save me, Johnny Sands!"
"I can't, my love, though much I wish,
  For you have tied my hands."

Poems and Songs

❖❖❖❖❖❖❖❖❖❖❖❖❖❖❖❖❖❖❖❖❖❖❖

JAMES WHITCOMB RILEY

(b. Greenfield, 1849–d. 1916) attended the Greenfield public schools, and though he did not go to college, he was ultimately awarded an honorary degree by Yale University. He composed verses in a mixture of Hoosier dialect and Riley idiolect, addressing them primarily to children (e.g., "The Raggedy Man" and "Little Orphant Annie") but reaching the child in readers of all ages. From 1900 to 1910 he was very much in demand for his readings and "recitations" in Indiana schools. A bachelor, and not particularly fond of children, he nevertheless opened his Indianapolis home (on Lockerbie Street) to boys and girls who sought to be photographed on his knee. For further information about Riley, see page 123.

When the Frost
Is on the Punkin

When the frost is on the punkin and the fodder's in the shock,
And you hear the kyouck and gobble of the struttin'
    turkey-cock,
And the clackin' of the guineys, and the cluckin' of the hens,
And the rooster's hallylooyer as he tiptoes on the fence;
O, it's then's the time a feller is a-feelin' at his best,
With the risin' sun to greet him from a night of peaceful rest,
And he leaves the house, bare-headed, and goes out to feed the
    stock,
When the frost is on the punkin and the fodder's in the shock.

They's something kindo' harty-like about the atmusfere
When the heat of summer's over and the coolin' fall is here—
Of course we miss the flowers, and the blossoms on the trees,
And the mumble of the hummin'-birds and buzzin' of the bees;
But the air's so appetizin'; and the landscape through the haze
Of a crisp and sunny morning of the early autumn days
Is a pictur' that no painter has the colorin' to mock—
When the frost is on the punkin and the fodder's in the shock.

The husky, rusty russel of the tossels of the corn,
And the raspin' of the tangled leaves, as golden as the morn;
The stubble in the furries—kindo' lonesome-like but still
A-preachin sermuns to us of the barns they growed to fill;

The strawstack in the medder, and the reaper in the shed;
The hosses in theyr stalls below—the clover overhead!
O, it sets my hart a-clickin' like the tickin' of a clock,
When the frost is on the punkin and the fodder's in the shock!

Then your apples all is gethered, and the ones a feller keeps
Is poured around the celler-floor in red and yeller heaps;
And your cider makin's over, and your wimmern-folks is
　　through
With their mince and apple-butter, and theyr souse and sausage
　　too!
I don't know how to tell it — but ef sich a thing could be
As the Angels wantin' boardin' and they'd call around on me —
I'd want to 'commodate 'em — all the whole-indurin' flock —
When the frost is on the punkin and the fodder's in the shock!

FRANKLIN PIERCE ADAMS

(b. 1881–d. 1960), although not a native of Indiana, was one of the
professed admirers of James Whitcomb Riley ("I think that he is
great") who at the same time poked fun at Riley's kind of verse.
A light-versifier himself, Adams won popularity for his columns in
newspapers in Chicago and New York — especially for his column
"The Conning Tower" in the *New York Post*. This poem appeared
in the March, 1906 issue of *The Reader Magazine*.

To Whom It May Concern

It's not for me to criticize; it's not for me to knock
A poem as refreshing as "The Fodder in the Shock."
For who am I that I should dare to criticize a rhyme
So likely to endure the chill corroding blasts of Time?
My quarrel's not with Riley—I think that he is great—
But with the bards that feebly try his work to imitate
And think they have a masterpiece if it should but contain
Some platitudy commonplace and obvious refrain.

The Cheerup School of Poetry is open night and day,
Its principles and principals are but to make you say
With "Keep-a-Smilin' " verses written by some doleful bard,
Whose bargain rate is just about one-forty-nine a yard.
"When Sunshine Is a Shinin' What's the Use to Mope and
　　Fret?"
"The Things We Don't Remember Are the Things that We
　　Forget."
"We Wouldn't Have No Rainbow If We Didn't Have No
　　Rain,"—
Or any other commonplace and obvious refrain.

Parnassus is macadamized; they've paved the road to Fame.
Jump on a rented Pegasus—you'll find him very tame.
"The Man Who Never Worries Is the Man Who Gets Along."
"When Trouble Comes to Bother You Just Sing a Little Song."
"The Man Who Makes You Hustle Is the Man Who's Just
　　Ahead."
"The People Who Are Living Ain't the People Who Are Dead."
O bardlets of the magazines, a word of warning plain
To ye that write the Commonplace and Obvious: REFRAIN!

PAUL DRESSER

(b. Terre Haute, 1857–d. 1906), whose name was originally
Dreiser, was the brother of Theodore Dreiser. He composed such
popular songs as "My Gal Sal," "The Blue and the Gray," and the
Wabash song, below, which became the official State song of Indiana. For the part that Theodore Dreiser had in the composition of
this song, see "My Brother Paul," page 133.

On the Banks of the Wabash,
Far Away

Round my Indiana homestead wave the cornfields,
In the distance loom the woodlands clear and cool.
Often times my thoughts revert to scenes of childhood,

Where I first received my lessons, nature's school.
But one thing there is missing in the picture,
Without her face it seems so incomplete.
I long to see my mother in the doorway,
As she stood there years ago, her boy to greet!

REFRAIN

Oh, the moonlight's fair tonight along the Wabash,
From the fields there comes the breath of new-mown hay.
Thro' the sycamores the candle lights are gleaming,
On the banks of the Wabash, far away.

Many years have passed since I strolled by the river,
Arm in arm with sweetheart Mary by my side.
It was there I tried to tell her that I loved her,
It was there I begged of her to be my bride.
Long years have passed since I strolled thro' the churchyard,
She's sleeping there, my angel Mary dear.
I loved her but she thought I didn't mean it,
Still I'd give my future were she only here.

COLE PORTER

(b. 1893, Peru, Indiana–d. 1964), by anybody's definition, is one of
the greatest American songwriters of all time. For biographical
information, see page 135.

A Member of the Yale
Elizabethan Club

VERSE

I'm a member very noted
Of a club that's often quoted
As the most exclusive club in college.
My medulla oblongata
Has an awful lot of data

On the sources of our springs of knowledge.
I delight in being chatty
With New Haven's literati
On the subject of a brand new binding.
All the critics sing my praises
In illuminated phrases;
As a literary light I'm blinding.
As a literary light, as a literary light
    he's blinding!
Did you get that metaphor?
I confess I could do better for—

REFRAIN

I'm a member of the Yale Elizabethan Club
In a very hypocritical way.
By belonging to the Yale Elizabethan Club
I've a terrible political sway.
I convert New Haven
To the bard of Avon,
And a highbrow must I be;
For I give support
To the latest college sporto,
Tea by the quart
And editions by the quarto.
Good Gadzooks! But I love those books.
With a fol, with a fol,
With a hey, with a hey,
With a toureloure tourelourelay,
With a tralalalala,
With a tralalalala,
And a noney, noney, noney, noney, ney,
For a member of the Yale Elizabethan Club am I!

By the Mississinewah

I'm a poor little squaw from Indiana,
Who embarked on a trip for fun,
I'm a poor little squaw who'll sing "Hosanna,"
When the dog-gone trip is done.
No, no more shall I roam
From my comfy, cozy, Hoosier home!

REFRAIN 1

By the Miss-iss-iss-iss-iss-iss-iss-iss-inewah,
There's a husband to whom I'm true,
By the Miss-iss-iss-iss-iss-iss-iss-iss-inewah,
There he waits in a wigwam built for two,
Since no love I've had since from that lad I've been awah,
Back by that stream I will scream "hoorah!"
Thank the Lord this trip is brief
So I can leap on my heap-big chief
By the Miss-iss-iss-iss-iss-iss-inewah, Wah-wah!
By the Miss-iss-iss-iss-iss-iss-inewah!

REFRAIN 2

By the Miss-iss-iss-iss-iss-iss-iss-iss-inewah,
There's a husband to whom I'm true,
By the Miss-iss-iss-iss-iss-iss-iss-iss-inewah,
There he waits in a wigwam built for two,
I'm a total loss since from the boss I've been awah,
'Cause for that Bo, I am so ga-ga,
Yes, the moment I get in
I'll blow the top with my pop red-skin
By the Miss-iss-iss-iss-iss-iss-inewah!
By the Miss-iss-iss-iss-iss-iss-inewah!

You'd Be So Nice to Come Home to

You'd be so nice to come home to,
You'd be so nice by the fire,
While the breeze, on high,
Sang a lullaby,
You'd be all that I
Could desire.
Under stars, chilled by the winter,
Under an August moon, burning above,
You'd be so nice,
You'd be Paradise
To come home to and love.

In the Still of the Night

In the still of the night,
As I gaze from my window
At the moon in its flight,
My thoughts all stray to you.
In the still of the night,
While the world is in slumber,
Oh, the times without number,
Darling, when I say to you,
"Do you love me as I love you?
Are you my life-to-be, my dream come true?"
Or will this dream of mine
Fade out of sight
Like the moon,
Growing dim
On the rim
Of the hill
In the chill,
Still
Of the night?

Night and Day

VERSE

Like the beat beat beat of the tom tom when the jungle
  shadows fall
Like the tick tick tock of the stately clock as it
  stands against the wall
Like the drip drip drip of the raindrops when the
  sum'r show'r is through
So a voice within me keeps repeating You—You—You.

REFRAIN

Night and day you are the one,
Only you beneath the moon and under the sun,
Whether near to me or far
It's no matter darling where you are
I think of you night and day.
Day and night, why is it so
That this longing for you follows wherever I go?
In the roaring traffic's boom

In the silence of my lonely room
I think of you night and day.
Night and day under the hide of me
There's an, oh, such a hungry, yearning burning
    inside of me
And its torment won't be through
Till you let me spend my life making love to you
Day and night, night and day.

Miss Otis Regrets

Miss Otis regrets she's unable to lunch today,
Madam, Miss Otis regrets she's unable to lunch today.
She is sorry to be delayed.
But last evening down in lover's lane she strayed,
Madam, Miss Otis regrets she's unable to lunch today.

When she woke up and found
That her dream of love was gone,
Madam, she ran to the man
Who had led her so far astray,
And from under her velvet gown
She drew a gun and shot her lover down,
Madam, Miss Otis regrets she's unable to lunch today.

When the mob came and got her
And dragged her from the jail,
Madam, they strung her upon
The old willow across the way,
And the moment before she died
She lifted up her lovely head and cried
Madam, "Miss Otis regrets she's unable to lunch today."

BESSIE MASON

(b. Bloomington, 1899–) was educated at Bloomington High School
and at Indiana University, from which she graduated with a Phi
Beta Kappa key. Many of her poems have been published in such
magazines as *Sparrow, Good Housekeeping,* and *Saturday Evening Post.* Some of her poems are collected in *Along the Creek*
(1967).

Winter Evening

The creekside willows are bleak and bare:
Snowflakes swirl through the cold black air.

Oak trees shiver against the dark,
Their crisp leaves rattle on ice-glazed bark.

The mad wind bursts through the sycamores
And whines for entrance at tight-latched doors.

Hearth wood crackles, bright and warm
And sputters saucily at the storm.

The people sit by the fire and see
Turning furrow and budding tree,

And muse and plan about what to sow
On the hillside patch or the field below.

Undaunted by weather or anything,
Their backs toward winter, their hearts toward spring.

JEAN GARRIGUE

(b. Evansville, 1914–d. 1973), the daughter of Allan Colfax and
Gertrude Garrigus, took as her pen name "Garrigus" changed to
its original French spelling. She was educated in the Evansville
schools and at the Universities of Chicago and Iowa. She taught at
several colleges, including Bard, Queens, and Smith. Her poems
appeared in distinguished literary journals and were collected in
a number of volumes, among them *The Ego and the Centaur*
(1947).

Forest

There is the star bloom of the moss
And the hairy chunks of light between the conifers;
There are alleys of light where the green leads to a funeral

Down the false floor of needles.
There are rocks and boulders that jut, saw-toothed and
    urine-yellow.
Other stones in a field look in the distance like sheep grazing,
Grey trunk and trunklike legs and lowered head.
There are short-stemmed forests so close to the ground
You would pity a dog lost there in the spore-budding
Blackness where the sun has never struck down.
There are dying ferns that glow like a gold mine
And weeds and sumac extend the Sodom of color.
Among the divisions of stone and the fissures of branch
Lurk the abashed resentments of the ego.
Do not say this is pleasurable!
Bats, skittering on wires over the lake,
And the bug on the water, bristling in light as he measures
    forward his leaps,
The hills holding back the sun by their notched edges
(What volcanoes lie on the other side
Of heat, light, burning up even the angels)
And the mirror of forests and hills drawing nearer
Till the lake is all forests and hills made double,
Do not say this is kindly, convenient,
Warms the hands, crosses the senses with promise,
Harries our fear.
Uneasy, we bellow back at the tree frogs
And, night approaching like the entrance of a tunnel,
We would turn back and cannot, we
Surprise our natures; the woods lock us up
In the secret crimes of our intent.

My Frantic Heart

My frantic heart awoke
In the middle of the night.
What foot trod the stairs?
Who sobbed below in the street?
The crawling silence told
Nothing, and my loud heart shrieked.

The image of the sufferer
Abides at every street.
These mourning crowds at noon
Numb to their exit, break

For entrance that has no retreat.
The concrete and the buildings sink
Imagination to a terrible use.
Our passion wastes against a vile produce.

Such darkness falls from day
How may you and I and they
Endure enschooled reality?
No taxi stops to let you out
No foot is running on the stair
And all forgiven, all forgot,
That makes you and redemption what
Frees a whole society
From the death that it knows not.

Their living death is in my heart.

And you, my only one, who've gone
And return not, nor will,
The image of your stricken face is they
And I am crying in the street miles away.

A. L. LAZARUS

(b. 1914–) has taught at Purdue since 1962. His poems have appeared in such magazines as *Saturday Review, New Republic,* and *Quarterly Review of Literature.* In 1970 he was elected to Poetry Society of America. He is the author or editor of twenty books and anthologies, including the Harbrace *Adventures in Modern Literature* series and the Grosset *Glossary of Literature & Composition.*

Boneless on the Monon (Winter, 1966 to 1866)

Riding on the Monon in December
just throw away your bones.
Let snowy fields glide by,
the breakable glass ponds,
the skaters in molasses

plaids and pompoms courtesy of Currier & Ives.
Depend upon this team of diesels
to neigh along the rails,
their tow chains clanking,
their sledges swaying,
their tails flying in our faces.
On, Percheron! On, Charger!
Shuck the sleighs—you've got us saddled!
Now we gallop past the silos,
corn cribs, hogs magnificent in mufti,
past the stilted tanks, the formal water
blessing out the towns
of Battle Ground and Chalmers,
Rensselaer and Hammond.
We must hoot at V-8 horses stalled at crossings,
buried in snow sidings.
Near the Windy City (past sticks and stones?)
if wind whips up harsh names
it cannot harm our bones:
by the Monon's horses hypnotized
equestrians pull boneless
into Dearborn and Van Buren.

Aubade for the Parishioners of New Paris, Indiana

This Paris too is surely worth a mass.
But from a tipsy sovereign's glass?
From the top of his tree
(Mais oui! Mais whee!)
in his land lord call
our c a r d i n a l
sings his head up.
At the drop of a ray
this Gaul greets the day
with a wine-soaked paean:
Paree
Paree
Paree
Such liturgy!
Whatever else he has to mean
our celebrant sings his red up.

An Indiana House
Named Sylvia

Wallflower by a mossy wall
in the shadow of maple and oak
she had stood too long neglected by lovers.
We were going to do her over
—or so we thought.
We lifted her face and furnace
scrubbed out her coal-smoked soul
painted sun to her clapboards
and after a fashion becoming to ladies
dusted her shingles blue-white.

But she spat diamonds to the winds
stuck to her zinc hatpin
winked at clouds
made pacts with tornadoes.

To inform our maudlin sunshine
her brown stain bled
and soot drifted from her pores.
Darkly from her chimney she sent signals;
her messages rolled from the hearth.
Conversant in more than one tongue
though resisting polyglot
she rehearsed us in substitution drills.

At night she ran labs and seminars
leading us mim-mem into restoring
her original weather-warped front tooth.
We learned from her the language of welcoming.

With a clock in each mouth
We smiled at forests.
For Sylvia we went into woods
we never came out of.

RUTH STONE

(b. Indianapolis, 1915–) was educated in Indianapolis high schools,
having attended Arsenal Tech for one year and Shortridge for
three years. She has served as one of the Poets-in-the-Schools and

has taught at Brandeis and Indiana Universities. Widely published, her poems are collected in such books as *In an Iridescent Time* (1959), *Topography & Other Poems* (1971), and *Cheap* (1975).

Love's Relative

The couple who remain in bed
Are not alike; he's tanned and hairy,
Has a fierce Egyptian head,
She's dimpled, brief; alas, contrary.

Rather defenseless on the sheet
When morning oozes in the cracks,
Her tiny toes, his monster feet,
Both of them upon their backs.

Her years are two and his are thirty.
He's long and bony, somewhat glum.
Her little peaceful feet are dirty.
She sucks a firmly calloused thumb.

At some point in the evil dawning
This oedipal arrangement grew,
The leap from crib to bed while yawning
Mother in disdain withdrew.

O man, whose waking breeds confusion,
Protect the comfort of her sleep.
Hers is the primal bright illusion
From which she makes the bridal leap.

Ballet

Three who are one in blood
Without the blessing of sun,
Wade in the brake, a flood
Down the hill, to run
The pheasant cock, gamely hid,
Male iridescence quelled
Under the weedy dun.

Two men and a boy dance
Rifles up, measures apart,

Waist high in the brake for a chance
At the pheasant's heart.
He runs like a hen, head down
In a cunning art.

It is a fine day in the open season,
Hounds on a nearby farm sweetly bay,
The ring like a charm closes upon the cock,
In a dream of frivolity
He rises before the stock.

Three who have disarrayed
A thousand feathers of gold
Mired in the weeds wade
Toward the marvelous cock turned cold,
With his armored spurs aglint,
By his cock-gold legs they hold.

Seat Belt Fastened?

Old Bill Pheasant won't trim his beard.
Weep, my daughters, and have you heard?
Sing, little otters; don't be afraid.
There's a rustle in the oak leaves
Down by the river. Oh, the moving mirror
And the hearer and the word.

Old Bill wandered in my waking dream,
A river dream; when I saw him come
I was riding by with my gas tank high
Down to Otter Creek from my just-right home.
And he put his beard in the window and said,
"It's sleazy and greasy but it's in your head.
Tell me woman, do you carry a comb?"
Too far from home to the river, I shammed.
"Better not come this far," I said.

But old Bill Pheasant said he'd be damned.
And we backfired down. Oh, daughters, do you tread
On the leaf fall, fern all—picked and pocketed?

Now tell me when we're passing, and tell me when we gain.
And laugh, little children, while our gas tank's high.

"Give thanks for desire," was all he said.
"It'll either clear up or snow or rain."
So we tweaked his beard and we punched his head.
Is your seat belt fastened? Do you sleep in your bed?
If you're stuck in the river can you shift to red?
If you're coming are you going?
If you're living are you dead?

And we drove him away where the otters play,
Where it's twice on Sunday in the regular way,

Where they say what they know and they know what they say,
And the good time's coming on yesterday.

MARY ELLEN SOLT

(b. 1920–), a leading American concretist poet, has lived in Bloomington since 1955. She is an Associate Professor of Comparative Literature at Indiana University, her poetry has appeared in many journals and anthologies, and she is editor of *Concrete Poetry: A World View* (1970). The poem below comes from her book *Flowers in Concrete* (1966); it relates the visual properties of the word to the shape of the flower.

Dogwood

FELIX STEFANILE

(b. 1920–) has taught at Purdue since 1961. His poems have appeared in *A Suit of Four* (Purdue Press, 1973) and in scores of distinguished places, including *Poetry* (Chicago). In 1972 he won the Emily Clark Balch Prize. Among his several volumes of verse the most representative, perhaps, remains *A Fig Tree in America* (1970).

How I Changed My Name Felice

In Italy a man's name, here a woman's,
transliterated so I went to school
for seven years, and no one told me different.
The teachers hardly cared, and in the class
Italian boys who knew me said Felice,
although outside they called me feh-LEE-tchay.
I might have lived, my noun so neutralized,
another seven years, except one day
I broke a window like nobody's girl,
and the old lady called a cop, whose sass
was wonderful when all the neighbors smiled
and said there was no boy named Felice.
And then it was it came on me, my shame,
and I stepped up, and told him, and he grinned.
My father paid a quarter for my sin,
called me inside to look up in a book
that Felix was American for me.
A Roman name, I read. And what he said
was that no Roman broke a widow's glass,
and fanned my little neapolitan ass.

The Mourning Dove

The mourning dove with the lump in her throat
has been tooting her little grey horn all afternoon:

I stand beneath the red-bud tree, and the sad parasol
of her nest, to catch a glimpse.

Once in a while I see the flick of her tail;
it is as though she turns her back on me.

She makes me want to run errands, she is so busy,
twisting and turning, smoothing her lumpy mattress,

and I say to myself, here is womanhood in action!
the least I can do is get out of the way but I don't.

Again, a ripple and chime, she is calling the tune
that reminds me of you—you always hum when you work.

I don't mean to flatter you by telling you this,
but you have that sadness in your voice, that lilt,

and you see, you are calling the tune, and I listen and listen,
and once in a while I write a poem for you.

Blizzard

The power's off, and our cold house
creaks like an ark in the storm;
even the candles are sneezing.

American Aubade

A crazy cardinal
is sitting on the fence; he sings
to the whole town, and counts us house by house.
Wives wake up to wisdom, as he brings
news of chores to men, and in a madrigal
pure yodel and carouse
daylight's plain reasoning
to anybody's dream.

Is his a music verse cannot declare?
All who had slept and started turn again
in a dawn honed by bells, as on the air

his red and sequin clapper startles them,
the taunt and the refrain,
toward wines of color that the windows wear.

DONALD BAKER

(b. 1923–) has been Poet in Residence at Wabash College since
1953. His poems have appeared in scores of literary journals,
among them the *Atlantic Monthly, Poetry* (Chicago), and the *Saturday Review*. He has also been widely anthologized.

Twelve Hawks

From the burning highway where I drove
with my small daughter, I saw their shapes,
blurred through the pane of August,
black lumps sticking to the bones of oak,
and my gorge filled with ancient sickness
and my daughter with strange fire.

When we had climbed the wire to invade
their wild land, and bleached in its blue shroud
the bone-bare tree grew taller,
hooked heads swiveled to our captured eyes,
and the song I had thought was silence
became a dirge of locusts.

A hot wind rustled in the grasses
where the small prey crouched. Close to the creek
a cardinal flashed and whistled.
And she, thigh-deep in briars, hands bright
with goldenrod, laid bare with wary foot
the tiny, broken skull.

Then the heavy, deliberate wings
shrugged loose, broke black against bright air,
exploded out of the bone,
a slow storm of brutal, beautiful
hawks, climbing the wind with heavy grace
and sun-raking symmetry,

until, shooting the blue cataracts,
coasting the cold mountains of the air
between our flesh and the sun,
the twelve circled through a zodiac,
trailing shadows that possessed the world
and my daughter's upraised face.

Full of the skull, sky, oak, and wild land,
I drove on, on the burning highway,
my daughter listening beyond
the wings, the music, and her father's voice
that fought hawk shadows fondling the earth
through an August of savage flight.

JOHN WOODS

(b. Martinsville, 1926–) was educated in the Martinsville schools
and at Indiana University. His poems, stories, and essays have appeared in many literary reviews, and the Library of Congress has
recorded his poetry. His books include *The Deaths at Paragon,
Indiana* (1955), *On the Morning of Color* (1961), *The Cutting Edge*
(1966), *Keeping Out of Trouble* (1968), and *Striking the Earth*
(1976).

The Deaths at Paragon, Indiana

1. Sandra, the waitress

Sun streaked the coffee urn
and wrote AL'S LUNCH across the cups.
I saw no harm in summer then,
and held against the scorching sun
a spring, touching the deepest earth,
that trickled in the bearded tub
behind the store. But nothing holds
when fire levels on the frying concrete.
Thermometer said *Go easy, girl.
Dodge trouble.* And so I fed
the truckers, watching the tube of coffee
twitch along the urn, the street

repeat itself across the mirror.
I washed an egg beneath the tap.

Then, too sudden for the mind,
the car came rolling, spraying parts
and boys across the road outside.
He came, and comes forever, sliding
headfirst into the curb.
The egg broke beneath my hand.
O this to say: his arm was bent
behind his back. Dust and leaves
crawled down the gutter.
O this to hope: someday his eyes
will close upon my dream.

2. *Goss, the ambulance driver*

My head spins in the siren
but I hold the road. Muscles
keep the old shapes. When oaks
are ripped by lightning, tip to root,
does sap spring out until the tree
hangs flat as an inner tube
from junkyard fences? Dr. Sweet,
this siren calls *I am the cross*
your training binds you to.
But hear, one behind is crucified
on a steering wheel, and bleeds
his heart away. Sew on him
a year, and he will lie unbuckled.
The highway whips my face,
and all my riders are emptying
behind me.
     O this to say:
lives are balloons. When the moorings
drop, the wind takes you sailing.
Someday the wind goes slack, and they
come spinning like my passengers.

3. *Chauncy, the junk man*

Scatter me, wind. I am the king
of bang and rattle, of fall apart
and rust in weeds. I am where
things wobble off to. My offerings
sail back from stoops: wires
distracted into sparks, handles

that give you pains, broken holders.
When I am mayor, every matron
will come unglued and hit the spot
with all her joints aglow.
But I can coax a shape in anything,
make it stick and tend and solder.
O this to say: today I dragged
a mash of wheels and sparking sides
into my shed. I cluttered ledges
and festooned rafters. But when
I gathered shape into my brain,
I cowered under fenders, reeling.
The shape was fall and spin and blast.
The shape was death. I let it go.

4. Doctor Sweet

Yesterday I fished for bass,
but now I fish for breath in bones
clasped as bottom roots. The pulse
nibbled like a chub but got away.
All five of you are dead.
Light beaks my eyes, and edges
my knives with fire. Though I link
you by my chart, you'll dangle empty.
Even Chauncey, with his shed of parts,
can never make you run. I know
he'll tow your flattened car away
and hang its pieces from his roof
like sausages and collarbones.
He'd bandage you with earth.
I know those visitors below.
Because you left them yet to be,
they come to lynch you with their tears.

Now I give you to their hands
for burial in summer earth.
O this to hope: that you will never
wake upon an empty world,
and cry for love, and hear no answer.

Guns

Surely the day will come
when they will bring in the guns to the memory

and be given an acre and seeds
by the old sergeant with frank tears.
In Quincy, they will burn them in the vacant lot,
where the feed store failed, you remember,
and the bulldozers coming in the morning.
Children in arms, and the drunks let out
among the parishioners.
And out near the ore fills, where the freshets ran brown,
Billy Joe Smith, the harelip cousin,
will tamp down the sour dirt over his squirrel rifle.
What will grow there? A cordite daisy,
a squirrel arching his leg over it.
All the animals back, like cats,
to be shooed out of the privies.

Remember, then, in your canines, in your
trigger fingers, in the blood of your temples,
the belts of blue cartridges, Bofors pocking
the Stuka sky, John Wayne searching for something
in his chaps, sorry, it's gone. His grandchildren
will have to look it up in Webster's.
It starts with G, like God.

Striking the Earth

As we strike the earth with our bodies,
for we are always falling, and standing up,
and falling again, though you call it dancing,
or walking, or flying, there is the sound of stone
coming to rest in quarries, the last spray of sand,
as we knock on earth's sullen, historical face.

If we are men with such manners, we lie down
on women and hold a heart length of warm earth.
You will ask me if we have deserved as much,
as men, so long from the mother. Yes,
but some of us would hold that pose forever.
Stones can leave scars on naked backs, remember,
and the backyard tom has a limited voice.

There are times we strike the earth
like coastal rain, thin but steady, when colors
fade from store fronts, and dawn

might as well be dusk, and both night.
The black box on the last page of the rural weekly,
passing of long cars with lights on, and flags,
as though they might become lost in that night
they have been chosen to carry, rainwet,
with police sanction, to the plain of skulls.
Funereal, we say of that clothing and steady rain,
when we hang our names and flags in a dark closet,
when the priest turns off the lights below,
and the sound of dirt falling reminds us
of rain through leaves, or the world's bedridden breath.

Every few years we need the quick downpour,
like rivers on end, seeing the oak stump
hammering the pilings, the car lights shining
at the bottom of deep wells. These are our wars.
Tonight, if you lie and listen to the soughing
râle of your breath, you may understand
why some men take up edged weapons, or stare
at ceilings from red bath water.

There are unique colloids of water and oil,
but white horses pull a box so light
they don't even lather up, so light even the gasses
are colorless. The skin can be read through,
and the book of the eyes slides back,
unread, into the case. The fingerprint rests
a moment on the flower, then sinks into its
dizzying spiral. A spring day can be a room
kept just the way it was when someone lived,
the black wreath blossoming. Though we eat
decay with both hands, the bruise
is the sweetest part of the apple.
Names that burned, that kissed deeply
to the brain stem, that owned the Tartar plain
from the high fur saddles, weather on stones,
coming to rest in quarries.

DAVID WAGONER

(b. 1926–) was brought up in Whiting, not far from the steel mills.
He was educated in Lake County schools and at Indiana Univer-
sity, among other universities. He began his teaching career at De
Pauw in 1949 but has been teaching at the University of Washing-

ton, Seattle, since 1954. He is Editor of the distinguished little literary magazine *Poetry Northwest.* Aside from several novels, his books of poetry include *Staying Alive* (1966), *Working Against Time* (1970), *Riverbed* (1972), and *Sleeping in the Woods* (1974).

The Breathing Lesson

"Sensations of smell are relatively homogeneous and untranslatable into the form of language. Nobody can enlarge upon an odor."—Oscar W. Firkins

> Around the compass, soap-flakes and burnt corn,
> A swamp, the acid cracked from boiling oil,
> Sulfur dioxide, plumage of soft coal,
> The yellow wreckage of Lake Michigan—
> The unpredictable first breath of a day
> Where I grew up depended on the wind.
>
> My life would turn tail like a weathervane
> And find attention wrung out on the line,
> My breath in dollops, dead frogs in the throat,
> The drill in the forehead, branches of membrane
> Flocking with soot, or the unhallowed dregs
> Of the lake come lapping up like burlap dogs.
>
> Led by the nose around the pit of self
> In all directions, I was washerwoman,
> The dying year-god, infidel at the gate,
> The egg of the world, machine-man, rancid goat.
> But if the wind was veering, backing off,
> They choked themselves on metamorphosis.
>
> O Lux, Mazola, Wolf Lake, Standard Oil,
> O city dump, O docks of Bethlehem—
> Though a mind, run through its middle, can't forget
> What creatures roamed its baffling passages,
> In the dead calm of morning once, I rose
> Breathless without your help, and walked away.

PHILIP APPLEMAN

(b. Kendallville, 1926–) has taught at Indiana University since 1955. Widely published, his poems have appeared in most of the distinguished reviews from A to Y (Antioch to Yale). Aside from his non-fiction, he is the author of a novel *In the Twelfth Year of the War* (1970) and of several collections of poetry, including *Kites on a Windy Day* (1967), *Summer Love & Surf* (1968), and *Open Doorways* (1976).

To the Garbage Collectors in Bloomington, Indiana, the First Pickup of the New Year

(the way bed is in winter, like an aproned lap,
like furry mittens,
like childhood crouching under tables)
The Ninth Day of Xmas, in the morning black
outside our window: clattering cans, the whir
of a hopper, shouts, a whistle, *move on* ...
I see them in my warm imagination
the way I'll see them later in the cold,
heaving the huge cans and running
(running!) to the next house on the street.

My vestiges of muscle stir
uneasily in their percale cocoon:
what moves those men out there, what
drives them running to the next house and the next?
Halfway back to dream, I speculate:
The Social Weal? "Let's make good old
    Bloomington a cleaner place
    to live in, right men? *Hup, tha!*"
Healthy Competition? "Come on, boys,
    let's burn up that rowt today and beat those dudes
    on truck thirteen!"
Enlightened Self-Interest? "Another can,
    another dollar—don't slow down, Mac, I'm puttin'
    three kids through Princeton."
Or something else?
Terror?

A half hour later, dawn comes edging over
Clark Street: layers of color, laid out like
a flattened rainbow—red, then yellow, green,
and over that the black-and-blue of night

still hanging on. Clark Street maples wave
their silhouettes against the red, and through
the twiggy trees, I see a solid chunk
of garbage truck, and stick-figures of men,
like windup toys, tossing little cans—
and *running*.

All day they'll go like that, till dark again,
and all day, people fussing at their desks,
at hot stoves, at machines, will jettison
tin cans, bare evergreens, damp Kleenex, all
things that are Caesar's.

O garbage men,
the New Year greets you like the Old;
after this first run you too may rest
in beds like great warm aproned laps
and know that people everywhere have faith:
putting from them all things of this world,
they confidently bide your second coming.

October 15

On one of those maple-red
Indiana noons,
a girl in a rusty Ford
smiled at me, for no reason,
and without one beat of transition,
scruffy kids in knickers
went skipping down the alleys
of little Hoosier towns,
yellow mongrels yapping
circles of joy around them;
and Model T's chugged past,
saying familiar things,
like a-HOO-ga;
and the maple-bright Indiana
noon was the color of bonfires
and the color of brick schoolhouses
and cherries in Mason jars
and firecrackers
and sunburn
and maple trees gone blazing . . .

Scruffy kids in knickers
are dropping their graying hairs
relentlessly on cashmere
and the carpets of Cadillacs:
in the grief of that sudden smile
I thought, only man can say
autumn.
And I bore the crushing miracle
of tears.

ETHERIDGE KNIGHT

(b. 1931–), a native of Mississippi, has lived in Indiana for several
years. "My literary career began," he writes, "while I was an in-
mate at the Indiana State Prison, Michigan City, where I served a
term (1960–1968) for robbery." In 1968, after his parole, he
became Poet-in-Residence at the University of Pittsburgh. In 1972
he was an NEA Fellow, and in 1974 a Guggenheim Fellow. His
poems are widely published in such collections as the Norton *Anthology of Modern Poetry* and New American Library's *New Black
Voices.* His books include *Poems From Prison* (1968), *Black Voices
from Prison* (1970), and *Born of a Woman* (1976).

He Sees Through Stone

He sees through stone
he has the secret
eyes this old black one
who under prison skies
sits pressed by the sun
against the western wall
his pipe between purple gums

the years fall
like overripe plums
bursting red flesh
on the dark earth

his time is not my time
but I have known him
in a time gone

he led me trembling cold
into the dark forest
taught me the secret rites
to take a woman
to be true to my brothers
to make my spear drink
the blood of my enemies

now black cats circle him
flash white teeth
snarl at the air
mashing green grass beneath
shining muscles
ears peeling his words
he smiles
he knows
the hunt   the enemy
he has the secret eyes
he sees through stone

RICHARD PFLUM

(b. Indianapolis, 1932–) attended Purdue and Indiana Universities
and was recently a Fellow of the MacDowell Colony. Co-Editor of
Stoney Lonesome, he has also served in the Indiana Arts Commission's Poets-in-the-Schools program. His most recent collection of
poems is *Moving Into Light* (1975).

Windfall

I have a little packet of money today
and I can go downtown
and buy an icecream cone
and think of all the things I could buy

like socks to replace the ones with holes
and shoes that don't take in water.
I could go to the laundromat and have enough
left over for a steak or book
or a magazine full of pretty girls,
or I could just walk along
feeling rich and looking at trees
and know that summer isn't far off now.
I have a little packet of money
singing inside my wallet
and the weather is suddenly warmer
and I won't have to ask my girl
if she would like an icecream cone just
so she'd buy me one, too.
My wallet is full of green leaves.
Summer won't be long.

Proem

Poets are always found dead
at the tops of their poems,
lying in state
under the eyes of their readers.

Flies' buzzing in the rich air
of flowers elicits murmurs
from hungry mourners.
Stage right to stage left

lines file by, everyone eager
to taste the curious food
heaped upon the platters.
Consensuses are reached

though the corpus is beyond this,
having found a new point of departure
beneath the stitched lips,
some new anger to grind

between the teeth.

ROGER PFINGSTON

(b. Evansville, 1940–) is a graduate of Evansville North High School
and Indiana University. He served in the U.S. Navy, and since 1967
he has been teaching in the Bloomington, Indiana, schools. His
poems are widely published in such magazines as *Quartet, Indiana
Writes,* and *The Nation;* and they have been widely reprinted in
anthologies, including *The New York Times Book of Verse.*

Father and Gun

My father, of German/Dutch descent,
southern Indiana, told me
the 12-gauge once belonged
to a Cherokee friend who used
to walk the wooded sand
on both sides of the Ohio River,
hoping to scare a duck or rabbit.
They would meet and talk
on Man's Beach (Indiana side)
owned by my grandfather, who died
when I was four. My father
was a lifeguard, and once
a girl drowned as he stood talking
with the Cherokee, admiring the gun.
He helped pull her in,
"her face so calm," he always said,
"I couldn't believe she was dead."
A few years later he married
my mother when he was twenty-two,
and soon drifted into the food
business, where he's been ever since.
The gun was given him as payment for
loans the Cherokee could never meet.
I used the gun one winter
when I was sixteen, learning
to hunt with a high-school friend,
and killed one rabbit the whole
season, so close that when he jumped
the shot wasted him to a bloody rag
of flesh and fur. A few years
after that I took to poetry,

and any shooting I do these days
is done with a Pentax.
My father, fifty-two, fishes now,
and at Thanksgiving or Christmas
is always called upon
to make the dumplings.

The Barn

The skeletal frame,
once tin-roofed and strong
with weather-blasted timber,
leans beyond repair. Still, you,
old grandfather dream,
walk the hollyhock path
down which a spring tornado spun,
gashed and spit your barnyard's flesh
and bone. Walking there
perhaps you remember
the hoary breath of cattle
rising to warm the spider's lair
of web-coated rafters;
the stacks of musty hay
where your daughter's children
leaped in heedless play
(The cattle wouldn't eat the hay,
you said, if they played upon it);
the feedbin stuffed
half the barn's leaning height.
Perhaps you remember,
at night when the wind is up,
and the clacking tongue
of a doorless hinge
stirs your tired despairing pulse,
how the earthen corners
shone with golden corn,
and the air lay thick
as fallen fruit.

JOHN MATTHIAS

(b. 1941–) has taught at the University of Notre Dame since 1967.
He is a graduate of Stanford and the University of London. His

poems are widely published and anthologized. His books include *Bucyrus* (1970) and *Turns* (1974). He has also edited the anthology *23 Modern British Poets* (1971).

Swimming in the Quarry at Midnight

Under a pine and confusion:
ah! Tangles of clothes: (come
on, silly, nobody's here:) and
naked as fish, a boy and a girl.
(Nobody comes here: nobody looks:
nobody watches us watching us watch.)
Thighs slide into the moon.
Humbly, into the stars: Mirrored,
flashes a father's red eye, a
blue-bitten mother's red lip: NO
Swimming Allowed in the Quarry
At Night. (Anyway, nevertheless
and moreover: feel how warm!) here,
among the reflections. (Feel the
water's mouth and its hands, feel
them imitate mine: can there truly
be any danger?) danger allowed in
the quarry at night? can people
really have drowned? (Now my body
is only water alive, and aeons
ago you were a fish growing
legs—) well, dust to dust, a
curious notion. But quarry water on
dust green with seed! Quarry water
forbidden on land after dark! What
young forms of vegetation emerge,
what new colors of light.

MICHAEL ALLEN

(b. Vincennes, 1947–) is a graduate of Indiana University. He has published poems in such magazines as *Indiana Writes, North American Review,* and *Carleton Miscellany.*

Of Worms,
the Earliest Harvest

The worms, lips in the earth,
have urged me to say things
they refuse to own.

This is not a promise but a path
winding in sod I take up
spadeful by spade cut, as I make
garden in March.

The worms weave as if earth were
skein of wool or cotton, not that body
beneath the house that holds on tight.

They bend the earth toward green
showers in trees.

        They eat what they know
of brown and red and puzzle their way
through all Indiana.

They are unashamed of their food,
their beds, and tell how to go from Monday
to Saturday by tunnel. I have ignored them
far too long, believing only in grass,
in its thin secret.

Look! how they never fail to take colors
of any winter or spring sky
deep into their skin!

JARED CARTER

Jared Carter was born in Elwood, Indiana in 1939 and attended
Yale and Goddard. Except for two years he served with the army
in France in the early 1960s, he has lived most of his life in Indiana.
His poetry has appeared in *Indiana Sesquicentennial Poets, Indiana Writes,* and *The Nation.* He lives in Indianapolis, where he
works as a freelance editor and book designer.

Early Warning

When the weather turned
Crows settled about the house
Cawing daylong among the new leaves.
It would be a hard spring,
Folks said, the crows—
They know. There are folks
Up near where I come from
In Mississinewa County
Who study such things.
Folks who believe tornadoes
Are alive: that polluted streams
Rise from their beds
Like lepers, following after
Some great churning, twisting cloud.
With their own eyes
They've seen a cyclone stop,
Lap up electricity
From a substation, then make
A right-angle turn
And peel the roof off some
Prefabricated egg factory.
Thousands of hens, who've never seen
The light of the sun, or
Touched earth with their beaks,
Go up the funnel like souls to God.

Pompeii: Calco del Cane

"Cast of a chained dog (from the 'Casa di Vesonio Primo') who was
caught by death while struggling with all his contracted sinews
against the restricting chain (Plate LXIV, *fig.* 111)."

Pompeii, Liberia Dello Stato

Exploding still, after two thousand years,
He writhes within his pen of iron and glass,
While we observe that fiery moment pass
And marvel at such anguish, without fear.

The mule driver hunched beneath his cloak,
The woman turned face down, the others skulked

To cellars, leaving behind the dog to balk
Against a vanished chain that never broke.

Time passed. Then archeologists came
To pour impartiality into
These hollow testaments to sudden flame;

Toward casual eyes the dog's pale limbs
Now send a pulse so strong it passes through
Unfelt—as when a white star flares and dims.

INDEX OF AUTHORS AND TITLES